Lecture Notes in Computer S

Commenced Publication in 1973
Founding and Former Series Editors:
Gerhard Goos, Juris Hartmanis, and Jan van Leeuwen

Editorial Board

David Hutchison
Lancaster University, UK

Takeo Kanade
Carnegie Mellon University, Pittsburgh, PA, USA

Josef Kittler
University of Surrey, Guildford, UK

Jon M. Kleinberg
Cornell University, Ithaca, NY, USA

Alfred Kobsa
University of California, Irvine, CA, USA

Friedemann Mattern
ETH Zurich, Switzerland

John C. Mitchell
Stanford University, CA, USA

Moni Naor
Weizmann Institute of Science, Rehovot, Israel

Oscar Nierstrasz
University of Bern, Switzerland

C. Pandu Rangan
Indian Institute of Technology, Madras, India

Bernhard Steffen
TU Dortmund University, Germany

Madhu Sudan
Microsoft Research, Cambridge, MA, USA

Demetri Terzopoulos
University of California, Los Angeles, CA, USA

Doug Tygar
University of California, Berkeley, CA, USA

Gerhard Weikum
Max Planck Institute for Informatics, Saarbruecken, Germany

Corina S. Păsăreanu   Gwen Salaün (Eds.)

Formal Aspects of Component Software

9th International Symposium, FACS 2012
Mountain View, CA, USA, September 12-14, 2012
Revised Selected Papers

 Springer

Volume Editors

Corina S. Păsăreanu
NASA Ames Research Center
Mail Stop 269-2
Moffett Field, CA 94035, USA
E-mail: corina.s.pasareanu@nasa.gov

Gwen Salaün
INRIA Grenoble - Rhône-Alpes/CONVECS
655, avenue de l'Europe
38330 Montbonnot Saint-Martin, France
E-mail: gwen.salaun@inria.fr

ISSN 0302-9743   e-ISSN 1611-3349
ISBN 978-3-642-35860-9   e-ISBN 978-3-642-35861-6
DOI 10.1007/978-3-642-35861-6
Springer Heidelberg Dordrecht London New York

Library of Congress Control Number: 2012954531

CR Subject Classification (1998): D.2.4, D.2, F.4, F.3, H.3.5, D.3, D.1, K.6.3

LNCS Sublibrary: SL 2 – Programming and Software Engineering

© Springer-Verlag Berlin Heidelberg 2013

This work is subject to copyright. All rights are reserved, whether the whole or part of the material is
concerned, specifically the rights of translation, reprinting, re-use of illustrations, recitation, broadcasting,
reproduction on microfilms or in any other way, and storage in data banks. Duplication of this publication
or parts thereof is permitted only under the provisions of the German Copyright Law of September 9, 1965,
in its current version, and permission for use must always be obtained from Springer. Violations are liable
to prosecution under the German Copyright Law.
The use of general descriptive names, registered names, trademarks, etc. in this publication does not imply,
even in the absence of a specific statement, that such names are exempt from the relevant protective laws
and regulations and therefore free for general use.

Typesetting: Camera-ready by author, data conversion by Scientific Publishing Services, Chennai, India

Printed on acid-free paper

Springer is part of Springer Science+Business Media (www.springer.com)

Preface

This volume contains the papers presented at FACS 2012, the 9th International Symposium on Formal Aspects of Component Software held during September 12–14, 2012, in Mountain View, California. This was the first international FACS Symposium held outside Europe. The symposium featured a strong technical program consisting of peer-reviewed presentations, two invited talks, and a panel. The event was organized by Carnegie Mellon University, Silicon Valley, and was held on the grounds of the NASA Ames Research Park.

The component-based software development approach has emerged as a promising paradigm to cope with the complexity of present-day software systems by bringing sound engineering principles into software engineering. The FACS Symposium is concerned with how formal methods can be used to make component-based software development succeed. The symposium targets challenging issues such as mathematical models for components, composition and adaptation, and rigorous approaches to verification, deployment, testing, and certification for component software. FACS 2012 addressed the applications of formal methods in all aspects of software components and services.

The first invited talk was titled "Analyzing Interactions of Asynchronously Communicating Software Components" and was given by Tevfik Bultan from the University of California at Santa Barbara. The second invited talk was titled "Safe Programming of Asynchronous Interaction: Can We Do It for Real?" and was given by Shaz Qadeer from Microsoft Research.

The panel was led by Natarajan Shankar, from the Stanford Research Institute, and it addressed the impact of emerging technologies, such as cloud computing, cyber-physical, biological and distributed systems, on component software. The panel participants were Dimitra Giannakopoulou (from NASA Ames Research Center), Shaz Qadeer, Natarajan Shankar, and the two Program Chairs. There were 40 submissions. Each submission was reviewed by at least three Program Committee members. The committee decided to accept 16 papers. The submission and reviewing of the papers was done via EasyChair.

We would like to thank Javier Camara, for his work as publicity chair, and Guy Power, Hector Rastrullo and Jose Miguel Rojas Siles for their help with the local organization.

September 2012

Corina S. Păsăreanu
Gwen Salaün

Organization

Program Committee

Erika Abraham	RWTH Aachen University, Germany
Farhad Arbab	CWI and Leiden University, The Netherlands
Christian Attiogbe	University of Nantes, France
Christel Baier	Technical University of Dresden, Germany
Luis Barbosa	Universidade do Minho, Portugal
Roberto Bruni	Università di Pisa, Italy
Carlos Canal	University of Málaga, Spain
Frank De Boer	CWI, The Netherlands
José Luiz Fiadeiro	University of Leicester, UK
Carlo Ghezzi	Politecnico di Milano, Italy
Rolf Hennicker	Ludwig-Maximilians-Universität München, Germany
Zhiming Liu	United Nations University - International Institute for Software Technology, Macao
Markus Lumpe	Swinburne University of Technology, Australia
Eric Madelaine	INRIA, France
John Mullins	Ecole Polytechnique de Montreal, Canada
Peter Olveczky	University of Oslo, Norway
Corina Pasareanu	CMU/NASA Ames Research Center, USA
Frantisek Plasil	Charles University, Prague, Czech Republic
Pascal Poizat	Université d'Evry Val d'Essonne and CNRS, France
Shaz Qadeer	Microsoft, USA
John Rushby	SRI International, USA
Gwen Salaun	Grenoble INP - INRIA - LIG, France
Bernhard Schatz	TU München, Germany
Nishant Sinha	NEC Labs, USA
Marjan Sirjani	Reykjavik University, Iceland
Volker Stolz	University of Oslo, Norway
Meng Sun	Peking University, China
Carolyn Talcott	SRI International, USA
Oksana Tkachuk	Fujitsu Laboratories of America
Sebastian Uchitel	University of Buenos Aires and Imperial College London, Argentina and UK
Gianluigi Zavattaro	University of Bologna, Italy

Additional Reviewers

Andre, Pascal
Blech, Jan Olaf
Cengarle, María Victoria
Chesani, Federico
Corzilius, Florian
Dan, Li
Faber, Johannes
Filieri, Antonio
Gerostathopoulos, Ilias
Greenyer, Joel
Izadi, Mohammad
Izadi, Mohammad-Javad
Jaghoori, Mohammad Mahdi
Jancik, Pavel
Jansen, Nils
Khamespanah, Ehsan
Klueppelholz, Sascha
Knapp, Alexander
Kofron, Jan
Koss, Dagmar
Krause, Christian

Kupke, Clemens
Lanoix, Arnaud
Lascu, Tudor
Lauer, Michaël
Loup, Ulrich
Malkis, Alexander
Malohlava, Michal
Mayer, Philip
Melgratti, Hernan
Meriem, Ouederni
Nellen, Johanna
Proenca, Jose
Qamar, Nafees
Rensink, Arend
Rot, Jurriaan
Salvaneschi, Guido
Savu, Alexandra
Schorp, Konstantin
Srba, Jiri
Stahl, Christian
Tuosto, Emilio

Table of Contents

Formal Patterns for Multi-rate Distributed Real-Time Systems*

Kyungmin Bae[1], José Meseguer[1], and Peter Csaba Ölveczky[2]

[1] University of Illinois at Urbana-Champaign
[2] University of Oslo

Abstract. Distributed real-time systems (DRTSs), such as avionics and automotive systems, are very hard to design and verify. Besides the difficulties of asynchrony, clock skews, and network delays, an additional source of complexity comes from the multirate nature of many such systems, which must implement several levels of hierarchical control at different rates. In this work we present several simple model transformations and a multirate extension of the PALS pattern which can be combined to reduce the design and verification of a virtually synchronous multirate DRTS to the much simpler task of specifying and verifying a single synchronous system. We illustrate the ideas with a multirate hierarchical control system where a central controller orchestrates control systems in the ailerons and tail of an airplane to perform turning maneuvers.

1 Introduction

Many cyber-physical systems such as cars, airplanes, and networked medical devices are *virtually synchronous distributed real-time systems* (DRTSs), where many components interact *asynchronously* through a network, yet must obey hard real-time synchronization constraints which are essential to their correctness. As these systems grow in complexity before our eyes, their safety-critical nature and associated certification requirements make their development increasingly challenging, to the point where verification efforts can easily dominate the cost of system development. The complexities of concurrency, network communication, clock skews, hard real-time constraints, and synchronization constraints make verification a daunting task. To make things worse, formal verification by automatic methods such as model checking is all but impossible even for small systems, due to the state space explosion caused by asynchrony. For these reasons, a component-based, modular approach to DRTS design based on reusable *complexity-reducing formal patterns* that can drastically reduce the effort and cost involved in DRTS design, implementation, and verification is sorely needed.

Several such formal patterns have been proposed. They offer impressive reductions in system complexity and make automatic verification possible where it was impossible before. For DRTSs that must obey virtual synchrony, both the PALS

---

* This work was partially supported by Boeing Corporation Grant C8088 and NSF Grant CCF 09-05584.

© Springer-Verlag Berlin Heidelberg 2013

("Physically Asynchronous Logically Synchronous") pattern developed with our colleagues at UIUC and Rockwell-Collins [11,10], and the TTA patterns proposed in [8,15] can greatly reduce system complexity and make verification much easier. For example, for an avionics case study considered in [10], the number of system states in the simplest possible distributed version with perfect clocks and no network delays was 3,047,832, but the PALS pattern reduced the number of states to be analyzed to a mere 185. This is certainly helpful; but the problem still remains that patterns such as PALS and TTA assume a *single period* for the virtually synchronous system. This excludes many DRTSs, in fact the majority, which are *multirate*. It is a fact of life that different sensors and effectors need to operate at different rates; and that this necessitates using slower rates in the distributed control hierarchies that orchestrate and synchronize their actions in, say, a car or an airplane.

The goal of the present work is to propose *Multirate PALS* as a formalized mathematical model providing a formal pattern that can drastically reduce the complexity of designing, verifying, and implementing multirate DRTSs. In particular, we prove that the entire DRTS design as a concurrent system of asynchronous components communication on a network is *bisimilar* to an enormously simpler *synchronous multirate ensemble* of state machines. This bisimilarity provides a very drastic reduction on the number of states, making model checking verification possible in many cases where it is unfeasible for the original DRTS. As we explain in more detail in Section 6, our work shares the same complexity-reducing goals as those of our colleagues in [1], who have made a similar, but substantially different, proposal of a multirate PALS architecture expressed in terms of the AADL modeling language. We differ from [1] not only on the model of Multirate PALS that is actually proposed, but more importantly in providing mathematical foundations for the Multirate PALS model, its asynchronous counterpart, and the bisimulation relation between both not available in [1].

Our approach, formalized in the Real-Time Maude specification language [13], is highly modular and consists of expressing Multirate PALS itself as the composition of several simple formal patterns, including a modified version of PALS. Based on those patterns, we give a formal specification of Multirate PALS as a model transformation $(\mathfrak{E}, T, \Gamma) \mapsto \mathcal{MA}(\mathfrak{E}, T, \Gamma)$, which maps a multirate ensemble $\mathfrak{E}$, where $\mathfrak{E}$ is a mathematical model of a collection of interconnected state machines running at different rates, yet synchronously in terms of their hyperperiod T, and performance parameters Γ, to a semantically equivalent specification of distributed components $\mathcal{MA}(\mathfrak{E}, T, \Gamma)$.

In summary, the new contributions of this work are:

1. The mathematical definitions of a number of simple formal patterns, and of a multirate ensemble $\mathfrak{E}$ and its synchronous composition $MRSC(\mathfrak{E})$.
2. The mathematical definition of Multirate PALS as a transformation $(\mathfrak{E}, T, \Gamma) \mapsto \mathcal{MA}(\mathfrak{E}, T, \Gamma)$, and a *bisimulation theorem*, proving that the state machine $MRSC(\mathfrak{E})$ and the real-time system $Stable(\mathcal{MA}(\mathfrak{E}, T, \Gamma))$ associated to $\mathcal{MA}(\mathfrak{E}, T, \Gamma)$ are bisimilar and satisfy the same CTL^* formulas.

3. An aeronautics case study showing the power of Multirate PALS in reducing the (in fact unfeasible) model checking of a hierarchical control system involved in the turning maneuvers of an airplane to the much simpler and feasible task of model checking a synchronous machine of the form $MRSC(\mathfrak{E})$.

2   Preliminaries: Single-Rate PALS and Real-Time Maude

Single-Rate PALS. Single-rate PALS was introduced in [9,11] to reduce the design and verification of a distributed real-time system that should behave as if it were virtually synchronous to the much simpler task of designing and verifying its synchronous version, assuming that the network infrastructure can guarantee bounds on the messaging delays and the skews of the local clocks. For a (single-rate) synchronous design SD, network bounds Γ, and period T of the asynchronous system, PALS defines the asynchronous system $PALS(SD, T, \Gamma)^1$. In [10] we formalize the synchronous models as the synchronous composition of an ensemble of typed machines, and the asynchronous models as object-oriented rewrite theories in Real-Time Maude, and prove that the synchronous design SD and the asynchronous distributed model $PALS(SD, T, \Gamma)$ satisfy the same temporal logic properties as explained below.

Synchronous Models. The synchronous model is the synchronous composition of a collection of *typed machines*, an *environment*, and a *wiring diagram* that connects the machines. A *typed machine* M is a tuple (D_i, S, D_o, δ_M), where $D_i = D_{i_1} \times \cdots \times D_{i_n}$ is M's *input set*, S is a set of *states*, $D_o = D_{o_1} \times \cdots \times D_{o_m}$ is M's *output set*, and $\delta_M \subseteq (D_i \times S) \times (S \times D_o)$ is M's *transition relation*. That is, a machine has n input ports and m output ports; an input to port k is an element of D_{i_k}, and an output from port j is an element of D_{o_j}.

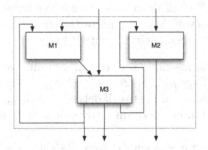

Fig. 1. A machine ensemble

Typed machines can be "wired together" into *machine ensembles*, as shown in Fig. 1. A single-rate machine ensemble is a tuple $\mathcal{E} = (J \cup \{e\}, \{M_j\}_{j \in J}, E, src)$, where: J is a finite set of *indices*, and $e \notin J$ is the *environment index*; $\{M_j\}_{j \in J}$

---

[1] PALS can also compute the optimal (shortest) period T for a given Γ.

is a family of typed machines; the *environment* is a pair $E = (D_i^e, D_o^e)$, with D_i^e the environment's *input set* and D_o^e its *output set*; and *src* is a function that assigns to each input port (j, n) (input port n of machine j) its "source."

An ensemble $\mathcal{E}$ has a *synchronous semantics*: the transitions of all machines are performed simultaneously, and if a machine has a feedback wire to itself and/or to another machine, then the output becomes an input at the *next* instant. The *synchronous composition* of an ensemble $\mathcal{E}$ is therefore equivalent to a *single machine* $M_{\mathcal{E}} = (D_o^e, S^{\mathcal{E}}, D_i^e, \delta_{\mathcal{E}})$, where: $S^{\mathcal{E}} = (\Pi_{j \in J} S_j) \times (\Pi_{j \in J} D_{OF}^j)$, where D_{OF}^j stores the "feedback outputs" of machine M_j; and the transition relation $\delta_{\mathcal{E}} \subseteq (D_i^{\mathcal{E}} \times S^{\mathcal{E}}) \times (S^{\mathcal{E}} \times D_o^{\mathcal{E}})$ "combines" the transitions of the single machines into a synchronous step as explained in [10]. The synchronous composition of the ensemble in Fig. 1 is the machine given by the outer box.

The transition system $ts(\mathcal{E}) = (S^{\mathcal{E}} \times D_o^e, \longrightarrow)$ defining the behaviors of $\mathcal{E}$ is defined by $((s, o_{fb}), i) \longrightarrow ((s', o'_{fb}), i')$ iff an ensemble in state (s, o_{fb}) with input i from the environment has a transition to state (s', o'_{fb}), and the environment can generate output i' in the next step. If $L : S^{\mathcal{E}} \times D_o^e \to \mathcal{P}(AP)$ is a *labeling function* that assigns to each state the atomic propositions that hold in the state, then $(ts(\mathcal{E}), L)$ is a *Kripke structure* associated to $(\mathcal{E}, L)$.

Asynchronous Models. The *asynchronous* model $\mathcal{A}(\mathcal{E}, T, \Gamma)$ adds a "wrapper" around each machine in $\mathcal{E}$. This wrapper has an input buffer, an output buffer, a local clock that deviates by less than ϵ from a global "perfect clock," and some timers. All components have the same period (the "PALS period" T) and the behavior of such an asynchronous component can be summarized as follows:

- Received messages are stored in the input buffer.
- When a new round begins (according to the local clock), the component:
  1. Reads input from the input buffer, performs a transition, and produces output which is put into the output buffer.
  2. Sets its output backoff timer to a value b (see below).
- When the output backoff timer expires or the transition has finished (whichever comes last), the messages in the output buffer are sent into the network.

We prove in [10] that all messages are read in a "round-consistent" way if $b \geq 2\epsilon$ monus μ_{min} and $T \geq \mu_{max} + 2\epsilon + \max(b, \alpha_{max})$, where μ_{min} and μ_{max} are the minimum and maximum network delays, and α_{max} is maximum time it takes a machine to read input, perform a transition, and produce output.

Relating the Synchronous and Asynchronous Systems. The *stable* states of the asynchronous model are the states where all components have full input buffers and empty output buffers. The idea is to consider "big step" transitions $t \longrightarrow_{st} t'$ between such stable states t and t'. The Kripke structures $(ts(\mathcal{E}), L)$ and $(Stable(\mathcal{A}(\mathcal{E}, T, \Gamma)), \longrightarrow_{st}, sync; L)$ satisfy the same CTL^* formulas for related initial states, where *sync* maps each stable asynchronous state to the corresponding synchronous state. We have also proved that $(ts(\mathcal{E}), L)$ satisfies a CTL^* formula ϕ if and only if $(\mathcal{A}(\mathcal{E}, T, \Gamma), sync; L)$ satisfies the CTL^* formula ϕ_{stable}.

Real-Time Maude. A Real-Time Maude [13] *theory* consists of:

- A *membership equational logic* [6] theory (Σ, E) with Σ a signature[2] and E a set of *confluent and terminating conditional equations*. (Σ, E) specifies the system's states as an algebraic data type.
- A set *IR* of (possibly conditional) *labeled instantaneous rewrite rules* specifying the system's *instantaneous* (i.e., zero-time) local transitions.
- A set *TR* of *tick rewrite rules* of the form   `crl [l] : {u} => {v} in time` τ `if` *cond*. Such a rule specifies a transition with duration τ and label l from an instance of the term u to the corresponding instance of the term v.

A *class* declaration   `class C | att`$_1$` : s`$_1$`, ..., att`$_n$` : s`$_n$ declares a class C with attributes att_1 to att_n of sorts s_1 to s_n. An *object* of class C is represented as a term `< O : C | att`$_1$` : val`$_1$`, ..., att`$_n$` : val`$_n$` >` where O is the object's *identifier*, and where val_1 to val_n are the current values of the attributes att_1 to att_n. The global state has the form $\{t\}$, where t is a term of sort `Configuration` that has the structure of a *multiset* of objects and messages, with multiset union denoted by a juxtaposition operator that is declared associative and commutative. The dynamic behavior of concurrent object systems is axiomatized by specifying each of its transition patterns by a rewrite rule. For example, the rule

```
rl [l] : m(O,w)  < O : C | a1 : x, a2 : O', a3 : z >   =>
                  < O : C | a1 : x + w, a2 : O', a3 : z >  dly(m'(O'),x) .
```

defines a parametrized family of transitions in which a message `m`, with parameters `O` and `w`, is read and consumed by an object `O` of class `C`. The transitions change the attribute `a1` of the object `O` and send a new message `m'(O')` *with delay* `x`. "Irrelevant" attributes (such as `a3`) need not be mentioned in a rule.

3   Multirate Machine Ensembles

This section formally defines multirate synchronous systems as a multirate machine ensemble of typed machines, and defines their semantics.

Virtually synchronized cyber-physical systems are typically networked real-time systems consisting of distributed devices controlled by a hierarchy of distributed controllers. The devices may operate at different rates, and, furthermore, in a perfectly synchronized distributed system, the synchronous changes of the local control applications can happen only at the hyperperiod boundary [1]. We therefore consider hierarchical multirate systems in which a set of controllers with the same rate may communicate with each other and with a number of faster components, so that the period of the higher-level controllers is a multiple of the period of each fast component, as illustrated in Figure 2.

There are in essence two ways of composing machines with different periods into a synchronous system in which all components operate in lock-step: One can "speed up" the slower components, or one can "slow down" the faster

---

[2] i.e., Σ is a set of declarations of *sorts*, *subsorts*, and *function symbols*.

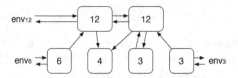

Fig. 2. A multirate system, with each machine/environment annotated by its period

components so that all components run at the slow rate. We follow the latter
approach, since we find it more natural to consider the system at the rate of
the "higher-level" components. An additional benefit of this choice is that there
are fewer reachable states to consider in model checking analyses, since multiple
"fast" transitions are combined into a single (slow) transition.

When a fast machine is composed with a slower machine, and the resulting
composition runs at the slower rate, the fast machine has to be *slowed*. A fast
machine that is slowed, or *decelerated*, by a factor k *performs k internal transitions* in one synchronous step. Since the fast machine consumes an input and
produces an output in each of these internal steps, the decelerated machine consumes and produces k-tuples of inputs and outputs in each synchronous step. A
k-tuple output from the fast machine must therefore be *adapted* so that it can
be read by the slow component. That is, the k-tuple must be transformed to a
single value (e.g., the average of the k values, the last value, or any other function
of the k values); this transformation is formalized as an *input adaptor*. Likewise,
since the fast component expects a k-tuple of input values in each input port, the
single output from a slow component must be transformed to a k-tuple of inputs
to the fast machine; this is also done by input adaptors which may, for example,
transform an input d to a k-tuple $(d, \perp, \ldots, \perp)$ for some "don't care" value $\perp$.
Since what the fast machine does when receiving $\perp$ is application-dependent, we
assume that this is defined in the transition relation δ_M of the fast machine M.

We define a *multirate machine ensemble* to be a network of typed machines
with different rates, satisfying the above constraints, and with given input adaptors. To define the synchronous composition of such a multirate ensemble, we
make use of several auxiliary *formal patterns*. Specifically, we:

1. Define the *"k-step machine" pattern*, which transforms a "fast" machine into
   a slow machine that performs k "internal transitions" in one transition step.
2. Define input adaptors and the *input adaptor pattern*, specifying how a machine with input adaptors can be transformed to an ordinary typed machine.
3. Using the input adaptors and the k-step machines, we formally define a
   multirate ensemble together with an associated *multirate synchronous composition pattern*, by which it can be composed into a single typed machine.

We start by defining the *input adaptor pattern*:

Definition 1. *An* input adaptor α *for a typed machine* $M = (\mathcal{D}_i, S, \mathcal{D}_o, \delta_M)$
with $\mathcal{D}_i = D_{i_1} \times \cdots \times D_{i_n}$ *is a family of functions* $\alpha = \{\alpha_k : D'_k \to D_{i_k}\}_{k \in \{1, \ldots, n\}}$.
If $\boldsymbol{d} = (d_1, \ldots, d_n) \in D'_1 \times \cdots \times D'_n$, *we also write* $\alpha(\boldsymbol{d})$ *for* $(\alpha_1(d_1), \ldots, \alpha_n(d_n))$.

A machine with an input adaptor can be regarded as another typed machine:

Definition 2. *The* adaptor closure *of a typed machine* $M = (\mathcal{D}_i, S, \mathcal{D}_o, \delta_M)$ *with an adaptor* $\alpha = \{\alpha_k : D'_k \to D_{i_k}\}_{k \in \{1,\ldots,n\}}$ *is a typed machine* $M_\alpha = ((D'_1 \times \cdots \times D'_n), S, \mathcal{D}_o, \delta_{M_\alpha})$ *where*

$$((\mathbf{d}_i, s), (s', \mathbf{d}_o)) \in \delta_{M_\alpha} \iff ((\alpha(\mathbf{d}_i), s), (s', \mathbf{d}_o)) \in \delta_M.$$

We next define the *k-step machine pattern* by which we can "slow down," or *decelerate*, a fast machine by a factor k. As already mentioned, the machine reads k inputs (in each port), performs a transition which corresponds to k "internal transition steps" and outputs k-tuples of values:

Definition 3. *The* k-*step deceleration of a typed machine* $M = (\mathcal{D}_i, S, \mathcal{D}_o, \delta_M)$, *with* $\mathcal{D}_i = D_{i_1} \times \cdots \times D_{i_n}$ *and* $\mathcal{D}_o = D_{o_1} \times \cdots \times D_{o_m}$, *for* $k \in \mathbb{N}_+$ *is a typed machine* $M^{\times k} = ((D_{i_1})^k \times \cdots \times (D_{i_n})^k,\ S,\ (D_{o_1})^k \times \cdots \times (D_{o_m})^k,\ \delta_{M^{\times k}})$ *where*

$$((((d_{i_{1_1}}, \ldots, d_{i_{1_k}}), \ldots, (d_{i_{n_1}}, \ldots, d_{i_{n_k}})), s),$$
$$(s', ((d_{o_{1_1}}, \ldots, d_{o_{1_k}}), \ldots, (d_{o_{m_1}}, \ldots, d_{o_{m_k}})))) \in \delta_{M^{\times k}}$$

iff there exists $s_1, \ldots, s_{k-1} \in S$ *such that*

$$(((d_{i_{1_1}}, \ldots, d_{i_{n_1}}), s),\ (s_1, (d_{o_{1_1}}, \ldots, d_{o_{m_1}}))) \in \delta_M$$
$$(((d_{i_{1_2}}, \ldots, d_{i_{n_2}}), s_1),\ (s_2, (d_{o_{1_2}}, \ldots, d_{o_{m_2}}))) \in \delta_M$$
$$\vdots \qquad\qquad \vdots$$
$$(((d_{i_{1_k}}, \ldots, d_{i_{n_k}}), s_{k-1}),\ (s', (d_{o_{1_k}}, \ldots, d_{o_{m_k}}))) \in \delta_M.$$

The "local" fast environments should be dealt with by the corresponding fast machine, and we therefore assume that fast local environments are already integrated with their corresponding fast machines.[3] That is, the environment at the (slow) global level is only the environment of the high-level controllers. Finally, we make the definition more abstract by considering only the relative rates instead of the concrete periods. For example, the multirate "system" in Fig. 2 corresponds to the multirate ensemble in Fig. 3.

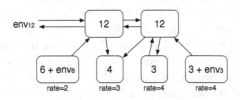

Fig. 3. A simple multirate ensemble (input adaptors not shown)

We now formally define *multirate ensembles* and the associated *multirate synchronous composition pattern*.

---

[3] An environment can be viewed as a nondeterministic typed machine [10]. Therefore, a faster machine's environment and the fast machine itself form a simple 2-machine ensemble, whose *ensemble composition* has now only wires from/to slow machines.

Definition 4. *A multirate ensemble is a tuple*

$$\mathfrak{E} = (J_S \cup J_F \cup \{e\}, \{M_l\}_{l \in J_S \cup J_F}, E, src, rate, adaptor)$$

where:

- J_S *is a nonempty set of ("controller component" or "slow machine") indices and J_F is a set of ("fast machine") indices with $J_S \cap J_F = \emptyset$;*
- *each M_l, with $l \in J_S \cup J_F$, is a typed machine;*
- *rate is a function rate : $J_F \to \mathbb{N} - \{0, 1\}$, assigning to each fast machine a value denoting how many times faster the machine runs compared to the slow machines; and*
- *src is a wiring diagram such that there is no connections between controlled components, or between the environment and a controlled component; i.e., if $src(l, q) = (k, p)$ then $l \in J_S \vee k \in J_S$; and*
- *adaptor is a function that assigns an input adaptor to each $l \in J_F \cup J_S$*

such that

$$\mathfrak{E}_{sr} = (J_S \cup J_F \cup \{e\}, \{(M_j)_{adaptor(j)}\}_{j \in J_S} \cup \{(M_j^{\times rate(j)})_{adaptor(j)}\}_{j \in J_F}, E, src)$$

is an ordinary (single-rate) typed machine ensemble.

By definition, the *multirate synchronous composition pattern* applied to $\mathfrak{E}$ is the transformation $\mathfrak{E} \mapsto MRSC(\mathfrak{E})$ assigning to a multirate ensemble $\mathfrak{E}$ the typed machine $MRSC(\mathfrak{E}) = M_{\mathfrak{E}_{sr}}$. Note that when J_F is empty and the input adaptors are identity functions, a multirate ensemble $\mathfrak{E}$ becomes an ordinary single-rate ensemble, and $MRSC(\mathfrak{E}) = M_{\mathfrak{E}}$. Therefore, $MRSC$ generalizes the single-rate synchronous composition pattern.

Furthermore, as for the single-rate synchronous composition pattern, the pattern $MRSC$ can be recursively applied. That is, the synchronous multirate composition $MRSC(\mathfrak{E})$ is itself a typed machine $M_{\mathfrak{E}_{sr}}$ which can appear as a component in another multirate ensemble, so that we can easily define hierarchical multirate systems. Such an architecture in common in, e.g., avionics, where, for redundancy purposes, there are *multiple* surface controllers for each aileron, the rudder, the elevator, etc. The controllers for a given device operate between themselves and the device at a fast rate, which might be different for different devices. These groups of surface controllers are again controlled by the main supervisory controllers, which operate at the slow rate and give commands so that the ailerons and rudder operate in lock-step to, e.g., turn the aircraft.

4   Multirate PALS

This section presents *Multirate PALS*, a formal pattern $(\mathfrak{E}, T, \Gamma) \mapsto \mathcal{MA}(\mathfrak{E}, T, \Gamma)$ that transforms a multirate ensemble $\mathfrak{E}$, together with its (global) period T and performance bounds Γ on clock skews, execution times, and network delays, into a formal specification $\mathcal{MA}(\mathfrak{E}, T, \Gamma)$ of a distributed real-time system where each machine performs at its own rate. We prove in Section 4.2 that the synchronous composition and the distributed asynchronous real-time model of a multirate ensemble satisfy the same properties. Since the *MRSC* pattern can be recursively applied, the Multirate PALS pattern can likewise be recursively applied. Due to space limitations, in this paper we apply Multirate PALS to non-hierarchical ensembles where fast machines do not have their own environments.

Since multirate PALS is based on a number of patterns, we could for modularity purposes use multiple "wrappers" to define the asynchronous model. The outermost wrapper would be the standard "PALS wrapper," which would enclose an input adaptor wrapper, which would enclose either a (slow) typed machine or a k-machine wrapper, which in turn would enclose an ordinary typed machine. However, in this paper we present a simpler "flat" model of the components in the asynchronous system where these wrappers have been combined.

Our definition of $\mathcal{MA}(\mathfrak{E},T,\Gamma)$ is in essence a reduction to PALS and roughly corresponds to $\mathcal{A}(\mathfrak{E}_{sr},T,\Gamma)$. There is, however, an important difference between the single-rate system $\mathcal{A}(\mathfrak{E}_{sr},T,\Gamma)$ and the multirate system $\mathcal{MA}(\mathfrak{E},T,\Gamma)$: in the former, fast machine with rate k performs all k transitions "in one shot," whereas in $\mathcal{MA}(\mathfrak{E},T,\Gamma)$ the fast machine operates according to its own fast period T/k and performs *one* transition at the beginning of each such fast period. Figure 4 presents a high-level view of the timeline of one round of a system with a fast (with $k=4$) and a slow component, where diagonal arrows denote message transmission and short horizontal lines denote the execution of a transition. The fast component may *not* be able to finish all of its internal transitions *before* the messages must be sent to the slow component to ensure that they arrive before the beginning of the next round (dashed diagonal arrow), even if T satisfies the constraints of the PALS period. The *fast* period T/k must satisfy $T/k \geq 2\epsilon + \mu_{\max} + \max(2\epsilon - \mu_{\min}, \alpha_{\max_f})$, where $\alpha_{\max_f}$ is the maximal transition execution time for the fast component, to ensure that the sending of messages can be delayed until all fast transitions in a slow round have been performed.

Using adaptors the above, quite stringent, constraint on fast machines can be avoided as follows. If there is not enough time for a fast machine to execute all of its k transitions before the messages must be sent to the slow component, but can only send $k' < k$ inputs, then the slow component should only consider

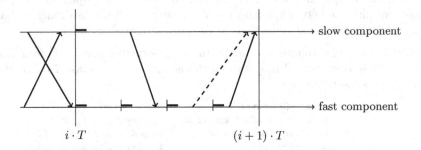

Fig. 4. Timeline for multirate asynchronous PALS system with $k=4$

these k' values. The number of transitions a fast component can perform in a global round before its output must be sent is given by

$$k' = \lfloor \frac{(T \text{ monus } (2\epsilon + \mu_{max} + \alpha_{max_f})) \cdot k}{T} \rfloor.$$

That is, if the source of the ith input port of a slow machine M_j is a fast machine whose k' is less than its rate k, then the adaptor function $adaptor(j)_i$ must satisfy $adaptor(j)_i (v_1, \ldots, v_{k'}, v_{k'+1}, \ldots, v_k) = adaptor(j)_i (v_1, \ldots, v_{k'}, v'_{k'+1}, \ldots, v'_k)$ for all values v_l and v'_l of appropriate types. Finally, we assume that a null value $\perp$ has been added to each type.

4.1 Formalizing the Asynchronous System in Real-Time Maude

This section presents the Real-Time Maude specification of the asynchronous real-time system $\mathcal{MA}(\mathfrak{E}, T, \Gamma)$ satisfying the above requirements. The model of slow components is essentially that of single-rate PALS [10], with the difference that the adaptor function should be applied to the input tuples to get a single input value for each input port. It can also be seen as the case $k = 1$ of the behavior of a fast component with rate k, which can be summarized as follows:

- At the beginning of each global round, the fast machine:
  - reads the received messages from its PALS input buffer;
  - uses its input adaptor to extract the "first" data value from each received message, performs a local transition, and places the resulting output in the PALS output buffer;
  - moves the received messages to another buffer, since the PALS input buffer is needed for the messages that arrive during the current round;
  - sets its output backoff timer to $T - 2\epsilon - \mu_{max}$, which is the latest local time (relative to the start of the slow round) that the messages can be sent out into the network while ensuring that they will be received by the beginning of the next global period.
- When the fast machine performs a local transition that does not take place at the beginning of a global round, it applies its input adaptor to the inputs stored in the additional input buffer, performs a transition, and adds the produced output to the output buffer.
- When the output backoff timer expires, the generated (tuples of) output are sent into the network, regardless of whether or not the fast machine has finished all of its local transitions in the current global period.

We model the asynchronous system in an object-oriented style, where a fast machine M_j is transformed into an object instance of a subclass FC_j of the following class FastMachine:

```
class FastMachine | state : DlyState,          clock : Time,
                    inBuffer : MsgConfiguration, prevInput : DataTuple,
                    outBuffer : DataTupleList,    outputBackoffTimer : TimeInf,
                    fastPeriodTimer : Time,       fastPeriodCounter : NzNat,
                    rate : NzNat,                 localWiring : LocalWiring .

class FC_1 .      ...      class FC_q .      subclass FC_1 ... FC_q < FastMachine .
```

The `inBuffer` attribute denotes the main input buffer that stores incoming messages; `prevInput` is the additional local input buffer; the output generated during the round is stored in `outBuffer` until it is sent into the network when the `outputBackoffTimer` expires; `fastPeriodTimer` expires whenever a local transition must be taken; the `fastPeriodCounter` attribute denotes *which* local transition this is during a global round (and has value 1 when a global round begins); and `clock` is the local clock. All timers advance at the rate of the imperfect local clock, as formalized in [10]. We do not show the definition of the various data types, many of which are explained in detail in [10], but note that, e.g., we assume that we have a supersort `Data` of all the data sorts.

The following rewrite rule models the reception of a message during a round; the received message is just added to the main input buffer:

```
vars j j' : Oid .     var p : Nat .     var d : Data .     var B : MsgConfiguration .

rl [receiveMsg] :
   (to j from j' (p, d))
   < j : FastMachine | inBuffer : B >
=>
   < j : FastMachine | inBuffer : B (to j from j' (p, d)) > .
```

The following rewrite rule models the beginning of a new global period (`fastPeriodTimer` has expired (i.e., is 0) and `fastPeriodCounter` is 1). The first single transition is performed, the output backoff timer is set to expire at the latest possible time, received input is stored in an internal buffer, and so on:

```
var X-DLY : Time .        vars S NEXT-STATE : State .        var W : LocalWiring .
var d_{j_1} : D^j_{o_1} .    ...    var d_{j_{m_j}} : D^j_{o_{m_j}} .    var RATE : NzNat .

crl [applyTrans] :
   < j : FC_j | inBuffer : B, fastPeriodTimer : 0, fastPeriodCounter : 1,
                rate : RATE, state : S >
=>
   < j : FC_j | inBuffer : none, fastPeriodTimer : T/RATE,
                fastPeriodCounter : if RATE == 1 then 1 else 2 fi,
                prevInput : vect(B), state : [NEXT-STATE, X-DLY],
                outputBackoffTimer : T - 2·ε - μ_max,
                outBuffer : [(d_{j_1}, ..., d_{j_{m_j}}), X-DLY] >
   if X-DLY >= α_min and X-DLY <= α_max
   /\ (π_1(adaptor(j)(vect(B))), S), (NEXT-STATE, (d_{j_1}, ..., d_{j_{m_j}}))) ∈ δ_{M_j} .
```

The function `vect` maps a set B of messages of the form

$$(\text{to } j \text{ from } j'_1 \ (1, d_1)) \quad \ldots \quad (\text{to } j \text{ from } j'_{n_j} \ (n_j, d_{n_j})) \quad (\dagger)$$

to the vector of inputs $(d_1, \ldots, d_{n_j})$, and π_i maps the tuple $((d_{1_1}, \ldots, d_{1_k}), \ldots, (d_{n_{j_1}}, \ldots, d_{n_{j_k}}))$ to the tuple $(d_{1_i}, \ldots, d_{n_{j_i}})$. Notice that any possible previous content in the output buffer is replaced by the generated output.

The following rule models the Ith transition ($2 \leq \text{I} \leq \text{RATE}$) of a fast machine, where `_::_` denotes list concatenation for lists of data tuples, and $[d, dly]$ and $[s, dly]$ denote "delayed" output/state that will be "undelayed" after time dly:

```
var I : NzNat .     var DT : DataTuple .     var DTL : DataTupleList .

crl [applyInternalTransition] :
    < j : FCj | prevInput : DT, fastPeriodTimer : 0, fastPeriodCounter : I,
                rate : RATE, state : S, outBuffer : DTL >
  =>
    < j : FCj | fastPeriodTimer : T/RATE,
                fastPeriodCounter : if I == RATE then 1 else I + 1 fi,
                state : [NEXT-STATE, X-DLY],
                outBuffer : DTL :: [(dj1, ..., djmj), X-DLY] >
  if X-DLY >= αmin and X-DLY <= αmax
    /\ (πI(adaptor(j)(DT)),S), (NEXT-STATE,(dj1, ..., djmj))) ∈ δMj .
```

The last rule for fast machines takes the tuples in the output buffers, generates the corresponding messages and sends the messages into the network when the output backoff timer expires. "Delayed" output, indicating that the transition generating that output is not yet finished, should of course not be sent:

```
crl [outputMsg] :
    < j : FastMachine | outBuffer : DTL, outputBackoffTimer : 0, rate : RATE,
                        localWiring : W >
  =>
    < j : FastMachine | outBuffer : nil, outputBackoffTimer : INF >
    dly(makeMsgs(j, W, DTL, RATE), μmin, μmax) .
```

where `makeMsgs` takes a list of outputs (ignoring the last vector if it is still "delayed" and adding ⊥ elements if there is less than `RATE` tuples to transmit) and the wiring diagram and generates the corresponding outgoing messages, and `dly` assigns the given network delay interval to each message [12].

The treatment of time (including updating the timers and delays) and of the environment is done in the same way as in [10] and is not shown.

4.2 Correctness of the Multirate PALS Transformation

This section formalizes the relationship between the synchronous composition $MRSC(\mathfrak{E})$ and the asynchronous multirate real-time system $\mathcal{MA}(\mathfrak{E},T,\Gamma)$, where the input adaptors in $\mathfrak{E}$ do not distinguish between inputs that cannot be generated early enough. We also assume, in addition to the single-rate PALS requirements in Section 2, that for a fast machine f with rate k, $\alpha_{max_f} < T/k - 2\epsilon$, which implies that the machine can finish one local transition before having to start the next one. Because of space limitations, we only give a brief overview of our correctness proof.

Our proof exploits that for single-rate ensembles $\mathcal{E}$, the transition system $ts(\mathcal{E})$ and the "big step" transition system $(Stable(\mathcal{A}(\mathcal{E},T,\Gamma)), \longrightarrow_{st})$ are bisimilar. Since $\mathfrak{E}_{sr}$ is a single-rate ensemble, the transition system $ts(\mathfrak{E}_{sr})$ of $MRSC(\mathfrak{E})$ (which equals $M_{\mathfrak{E}_{sr}}$) and $(Stable(\mathcal{A}(\mathfrak{E}_{sr},T,\Gamma)), \longrightarrow_{st})$ are bisimilar. The part remaining is to define the stable states in $\mathcal{MA}(\mathfrak{E},T,\Gamma)$ and show that its big-step transition system $Stable(\mathcal{MA}(\mathfrak{E},T,\Gamma), \longrightarrow_{st})$ is bisimilar and satisfies the same properties as $Stable(\mathcal{A}(\mathfrak{E}_{sr},T,\Gamma))$. We start by defining the stable states in $\mathcal{MA}(\mathfrak{E},T,\Gamma)$ and its associated transition system.

Definition 5. *A state t in $\mathcal{MA}(\mathfrak{E}, T, \Gamma)$ is stable iff (i) it is reachable from a legitimate initial state of the system; (ii) all its input buffers are full; (iii) there are no messages in transit; (iv) there is nothing in the output buffers of the slow components; and (v) the* `fastRateCounter` *attribute of each fast component equals 1 and its state is "undelayed."*

A stable state corresponds to a state (s, o_{fb}) in $MRSC(\mathfrak{E})$, where the values of the objects' `state` attributes give s and the content in the input buffers give the content o_{fb} in the feedback wires. A "big step" stable transition $t \longrightarrow_{st} t'$ between two stable states t and t' is a sequence of rewrite steps

$$t = t_0 \longrightarrow t_1 \longrightarrow \cdots \longrightarrow t_i \longrightarrow \cdots \longrightarrow t_{i'} = t'$$

in $\mathcal{MA}(\mathfrak{E}, T, \Gamma)$, for some $i \geq 0$ such that each step $t_l \longrightarrow t_{l+1}$, for $l < i$, is a tick step between stable states, the states $t_{i+1}, \ldots, t_{i'-1}$ are not stable, and there is at least one application of an instantaneous rewrite rule in the sequence. Intuitively, a stable transition consists of (possibly) some applications of the tick rule to advance time in stable states, and then a sequence of both instantaneous and tick steps leading to a stable state corresponding to the beginning of the *next* round. We denote by $Stable(\mathcal{MA}(\mathfrak{E}, T, \Gamma))$ the set of stable states of $\mathcal{MA}(\mathfrak{E}, T, \Gamma)$.

There is in general no straight-forward correspondence between the stable states in $\mathcal{MA}(\mathfrak{E}, T, \Gamma)$ and the states in $M_{\mathfrak{E}_{sr}}$ (and hence $Stable(\mathcal{A}(\mathfrak{E}_{sr}, T, \Gamma)))$ since in both $M_{\mathfrak{E}_{sr}}$ and $\mathcal{A}(\mathfrak{E}_{sr}, T, \Gamma)$, the fast machines perform all k transitions in one step. Since a fast machine in $\mathcal{MA}(\mathfrak{E}, T, \Gamma)$ may not finish all k transitions before its output must be sent into the network, some of its outputs will be '$\perp$' where $M_{\mathfrak{E}_{sr}}$ and $\mathcal{A}(\mathfrak{E}_{sr}, T, \Gamma)$ output "real" values. Since the content of the "feedback wires" is part of a state of $M_{\mathfrak{E}_{sr}}$, the states in $M_{\mathfrak{E}_{sr}}$ and $Stable(\mathcal{MA}(\mathfrak{E}, T, \Gamma))$ will not be the "same." However, since input adaptors cannot distinguish between the two outputs in these cases, the outputs are equivalent for all practical purposes. We therefore define an equivalence $\equiv_A$ ("adaptor equivalence") on $S^{\mathfrak{E}_{sr}} \times D_o^e$ such that $((s, o_{fb}), i) \equiv_A ((s, o'_{fb}), i)$ if no input adaptor in $\mathfrak{E}$ can distinguish between o_{fb} and o'_{fb} and state our main result:

Theorem 1. *Let $L : S^{\mathfrak{E}_{sr}} \times D_o^e \to \mathcal{P}(AP)$ be a function such that $((s, o_{fb}), i) \equiv_A ((s, o'_{fb}), i)$ implies $L((s, o_{fb}), i) = L((s, o'_{fb}), i)$. For any CTL^* formula ϕ over AP and initial state t_0 we have $(Stable(\mathcal{MA}(\mathfrak{E}, T, \Gamma)), \longrightarrow_{st}), sr; sync; L, t_0 \models \phi$ if and only if $ts(\mathfrak{E}_{sr}), L, sync(sr(t_0)) \models \phi$, where sr maps a stable state in $\mathcal{MA}(\mathfrak{E}, T, \Gamma)$ to the corresponding stable state in $\mathcal{A}(\mathfrak{E}_{sr}, T, \Gamma)$.*

The proof "lifts" $\equiv_A$ to $\mathcal{A}(\mathfrak{E}_{sr}, T, \Gamma)$, proves that $sr; \equiv_A$ is a bisimulation between $(Stable(\mathcal{MA}(\mathfrak{E}, T, \Gamma)), \longrightarrow_{st})$ and $(Stable(\mathcal{A}(\mathfrak{E}_{sr}, T, \Gamma)), \longrightarrow_{st})$, and that $\equiv_A$-equivalent states in $Stable(\mathcal{A}(\mathfrak{E}_{sr}, T, \Gamma)$ satisfy the same atomic propositions w.r.t. the labeling function $sync; L$.

5   An Aeronautics Case Study

We illustrate Multirate PALS with a simple model of a control system to turn an aircraft. This case study is explained in detail in [4]. When an aircraft makes a turn, it rolls towards the direction of the turn, so that the lift force caused by the two wings acts as the centripetal force and the aircraft moves in a circular motion. If the direction of the aircraft is given by an angle ψ, the turning rate can be given by $d\psi = (g/v) * \tan\phi$, where ϕ is the roll angle, g is the gravity constant, and v is the velocity of the aircraft [2]. The ailerons[4] are used to control the rolling angle of the aircraft by generating different amount of lift force in the left and the right wings. However, the roll of the aircraft causes a difference in the drag on the left and the right wings, which causes adverse yaw. This is countered by using the rudder[5], which generates the side lift force on the vertical tail that opposes the adverse yaw. To turn an aircraft, its roll angle should be increased towards the desired direction while its yaw angle stays at 0. The roll angle ϕ and the yaw angle β can be modeled by the following equations [2]:

$$d\phi^2 = (\textit{Lift Right} - \textit{Lift Left})/(\textit{Weight} * \textit{Length of Wing})$$
$$d\beta^2 = \textit{Drag Ratio} * (\textit{Lift Right} - \textit{Lift Left})/(\textit{Weight} * \textit{Length of Wing})$$
$$+ \textit{Lift Vertical}/(\textit{Weight} * \textit{Length of Aircraft})$$

The lift from the left, the right, or the vertical wing is given by the equation

$$\textit{Lift} = \textit{Lift constant} * \textit{Angle with respect to free stream}$$

where the lift constant depends on the geometry of the corresponding wing, and the drag ratio is given by the size and the shape of the entire aircraft.

We model the airplane turning control system as the multirate ensemble of 4 typed machines: the main controller, the left wing controller, the right wing controller, and the rudder controller. Each subcontroller moves the surface of the wing towards the goal angle specified by the main controller, which sends the desired angles to the subcontrollers to make a coordinated turn whose goal direction is given by a pilot (the environment). The main controller also models sensors that measure the roll, the yaw, and the direction, by the formulas above. We assume that the main controller has period 60 ms, the left and the right wing controllers have period 15 ms, and the rudder controller has period 20 ms.

In [4] we present a modeling framework for multirate ensembles in Maude. Each machine is modeled as an object instance of a subclass of `Component`, whose attribute `ports` contains the component's ports. We support the definition of hierarchical ensembles by letting an ensemble be a `Component` containing also the wiring diagram (`connections`) and the `machines` in the ensemble:

```
class Component | ports : Configuration, rate : NzNat .
class Ensemble | machines : Configuration,  connections : Set{Connection} .
subclass Ensemble < Component .
```

For each machine, the user must define its subclass, the function `delta` defining the transition function, and the `adaptor` function for each input port:

---

[4] A flap attached to the end of the left or the right wing in the aircraft.
[5] A flap attached to the vertical tail of the aircraft.

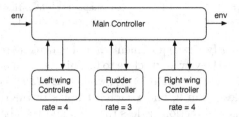

Fig. 5. The architecture of the airplane turning control system

```
op delta : Object ~> Object [frozen] .
op adaptor : ComponentId PortId NeList{Data} ~> NeList{Data} .
```

Given these definitions, our framework then provides an executable Maude model of the synchronous composition of the ensemble as explained in [4].

In our case study, the subcontrollers for the ailerons and the rudder are modeled as object instances of the following class SubController:

```
class SubController | curr-angle : Float, goal-angle : Float, diff-angle : Float .
subclass SubController < Component .
```

diff-angle indicates the maximal angle of the wing that can be changed during each fast period. The transition function is defined by the following equation.

```
ceq delta(< C : SubController | ports : < input : InPort | content : D LI >
                                < output : OutPort | content : LO >,
                      curr-angle : CA, goal-angle : GA, diff-angle : DA >)
 = < C : SubController | ports : < input : InPort | content : LI >
                         < output : OutPort | content : LO d(CA') >,
               curr-angle : CA', goal-angle : GA' >
 if CA' := adjAngle(moveAngle(CA,GA,DA))
 /\ GA' := adjAngle(if D == ⊥ then GA else float(D) fi) .
```

moveAngle(CA,GA,DA) increases or decreases the current angle CA by up to the maximum angle difference DA towards the goal angle GA. adjAngle keeps the angle value between −180 and 180. delta updates the goal angle according to input from the main controller, and keeps the previous goal if it receives ⊥.

We refer to [4] for the specification of the main controller. The airplane turning control system is represented as an ensemble as follows:

```
< system : Ensemble | rate : 1, ports : ...
          machines : < left : SubController | rate : 4, ... >
                     < right : SubController | rate : 4, ... >
                     < rudder : SubController | rate : 3, ... >
                     < main : MainController | rate : 1, ... >,
            connections : (input --> main . input) ; (main . output --> output) ;
                          (left . output --> main . inLW) ; ... > .
```

The input adaptors for the subcontrollers generate a vector with extra ⊥'s and the adaptor for the main controller selects the last value of the input vector:

```
eq adaptor(left, input, D) = D ⊥ ⊥ ⊥ .    eq adaptor(right, input, D) = D ⊥ ⊥ ⊥ .
eq adaptor(rudder, input, D) = D ⊥ ⊥ .    eq adaptor(main, PI, LI D) = D .
```

Our system should satisfy the requirement that the airplane reaches the desired direction while keeping the yaw angle close to 0. This requirement is formalized as the LTL formula safeYaw U reach(60.0), where safeYaw holds iff the absolute value of the yaw is less than 2, and reach(F) holds iff the difference between the current and the goal directions is less than 0.5 and the absolute value of the roll is less than 0.1. The initial state init(60.0) defines a model where the goal direction of the main controller is 60, and where the environment always outputs ⊥, since the goal never changes. The following model checking command shows that the property holds:

```
Maude> (red modelCheck(init(60.0), safeYaw U reach(60.0)) .)
result Bool :   true
```

6   Related Work

The most closely related work is a paper on the same topic [1] by colleagues with whom we developed the original PALS pattern. Both our paper and theirs share a common goal, namely, drastically simplifying the complexity of multi-rate distributed real-time systems; but they address this topic in quite different ways. By using AADL to describe their version of multirate PALS, the authors of [1] achieve a useful engineering description of the pattern that can be directly used in model-based software engineering. What is not attempted in [1] is to give *mathematical* models of either synchronous multirate systems or their multirate PALS transformation as distributed real-time systems, or to justify why the synchronous multirate system and its multirate PALS counterpart satisfy the same temporal logic properties; in fact, AADL is totally unsuited for such tasks. This is exactly what we do in this paper, and why both papers are complementary. It is also important to remark that our model of multirate PALS and theirs *have some important differences*, including the following: (i) their model lacks a systematic notion of *input adaptor*, and therefore the issue of what to do with the multiple outputs of a faster component is left somewhat open; (ii) their model assumes that if a component runs k times faster than the common period, then the *last* output from that component will be the one provided before the end of the common period to other components; we think that for k fast enough this may easily become impossible due of communication delays; our model is more flexible and can easily handle arbitrarily faster rates; and (iii) their model allows "sideways" communication between different fast components with different rates; but it is unclear how these different components will behave at different rates at times when they lack the needed inputs from other components; instead, our communication is hierarchical and avoids this problem.

More generally, the PALS pattern can be seen as part of a body of work on so-called *synchronizers*, which relate (single-rate) synchronous and asynchronous systems. Very general synchronizers such as those in [3] place no a priori bounds on message delays, so that *physical time* in the original synchronous system is simulated by *logical time* in its asynchronous counterpart. More recent work has developed synchronizers for the Asynchronous Bounded Delay (ABD) network model [16], in which a bound can be given for the delay of message transmissions. PALS also assumes the ABD model (plus clock synchronization) but provides *hard real-time guarantees* needed for embedded systems, whereas in the synchronizers in [16], two nodes could be in completely different (local) rounds at the same physical time. Work by Tripakis et al. [17] relates a synchronous Mealy machine model to a loosely timed triggered architecture with local clocks that can advance at different rates with no clock synchronization. The main difference with PALS is that it does not seem possible to give hard real time bounds for the behavior of the asynchronous system realization. In the Globally Synchronous Locally Asynchronous (GALS) Architecture [7,14], systems may be widely distributed and it may not be possible to assume that all message communication delays are bounded, although such delays may be bounded within a synchronous subdomain. Consequently, no hard real-time guarantees can be given for a GALS implementation. Single-rate PALS is also closely related to the *time-triggered systems* of Kopetz and Rushby [8,15], where the goal is also to reduce an asynchronous real-time system to a simpler, synchronous one. One important difference is that the smallest period of the asynchronous system of Kopetz and Rushby may be significantly larger than the optimal PALS period.

7   Conclusions

We have argued that the design, verification, and implementation of a DRTS is a big challenge that requires new methods to tame the enormous complexities involved. We have poposed Multirate PALS as an answer to this challenge in the case of a multirate DRTS where virtual synchrony must be ensured between its components. To achieve this in a rigorous way we have defined the mathematical semantics of synchronous multirate ensembles of machines and of several key component transformations that together allow us to give a precise mathematical definition of Multirate PALS and prove its bisimilarity with the synchronous composition of the original multirate ensemble. Multirate PALS is supported by Maude and Real-Time Maude for specification and model checking purposes. We have illustrated its power as a complexity-reducing pattern by showing how it can be used to verify properties about the turning maneuvers of an airplane.

One obvious next step is to make the formal verification capabilities associated to Multirate PALS available to DRTS engineers using the AADL modeling system in the same way as we did for PALS through the *SynchAADL2Maude* system [5]. This will require further extending the AADL synchronous annex with multirate capabilities, and making Maude-based model checking available at the level of AADL models of synchronous multirate ensembles.

References

1. Al-Nayeem, A., Sha, L., Cofer, D.D., Miller, S.M.: Pattern-based composition and analysis of virtually synchronized real-time distributed systems. In: Proc. Cyber-Physical Systems (IEEE/ACM ICCPS 2012) (2012)
2. Anderson, J.: Introduction to flight. McGraw-Hill (2005)
3. Awerbuch, B.: Complexity of network synchronization. J. ACM 32(4), 804–823 (1985)
4. Bae, K., Krisiloff, J., Meseguer, J., Ölveczky, P.C.: PALS-based analysis of an airplane multirate control system in Real-Time Maude. In: Proc. FTSCS 2012 (2012); To appear in Electronic Proceedings in Theoretical Computer Science
5. Bae, K., Ölveczky, P.C., Al-Nayeem, A., Meseguer, J.: Synchronous AADL and Its Formal Analysis in Real-Time Maude. In: Qin, S., Qiu, Z. (eds.) ICFEM 2011. LNCS, vol. 6991, pp. 651–667. Springer, Heidelberg (2011)
6. Clavel, M., Durán, F., Eker, S., Lincoln, P., Martí-Oliet, N., Meseguer, J., Talcott, C.: All About Maude. LNCS, vol. 4350. Springer, Heidelberg (2007)
7. Girault, A., Ménier, C.: Automatic Production of Globally Asynchronous Locally Synchronous Systems. In: Sangiovanni-Vincentelli, A.L., Sifakis, J. (eds.) EMSOFT 2002. LNCS, vol. 2491, pp. 266–281. Springer, Heidelberg (2002)
8. Kopetz, H., Grünsteidl, G.: TTP - a protocol for fault-tolerant real-time systems. IEEE Computer 27(1), 14–23 (1994)
9. Meseguer, J., Ölveczky, P.C.: Formalization and Correctness of the PALS Architectural Pattern for Distributed Real-Time Systems. In: Dong, J.S., Zhu, H. (eds.) ICFEM 2010. LNCS, vol. 6447, pp. 303–320. Springer, Heidelberg (2010)
10. Meseguer, J., Ölveczky, P.C.: Formalization and correctness of the PALS architectural pattern for distributed real-time systems. Theor. Comp. Sci. 451, 1–37 (2012)
11. Miller, S.P., Cofer, D.D., Sha, L., Meseguer, J., Al-Nayeem, A.: Implementing logical synchrony in integrated modular avionics. In: Proc. DASC 2009. IEEE (2009)
12. Ölveczky, P.C.: Towards formal modeling and analysis of networks of embedded medical devices in Real-Time Maude. In: Proc. SNPD 2008. IEEE (2008)
13. Ölveczky, P.C., Meseguer, J.: Semantics and pragmatics of Real-Time Maude. Higher-Order and Symbolic Computation 20(1-2), 161–196 (2007)
14. Potop-Butucaru, D., Caillaud, B.: Correct-by-construction asynchronous implementation of modular synchronous specifications. Fundam. Inform. 78(1), 131–159 (2007)
15. Rushby, J.: Systematic formal verification for fault-tolerant time-triggered algorithms. IEEE Trans. Software Eng. 25(5), 651–660 (1999)
16. Tel, G., Korach, E., Zaks, S.: Synchronizing ABD networks. IEEE Trans. Networking 2(1), 66–69 (1994)
17. Tripakis, S., Pinello, C., Benveniste, A., Sangiovanni-Vincentelli, A., Caspi, P., DiNatale, M.: Implementing synchronous models on loosely time triggered architectures. IEEE Trans. on Computers 1 (2008)

Component Interfaces with Contracts on Ports*

Sebastian Bauer[1], Rolf Hennicker[1], and Axel Legay[2]

[1] Ludwig-Maximilians-Universität München, Germany
[2] INRIA/IRISA Rennes, France

Abstract. We show how the abstract concept of a (labeled) interface theory can be canonically extended to an abstract framework for component interfaces with ports. The resulting component framework satisfies itself the general laws of an interface theory (concerning the composition, refinement, and environment correctness notions). The ports of a component interface represent the interaction points of a component. Each port is equipped with a contract specifying the assumptions on and the guarantees for the environment of a component. As a particular instance we consider modal component interfaces such that component behaviors and the assume and guarantee behaviors of ports are given in terms of modal I/O-transition systems with weak modal refinement and with a weak modal environment correctness notion. The modal approach is particularly useful to specify loose environment assumptions.

1 Introduction

The development of large, reliable component systems relies heavily on the use of interfaces. Hence, rigorous development methods are mandatory which support interface composition, stepwise refinement and the consideration of compatibility issues when a component is put in an environment. These requirements together with concise rules how the different dimensions of system development should work together are formulated in an abstract way in the seminal work of De Alfaro and Henzinger [10]. There the notion of an *interface theory* has been introduced which consists of an interface algebra together with a component algebra thus distinguishing interface specifications and component implementations.

In this paper we follow the idea of De Alfaro and Henzinger to study abstract concepts and rules that later on can be instantiated by concrete frameworks. But we will focus more specifically on the domain of reactive component systems such that interfaces should be equipped with additional structure that makes more explicit their possible connections. For that purpose we rely on ports as interaction points of a component as it is quite standard in many design languages.

Independently, a number of contract theories, based on assume-guarantee (AG) reasoning have been developed, with a similar aim of approaching compositional design. Contract theories differ from interface theories in that they strictly follow the principle of separation of concerns. They separate the specification of assumptions from specification of guarantees, a choice largely inspired

---

* This work has been partially sponsored by the EU project ASCENS, 257414.

C.S. Păsăreanu and G. Salaün (Eds.): FACS 2012, LNCS 7684, pp. 19–35, 2013.
© Springer-Verlag Berlin Heidelberg 2013

by early ideas on manual proof methods of Misra, Chandy [25] and Jones [18], along with the wide acceptance to pre-/post-condition style of specification in programming [24,30], and more general semantical rules independent from language representation [8].

In [4], we have shown how a theory of contracts can be built on top of a given abstract specification theory. Contracts are just pairs (A, G) of an assumption and a guarantee specification. We have shown in [4] how the contract theory can be instantiated by using modal transitions systems [29] with strong modal refinement. This approach, however, did only work for specification theories which admit a "quotient" construction as specification building primitive and therefore could not be applied to instances that support weak refinement abstracting away silent τ-transitions [5] which is much more powerful. Compatibility issues concerning the communication between modal transition systems have not been integrated in [4]. On the other hand, the entities of our contract theory were just pairs (A, G) disallowing any structural splitting which is necessary if we want to deal with components with more than one port.

In the current paper we first introduce the notion of a labeled interface theory in Sect. 2, which resembles an interface theory in the sense of De Alfaro and Henzinger with the additional provision that a set of labels is assigned to any interface (which intuitively represents an action alphabet). Moreover, in addition to interface refinement, we introduce an environment correctness relation $S \rightarrow E$ to express when an environment E satisfies the interaction requirements of an interface S. We show, in Sect. 3, how a theory of component interfaces can be defined on top of any framework satisfying our abstract rules of an interface theory. A distinguished feature of component interfaces is that they have a set of ports such that each port P is equipped with a port contract (A^P, G^P) specifying the assumptions on the environment that is going to be connected on this particular port, and the guarantees of the component on that port. Hence our approach deviates from approaches that use single port protocols not allowing to extract distinguished assumptions and guarantees. All notions of an interface theory, i.e. composition, refinement and environment correctness, are propagated to the level of component interfaces which themselves are shown to satisfy the requirements of an interface theory. We also discuss reliability of component interfaces which means that the component frame, intended to specify the overall visible behavior of a component, supports the guarantees shown on the ports. We prove that reliability is compositional.

As a proof of concept, we instantiate in Sect. 4 our generic constructions and build a modal theory of component interfaces on top of a labeled interface theory with modal I/O-transitions systems and weak modal refinement as a basis [21],[5]. In particular, we consider a small case study in Sect. 4.2.

Related Work. As observed above, our work extends classical interface theories [10,12,7] with an explicit treatment of assumptions-guarantees. Other works on interface automata, e.g. [14], exploit the concept of assumption and guarantee to improve the efficiency of compatibility checking. However, they are not comparable to our approach as they exploit assumption and guarantee at the operational level, but not at the design one. An intermediary step between those approaches is the work of Parizek and Plasil [26] that proposes a compositional methodology to reduce the verification of a composite component to the one of a series of smaller verifications on single components. Recently, a similar approach to the one of [26] was followed in the BIP toolset developed by Sifakis et al. [3].

Independently, a number of contract theories, based on explicit assume-guarantee reasoning have been developed, with a similar aim of approaching the compositional design. Among them, one finds the work of Meyer [24], that is based on pre and post conditions as state predicates and invariants for the system itself. This approach, which builds on seminal ideas proposed by Dijkstra and Lamport [13,19], is similar to ours in the sense that pre and post conditions shall be viewed as assumption and guarantee, respectively.

Some works [2] introduced contracts in the refinement calculus. In this formalism, processes are described with guarded command operating on shared variables. This formalism is best suited to reason on untimed system, while our approach is general and could be instantiated on other types of data. Additionally, each of the above mentioned work suffers from the absence of multiple treatment of assumptions/guarantees and rely on a unique language while our abstract language can work with arbitrary interface theories.

More recently, Benveniste et al.[6] proposed a contract theory in where assumption and guarantees are represented by trace structures. While this work is of clear interest, it suffers from the absence of effective representation for the embedded interface theory. Extensions such as the one proposed in [28,15] leverage this problem but ignore the multiple treatment of assumptions and guarantees.

2 Labeled Interface Theories

The idea of an interface theory is to capture basic requirements that should be satisfied by any formal framework supporting behavior specifications of components. We assume given a set $\mathfrak{S}$ of interface specifications such that any interface is equipped with a finite set of labels (representing the alphabet of actions an interface may perform). An interface theory includes a composition operator $\otimes$ to combine interfaces to larger ones. The composition operator is, in general, partial since it is not always syntactically meaningful to compose interfaces, due to syntactic constraints. Additionally, an interface theory must offer a refinement relation $\leq$ to relate "concrete" and "abstract" specifications, i.e. $S \leq T$ means that S is a correct refinement of T. Intuitively, the refinement relation expresses that the implementation requirements of the (abstract) interface T are respected by the refinement S. Refinement must be compositional in the sense that it must be preserved by the composition operator expressed by requirement (A1) below. An interface theory must also address the relationship between components and their environment. For this purpose we introduce an environment correctness relation $\rightarrow$ such that $S \rightarrow E$ means that E is a correct environment for S. Intuitively, this relation expresses that the communication requirements of S are satisfied by the environment E (which is itself just another interface); we may say that S "feels well" in the environment E. Hence, the environment correctness relation is unidirectional and it is orthogonal to the refinement relation; the former concerns the "horizontal" dimension while the latter concerns the "vertical" dimension of system development. Both relations must be compatible in the sense that environment correctness must be preserved by refinement as stated in requirement (A2) below. This means that interface specifications and correct environments can be replaced by specialized versions without disrupting the correctness of the environment. Requirement (A3) concerns the relation between interface composition and environment correctness. Intuitively, it states that correct environments can be composed to a larger correct environment. More precisely, if S in the context of E feels well in E' and if S in the context of E' feels well in E, then S feels well in the larger environment $E \otimes E'$.

Definition 1 (Labeled Interface Theory). *A labeled interface theory is a quadruple* $(\mathfrak{S}, \mathcal{L}, \ell, \otimes, \leq, \rightarrow)$ *consisting of*

- *a set $\mathfrak{S}$ of interface specifications,*
- *a set $\mathcal{L}$ of labels,*
- *a function $\ell : \mathfrak{S} \rightarrow \wp_{\mathrm{fin}}(\mathcal{L})$ assigning a finite set of labels to each interface,*
- *a partial, commutative[1] composition operator $\otimes : \mathfrak{S} \times \mathfrak{S} \rightarrow \mathfrak{S}$; we call S and E composable, if $S \otimes E$ is defined and require the following rules for composable interfaces:*
  C1. If $S \otimes E$ is defined, then $\ell(S \otimes E) = (\ell(S) \cup \ell(E)) \setminus (\ell(S) \cap \ell(E))$.
  C2. If $\ell(S) \cap \ell(E) = \emptyset$, then $S \otimes E$ is defined.
  C3. Pseudo-associativity: If S, E and E' are pairwise composable and $\ell(S) \cap \ell(E) \cap \ell(E') = \emptyset$, then $(S \otimes E) \otimes E'$ and $S \otimes (E \otimes E')$ are defined and $(S \otimes E) \otimes E' = S \otimes (E \otimes E')$.
- *a reflexive and transitive refinement relation $\leq \subseteq \mathfrak{S} \times \mathfrak{S}$ such that $S \leq T$ implies $\ell(S) = \ell(T)$,*
- *an environment correctness relation $\rightarrow \subseteq \mathfrak{S} \times \mathfrak{S}$ such that, if $S \rightarrow E$ then $S \otimes E$ is defined; we write $S \leftrightarrows E$ and call S and E compatible, if $S \rightarrow E$ and $E \rightarrow S$.*

For all interfaces $S, S', E, E' \in \mathfrak{S}$ the following properties must hold:

A1. *Compositional Refinement:*
   If $S \otimes E$ is defined, $S' \leq S$ and $E' \leq E$, then $S' \otimes E'$ is defined and $S' \otimes E' \leq S \otimes E$.
A2. *Preservation of Environment Correctness:*
   If $S \rightarrow E$ and $S' \leq S$, $E' \leq E$, then $S' \rightarrow E'$.
A3. *Environment Composition:*
   If $S \otimes E \rightarrow E'$ and $S \otimes E' \rightarrow E$ and $\ell(E) \cap \ell(E') = \emptyset$, then $S \rightarrow E \otimes E'$.[2]

---

[1] Commutativity means that for all $S, E \in \mathfrak{S}$, if $S \otimes E$ is defined then $E \otimes S$ is defined and $S \otimes E = E \otimes S$; "$=$" means set-theoretic equality of elements.
[2] In particular, $S \otimes (E \otimes E')$ must be defined.

A formal notion of an *interface theory* was, to our knowledge, first proposed by de Alfaro and Henzinger in [10]. In their work, an interface theory consists of an interface algebra together with a component algebra thus distinguishing between interface specifications and component implementations. Later, in [11], the authors introduced the term *interface language* which simplifies the approach by considering just interfaces with the requirements that independent implementability and incremental design are supported. Our notion of an interface theory is close to an interface language in the sense of [11]. The differences are the following: (1) We associate a set of labels to each interface. (2) We require that interface composition is commutative and pseudo-associative. (3) Instead of using a binary compatibility predicate to express that two interfaces can work properly together, we introduce a unidirectional environment correctness relation. If it is applied in both directions we obtain compatibility. (4) We require compositional refinement for any composable interfaces and not only for compatible ones. (5) Our notion of environmental composition is a variant of incremental design in [11]. For any finite index set I we consider I-sorted sets $(S_i)_{i \in I}$ (i.e. finite families) of interfaces. We call $(S_i)_{i \in I}$ *composable*, if the single interfaces S_i are pairwise composable and if labels of each S_i are shared with at most one other interface S_j ($j \neq i$) of the family. Obviously, any subset of a composable set of interfaces is composable.

For non-empty index sets I we extend the binary notion of interface composition to I-sorted sets of composable interfaces by the following inductive definition along the size $|I|$ of I:

- If $|I| = 1$, then $\otimes(S_i)_{i \in I} = S_i$ where $I = \{i\}$.
- If $|I| > 1$ and $(S_i)_{i \in I}$ is composable, then $\otimes(S_i)_{i \in I} \triangleq \otimes(S_i)_{i \in I'} \otimes S_j$ for some subset $I' \subseteq I$ with $|I'| = |I| - 1$ and for S_j with $I \setminus I' = \{j\}$.

$\otimes(S_i)_{i \in I}$ is well-defined, since by commutativity and pseudo-associativity of the binary composition the definition is independent of the choice of I'.

3   A Theory of Component Interfaces with Port Contracts

In this section we show how a theory of component interfaces can be constructed on top of any arbitrary labeled interface theory. Our goal is not to define yet another language for component-based design but to focus on fundamental, abstract properties of component interfaces which refines the concept of an interface theory of Sect. 2 by introducing more structure. In addition to pure interfaces, we require that component interfaces define access points in terms of distinguished ports which are used for the composition of component interfaces. In the remainder of this section we assume given an arbitrary labeled interface theory $(\mathfrak{S}, \mathcal{L}, \ell, \otimes, \leq, \rightarrow)$.

3.1   Port Contracts and Component Interfaces

We follow the idea that a port is an interaction point of a component. To specify the legal interactions on a port often port protocols are used, e.g. [1,16]. The disadvantage of using such port protocols is that they usually mix up assumptions

and guarantees. Mostly it is rather difficult or even not feasible to figure out what
are the guarantees of a component at a port and what is assumed from the environment for communication on that port. To overcome this deficiency we propose
to use explicit distinguished guarantee and assumption behavior specifications
for each port of a component following the principles of assume/guarantee reasoning; cf. e.g. [18]. Hence we consider contracts on ports where assumptions
and guarantees are both provided by an interface specification of our underlying
interface theory.

Definition 2 (Port Contract). *A port contract is a pair (A, G) with $A, G \in \mathfrak{S}$
such that $\ell(A) = \ell(G)$ and $G \to A$, i.e. A is a correct environment for G.[3] We
write $\ell(P)$ for $\ell(A)$ $(= \ell(G))$ and call $\ell(P)$ the* port labels *of P.*

The condition $G \to A$ is motivated by the intuition that any port contract should
specify the assumptions on the environment in such a way that the guaranteed
behavior (shown at this port) works fine in any such environment. Port contracts
can be refined following the co/contravariant approach where assumptions can
be relaxed in the refinement while guarantees may be strengthened.

Definition 3 (Port Contract Refinement). *A port contract $P' = (A', G')$
refines a port contract $P = (A, G)$, written $P' \sqsubseteq P$, if $G' \leq G$ and $A \leq A'$.[4]*

A component interface consists of two parts. First, any component interface has
a finite set of ports with associated contracts. Formally, the ports are given by a
finitely indexed set of port contracts. Secondly, following the terminology in [27],
there is a *frame* specification describing the possible visible behaviors of the full
component. The idea is that the frame shows the dependencies of actions on
the single ports. We assume that the label sets of the ports are pairwise disjoint
and that the label set of the component frame is the disjoint union of the port
labels. Moreover, the set of assumed behaviors on each port together with the
frame must be composable. This is necessary to guarantee that whenever the
assumptions on the ports are met by the environment one can indeed construct
the composition of the frame with the environment.

Definition 4 (Component Interface). *A component interface C is a pair
$C = ((P_i)_{i \in I}, F)$ such that $(P_i)_{i \in I}$ is a finitely indexed set of port contracts
$P_i = (A_i, G_i)$ and $F \in \mathfrak{S}$ is an interface, called* component frame, *such that the
following conditions are satisfied:*

1. *For all $i, j \in I$ with $i \neq j$, $\ell(P_i) \cap \ell(P_j) = \emptyset$.*
2. *$\ell(F) = \bigcup_{i \in I} \ell(P_i)$.*
3. *$(A_i)_{i \in I} \cup \{F\}$ is a composable set of interfaces.*

The set of labels of the component interface C is given by $\ell(C) = \ell(F)$.

---

[3] In particular, A and G are composable.
[4] Note that $P' \sqsubseteq P$ implies $\ell(P') = \ell(P)$.

3.2   Composition of Component Interfaces

In this section we describe the composition of component interfaces merely based on syntactic considerations. In particular, we do not require yet that guarantees of one component port must satisfy the assumptions of the connected port of the other component.[5] Semantic requirements like this are studied in Sects. 3.4 and 3.5. The composition of two component interfaces C and D is only possible if ports of C can be connected to ports of D in a syntactically meaningful way. The simplest solution would be to require that there is exactly one port of C which can be syntactically matched with exactly one port of D. In that way we would, however, not be able to construct cyclic architectures. Therefore we consider the case in which several binary port connections can be established between two component interfaces (even none). For a binary port connection between two ports, say P^C of C and P^D of D, we assume that P^C and P^D have the same set of labels and that the guarantee interfaces of the two ports are composable.[6] Then C and D can be composed if there is a set of binary connections between ports of the two components such that the non-connected ports of C and D have pairwise disjoint labels and if the two component frames are composable. The non-connected ports become the ports of the composition.

Definition 5 (Component Interface Composition).
Let $C = ((P_i^C)_{i \in I}, F^C)$ and $D = ((P_j^D)_{j \in J}, F^D)$ be component interfaces. C and D are composable if there exist subsets $I_0 \subseteq I$, $J_0 \subseteq J$ and a bijective connector function $\kappa : I_0 \to J_0$ such that

1. for all $i \in I_0$, $P_i^C = (A_i^C, G_i^C)$ and $P_{\kappa(i)}^D = (A_{\kappa(i)}^D, G_{\kappa(i)}^D)$, the pair $G_i^C, G_{\kappa(i)}^D$ is composable and $\ell(P_i^C) = \ell(P_{\kappa(i)}^D)$,
2. $\ell(C) \cap \ell(D) = \bigcup_{i \in I_0} \ell(P_i)$,
3. F^C and F^D are composable.

Then the composition of C and D is defined by

$$C \boxtimes D = ((P_i^C)_{i \in (I \setminus I_0)} \cup (P_j^D)_{j \in (J \setminus J_0)}, F^C \otimes F^D).$$

Obviously, $\boxtimes$ is commutative since the underlying composition operator $\otimes$ and the set-theoretic union of (non-connected) ports is commutative. It is also straightforward to prove that the rules (C1) - (C3) of Def. 1 are satisfied for the composition of component interfaces. Moreover, it is easy to see that whenever C and D are composable component interfaces, then $C \boxtimes D$ is a component interface.

3.3   Refinement of Component Interfaces

Our definition of component interface refinement relies on refinement of ports, see Def. 3, which has been inspired by assume/guarantee reasoning and the

---

[5] Similarly to interface specifications which may be syntactically composable without being semantically compatible.

[6] Since $\ell(P^C) = \ell(P^D)$ one could equivalently require (taking into account the properties of a port contract) that the assumption interfaces are composable.

notions of behavioral subtyping, see e.g. [23]. A component interface C refines another one D if, first, both have the same number of ports which are pairwise refined and, secondly, the frame of C refines the frame of D in accordance with the refinement relation of the underlying interface theory. Hence component behaviors and guarantees are specialized in the refinement while assumptions are relaxed.

Definition 6 (Component Interface Refinement). *Let $C = ((P_i^C)_{i \in I}, F^C)$ and $D = ((P_j^D)_{j \in J}, F^D)$ be two component interfaces. C refines D, written $C \sqsubseteq D$, if there exists a bijection $\rho : I \to J$ such that*

1. $P_i^C \sqsubseteq P_{\rho(i)}^D$ *for all $i \in I$, and*
2. $F^C \leq F^D$.

Note that $C \sqsubseteq D$ implies $\ell(C) = \ell(D)$ and that reflexivity and transitivity of $\sqsubseteq$ is inherited from the underlying refinement relation $\leq$ for interfaces.

Next, we show that the property of compositional refinement required by condition (A1) of an interface theory is also valid for the refinement relation between component interfaces.

Theorem 1 (Compositional Refinement for Component Interfaces). *Let C, C', D, and D' be component interfaces such that C and D are composable and $C' \sqsubseteq C$ as well as $D' \sqsubseteq D$ holds. Then C' and D' are composable and $C' \boxtimes D' \sqsubseteq C \boxtimes D$.*

3.4 Correct Component Environments

Finally, in order to obtain an interface theory for component specifications, we need to define a suitable environment correctness relation. The idea is that the communication requirements of a component interface C are satisfied by another component interface D, playing the role of the environment for C, if (1) C and D are composable, and (2) all port connections that can be established between C and D have the property, that each (environment) assumption, say A_i^C of a connected port of C is satisfied by the guarantee $G_{\kappa(i)}^D$ of the corresponding port of D; i.e. $G_{\kappa(i)}^D \leq A_i^C$.

Definition 7. *Let $C = ((P_i^C)_{i \in I}, F^C)$ and $D = ((P_j^D)_{j \in J}, F^D)$ be two component interfaces which are composable according to a bijective connector function $\kappa : I_0 \to J_0$ for subsets $I_0 \subseteq I$ and $J_0 \subseteq J$. D is a correct environment for C, denoted by $C \twoheadrightarrow D$, if for all $i \in I_0$, $G_{\kappa(i)}^D \leq A_i^C$.*

Theorem 2 (Preservation of Environment Correctness). *Let C, C', D, and D' be component interfaces such that $C' \sqsubseteq C$ and $D' \sqsubseteq D$. If $C \twoheadrightarrow D$, then also $C' \twoheadrightarrow D'$.*

Corollary 1. *Component interfaces together with their composition, refinement and environment correctness relation form a labeled specification theory with labels $\mathcal{L}$ over any labeled interface theory $(\mathfrak{S}, \mathcal{L}, \ell, \otimes, \leq, \twoheadrightarrow)$.*

3.5 Reliability of Component Interfaces

Up to know, we have not studied the relation between the frame of a component and the guarantees at the ports of the component. Thus it could be possible that a component C states a guarantee on a port, which is not really supported by the component frame. In such a case the component interface would not be reliable on that port. Indeed the actual behavior of a component is specified by its frame and a user who wants to connect to a certain port is trusting the guarantee on that port which should be established by any component implementation that is a refinement of the component frame. In general, we can still relax this consideration, since we can assume that the component is put into a context where the assumptions on all other ports are met. Consider, for instance, a component interface C and the port $P_1 = (A_1, G_1)$ of C. Then G_1 shows the guarantee of C on port P_1 whenever the component is put in the environment $A_2 \otimes \ldots \otimes A_n$ for the other ports. In other words, the frame F, which specifies the dependencies between the ports, should produce in the context of the environment $A_2 \otimes \ldots \otimes A_n$ a behavior that satisfies the guarantee G_1 on the first port. Formally, this can be expressed by requiring that $A_2 \otimes \ldots \otimes A_n \otimes F$ is a refinement of G_1. Hence A_1 is not used as an assumption for G_1 but only as an assumption for the other guarantees G_j with $j > 1$.[7]

Definition 8 (Reliable Component Interface). *Let $C = ((P_i)_{i \in I}, F)$ be a component interface with port contracts $P_i = (A_i, G_i)$ for all $i \in I$. C is reliable on a port P_j ($j \in I$), if $\otimes(A_i)_{i \in I \setminus \{j\}} \otimes F \leq G_j$. C is reliable if C is reliable on all ports P_i for all $i \in I$.*

The next proposition shows that reliable components can themselves rely on all environments which satisfy the assumptions on each port of the component; i.e. the component frame (as well as all refinements F' of F) "feel well" in each environment made up by the composition of single environments that satisfy the assumptions on each port.

Proposition 1. *Let $C = ((P_i)_{i \in I}, F)$ be a reliable component interface with port contracts $P_i = (A_i, G_i)$ for all $i \in I$. For all $i \in I$, let E_i be interfaces such that $E_i \leq A_i$. Then $F \to \otimes(E_i)_{i \in I}$.*

An important issue is, of course, to study to what extent reliability of component interfaces is preserved by composition. We can show that this is indeed the case if reliable components are correct environments for each other and if the composition relies on the connection of two ports. If there are more port connections used for the composition, then the ports of each single component (used for the connections) must be independent to achieve this result. Intuitively this means, that the frame allows arbitrary interleaving between the behaviors of those ports. Formally we require that under the assumptions of the other ports

---

[7] It would be desirable to use all assumptions $A_1 \otimes \ldots \otimes A_n$ for each guarantee G_j. But this can raise serious problems if there are cyclic dependencies between assumptions and guarantees on connected ports.

the frame is a refinement of the product of the behaviors (i.e. guarantees) of the ports under consideration.

Definition 9. *Let* $C = ((P_i)_{i \in I}, F)$ *be a component interface with port contracts* $P_i = (A_i, G_i)$ *for all* $i \in I$ *and let* $I_0 \subseteq I$. *The ports* $(P_i)_{i \in I_0}$ *are independent w.r.t.* F, *if*

1. $\otimes(A_i)_{i \in I \setminus I_0} \otimes F \leq \otimes(G_j)_{j \in I_0}$, *and*
2. $\otimes(G_j)_{j \in I_0} \to \otimes(A_j)_{j \in I_0}$.

Of course, any single port is independent and a set of ports is independent if and only if it could be collapsed into a single port.

Theorem 3 (Contract Composition Preserves Reliability). *Let* C *and* D *be two reliable and composable component interfaces such that the connected ports on each side are independent (which is trivially satisfied if only two ports are connected). Then* $C \leftrightsquigarrow D$ *implies that* $C \boxtimes D$ *is reliable.*

We can further prove that whenever $C \leftrightsquigarrow D$ then the composition of F^C with any environments of non-connected ports of C is compatible with the composition of F^D with any environments of non-connected ports of D.

Lemma 1. *Let* $C = ((P_i^C)_{1 \leq i \leq m}, F^C)$ *and* $D = ((P_i^D)_{1 \leq i \leq n}, F^D)$ *be reliable component specifications which are composable according to a bijective connector function* $\kappa : I_0 \to J_0$ *for subsets* $I_0 \subseteq I$ *and* $J_0 \subseteq J$. *Assume that the ports* $(P_i^C)_{i \in I_0}$ *and* $(P_j^D)_{j \in J_0}$ *are independent w.r.t.* F^C *and* F^D, *respectively. If* $C \leftrightsquigarrow D$ *then it holds that*

$$\left(\otimes(A_i^C)_{i \in (I \setminus I_0)} \otimes F^C\right) \leftrightsquigarrow \left(F^D \otimes (\otimes(A_j^D)_{j \in (J \setminus J_0)})\right).$$

4 Component Interfaces with MIOs

As a concrete instance of our approach we will use modal I/O-transition systems (MIOs) for the representation of component frames and for the specification of assumptions and guarantees on ports. Modal transition systems have been introduced in [22] and later extended to MIOs in [21]. We have chosen MIOs as our basic formalism since they allow us to distinguish between transitions which are optional (*may*) or mandatory (*must*) and thus support well loose specifications and refinements. In particular the ability for may-transitions is very useful to specify contracts with loose assumptions. In Sect. 4.1 we construct a labeled modal interface theory on the basis of [5], which will then be used, in Sect. 4.2, to build modal component interfaces along the lines of our abstract framework in Sect. 3.

4.1 Labeled Modal Interface Theory

We assume a global set of (observable) action labels $\mathcal{L}^{act}$ and a distinguished (non-observable) action $\tau \notin \mathcal{L}^{act}$. Each MIO is based on an *I/O-labeling* $L =$

(I_L, O_L) consisting of disjoint sets of *input labels* $I_L \subseteq \mathcal{L}^{act}$ and *output labels* $O_L \subseteq \mathcal{L}^{act}$. A *modal I/O-transition system* $M = (L_M, S_M, s_{0,M}, {\dashrightarrow}_M, {\rightarrow}_M)$ consists of an I/O-labeling $L_M = (I_M, O_M)$, a finite set of *states* S_M, an *initial state* $s_{0,M} \in S_M$, a *may-transition relation* ${\dashrightarrow}_M \subseteq S_M \times (\bigcup L_M \cup \{\tau\}) \times S_M$, and a *must-transition relation* ${\rightarrow}_M \subseteq {\dashrightarrow}_M$, i.e. any must-transition is also a may-transition. The set of the *reachable states* of M is denoted by $\mathscr{R}(M)$ with $s \in \mathscr{R}(M)$ if, and only if there is a finite sequence of may-transitions from $s_{0,M}$ to s in M.

All facts and definitions that we provide for particular MIOs are independent of the names of the states of the MIO. In fact we will use MIOs as representatives of their isomorphism classes w.r.t. bijections on states and the set of those isomorphism classes is denoted by $\mathfrak{S}^{MIO}$. The labeling function $\ell^{act} : \mathfrak{S}^{MIO} \rightarrow \wp_{fin}(\mathcal{L}^{act})$ is defined by $\ell^{act}(M) = I_L \cup O_L$ for each MIO M with I/O-labeling $L = (I_L, O_L)$.

Figure 1 shows the pictorial representation of MIOs used in the following. The I/O-labeling of a MIO is shown on its frame. Input and output labels are indicated by the names on the incoming and outgoing arrows. On the transitions, input labels are suffixed with "?" and output labels are suffixed with "!". May-transitions are drawn with a dashed arrow; must-transitions with a solid arrow.

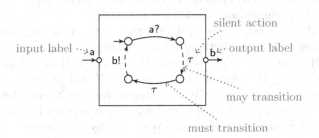

Fig. 1. Modal I/O-transition system

Composable MIOs and Their Synchronous Composition. Two MIOs can be composed if their labels overlap only on complementary types. This means that whenever a label is shared, then the label is either an output label of the first MIO and an input label of the second one or an input label of the first MIO and an output label of the second one. Formally, for two I/O-labelings $K = (I_K, O_K)$ and $L = (I_L, O_L)$, their intersection is denoted by $K \bowtie L = (I_K \cup O_K) \cap (I_L \cup O_L)$. K and L are *composable* if $K \bowtie L = (I_K \cap O_L) \cup (I_L \cap O_K)$. Two MIOs M and N are *composable* if their I/O-labelings are composable. A finitely indexed set $(M_i)_{i \in I}$ of MIOs is composable, if the single interfaces M_i are pairwise composable. Then labels of each M_i can only be shared with at most one other MIO M_j $(j \neq i)$ of the family.

Synchronous composition means that single transitions of two MIOs with shared actions are performed simultaneously. After composition the shared labels become invisible modeled by τ. Formally, the *synchronous composition* of two composable I/O-labelings K and L removes shared labels from inputs and outputs, i.e., it yields the I/O-labeling $K \otimes^{sy} L = ((I_K \cup I_L) \setminus (K \bowtie L), (O_K \cup O_L) \setminus (K \bowtie L))$.

The synchronous composition is defined for composable MIOs M and N and denoted (also) by $M \otimes^{sy} N$. It is defined as the usual product of automata with synchronization on shared labels, which become τ in the product; a synchronization transition in $M \otimes^{sy} N$ is a must-transition if both synchronizing transitions are must-transitions. If one of the single synchronizing transitions is a proper may-transition, then the synchronization transition is also a proper may-transition. An example for synchronous composition of MIOs will be given in Sect. 4.2 when the frames of the interfaces of a Broker and a Client component are composed. The synchronous composition of MIOs is commutative (since we consider MIOs up to bijections between the sets of states). Also the rules (C1) to (C3) required for a labeled interface theory are true for MIOs.

Weak Modal Refinement. The basic idea of *modal* refinement is that required (*must*) transitions of an abstract specification must also occur in the concrete specification. Conversely, allowed (*may*) transitions of the concrete specification must be allowed by the abstract specification. We will use the weak form of modal refinement introduced by Hüttel and Larsen [17] which supports observational abstraction, i.e., τ-transitions can be dropped and inserted as long as the modalities and the simulation relation are preserved.

M is a *weak modal refinement* of N, written $M \leq_m^* N$, if there exists a weak modal refinement relation R between M and N such that $(s_{0,M}, s_{0,N}) \in R$. Two MIOs M and N are *equivalent*, written $M \approx_m^* N$, if M co-simulates N, i.e. $M \leq_m^* N$ and $N \leq_m^* M$. Weak modal refinement $\leq_m^*$ is reflexive and transitive. If all transitions of the abstract MIO are must-transitions it coincides with weak bisimulation. An example of weak modal refinement is given later in Fig. 4. As a crucial fact, weak modal refinement is preserved by synchronous composition.

Theorem 4 (Compositional Refinement (A1)). *For $i = 1, 2$, let M_i, N_i be MIOs such that $M_i \leq_m^* N_i$ and let M_1 and M_2 be composable. Then M_1 and M_2 are composable and $M_1 \otimes^{sy} M_2 \leq_m^* N_1 \otimes^{sy} N_2$.*

Modal Environment Correctness Relation. To discuss correctness of environments we follow the implicit assumption, taken from interface automata [9,11], that outputs are autonomous and must be accepted by a communication partner while inputs are subject to external choice and need not to be served. Hence, output transitions of a MIO express requirements on its environment. For the formal definition, we use one direction of the weak compatibility relation of [5]:

A MIO E is a *modally correct environment* for a MIO M, written $M \rightarrow_m^* E$, if M and E are composable and if for each reachable state $(s, t) \in \mathscr{R}(M \otimes^{sy} E)$, if M *may* send out in state s a message a shared with E, i.e. if there exists $s \xrightarrow{a}_M s'$ with $a \in O_M \cap I_E$, then E *must* be able to receive the message possibly after a series of internal must-transitions have been performed by E starting from state t, i.e. there exists $t \xrightarrow{\hat{\tau}}_E t'' \xrightarrow{a}_E t'$. The notation $t \xrightarrow{\hat{\tau}}_E t''$ expresses arbitrary many (must) τ-transitions.

Examples of weak modal refinement are given below in Sect. 4.2. Both requirements (A2) and (A3) of labeled interface theories are satisfied by MIOs with weak modal refinement and modal environment correctness.

Theorem 5 (Preservation of Environment Correctness (A2), Environmental Composition (A3)). *Let* $M, M', E, E' \in \mathfrak{S}^{MIO}$.

1. *If* $M \to_m^* E$ *and* $M' \leq_m^* M$, $E' \leq_m^* E$, *then* $M' \to_m^* E'$.
2. *If* $M \otimes^{sy} E \to_m^* E'$ *and* $M \otimes^{sy} E' \to_m^* E$ *and* E, E' *are composable, then* $M \to_m^* E \otimes^{sy} E'$.

As a consequence of the definitions and results from above, the MIO framework satisfies the requirements of a labeled interface theory according to Def. 1.

Corollary 2. $(\mathfrak{S}^{MIO}, \mathcal{L}^{act}, \ell^{act}, \otimes^{sy}, \leq_m^*, \to_m^*)$ *is a labeled interface theory.*

4.2 Modal Component Interfaces

On top of the modal interface theory defined in the last section we construct, along the lines of Sect. 3, a theory of modal component interfaces, cf. Cor. 1, represented by $(\mathcal{C}^{MIO}, \mathcal{L}^{act}, \ell^{act}, \boxtimes^{sy}, \sqsubseteq^m, \to_m^*)$.

As an illustration we consider a simple message transmission system which consists of two components: a broker component delivers received messages to a client component. A standard message is immediately delivered while a confidential message is only delivered after successful authentication of the client. The static structure of this component system is shown in Fig. 2. The meaning of the input and output actions is summarized in Table 1.

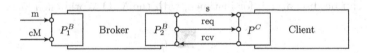

Fig. 2. The static structure of the message transmission system

Component Interface of the Broker Component. We first discuss the component interface of the broker component shown in Figure 3. It has a frame specification F^B and two port contracts $P_1^B = (A_1^B, G_1^B)$ and $P_2^B = (A_2^B, G_2^B)$.

Frame F^B. The frame specification F^B specifies the reaction to the reception of messages on port P_1^B. If a standard message is received $(m?)$, the message is delivered immediately to the client $(s!)$ via port P_2^B and the broker is again ready to receive new messages. If a confidential message is received $(cM?)$, the client is first asked for authentication $(req!)$, and only after the reception of the valid authentication information $(rcv?)$, the message is delivered $(s!)$.

Table 1. Intuitive meaning of actions

Broker B		Client C	
$m?$	receive a message		
$cM?$	receive a confidential message		
$s!$	deliver the message to the client	$s?$	receive the message
$req!$	send out an authentication request	$req?$	receive an authentication request
$rcv?$	receive the (valid) authentication information	$rcv!$	send the authentication information

Port Contracts P_1^B, P_2^B. The assumption A_1^B of the port contract P_1^B allows the environment to generate new messages of any type at any time and the guarantee G_1^B ensures that the broker must always accept standard as well as confidential messages. Obviously, $G_1^B \to_m^* A_1^B$ since G_1^B does not have any outputs.

The second port contract P_2^B specifies the interaction with the client environment. The assumption A_2^B requires that the client must accept messages and is obliged to answer any authentication request. The guarantee G_2^B expresses that the broker may directly send a message to the client but the broker may also ask the client for authentication before, and then it guarantees to take the authentication response. The port contract P_2^B is valid since $G_2^B \to_m^* A_2^B$: every possible output of G_2^B must be accepted by any environment satisfying A_2^B.

Component Interface. The interface of the broker component is given by $B = (\{P_1^B, P_2^B\}, F^B)$. Obviously it is well-formed, since the syntactic conditions of Def. 4 are satisfied. In particular, $\{A_1^B, A_2^B, F^B\}$ is a composable set of modal interfaces: every action label occurs in at most two interfaces in this set, with complementary action types (input vs. output). The broker interface is also reliable. According to Def. 8 the proof obligations are $A_1^B \otimes^{sy} F^B \leq_m^* G_2^B$ and $A_2^B \otimes^{sy} F^B \leq_m^* G_1^B$. They are detailed in Fig. 4 and the weak modal refinement relations can be discharged, for instance, with the MIO Workbench [5].

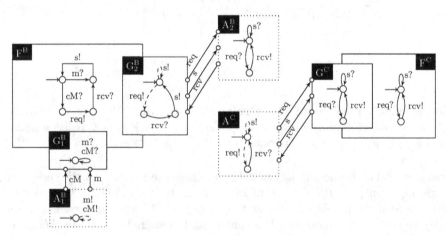

Fig. 3. Component interfaces of the broker and client component

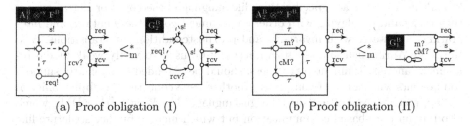

(a) Proof obligation (I)   (b) Proof obligation (II)

Fig. 4. Proof obligations for reliability of the component interface C^B

Component Interface of the Client Component. The interface C of the client component is much simpler; cf. Fig. 3. There is only one port such that the guarantee of the port coincides with the frame which immediately implies reliability The specifications are self-explanatory. Just note, that the assumptions A^C require that the environment must receive any answer to an authentication request; hence $G^C \rightarrow_m^* A^C$.

Composing Broker and Client Interfaces. Clearly, the two component interfaces B and C are (syntactically) composable by connecting the ports P_2^B and P_1^C, which both have the same labels and composable guarantees (and assumptions). The component interface $B \boxtimes^{sy} C$ resulting from the composition is shown in Fig. 5. Due to Thm. 3 the interface $B \boxtimes^{sy} C$ is reliable since the single interfaces are reliable and since they are correct environments for each other, i.e. $B \leftrightsquigarrow_m^* C$. For the latter the proof obligations are $G^C \leq_m^* A_2^B$ (which is trivially valid) and $G_2^B \leq_m^* A^C$ which can be discharged, for instance, with the MIO Workbench.

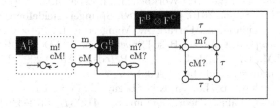

Fig. 5. Composition of broker and client component interfaces

5   Conclusion

We have presented an abstract framework how to construct a theory of component interfaces with port contracts on top of a given interface theory and we have instantiated this approach to obtain modal component interfaces on the basis of modal I/O-transition systems whose modalities are particularly useful for describing loose assumptions. In future work we plan to study other instantiations of our abstract component theory, on the one hand on the basis of other formalisms for interface specifications like language-based ones or Petri nets, on the other hand by playing with other environment correctness notions and integrating data states with invariants and pre/postconditions on transitions. Also the MIO Workbench [5], which can actually be used to verify weak modal refinement and environment correctness, should be extended to explicitly support components with contracts on ports. Another issue concerns the applicability of our approach to well established design-languages like Wright [1] or UML which also rely on port-based communication but which include further structure like explicit connectors as in Wright or ports consisting of provided and required interfaces as in UML.

Acknowledgement. We would like to thank the reviewers of the submitted version of this paper for their useful hints and remarks.

References

1. Allen, R., Garlan, D.: A formal basis for architectural connection. ACM Trans. Softw. Eng. Methodol. 6(3), 213–249 (1997)
2. Back, R.-J., von Wright, J.: Refinement calculus - a systematic introduction. Undergraduate texts in computer science. Springer (1999)
3. Basu, A., Bensalem, S., Bozga, M., Combaz, J., Jaber, M., Nguyen, T.-H., Sifakis, J.: Rigorous component-based system design using the bip framework. IEEE Software 28(3), 41–48 (2011)
4. Bauer, S.S., David, A., Hennicker, R., Larsen, K.G., Legay, A., Nyman, U., Wąsowski, A.: Moving from Specifications to Contracts in Component-Based Design. In: de Lara, J., Zisman, A. (eds.) FASE 2012. LNCS, vol. 7212, pp. 43–58. Springer, Heidelberg (2012)
5. Bauer, S.S., Mayer, P., Schroeder, A., Hennicker, R.: On Weak Modal Compatibility, Refinement, and the MIO Workbench. In: Esparza, J., Majumdar, R. (eds.) TACAS 2010. LNCS, vol. 6015, pp. 175–189. Springer, Heidelberg (2010)
6. Benveniste, A., Caillaud, B., Ferrari, A., Mangeruca, L., Passerone, R., Sofronis, C.: Multiple Viewpoint Contract-Based Specification and Design. In: de Boer, F.S., Bonsangue, M.M., Graf, S., de Roever, W.-P. (eds.) FMCO 2007. LNCS, vol. 5382, pp. 200–225. Springer, Heidelberg (2008)
7. Caillaud, B., Delahaye, B., Larsen, K.G., Legay, A., Pedersen, M.L., Wasowski, A.: Constraint markov chains. Theor. Comput. Sci. 412(34), 4373–4404 (2011)
8. Cau, A., Collette, P.: Parallel composition of assumption-commitment specifications: A unifying approach for shared variable and distributed message passing concurrency. Acta Inf. 33(2), 153–176 (1996)
9. de Alfaro, L., Henzinger, T.A.: Interface automata. Software Engineering Notes, 109–120 (2001)
10. de Alfaro, L., Henzinger, T.A.: Interface Theories for Component-Based Design. In: Henzinger, T.A., Kirsch, C.M. (eds.) EMSOFT 2001. LNCS, vol. 2211, pp. 148–165. Springer, Heidelberg (2001)
11. de Alfaro, L., Henzinger, T.A.: Interface-based Design. In: Broy, M., Grünbauer, J., Harel, D., Hoare, C.A.R. (eds.) Engineering Theories of Software-intensive Systems. NATO Science Series: Mathematics, Physics, and Chemistry, vol. 195, pp. 83–104. Springer (2005)

12. de Alfaro, L., Henzinger, T.A., Stoelinga, M.I.A.: Timed Interfaces. In: Sangiovanni-Vincentelli, A.L., Sifakis, J. (eds.) EMSOFT 2002. LNCS, vol. 2491, pp. 108–122. Springer, Heidelberg (2002)

13. Dijkstra, E.W.: Guarded Commands, Non-determinancy and A Calculus for the Derivation of Programs. In: Bauer, F.L., Samelson, K. (eds.) Language Hierarchies and Interfaces. LNCS, vol. 46, pp. 111–124. Springer, Heidelberg (1976)

14. Emmi, M., Giannakopoulou, D., Păsăreanu, C.S.: Assume-Guarantee Verification for Interface Automata. In: Cuellar, J., Maibaum, T., Sere, K. (eds.) FM 2008. LNCS, vol. 5014, pp. 116–131. Springer, Heidelberg (2008)

15. Goessler, G., Raclet, J.-B.: Modal contracts for component-based design. In: SEFM, pp. 295–303. IEEE Computer Society (2009)

16. Hennicker, R., Janisch, S., Knapp, A.: On the observable behaviour of composite components. Electr. Notes Theor. Comput. Sci. 260, 125–153 (2010)

17. Hüttel, H., Larsen, K.G.: The Use of Static Constructs in A Modal Process Logic. In: Meyer, A.R., Taitslin, M.A. (eds.) Logic at Botik 1989. LNCS, vol. 363, pp. 163–180. Springer, Heidelberg (1989)

18. Jones, C.B.: Development methods for computer programs including a notion of interference. PhD thesis, Oxford University Computing Laboratory (1981)

19. Lamport, L.: *win* and *sin*: Predicate transformers for concurrency. ACM Trans. Program. Lang. Syst. 12(3), 396–428 (1990)

20. Larsen, K.G.: Modal Specifications. In: Sifakis, J. (ed.) CAV 1989. LNCS, vol. 407, pp. 232–246. Springer, Heidelberg (1990)

21. Larsen, K.G., Nyman, U., Wąsowski, A.: Modal I/O Automata for Interface and Product Line Theories. In: De Nicola, R. (ed.) ESOP 2007. LNCS, vol. 4421, pp. 64–79. Springer, Heidelberg (2007)

22. Larsen, K.G., Thomsen, B.: A Modal Process Logic. In: 3rd Annual Symp. Logic in Computer Science, LICS 1988, pp. 203–210. IEEE Computer Society (1988)

23. Liskov, B., Wing, J.M.: A behavioral notion of subtyping. ACM Trans. Program. Lang. Syst. 16(6), 1811–1841 (1994)

24. Meyer, B.: Applying "design by contract". IEEE Computer 25(10), 40–51 (1992)

25. Misra, J., Mani Chandy, K.: Proofs of networks of processes. IEEE Trans. Software Eng. 7(4), 417–426 (1981)

26. Parizek, P., Plasil, F.: Modeling environment for component model checking from hierarchical architecture. Electr. Notes Theor. Comput. Sci. 182, 139–153 (2007)

27. Plasil, F., Visnovsky, S.: Behavior protocols for software components. IEEE Trans. Software Eng. 28(11), 1056–1076 (2002)

28. Quinton, S., Graf, S.: Contract-based verification of hierarchical systems of components. In: SEFM, pp. 377–381. IEEE Computer Society (2008)

29. Raclet, J.-B., Badouel, E., Benveniste, A., Caillaud, B., Legay, A., Passerone, R.: A modal interface theory for component-based design. Fundam. Inform. 108(1-2), 119–149 (2011)

30. Xu, Q., Cau, A., Collette, P.: On Unifying Assumption-commitment Style Proof Rules for Concurrency. In: Jonsson, B., Parrow, J. (eds.) CONCUR 1994. LNCS, vol. 836, pp. 267–282. Springer, Heidelberg (1994)

Avoiding Diamonds in Desynchronization

Harsh Beohar and Pieter J.L. Cuijpers

Department of Mathematics and Computer science
Eindhoven University of Technology, Eindhoven, The Netherlands
{H.Beohar,P.J.L.Cuijpers}@tue.nl

Abstract. The design of concurrent systems often assumes synchronous communication between different parts of a system. When system components are physically apart, this assumption becomes inappropriate. Desynchronization is a technique that aims to implement a synchronous design in an asynchronous manner by placing buffers between the components of the synchronous design. When queues are used as buffers, the so-called 'diamond property' (among others) ensures correct operation of the desynchronized design. However, this property is difficult to establish in practice. In this paper, we formally prove that the conditions for desynchronizability can be relaxed, and in particular the diamond property is no longer needed, when half-duplex queues are used as a communication buffer. Furthermore, we discuss how the half-duplex condition can be further relaxed when the diamond property can be partially guaranteed.

1   Introduction

Message passing [14] is a programming paradigm in which software components send and receive messages either synchronously or asynchronously. In synchronous communication components must be physically coupled, making it possible to execute corresponding send and receive messages simultaneously. Asynchronous communication is used when components are placed physically apart. The corresponding send and receive messages are then decoupled and the messages travel via a buffer from a sender to its recipient.

A problem with asynchronous communication is that the presence of buffers makes ensuring the correctness of a system a non-trivial task. In general, if the buffers are modeled to have infinite capacity, analyzing correctness of such systems is undecidable [8]. But also, if the buffers are modeled to have finite capacity, we may still face the state-space explosion problem.

It helps to separate concerns by first designing a correct synchronous system and then desynchronizing it. The challenge is then to design the synchronous system in such a way that the addition of communication buffers does not alter its behavior (in any relevant way) [10]. A synchronous system that is not altered by the addition of communication buffers is called *desynchronizable*.

In the context of web-services [4,5], the focus is on effective analysis (like deadlock freedom, choreography analysis) of an asynchronous system by developing

C.S. Păsăreanu and G. Salaün (Eds.): FACS 2012, LNCS 7684, pp. 36–54, 2013.
© Springer-Verlag Berlin Heidelberg 2013

synchronizability techniques. The idea is to make an asynchronous system synchronous, which is in contrast to desynchronizability, where a synchronous system is made asynchronous. Thus, synchrononizability techniques are applicable when the components of a system are designed under asynchronous communication from the start (for instance, in web-services), whereas desynchronizatbility techniques are applicable when the components of a system are designed under synchronous communication from the start (for instance, in supervisory control). Despite these differences both approaches aim to establish an equivalence between a synchronous system and its asynchronous version. In [4], the authors showed that weak bisimulation between a deterministic synchronous system and its asynchronous system with one place queues is sufficient and necessary for synchronizability modulo weak bisimulation. In this respect, our work differs from [4] by finding conditions solely on a given synchronous system.

In this paper, we show that the conditions *well-posedness, independence of external actions, input determinism*, and *diamond property* on a synchronous system are necessary and sufficient for desynchronizability. Intuitively,

- two communicating processes in a synchronous system are well-posed if both the processes are able to receive each other requests.
- the external actions (i.e., actions that are not involved in synchronization) are independent in a synchronous system if a receiver can always delay the execution of its own external action in favour of receiving a sequence of messages, without any consequence on its future behavior of the system.
- input determinism states that the communicating processes should not make nondeterministic choices upon the reception of messages.
- the essence of the diamond property is that when two components both wish to communicate a message, say α and β, then communication of α will not block communication of β, and vice versa. Furthermore, the order of communication will not influence the future behavior of the system.

In previous research [3,7,10,21], well-posedness and the diamond property were already present in the sufficient condition for desynchronizability, while the other two properties are new with respect to these references.

As it turns out, the diamond property is difficult to establish in practice, while in particular well-posedness and input determinism can be easily obtained by construction, at least for supervisory control synthesis [18].

As an example why this leads to practical problems, consider a simplified model of a controlled drive-motor [11]. The drive-motor can move in a forward direction '*fwmove*' or in a backward direction '*bwmove*', and it has a signal *chdir* indicating when it is safe to change this direction. A controller communicates with the drive-motor to ensure that the event '*chdir*' always executes before altering the direction of the motor. The models of the drive motor, the controller, and the synchronous system are shown in Fig. 1, where !a (?a) denotes that an action a is sent (received) and a denotes the synchronization of !a and ?a.

Observe in the synchronous system of drive-motor that the execution of the event *chdir* from state 1 to state 2 disables the execution of the event *fwmove*; thus, violating the commutativity of the traces *chdir.fwmove* and *fwmove.chdir*.

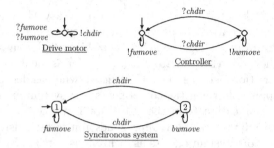

Fig. 1. An illustration showing the impossibility of establishing the diamond property in certain synchronous systems

Similarly, the commutativity of the traces *chdir.bwmove* and *bwmove.chdir* is prohibited in this synchronous system. As a result, the synchronous system in Fig. 1 does not satisfy the diamond property. In fact, the control requirement implicitly requires the diamond property to be broken. Therefore, it is impossible to desynchronize this system unless we adapt the model of plant or supervisor, or we adapt the way in which the desynchronization is performed.

Studying the origin of the diamond property, we notice that it is caused by the type of buffer that is used for communication. The authors of [3,10,21] follow [8] in taking two unidirectional FIFO queues as a means of communication. In [10] a separate unidirectional FIFO queue is used for each type of message, which effectively leads to a *bag*-type of buffering (cf. [7]). Both types of buffer are useful abstractions of a physical communication layer with a protocol layer on top. For example, queues nicely represent the use of the TCP/IP protocol, while bags represent a UDP-like protocol [20]. Note that both approaches require the diamond property, essentially because both approaches allow the messages α and β to be present in the buffer at the same time and arrive in arbitrary order.

Our research hypothesis is that it may be possible to find better desynchronizability conditions by changing the properties of the communication protocol. So far, research has focussed on the properties that the communicating components should have in order to ensure desynchronizability. The buffer is usually taken to be a queue or, incidentally, a bag. In this paper, we reconsider these properties, and alter them by changing the communication protocol if desired.

A first step in that direction is shown in this paper. We prove that the troublesome diamond property can be avoided by changing the type of buffer used for desynchronization to so-called *half-duplex* communication (also used in [9] for model-checking asynchronous systems). In the context of two communicating processes, half-duplex communication means that a component is only allowed to send a message when its input buffer is empty. As a result, the buffering between the two processes alternates in each direction, having to become empty before alternating. We show that in this case a synchronous composition is desynchronizable if and only if it is *well-posed, independent of external actions*, and *input deterministic*. These properties are generally weaker than the properties in [3,7,10,21], and we are able to give a general method to adapt systems that are synthesized using supervisory control theory to satisfy these properties. It is our hope that this paper will initiate discussion on the separation of concerns regarding desynchronization. Our use of a half-duplex buffering strategy indicates that the communication protocol is essential in this separation.

Admittedly, the choice for half-duplex communication is an odd one from the perspective of efficiency. The half-duplex protocol essentially makes components wait for each other, which makes communication slow. In Section 5, we sketch a first step to remedy this by recognizing when actions are independent of each-other. Independent messages satisfy the diamond property and can therefore be processed in a full-duplex way. However, more research is needed to complete this claim and to find out when the half-duplex condition is in fact necessary for desynchronizability, and when it can be dropped for the sake of efficiency.

The methods we use for studying desynchronizability in this paper stem from process algebra and concurrency theory (see e.g. [2]). We do not fix a set of desirable properties a priori, but rather aim for desynchronizability modulo a behavioral equivalence that preserves a large set of possibly desirable properties. The desynchronizability question is therefore posed as: *given two processes p and s, under which conditions are the synchronous composition and the asynchronous composition of p and s behaviorally equivalent?* To be as general as possible, we take *branching bisimulation* as our behavioral equivalence of choice, which is the strongest equivalence used in concurrency theory [12].

Organisation of the Paper. In Section 2, we describe the mathematical notations and formal definitions required to define desynchronizability using two unidirectional FIFO buffers. Section 3 discusses necessary and sufficient conditions for desynchronizability, including the unwanted diamond property. In Section 4, we show how the diamond property can be eliminated by using half-duplex buffers for desynchronization. Lastly, Section 5 discusses ways to relax this half-duplex condition and apply desynchronization in the context of supervisory control.

2   Basic Definitions

In this paper, we model the world as a single transition system in which all behaviors of interest are represented. Components of a system as well as their compositions are called *processes* and are represented by pointing out an *initial state* $q \in \mathbb{P}$ in the labelled transition system. A *process* q is then formed by all reachable states from the initial state $q \in \mathbb{P}$.

Definition 1. *A* labelled transition system *is a tuple* $(\mathbb{P}, A, \rightarrow, \sqcup)$, *where*

- $\mathbb{P}$ *is a set of states.*
- A *is a set of actions.*
- $\rightarrow \subseteq \mathbb{P} \times A \times \mathbb{P}$ *is a transition relation.*
- $\sqcup \subseteq \mathbb{P}$ *is the empty-buffer predicate and its purpose is to observe the states of an asynchronous system that consists of empty buffer contents.*

The notation $q \xrightarrow{\alpha} q'$ *denotes an element* $(q, \alpha, q') \in \rightarrow$, *the notation* $q\sqcup$ *denotes that state* q *satisfies the empty-buffer predicate. For a given initial state* $q \in \mathbb{P}$, *the set of* reachable states $\mathfrak{R}(q)$ *is defined as the smallest set such that:*

- $q \in \mathfrak{R}(q)$, and
- $\forall_{q_1, q_2 \in \mathbb{P}} \forall_{\alpha \in A} \cdot \left[\left(q_1 \in \mathfrak{R}(q) \wedge q_1 \xrightarrow{\alpha} q_2 \right) \Rightarrow q_2 \in \mathfrak{R}(q) \right].$

In what follows, the letter q and its decorations like $q', q_1, q_2, \cdots$ are used to reason about the arbitrary processes, whereas the letters p, s and their corresponding decorations are reserved for special purposes (see the next paragraph).

Considering a synchronous system as depicted in Fig. 2, we identify two basic components p, s, which we assume to be processes in our labeled transition system. These processes are composed into a synchronous process $p \parallel s$. The process $p \parallel s$ can perform four kinds of events; namely, the *external* actions of p and s that belong to the sets E_p and E_s, respectively, and *messages* from p and s that belong to the sets M_p and M_s, respectively.

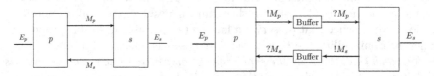

Fig. 2. A synchronous system   **Fig. 3.** An asynchronous system

When the system is *desynchronized* we obtain an asynchronous system as depicted in Fig. 3, consisting of the same processes p, s, which are now composed into an asynchronous process $p \, [\epsilon, \epsilon] \, s$ (with ϵ indicating initially empty buffer contents). In the asynchronous process, the external actions of p and s remain the same, but we now make a distinction between the sending of a message (modeled for p by the set $!M_p = \{!m \mid m \in M_p\}$) and the receiving of that message (modeled for p by the set $?M_p = \{?m \mid m \in M_p\}$). We assume that the so obtained sets of actions are all part of our alphabet and are all pairwise disjoint: $E_p \uplus E_s \uplus M_p \uplus !M_p \uplus ?M_p \uplus M_s \uplus !M_s \uplus ?M_s \subseteq A$.

Assuming that the processes p and s are already part of our labeled transition system, where p makes use of the actions $!M_p \uplus ?M_p \uplus E_p$ and s makes use of the actions $!M_s \uplus ?M_s \uplus E_s$, we can define the synchronous and asynchronous composition of p and s through structural operational semantic rules (SOS) on the states of the transition system [17]. The premise of each rule states the assumption on the states of the composed processes, and the conclusion gives the resulting transition for the composed state.

In Table 1, we give the SOS rules for synchronous composition and asynchronous composition using two unidirectional lossless FIFO queues. The notation $p \, [\mu, \nu] \, s$ denotes the asynchronous composition of states p and s with sequences of messages $\nu \in M_p^*$ and $\mu \in M_s^*$ in the respective queues. Note how the empty-buffer predicate is always true for synchronous compositions, while it is only true for asynchronous compositions if both queues are empty.

As explained in the introduction, a composition $p \parallel s$ is desynchronizable if it is equivalent to its asynchronous composition $p \, [\epsilon, \epsilon] \, s$. One problem with defining equivalence between the two is that asynchronous composition needs two actions for the communication of a message while synchronous composition

Table 1. SOS rules for synchronous and asynchronous parallel composition

$$\frac{p_1 \xrightarrow{!m} p_2,\ s_1 \xrightarrow{?m} s_2,\ m \in M_p}{p_1 \parallel s_1 \xrightarrow{m} p_2 \parallel s_2} \qquad \frac{p_1 \xrightarrow{?n} p_2,\ s_1 \xrightarrow{!n} s_2,\ n \in M_s}{p_1 \parallel s_1 \xrightarrow{n} p_2 \parallel s_2}$$

$$\frac{p_1 \xrightarrow{e} p_2,\ e \in E_p}{p_1 \parallel s_1 \xrightarrow{e} p_2 \parallel s_1} \quad \frac{s_1 \xrightarrow{e} s_2,\ e \in E_s}{p_1 \parallel s_1 \xrightarrow{e} p_1 \parallel s_2} \quad (p \parallel s) \sqcup$$

$$\frac{p \xrightarrow{!m} p',\ m \in M_p}{(p \,|[\mu, \nu]|\, s) \xrightarrow{!m} (p' \,|[\mu, \nu.m]|\, s)} \quad \frac{s \xrightarrow{!n} s',\ n \in M_s}{(p \,|[\mu, \nu]|\, s) \xrightarrow{!n} (p \,|[\mu.n, \nu]|\, s')}$$

$$\frac{p \xrightarrow{?n} p',\ \mu = n.\mu',\ n \in M_s}{(p \,|[\mu, \nu]|\, s) \xrightarrow{?n} (p' \,|[\mu', \nu]|\, s)} \quad \frac{s \xrightarrow{?m} s',\ \nu = m.\nu',\ m \in M_p}{(p \,|[\mu, \nu]|\, s) \xrightarrow{?m} (p \,|[\mu, \nu']|\, s')}$$

$$\frac{p \xrightarrow{e} p',\ e \in E_p}{(p \,|[\mu, \nu]|\, s) \xrightarrow{e} (p' \,|[\mu, \nu]|\, s)} \quad \frac{s \xrightarrow{e} s',\ e \in E_s}{(p \,|[\mu, \nu]|\, s) \xrightarrow{e} (p \,|[\mu, \nu]|\, s')} \quad (p \,|[\epsilon, \epsilon]|\, s) \sqcup$$

only needs one. The usual process algebraic way to solve this issue is by defining an abstraction scheme, translating certain actions from the asynchronous system to actions from the synchronous system while hiding others.

In Table 2, we define the abstraction operator $\Delta()$ that maps all the send-messages of the asynchronous system to communicated messages in the synchronous system, while the receive-messages are mapped to a so-called *internal action*, denoted by τ. Subsequently, we define *branching bisimulation* (see [2,12]) as an equivalence between processes that abstracts from internal actions.

Table 2. SOS rules for the abstraction operator $\Delta()$

$$\frac{x_1 \xrightarrow{!m} x_2,\ m \in M_p \cup M_s}{\Delta(x_1) \xrightarrow{m} \Delta(x_2)} \quad \frac{x_1 \xrightarrow{e} x_2,\ e \in E_p \cup E_s}{\Delta(x_1) \xrightarrow{e} \Delta(x_2)} \quad \frac{x_1 \xrightarrow{?m} x_2,\ m \in M_p \cup M_s}{\Delta(x_1) \xrightarrow{\tau} \Delta(x_2)} \quad \frac{x \sqcup}{\Delta(x) \sqcup}$$

Definition 2. *The* reachability relation $\longrightarrow\ \subseteq \mathbb{P} \times A^* \times \mathbb{P}$ *is derived from the transition relation* $\to$ *as the smallest relation satisfying:*

$$q_1 \xrightarrow{\epsilon} q_1\ , \quad \frac{q_1 \xrightarrow{w} q',\ q' \xrightarrow{\tau} q_2}{q_1 \xrightarrow{w} q_2}\ , \quad \frac{q_1 \xrightarrow{w} q',\ q' \xrightarrow{\alpha} q_2,\ \alpha \neq \tau}{q_1 \xrightarrow{w.\alpha} q_2}\ .$$

Definition 3. *A binary relation $\mathcal{B} \subseteq \mathbb{P} \times \mathbb{P}$ on the states of the transition system is a* branching bisimulation *relation iff the following conditions are satisfied.*

- $\forall_{q,q_1,q',\alpha}.\Big[\big((q,q') \in \mathcal{B} \wedge q \xrightarrow{\alpha} q_1\big) \Rightarrow (\alpha = \tau \wedge (q_1,q') \in \mathcal{B}) \vee$

$$\exists_{q_1',q_2'}.[q' \xrightarrow{\epsilon} q_1' \xrightarrow{\alpha} q_2' \wedge (q,q_1') \in \mathcal{B} \wedge (q_1,q_2') \in \mathcal{B}]\Big];$$

- $\forall_{q,q'}.\Big[\big((q,q') \in \mathcal{B} \wedge q \sqcup\big) \Rightarrow \exists_{q''}.\big[q' \xrightarrow{\epsilon} q'' \wedge q'' \sqcup \wedge (q,q'') \in \mathcal{B}\big]\Big];$

- $\forall_{q,q',q_1',\alpha}.\Big[\big((q,q') \in \mathcal{B} \wedge q' \xrightarrow{\alpha} q_1'\big) \Rightarrow (\alpha = \tau \wedge (q,q_1') \in \mathcal{B}) \vee$

$$\exists_{q_1,q_2}.[q \xrightarrow{\epsilon} q_1 \xrightarrow{\alpha} q_2 \wedge (q_1,q') \in \mathcal{B} \wedge (q_2,q_1') \in \mathcal{B}]\Big];$$

- $\forall_{q,q'}.\Big[\big((q,q') \in \mathcal{B} \wedge q' \sqcup\big) \Rightarrow \exists_{q''}.\big[q \xrightarrow{\epsilon} q'' \wedge q'' \sqcup \wedge (q'',q') \in \mathcal{B}\big]\Big].$

Two processes q and q' are said to be branching bisimilar, *denoted $q \leftrightarrow_{\mathbf{b}} q'$, if there exists a branching bisimulation relation $\mathcal{B}$ such that $(q,q') \in \mathcal{B}$.*

Now we have all the preliminaries that are necessary to define what desychronization formally means.

Definition 4. *A synchronous system $p \parallel s$ is* desynchronizable *if*

$$p \parallel s \leftrightarrow_{\mathbf{b}} \Delta(p\,\|[\epsilon,\epsilon]\|\, s).$$

3   Properties of Desynchronizable Systems

In this section, we prove a number of properties of desynchronizable systems modulo branching bisimulation. A new result (cf. [3,7,10,21]) is that the observation of the empty-buffer predicate makes that these properties are necessary as well as sufficient for desynchronizability. A technical assumption used to show necessity in this case, is that the desynchronized systems p and s are *concrete*, meaning they do not have internal behavior themselves.

Definition 5. *A process $q \in \mathbb{P}$ is* concrete *if $\nexists_{q',q''}.\big[q' \in \mathfrak{R}(q) \wedge q' \xrightarrow{\tau} q''\big]$. A transition $q_1 \xrightarrow{\tau} q_2$ is* inert *modulo $\leftrightarrow_{\mathbf{b}}$ iff $q_1 \leftrightarrow_{\mathbf{b}} q_2$.*

Lemma 1. *Let $p \parallel s$ be a concrete and desynchronizable system. Then, all the τ-transitions in $\Delta(p\,\|[\epsilon,\epsilon]\|\, s)$ are inert modulo branching bisimulation.*

Proof. Since $p \parallel s$ is a concrete process, none of the τ-transitions in the asynchronous system can be matched by any related state in the synchronous system. Thus, all τ-transitions in the asynchronous system have to be inert [2].   □

A key step in understanding the necessary conditions for desynchronizability, is to see that any reachable state $p' \parallel s' \in \mathfrak{R}(p \parallel s)$ of some desynchronizable system $p \parallel s$ is desynchronizable itself. This property seems both desirable and trivial, but its proof turned out to be more involved than expected. In particular, the proof turns out to rely on the chosen abstraction scheme, the fact that p and s are concrete processes, disjointness of the message sets, and the fact that we observe the empty-buffer predicate.

Theorem 1. *Let $p \parallel s$ be concrete and desynchronizable, then any $p' \parallel s' \in \mathfrak{R}(p \parallel s)$ is desynchronizable.*

Proof. As a base case, the initial state of $p \parallel s$ is desynchronizable by assumption. By induction, assume that we have a reachable desynchronizable state $p' \parallel s' \in \mathfrak{R}(p \parallel s)$ and consider any p'' and s'' with $p' \parallel s' \xrightarrow{\alpha} p'' \parallel s''$. Following the SOS rules, one of the following transitions must exist in the asynchronous process:

1. a transition $\Delta(p' \,||[\epsilon, \epsilon]||\, s') \xrightarrow{\alpha} \Delta(p'' \,||[\epsilon, \alpha]||\, s')$ with $\alpha \in M_p$, and a hidden transition $\Delta(p'' \,||[\epsilon, \alpha]||\, s') \xrightarrow{\tau} \Delta(p'' \,||[\epsilon, \epsilon]||\, s'')$ that is inert because $p \parallel s$ is concrete, i.e. $\Delta(p'' \,||[\epsilon, \alpha]||\, s') \leftrightarrow_b \Delta(p'' \,||[\epsilon, \epsilon]||\, s'')$;
2. a transition $\Delta(p' \,||[\epsilon, \epsilon]||\, s') \xrightarrow{\alpha} \Delta(p' \,||[\alpha, \epsilon]||\, s'')$ with $\alpha \in M_s$, and a hidden transition $\Delta(p' \,||[\alpha, \epsilon]||\, s'') \xrightarrow{\tau} \Delta(p'' \,||[\epsilon, \epsilon]||\, s'')$ that is inert because $p \parallel s$ is concrete, i.e. $\Delta(p' \,||[\alpha, \epsilon]||\, s') \leftrightarrow_b \Delta(p'' \,||[\epsilon, \epsilon]||\, s'')$;
3. a transition $\Delta(p' \,||[\epsilon, \epsilon]||\, s') \xrightarrow{\alpha} \Delta(p'' \,||[\epsilon, \epsilon]||\, s'')$ with $\alpha \in E_p$ ($\alpha \in E_s$), in which case we find that $s' = s''$ ($p' = p''$).

Because $p' \parallel s' \leftrightarrow_b \Delta(p' \,||[\epsilon, \epsilon]||\, s')$, the properties of branching bisimulation (applied to concrete processes) dictate that we can relate those asynchronous transitions to synchronous transitions. I.e. there exist p''' and s''' such that $p' \parallel s' \xrightarrow{\alpha} p''' \parallel s'''$ and $p''' \parallel s''' \leftrightarrow \Delta(p'' \,||[\epsilon, \epsilon]||\, s'')$. Finally, to prove that this implies that $p'' \parallel s''$ is desynchronizable, we study the relation:

$$\mathcal{S} = \big\{ (p_1 \parallel s_1, p_2 \parallel s_2) \mid p_1 \parallel s_1 \in \mathfrak{R}(p'' \parallel s'') \wedge$$
$$\Delta(p_2 \,||[\epsilon, \epsilon]||\, s_2) \in \mathfrak{R}(\Delta(p'' \,||[\epsilon, \epsilon]||\, s'')) \wedge p_1 \parallel s_1 \leftrightarrow_b \Delta(p_2 \,||[\epsilon, \epsilon]||\, s_2) \big\}$$

It remains to show that this is a witnessing branching bisimulation relation for $p''' \parallel s''' \leftrightarrow_b p'' \parallel s''$. For this, consider the following cases.

1. Let $p_1 \parallel s_1 \xrightarrow{m} p_3 \parallel s_3$, $(p_1 \parallel s_1, p_2 \parallel s_2) \in \mathcal{S}$, and $m \in M_p$ (the case when $m \in M_s$ is symmetric). By construction of $\mathcal{S}$ we have $p_1 \parallel s_1 \leftrightarrow_b \Delta(p_2 \,||[\epsilon, \epsilon]||\, s_2)$. By applying concreteness and disjointness of M_p and M_s and the transfer condition of branching bisimulation we get $\Delta(p_2 \,||[\epsilon, \epsilon]||\, s_2) \xrightarrow{m} \Delta(p_4 \,||[\epsilon, m]||\, s_2)$ and $p_3 \parallel s_3 \leftrightarrow_b \Delta(p_4 \,||[\epsilon, m]||\, s_2)$ for some $p_4 \in \mathbb{P}$. Since $p_3 \parallel s_3 \!\downarrow$, branching bisimulation gives us $\Delta(p_4 \,||[\epsilon, m]||\, s_2) \xrightarrow{\tau} \Delta(p_4 \,||[\epsilon, \epsilon]||\, s_4)$ and $p_3 \parallel s_3 \leftrightarrow_b \Delta(p_4 \,||[\epsilon, \epsilon]||\, s_4)$, for some $s_4 \in \mathbb{P}$. Thus, we derive $p_2 \xrightarrow{!m} p_4$ and $s_2 \xrightarrow{?m} s_4$; hence, $p_2 \parallel s_2 \xrightarrow{m} p_4 \parallel s_4$ and $(p_3 \parallel s_3, p_4 \parallel s_4) \in \mathcal{S}$.
2. Let $p_1 \parallel s_1 \xrightarrow{e} p_3 \parallel s_1$, $(p_1 \parallel s_1, p_2 \parallel s_2) \in \mathcal{S}$, and $e \in E_p$ (the case when $e \in E_s$ is symmetric). By construction of $\mathcal{S}$ we have $p_1 \parallel s_1 \leftrightarrow_b \Delta(p_2 \,||[\epsilon, \epsilon]||\, s_2)$. By concreteness and disjointness of E_p and E_s and the transfer condition of branching bisimulation we get $\Delta(p_2 \,||[\epsilon, \epsilon]||\, s_2) \xrightarrow{e} \Delta(p_4 \,||[\epsilon, \epsilon]||\, s_2)$ and $p_3 \parallel s_1 \leftrightarrow_b \Delta(p_4 \,||[\epsilon, \epsilon]||\, s_2)$. Thus, $p_2 \parallel s_2 \xrightarrow{e} p_4 \parallel s_2$ and $(p_3 \parallel s_1, p_4 \parallel s_2) \in \mathcal{S}$.

3. The cases where the transitions originates from $p_2 \parallel s_2$ when $(p_1 \parallel s_1, p_2 \parallel s_2) \in \mathcal{S}$ can be proved along the above lines.

Finally, by transitivity and symmetry, we get $p'' \parallel s'' \underset{\mathbf{b}}{\leftrightarrow} \Delta(p'' \,|[\epsilon, \epsilon]|\, s'')$.   □

Corollary 1. *If p, s, p', s' are concrete processes and $p \parallel s \underset{\mathbf{b}}{\leftrightarrow} \Delta(p' \,|[\epsilon, \epsilon]|\, s')$ then $p \parallel s \underset{\mathbf{b}}{\leftrightarrow} p' \parallel s'$.*

3.1 Well-Posedness

The first actual implication of desynchronizability that we would like to discuss, is that a desynchronizable system is always *well-posed*. This was already observed in [10] for desynchronizability modulo failure equivalence. Well-posedness means that whenever a process p would like to send a message, s should be willing to receive it and vice versa. In a synchronous composition such messages may be blocked, but in an asynchronous composition they lead to *orphans*, i.e., messages that remain forever in the buffer. In turn, orphans lead to deadlocking communication (except in a few pathological cases).

Definition 6. *A binary relation $\mathcal{W} \subseteq \mathbb{P} \times \mathbb{P}$ is called a well-posedness relation iff the following conditions are satisfied.*

1. $\forall_{p,s,p',m} \cdot \left[p \xrightarrow{!m} p' \wedge (p,s) \in \mathcal{W} \Rightarrow \exists_{s'} \cdot [s \xrightarrow{?m} s'] \wedge \forall_{s'} \cdot [s \xrightarrow{?m} s' \Rightarrow (p', s') \in \mathcal{W}] \right]$,
2. $\forall_{p,s,p',e \in E_p} \cdot \left[p \xrightarrow{e} p' \wedge (p,s) \in \mathcal{W} \Rightarrow (p', s) \in \mathcal{W} \right]$,
3. *Respectively Conditions 1 and 2 with the role of p and s interchanged.*

A composition $p \parallel s$ is well-posed if there exists a well-posedness relation $\mathcal{W}$ such that $(p, s) \in \mathcal{W}$.

Theorem 2. *If $p \parallel s$ is concrete and desynchronizable then it is well-posed.*

Proof. Define a relation $\mathcal{W} = \{(p_1, s_1) \mid \Delta(p_1 \,|[\epsilon, \epsilon]|\, s_1) \in \mathfrak{R}(\Delta(p \,|[\epsilon, \epsilon]|\, s))\}$. To show that $\mathcal{W}$ is a well-posedness relation, let $p_1 \xrightarrow{\alpha} p_2$ and $(p_1, s_1) \in \mathcal{W}$.

1. Let $\alpha \in !M_p$. Then, by the construction of $\mathcal{W}$ we have $\Delta(p_1 \,|[\epsilon, \epsilon]|\, s_1) \in \mathfrak{R}(\Delta(p \,|[\epsilon, \epsilon]|\, s))$ and using $p_1 \xrightarrow{\alpha} p_2$ we get $\Delta(p_1 \,|[\epsilon, \epsilon]|\, s_1) \xrightarrow{m} \Delta(p_2 \,|[\epsilon, m]|\, s_1)$. Since $p \parallel s$ is desynchronizable, we know that there exists $q \in \mathfrak{R}(p \parallel s)$ such that $q \underset{\mathbf{b}}{\leftrightarrow} \Delta(p_2 \,|[\epsilon, m]|\, s_1)$. Clearly, we have $q \sqcup$. Furthermore by the transfer property of branching bisimulation and under the assumption of concrete processes we get $\exists s_2 \cdot \left[\Delta(p_2 \,|[\epsilon, m]|\, s_1) \xrightarrow{\tau} \Delta(p_2 \,|[\epsilon, \epsilon]|\, s_2) \wedge \Delta(p_2 \,|[\epsilon, \epsilon]|\, s_2) \sqcup \right]$. Thus, $s_1 \xrightarrow{?m} s_2$. Next, we need to show that for every s_2', whenever $s_1 \xrightarrow{?m} s_2'$ then $(p_2, s_2') \in \mathcal{W}$. So let $s_1 \xrightarrow{?m} s_2'$, thus $\Delta(p_2 \,|[\epsilon, m]|\, s_1) \xrightarrow{\tau} \Delta(p_2 \,|[\epsilon, \epsilon]|\, s_2')$. Hence, by the construction of $\mathcal{W}$ it is clear that $(p_2, s_2') \in \mathcal{W}$.
2. Let $\alpha \in E_p$. Then, by the construction of $\mathcal{W}$ we have $\Delta(p_1 \,|[\epsilon, \epsilon]|\, s_1) \in \mathfrak{R}(\Delta(p \,|[\epsilon, \epsilon]|\, s))$ and using the above transition we get $\Delta(p_1 \,|[\epsilon, \epsilon]|\, s_1) \xrightarrow{e} \Delta(p_2 \,|[\epsilon, \epsilon]|\, s_1)$. Clearly, $(p_2, s_1) \in \mathcal{W}$.

Likewise, the symmetric case can be proved for the process s_1.   □

3.2   Independence of External Actions

The second implication of desynchronizability that we would like to discuss is *independence of external actions*. Intuitively, it means that a receiver can always delay the execution of its own external action in favor of receiving a sequence of messages from the other process, without any consequence on its future behavior modulo $\underleftrightarrow{}_b$. The reception of messages becomes *independent* of the external behavior in this way.

In the following, we define independence on the composition $p \parallel s$ rather than on the separate processes p and s because we aim for necessary conditions. The pathological case in which a process p is not independent in a part of its state-space that becomes unreachable when interacting with s has no effects on desynchronizability. Of course, independence of external actions of the separate processes would be a natural part of a sufficient condition for desynchronizability.

Definition 7. *A synchronous system $p \parallel s$ is* independent of external actions *modulo $\underleftrightarrow{}_b$ if the following conditions holds for every $p_1 \parallel s_1 \in \Re(p \parallel s)$.*

1. $\forall_{p_2, p_2', s_2, u, e} \cdot \left[e \in E_p \wedge u \in (M_s \cup E_s)^* \wedge p_1 \parallel s_1 \xrightarrow{e} p_2 \parallel s_1 \xrightarrow{u} p_2' \parallel s_2 \Rightarrow \right.$
$$\left. \exists_{p_3, p_3'} \cdot \left[p_1 \parallel s_1 \xrightarrow{u} p_3 \parallel s_2 \xrightarrow{e} p_3' \parallel s_2 \wedge p_3 \parallel s_2 \underleftrightarrow{}_b p_3' \parallel s_2 \right] \right].$$

2. $\forall_{p_2, s_2, s_2', v, e} \cdot \left[e \in E_s \wedge v \in (M_p \cup E_p)^* \wedge p_1 \parallel s_1 \xrightarrow{e} p_1 \parallel s_2 \xrightarrow{v} p_2 \parallel s_2' \Rightarrow \right.$
$$\left. \exists_{s_3, s_3'} \cdot \left[p_1 \parallel s_1 \xrightarrow{v} p_2 \parallel s_3 \xrightarrow{e} p_2 \parallel s_3' \wedge p_2 \parallel s_2' \underleftrightarrow{}_b p_2 \parallel s_3' \right] \right].$$

Theorem 3. *If $p \parallel s$ is concrete and desynchronizable then it is independent of external actions modulo $\underleftrightarrow{}_b$.*

Proof. Let $x = x_p \uplus x_s$, $yM = yM_p \uplus yM_s$, $x \in \{M, E\}$, and $y \in \{!, ?\}$. By abuse of notations, define two renaming functions $! : (M \cup E)^* \to (!M \cup E)^*$, $? : (M \cup E)^* \to ?M^*$ and a projection function $^- : (M \cup E)^* \to M^*$:

1. $?\epsilon = \epsilon$, $?(e.w) = w$, $?(m.w) = ?m.?w$, where $e \in E$ and $w \in (M \cup E)^*$.
2. $!\epsilon = \epsilon$, $!(e.w) = e.!w$, $!(m.w) = !m.!w$, where $e \in E$ and $w \in (M \cup E)^*$.
3. $\bar{\epsilon} = \epsilon$, $\overline{e.w} = \bar{w}$, and $\overline{m.w} = m.\bar{w}$, where $e \in E$ and $w \in (M \cup E)^*$.

Now, assume we have a reachable (Theorem 1) desynchronizable state $p_1 \parallel s_1 \in \Re(p \parallel s)$ with solid transitions as in Fig. 4, where $e \in E_p$ and $u \in (M_s \cup E_s)^*$. Using the above renaming functions and the semantics, we derive $p_1 \xrightarrow{e} p_2$, $s_1 \xrightarrow{!u} s_2$, and $p_2 \xrightarrow{?u} p_2'$. As well-posedness is necessary for desynchronizability, we may use it to obtain $p_1 \xrightarrow{?u} p_3$ (for some p_3). Thus, we get $p_1 \parallel s_1 \xrightarrow{u} p_3 \parallel s_2$ (dashed in Fig. 4). From these transitions we then derive the solid transitions in the asynchronous system depicted in Fig. 4, where $\mu = \bar{u}$.

Since τ-transitions are inert we have $\Delta(p_1 \Vert [\mu, \epsilon] \Vert s_2) \underleftrightarrow{}_b \Delta(p_3 \Vert [\epsilon, \epsilon] \Vert s_2)$. Branching bisimulation, under the assumption of concrete processes and disjointness of the sets E_p, E_s, gives us the existence of p_3' such that $\Delta(p_3 \Vert [\epsilon, \epsilon] \Vert s_2) \xrightarrow{e}$

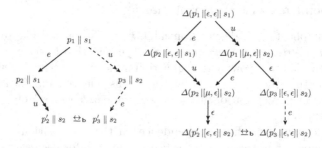

Fig. 4. The role of independence of external actions

$\Delta(p_3'\,|[\epsilon,\epsilon]|\,s_2)$ and $\Delta(p_3'\,|[\epsilon,\epsilon]|\,s_2) \; \underline{\leftrightarrow}_{\mathbf{b}} \; \Delta(p_2\,|[\mu,\epsilon]|\,s_2)$. Thus, by the SOS-rules we get $p_3 \parallel s_2 \xrightarrow{e} p_3' \parallel s_2$. Next, we need to show that $p_2' \parallel s_2 \; \underline{\leftrightarrow}_{\mathbf{b}} \; p_3' \parallel s_2$. From above we have $\Delta(p_3'\,|[\epsilon,\epsilon]|\,s_2) \; \underline{\leftrightarrow}_{\mathbf{b}} \; \Delta(p_2\,|[\mu,\epsilon]|\,s_2)$ and since τ-transition are inert we get $\Delta(p_2\,|[\mu,\epsilon]|\,s_2) \; \underline{\leftrightarrow}_{\mathbf{b}} \; \Delta(p_2'\,|[\epsilon,\epsilon]|\,s_2)$. Thus, by transitivity we get $\Delta(p_3'\,|[\epsilon,\epsilon]|\,s_2) \; \underline{\leftrightarrow}_{\mathbf{b}} \; \Delta(p_2'\,|[\epsilon,\epsilon]|\,s_2)$. By Theorem 1 we get $p_3' \parallel s_2 \; \underline{\leftrightarrow}_{\mathbf{b}} \; \Delta(p_3'\,|[\epsilon,\epsilon]|\,s_2)$, $p_2' \parallel s_2 \; \underline{\leftrightarrow}_{\mathbf{b}} \; \Delta(p_2'\,|[\epsilon,\epsilon]|\,s_2)$, from which we ultimately conclude $p_2' \parallel s_2 \; \underline{\leftrightarrow}_{\mathbf{b}} \; p_3' \parallel s_2$. Likewise, Condition 2 of Definition 7 can be proved. $\square$

3.3 Input Determinism

The next implication of desynchronizability, is that desynchronizable systems should be *input deterministic*. In other words, the synchronous system $p \parallel s$ should not make non-deterministic choices upon the reception of messages. It may perform non-deterministic external behavior, and it may also be non-deterministic when sending messages. The reason for this, is that desynchronization *delays* any non-deterministic choice on the input.

Like in the case of independence of external actions, we define the condition input-determinism on the synchronous process $p \parallel s$ rather than on the individual processes p and s (cf. [1]) because we are aiming for necessary conditions. As before, input-determinism of the individual processes would be a natural part of a sufficient condition for input-determinism of the composition.

Definition 8. *A synchronous system $p \parallel s$ is input deterministic modulo $\underline{\leftrightarrow}_{\mathbf{b}}$ if every reachable state $p_1 \parallel s_1 \in \Re(p \parallel s)$ satisfies the following conditions.*

1. *for all p_2, s_2, p_3, whenever $p_1 \parallel s_1 \xrightarrow{u} p_2 \parallel s_2$ and $p_1 \parallel s_1 \xrightarrow{u} p_3 \parallel s_2$ for some $u \in (M_s \cup E_s)^*$, then $p_2 \parallel s_2 \; \underline{\leftrightarrow}_{\mathbf{b}} \; p_3 \parallel s_2$.*
2. *for all p_2, s_2, s_3, whenever $p_1 \parallel s_1 \xrightarrow{v} p_2 \parallel s_2$ and $p_1 \parallel s_1 \xrightarrow{v} p_2 \parallel s_3$ for some $v \in (M_p \cup E_p)^*$, then $p_2 \parallel s_2 \; \underline{\leftrightarrow}_{\mathbf{b}} \; p_2 \parallel s_3$.*

Theorem 4. *Let $p \parallel s$ be concrete and desynchronizable, then it is input deterministic modulo $\underline{\leftrightarrow}_{\mathbf{b}}$.*

Proof. Pick a reachable state $p_1 \parallel s_1 \in \Re(p \parallel s)$ (see Fig. 5) such that $p_1 \parallel s_1 \xrightarrow{u} p_2 \parallel s_2$ and $p_1 \parallel s_1 \xrightarrow{u} p_3 \parallel s_2$, for some $u \in (M_s \cup E_s)^*, p_2, p_3, s_2 \in \mathbb{P}$. By Theorem 1 we have $p_1 \parallel s_1 \underline{\leftrightarrow}_{\mathbf{b}} \Delta(p_1 \,|[\epsilon, \epsilon]|\, s_1)$. Using the renaming functions from Theorem 3 we have $s_1 \xrightarrow{!u} s_2$ and $p_1 \xrightarrow{?u} p_2$ and $p_1 \xrightarrow{?u} p_3$. For the asynchronous system we then find the transitions as shown in Fig. 5, where $\mu = \bar{u}$. As $p \parallel s$ is concrete, all τ-transitions in the asynchronous system are inert, so we get $\Delta(p_1 \,|[\mu, \epsilon]|\, s_2) \underline{\leftrightarrow}_{\mathbf{b}} \Delta(p_2 \,|[\epsilon, \epsilon]|\, s_2) \underline{\leftrightarrow}_{\mathbf{b}} \Delta(p_3 \,|[\epsilon, \epsilon]|\, s_2)$. Finally,

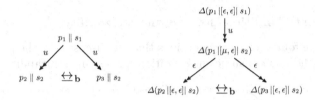

Fig. 5. The role of input-determinism

using Theorem 1 twice we ultimately get $p_2 \parallel s_2 \underline{\leftrightarrow}_{\mathbf{b}} p_3 \parallel s_2$. Likewise Condition 2 of Definition 8 can be proved. $\qquad\square$

3.4   The Diamond Property

The final implication of desynchronizability that we would like is the *diamond property*. Intuitively, the diamond property says that sending a message from one component does not disable the sending of message from the other component. Moreover, any order of execution leads to behaviorally equivalent states.

Definition 9. *A synchronous system $p \parallel s$ has the* diamond property modulo $\underline{\leftrightarrow}_{\mathbf{b}}$ *if for every reachable state $p_1 \parallel s_1$ and transitions $p_1 \parallel s_1 \xrightarrow{m} p_2 \parallel s_2$ and $p_1 \parallel s_1 \xrightarrow{n} p_3 \parallel s_3$ with $m \in M_p$ and $n \in M_s$ there exist transitions $p_2 \parallel s_2 \xrightarrow{n} p_4 \parallel s_4$ and $p_3 \parallel s_3 \xrightarrow{m} p_5 \parallel s_5$ with $p_4 \parallel s_4 \underline{\leftrightarrow}_{\mathbf{b}} p_5 \parallel s_5$.*

Theorem 5. *Let $p \parallel s$ be concrete and desynchronizable, then $p \parallel s$ has the diamond property modulo $\underline{\leftrightarrow}_{\mathbf{b}}$.*

Proof. Assume a state $p_1 \parallel s_1 \in \Re(p \parallel s)$, $p_1 \parallel s_1 \xrightarrow{m} p_2 \parallel s_2$ $(m \in M_p)$ and $p_1 \parallel s_1 \xrightarrow{n} p_3 \parallel s_3$ $(n \in M_s)$, as depicted in Fig. 6. From Theorem 1 we know that $p_i \parallel s_i \underline{\leftrightarrow}_{\mathbf{b}} p_i \,|[\epsilon, \epsilon]|\, s_i$, for $i \in \{1, 2, 3\}$. From the SOS rules we get $p_1 \xrightarrow{!m} p_2$, $s_1 \xrightarrow{?m} s_2$, $p_1 \xrightarrow{?n} p_3$, and $s_1 \xrightarrow{!n} s_3$. Using these transitions we find the transitions at the state $\Delta(p_1 \,|[\epsilon, \epsilon]|\, s_1)$ as shown in Fig. 6.

Since τ-transitions are inert we get $\Delta(p_2 \,|[\epsilon, m]|\, s_1) \underline{\leftrightarrow}_{\mathbf{b}} \Delta(p_3 \,|[\epsilon, \epsilon]|\, s_3)$. And from Theorem 1 we get $p_2 \parallel s_2 \underline{\leftrightarrow}_{\mathbf{b}} \Delta(p_2 \,|[\epsilon, \epsilon]|\, s_2)$. Thus, by transitivity we have $p_2 \parallel s_2 \underline{\leftrightarrow}_{\mathbf{b}} p_2 \,|[\epsilon, m]|\, s_1$. And, the transfer conditions of branching bisimulation gives the dashed transition labeled n shown in Fig. 6 with $p_4 \parallel s_4 \underline{\leftrightarrow}_{\mathbf{b}} \Delta(p_2 \,|[n, m]|\, s_2)$. Likewise we derive the dashed transition labeled m in Fig. 6 with $p_5 \parallel s_5 \underline{\leftrightarrow}_{\mathbf{b}} p_2 \,|[n, m]|\, s_3$. Finally, by transitivity $p_4 \parallel s_4 \underline{\leftrightarrow}_{\mathbf{b}} p_5 \parallel s_5$. $\qquad\square$

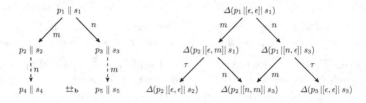

Fig. 6. The role of the diamond property

3.5 Sufficient Conditions for Desynchronizability

Conversely, the four necessary conditions that we discussed in the previous subsections, together form a sufficient condition for desynchronizability.

Theorem 6. *Let $p \parallel s$ be concrete, well-posed, independent of external actions, input deterministic, and have the diamond property, then $p \parallel s \underline{\leftrightarrow}_b \Delta(p \,|[\epsilon, \epsilon]|\, s)$.*

Proof. See [6].   □

4 Half-Duplex Communication Eliminates the Diamonds

In the previous section, we showed that the diamond property is a necessary condition for desynchronizability, while we expressed a desire in the introduction to desynchronize systems that do not possess this property as well. This leads us to rethink our model of desynchronization.

Changing the notion of equivalence or the observation of the predicate is not likely to help. Previous research [3,10] has been performed on weaker notions of equivalence, and although the diamond property was not identified as a necessary condition there, it did come up as a natural sufficient condition that the authors could not work around. This is why we decided to experiment with the properties of the buffer instead.

Inspired by the observation that the problem occurs when both communicating parties would like to send a message at the same time, we decided to see if *half-duplex communication*, in which only one party can communicate at a time, would give a solution. We model half-duplex communication between processes p and s as a process $p \,|[\epsilon, \epsilon]|_h\, s$, of which the structured operational semantics are given in Table 3. Observe that the rules are similar to those we used before, except that either the left or the right queue remains empty at all times.

Definition 10. *A synchronous system $p \parallel s$ is half-duplex desynchronizable if $p \parallel s \underline{\leftrightarrow}_b \Delta(p \,|[\epsilon, \epsilon]|_h\, s)$.*

Next, we find that the diamond property can be dropped from the necessary and sufficient conditions.

Theorem 7. *Let $p \parallel s$ be concrete and half-duplex desynchronizable, then it is well-posed, independent of external actions, and input deterministic.*

Table 3. SOS rules for asynchronous systems with half-duplex queues

$$\frac{p \xrightarrow{!m} p'}{(p\,|[\epsilon,\nu]|_{\mathrm{h}}\, s) \xrightarrow{!m} (p'\,|[\epsilon,\nu.m]|_{\mathrm{h}}\, s)} \qquad \frac{s \xrightarrow{!n} s'}{(p\,|[\mu,\epsilon]|_{\mathrm{h}}\, s) \xrightarrow{!n} (p\,|[\mu.n,\epsilon]|_{\mathrm{h}}\, s')}$$

$$\frac{p \xrightarrow{?n} p',\ \mu = n.\mu',\ n \in M_s}{(p\,|[\mu,\nu]|_{\mathrm{h}}\, s) \xrightarrow{?n} (p'\,|[\mu',\nu]|_{\mathrm{h}}\, s)} \qquad \frac{s \xrightarrow{?m} s',\ \nu = m.\nu',\ m \in M_p}{(p\,|[\mu,\nu]|_{\mathrm{h}}\, s) \xrightarrow{?m} (p\,|[\mu,\nu']|_{\mathrm{h}}\, s')}$$

$$\frac{p \xrightarrow{e} p',\ e \in E_p}{(p\,|[\mu,\nu]|_{\mathrm{h}}\, s) \xrightarrow{e} (p'\,|[\mu,\nu]|_{\mathrm{h}}\, s)} \qquad \frac{s \xrightarrow{e} s',\ e \in E_s}{(p\,|[\mu,\nu]|_{\mathrm{h}}\, s) \xrightarrow{e} (p\,|[\mu,\nu]|_{\mathrm{h}}\, s')} \qquad \frac{}{(p\,|[\epsilon,\epsilon]|_{\mathrm{h}}\, s)\sqcup}.$$

Proof. Along the same lines as the proofs in the previous section.   □

Theorem 8. *Suppose a concrete process $p \parallel s$ is well-posed, independent of external actions, and input deterministic, then it is half-duplex desynchronizable.*

Proof. See [6].   □

5 Discussion

5.1 Relaxing the Half-Duplex Condition

As already mentioned, the half-duplex mechanism leads to an inefficient design of an asynchronous system because a sender is prohibited to send messages while its input queue is non-empty. Moreover, we required half-duplex communication because we could not guarantee the diamond property for our synchronous system. In essence, the half-duplex property ensures a certain level of synchronization over the communication buffer. Half-duplex communication, namely, can only be implemented if some kind of semaphore is in place on top of the physical layer.

Table 4. SOS rules for semi-duplex communication over a set I

$$\frac{p \xrightarrow{!m} p',\ m \in M_p,\ (\mu \in I^* \vee m \in I)}{(p\,|[\mu,\nu]|\, s) \xrightarrow{!m} (p'\,|[\mu,\nu.m]|_I\, s)} \qquad \frac{s \xrightarrow{!n} s',\ n \in M_s,\ (\nu \in I^* \vee n \in I)}{(p\,|[\mu,\nu]|\, s) \xrightarrow{!n} (p\,|[\mu.n,\nu]|_I\, s')}$$

$$\frac{p \xrightarrow{?n} p',\ \mu = n.\mu',\ n \in M_s}{(p\,|[\mu,\nu]|\, s) \xrightarrow{?n} (p'\,|[\mu',\nu]|_I\, s)} \qquad \frac{s \xrightarrow{?m} s',\ \nu = m.\nu',\ m \in M_p}{(p\,|[\mu,\nu]|\, s) \xrightarrow{?m} (p\,|[\mu,\nu']|_I\, s')}$$

$$\frac{p \xrightarrow{\alpha} p',\ \alpha \in E_p}{(p\,|[\mu,\nu]|\, s) \xrightarrow{\alpha} (p'\,|[\mu,\nu]|_I\, s)} \qquad \frac{s \xrightarrow{\alpha} s',\ \alpha \in E_s}{(p\,|[\mu,\nu]|\, s) \xrightarrow{\alpha} (p\,|[\mu,\nu]|_I\, s')} \qquad \frac{}{(p\,|[\epsilon,\epsilon]|_I\, s)\sqcup}$$

Now, suppose that we do have the diamond property for certain pairs of actions in the synchronous system. In such a case, a specialized semaphore could be put in place that verifies whether there are actions in the incoming buffer that conflict with a specific outgoing action. For example, suppose we can identify a subset $I \subseteq M_p \cup M_s$ of actions that satisfy the diamond property with respect to all other messages in $M_p \cup M_s$. As long as there are only actions from I in the buffer, it is safe to send any message, and at any time it is safe to send actions from I. Such a type of communication is captured in the SOS rules of Table 4.

We conjecture that the necessary and sufficient conditions for desynchronization using such a buffer are well-posedness, independence of external actions, input determinism, and the diamond property for pairs of messages modeled by the set I. We actually expect the proof to be along the same lines of Theorem 6.

However, before going into detailed proofs of such theorems, we would like to point out that the selection of a semi-duplex buffering strategy does not only depend on the particular diamonds that can be proven, but also on the particular kinds of semaphores / semi-duplex buffering strategies that are implementable. If we want to distinguish different classes of messages that share the diamond property, we also need to use different semaphores to ensure the associated semi-duplex buffer (reminiscent of [16]). Which semaphores are actually implementable is highly dependent on the application domain, so we would like to concentrate future research on finding out which possibilities we have in practice (in our case, in practical cases of supervisory control) to put semaphores on a communication buffer.

5.2   Desynchronization in Supervisory Control

Regarding supervisory control theory, we should still check whether the conditions we have gotten so far are reasonable. That is the topic of this subsection.

Supervisory control theory [18] aims at controlling the behavior of a *plant p* to fit a requirement r by synthesizing a *supervisor s* such that $p \parallel s \leftrightarrow_{\mathbf{b}} r$. For this purpose, a plant and its supervisor perform two kinds of actions: *controllable* and *uncontrollable* actions. We model uncontrollable actions as the send messages from a plant to its supervisor, while the controllable actions are modeled as the send messages from the supervisor to the plant.

To make supervisory control synthesis feasible, it is usually assumed that p is deterministic. The result of the synthesis is then also a deterministic s.

In order to synthesize a supervisor that is well-posed, consider the procedure of taking the process $p \parallel s$ and renaming all communication actions to send-actions if they originated from s and to receive actions if they originated from p. In other words, define a function $\gamma : \mathbb{P} \to \mathbb{P}$ such that

$$\gamma(m) = \begin{cases} !m & ; \text{if } m \in M_s \\ ?m & ; \text{if } m \in M_p \\ m & ; \text{otherwise} \end{cases}$$

and consider the process $\gamma(p \parallel s)$ defined using the SOS rules of Table 5.

Table 5. SOS rules for renaming using a function γ

$$\frac{p \xrightarrow{m} p'}{\gamma(p) \xrightarrow{\gamma(m)} \gamma(p')} \qquad \frac{p\sqcup}{\gamma p\sqcup}$$

We obtain the following theorem, which gives us a well-posed and input-deterministic supervisor for p.

Theorem 9. *If p and s are deterministic, then p and $\gamma(p \parallel s)$ are well-posed, $p \parallel \gamma(p \parallel s)$ is input-deterministic, and $p \parallel s \underline{\leftrightarrow}_b p \parallel \gamma(p \parallel s) \underline{\leftrightarrow}_b r$.*

Proof. It is easy, but tedious, to verify that well-posedness of $p \parallel \gamma(p \parallel s)$ follows from the witnessing relation $\mathcal{W} = \{(p_1, \gamma(p_1 \parallel s_1)) \mid p_1 \parallel s_1 \in \mathfrak{R}(p \parallel s)\}$, while the fact that we have constructed a valid supervisor is witnessed by the branching bisimulation relation $\mathcal{B} = \{(p_1 \parallel s_1, p_1 \parallel \gamma(p_1 \parallel s_1)) \mid p_1 \parallel s_1 \in \mathfrak{R}(p \parallel s)\}$. Both witnesses rely on determinism of p and s, but we have to leave out the details for reasons of space. Obviously, if p and s are deterministic so is $\gamma(p \parallel s)$ (using disjointness of the message sets), hence it is input-deterministic.   □

The issue of ensuring independence of external actions is more involved. Intuitively, independence of external actions says that an external action can always be delayed in favor of an internal communication. Of course, since the role of a supervisor is just to limit the behavior of the plant, it has no direct need for external actions. However, if the plant's communication is dependent on the external behavior – for example, external behavior is processed with higher priority than internal communication – desynchronizability is still at risk.

5.3   Desynchronization of Non-Concrete Synchronous Systems

In this subsection, we focus on the desynchronization of synchronous systems that allow τ-transitions in their definitions.

The introduction of τ-transitions in a synchronous system makes it impossible to know from the semantics whether the process p or[1] s performed a τ-transition, whenever the synchronous system $p \parallel s$ executes the τ-transition. Such an information is vital in the definition of witnessing branching bisimulation relation between a synchronous system, and its asynchronous version.

One way to circumvent this problem is by renaming the label τ of every τ-transitions present in the processes p and s by the labels τ_p and τ_s, respectively. Furthermore, by assuming that the labels τ_p, τ_s are present in the external actions of the processes p, s, respectively, the conditions of Theorem 6 (Theorem 8) can still be used to assert whether a non-concrete synchronous system is desynchronizable (half-duplex desynchronizable) or not. However, despite this

---

[1] The word 'or' is used in the exclusive sense.

soundness result, more research is required in order to examine to what extent are these conditions necessary in the absence of concreteness assumption.

5.4 Conclusions

In this paper, we studied necessary and sufficient conditions for desynchroniz-ability modulo branching bisimulation, and we showed that reverting to half-duplex communication, or variants of it, can help in avoiding a troublesome condition known as the diamond property. To the best of our knowledge, this is the first characterization of desynchronizability modulo branching bisimulation; moreover, the previous works (cf. [3,7,10,21]) on weaker equivalences focused on giving sufficient conditions for desynchronizability.

Our results indicate that the study of desynchronizability should no longer focus on the properties one needs to retain equivalence of behavior in a certain communication context, but rather should focus on changing the communication context in such a way that these properties actually become attainable. Furthermore, we have shown that reasonable desynchronizability results can be obtained even for the finest equivalence in the van Glabbeek spectrum. Perhaps some of the necessary conditions can be relaxed by weakening this equivalence. For example, we know that we can eliminate the need for input determinism by studying desynchronizability modulo contra-simulation [12]. But so far the properties obtained using weaker equivalences are very similar to the ones we found, which indicates that there is not much to be gained there.

Another observation we made is that the choice of abstraction scheme is crucial in obtaining useful results. On the one hand, if we had chosen to abstract from outputs rather than from inputs in our definition of the operator $\Delta()$, there would have been an additional necessary condition saying that at any reachable state of $p \parallel s$ only one send-transition is allowed (the details of this are outside the scope of this paper, see [6]). On the other hand, we obtained interesting results in [7] using an abstraction scheme that abstracted from send- and receive actions from the plant using bags as a communication buffer, but that abstraction scheme did not work out for queues.

For deterministic supervisory control, we showed that it is possible to synthesize a controller that satisfies the well-posedness property by construction. For other systems, however, this may not be so easy. Therefore, it would be beneficial if tools for model checking asynchronous systems, like mCRL2 [13] and CADP [15], could be optimized to check for well-posedness as well.

Finally, we observe a similarity between our work and the work on chore-ographies and contracts, which turns out to be useful in model checking of asynchronous systems [4,5,19]. Basically, such choreographies serve to restrict the occurrence of diamonds in an asynchronous system, which means that it becomes synchronizable [5]. Perhaps it is also possible to use this idea in the other direction, i.e., to desynchronize a system using a choreography on the communication buffer. It would be interesting to see if, for example, the proposed semi-duplex buffer discussed in Section 5 can be implemented using a choreography.

Acknowledgements. The authors thank the anonymous reviewers for their feedbacks on an earlier draft of this paper. The authors also thank Jos Baeten, Koos Rooda, Bert van Beek, and Damian Nadales, for various discussions regarding this work and for putting us on the track of this problem.

This work has been performed as part of the "Integrated Multi-formalism Tool Support for the Design of Networked Embedded Control Systems" (MULTIFORM) project, supported by the Seventh Research Framework Programme of the European Commission (Grant agreement number: INFSO-ICT-224249).

References

1. Alfaro, L., Henzinger, T.: Interface-Based Design. In: Broy, M., Grünbauer, J., Harel, D., Hoare, C.A.R. (eds.) Engineering Theories of Software Intensive Systems. NATO Science Series, vol. 195, pp. 83–104. Springer Netherlands (2005)

2. Baeten, J.C.M., Basten, T., Reniers, M.A.: Process Algebra: Equational Theories of Communicating Processes, 1st edn. Cambridge University Press, New York (2009)

3. Balemi, S.: Control of Discrete Event Systems: Theory And Application. Ph.D. thesis, Swiss Federal Institute of Technology, Automatic Control Laboratory, ETH Zurich (May 1992)

4. Basu, S., Bultan, T.: Choreography conformance via synchronizability. In: Proceedings of the 20th International Conference on World Wide Web, WWW 2011, pp. 795–804. ACM, New York (2011)

5. Basu, S., Bultan, T., Ouederni, M.: Synchronizability for Verification of Asynchronously Communicating Systems. In: Kuncak, V., Rybalchenko, A. (eds.) VMCAI 2012. LNCS, vol. 7148, pp. 56–71. Springer, Heidelberg (2012)

6. Beohar, H.: Refinement of communication and states in models of embedded systems. Ph.D. thesis, Eindhoven university of technology (in preparation)

7. Beohar, H., Cuijpers, P.J.L.: Desynchronizability of (partial) synchronous closed loop systems. Scientific Annals of Computer Science 21, 5–38 (2011)

8. Brand, D., Zafiropulo, P.: On communicating finite-state machines. J. ACM 30, 323–342 (1983)

9. Cécé, G., Finkel, A.: Verification of programs with half-duplex communication. Inf. Comput. 202, 166–190 (2005)

10. Fischer, C., Janssen, W.: Synchronous Development of Asynchronous Systems. In: Montanari, U., Sassone, V. (eds.) CONCUR 1996. LNCS, vol. 1119, pp. 735–750. Springer, Heidelberg (1996)

11. Forschelen, S.T.J.: Supervisory control of theme park vehicles. Master's thesis, Eindhoven University of Technology, System Engineering Group, Dept. of Mechanical Engineering (2010)

12. van Glabbeek, R.J.: The Linear Time - branching Time Spectrum II. In: Best, E. (ed.) CONCUR 1993. LNCS, vol. 715, pp. 66–81. Springer, Heidelberg (1993)

13. Groote, J.F., Mathijssen, A., Reniers, M., Usenko, Y., van Weerdenburg, M.: The formal specification language mCRL2. In: MMOSS 2006 (2006)

14. Hoare, C.A.R.: Communicating sequential processes. Commun. ACM 21(8), 666–677 (1978)

15. Mateescu, R.: Specification and Analysis of Asynchronous Systems using CADP, pp. 141–169. ISTE (2010), http://dx.doi.org/10.1002/9780470611012.ch5

16. Peters, K., Schicke, J.-W., Nestmann, U.: Synchrony vs causality in asynchronous pi-calculus. In: Luttik, B., Valencia, F. (eds.) 18th International Workshop on Expressiveness in Concurrency, EXPRESS. EPTCS, vol. 64, pp. 89–103 (2011)

17. Plotkin, G.D.: A Structural Approach to Operational Semantics. Tech. Rep. DAIMI FN-19, University of Aarhus (1981)

18. Ramadge, P.J., Wonham, W.M.: Supervisory control of a class of discrete event processes. SIAM Journal on Control and Optimization 25(1), 206–230 (1987)

19. Salaün, G., Bultan, T.: Realizability of Choreographies Using Process Algebra Encodings. In: Leuschel, M., Wehrheim, H. (eds.) IFM 2009. LNCS, vol. 5423, pp. 167–182. Springer, Heidelberg (2009)

20. Tanenbaum, A.: Computer Networks, 4th edn. Prentice Hall Professional Technical Reference (2002)

21. Udding, J.: Classification and Composition of Delay-Insensitive Circuits. Ph.D. thesis, Eindhoven University of Technology, Eindhoven (1984)

The Tale of SOLOIST: A Specification Language for Service Compositions Interactions

Domenico Bianculli[1], Carlo Ghezzi[2], and Pierluigi San Pietro[2]

[1] University of Luxembourg - SnT Centre, Luxembourg
domenico.bianculli@uni.lu
[2] Politecnico di Milano - DEI - DEEP-SE Group, Italy
{carlo.ghezzi,pierluigi.sanpietro}@polimi.it

Abstract. Service-based applications are a new class of software systems that provide the basis for enterprises to build their information systems by following the principles of service-oriented architectures. These software systems are often realized by orchestrating remote, third-party services, to provide added-values applications that are called service compositions. The distributed ownership and the evolving nature of the services involved in a service composition make verification activities crucial. On a par with verification is also the problem of formally specifying the interactions—with third-party services—of service compositions, with the related issue of balancing expressiveness and support for automated verification.

This paper showcases SOLOIST, a specification language for formalizing the interactions of service compositions. SOLOIST has been designed with the primary objective of expressing the most significant specification patterns found in the specifications of service-based applications. The language is based on a many-sorted first-order metric temporal logic, extended with new temporal modalities that support aggregate operators for events occurring in a certain time window. We also show how, under certain assumptions, the language can be reduced to linear temporal logic, paving the way for using SOLOIST with established verification techniques, both at design time and at run time.

1 Introduction

Modern-age software engineering has to deal with novel kinds of software systems, which exhibit new features that often demand for rethinking and extending the traditional methodologies and the accompanying methods and techniques. One class of new software systems is constituted by *open-world* software [5], characterized by a dynamic and decentralized nature; service-based applications (SBAs) represent an example of this class of systems. SBAs are often defined as service compositions, obtained by orchestrating—with languages such as BPEL [2]—existing services, possibly offered by third-parties. This kind of applications has seen a wide adoption in enterprises, which nowadays develop their information systems using the principles of service orientation [20].

C.S. Păsăreanu and G. Salaün (Eds.): FACS 2012, LNCS 7684, pp. 55–72, 2013.
© Springer-Verlag Berlin Heidelberg 2013

The development of SBAs is usually spread across multiple organizations or multiple divisions within a single organization, and promotes a loose organizational coupling between service providers and service integrators. Moreover, in open-world software, changes are frequent, unexpected, and welcome [29]. On one hand, services are developed, deployed, operated, and evolved (e.g., by changing the interface, the implementation, the business protocol, or the quality of service guarantees) autonomously by service providers. On the other hand, service integrators may leverage dynamic binding as well as self-adaptation techniques to change a composite service at run time. These factors lead to a distributed ownership and to an evolving nature of service compositions, which affect the notions of correctness, dependability and in general all quality attributes of SBAs.

Guaranteeing quality attributes of SBAs poses new challenges to the definition of verification methodologies. This challenge has been taken on in the last years by the research community, which has proposed several techniques for the verification of SBAs, both at design time and at run time; see for example [4,10,35]. Equal in importance to verification techniques are the specification languages used to express the requirements of the service interactions that one wants to check. In most of the cases, the specification language is some logical language, such as the CTL and LTL temporal logics and the Event Calculus, or a domain-specific language defined to represent some non-functional attributes (e.g., response time).

Despite significant advances in research and in prototype implementation, these approaches did not spread to the world of practitioners. One of the reasons is that proposed specification languages do not meet the expressiveness requirements of SBAs. In a previous work [8], some of the authors performed an extensive analysis of requirements specifications of SBAs, written both in research settings and in industrial settings, to characterize the use of property specifications patterns in SBAs. The results of this study showed that: a) the majority of requirements specifications stated in industrial settings refers to specific aspects of service provisioning, which can be characterized as a new class of specification patterns; b) the specification patterns proposed in the research literature are barely used in industrial settings.

The outcome of the study described in [8] drove the design of a new formal specification language, with the primary objective to meet the most significant expressiveness requirements emerged from the study[1]. This paper introduces this new language, called SOLOIST (*SpecificatiOn Language fOr servIce compoSitions inTeractions*). The language is based on a many-sorted first-order metric temporal logic, which has been extended with new temporal modalities that support aggregate operators for events occurring in a certain time window. Expressiveness was not the sole requirement in designing this language. We also wanted the language to express specifications that could lead to automatic formal verification. Indeed, we also show that SOLOIST, under certain assumptions, can

---

[1] The language can be viewed as a profound revision of a previous attempt [3], driven by the feedback from the field study reported in [8].

be translated into linear temporal logic, allowing for its use with established techniques and tools, both for design-time and for run-time verification.

The rest of this paper is structured as follows. In Sect. 2 we describe the requirements elicitation process for the language and discuss some of the issues faced during its design. Section 3 describes some examples of properties, associated with a BPEL process, which can be expressed with the language. Section 4 introduces SOLOIST, its syntax, and its semantics (both informally and formally); it also shows the use of the language to specify the properties presented in Sect. 3. Section 5 illustrates the translation of SOLOIST to linear temporal logic. Section 6 discusses related work and Sect. 7 concludes the paper, providing some hints for future research.

2   Requirements Elicitation and Design of the Language

2.1   Eliciting Language Requirements from Usage of Specification Patterns in SBAs

In [8] some of the authors presented a study on the use of specification patterns in SBAs. The study analyzed the requirements specifications of two sets of case studies. One set consisted of 104 cases extracted from research papers in the area of specification, verification and validation of SBAs published in the last ten years; the other included 100 service interfaces developed by an industrial partner for its service-oriented information system in the last ten years. During the study, each requirement specification was matched against a specification pattern; in total, we analyzed and classified 290 + 625 requirements specifications from research and industrial data, respectively.

The study classified the requirements specifications according to four classes of property specification patterns. Three of them correspond to the systems of specification patterns proposed by Dwyer et al. [12], by Konrad and Cheng [23], and by Gruhn and Laue [16]; these patterns have been widely used for the specification and verification of concurrent and real-time systems. The fourth group includes patterns that are specific to service provisioning, and have emerged during the study; these new patterns are:

Average response time (S1) is a variant of the bounded response pattern defined in [23] that uses the average operator to aggregate the response time over a certain time window.

Counting the number of events (S2) is used to express common non-functional requirements such as reliability (e.g., "number of errors in a given time window") and throughput (e.g., "number of requests that a client is allowed to submit in a given time window").

Average number of events (S3) is a variant of the previous pattern that states the average number of events occurred in a certain time interval within a certain time window, as in "the average number of client requests per hour computed over the daily business hours".

Maximum number of events (S4) is a variant of pattern S3 that aggregates events using the maximum operator.

Absolute time (S5) indicates events that should occur at a time that satisfies an absolute time constraint, as in "if the booking is done in the first week of March, a discount is given".

Unbounded elapsed time (S6) indicates the time elapsed since the last occurrence of a certain event.

Data-awareness (S7) (inspired by [11,18]) is a pattern denoting properties that refer to the actual data content of messages exchanged between services as in "every ID present in a message cannot appear in any future message".

Summarizing the results of the study, we report that:

– The majority of requirements specifications stated in industrial settings referred to non-functional properties expressed using aggregate operators (e.g., average, count, maximum); more specifically, the combined usage of patterns S1-S3-S4 accounted for the 81.9% of the specifications, with S3 and S4 being the two most used patterns. Similar requirements were found only rarely in the research literature and when so, they were expressed using the non-aggregated versions of the patterns.
– The two most used patterns in research settings were the "response" and the "bounded response" patterns, defined respectively in [12] and [23].
– The usage of specification patterns from the first three groups in the SBAs research literature were similar to existing data available in literature for other domains.
– The specification patterns proposed in the research literature were barely used in industrial settings.
– The usage of pattern S7 was the same in both set of case studies, ranking at the third place.

2.2   Design Choices

The results reported above have deeply influenced the design of SOLOIST. Our main goal has been to design a formal language that is both expressive—to meet the requirements derived from our field study [8]—and suitable for use with automated verification techniques and tools.

Our starting point has been a temporal logic with metrics: this allows us to support the patterns defined in [12,23,16], i.e., the ones prescribing constraints on the order and/or the occurrence of events, possibly with (real-)time information. Note that this subset is enough to express common patterns such as "response" or "bounded response", defined respectively in [12] and [23]. The logic assumes a discrete time domain, with each occurrence of an event denoted by a time-stamp.

As for supporting the *service provisioning* patterns, we made different decisions. First, we decided not to support patterns referring to absolute or elapsed time (patterns S5 and S6), since this would have notably impacted on the complexity of the translation. Moreover, our field study [8] showed that both of them are used in less than 1% of the specifications; given these data, we maintain this decision does not critically affect the expressiveness of the language as well as its reception by practitioners.

Pattern S7 is supported by adding a first-order quantification to the logic, following the approach proposed in [18]. By making the simplifying assumption that domains over which the quantification ranges are finite, the first-order quantification is mere syntactic sugar, which does not impact on the decidability of the language, but helps to improve its readability. The logic is also many-sorted, to support the different types of the messages exchanged among services.

Regarding patterns S3 and S4, which define properties related to the aggregation[2] of events occurred in a certain time interval h within a certain time window K as in "the average number of service invocations per hour over the last 11.5 hours of operation", we run into different possibilities to represent the observation interval h (i.e., one hour in the example) within the time window K (i.e., 11.5 hours in the example) considered to compute the aggregate value. It could be defined either as a fixed window over adjacent, non-overlapping intervals, or as a sliding window over overlapping intervals. The latter interpretation would require also to define a minimal distance corresponding to the shift of the sliding window, which could be either a fixed value, such as a system tick, or a variable value, such as the time-stamp of each event occurrence (meaning that the window slides variably, according to the occurrences of the events). Furthermore, in both interpretations, one has to make a decision on how to deal with time windows whose length is not an exact multiple of the observation interval; in other words, how to consider the tail of the window whose length is less than the one of the observation interval. After consulting with our industrial partner and evaluating its needs, we decided to support the interpretation with adjacent, non-overlapping observation intervals, where tail intervals whose length is shorter then the observation interval are ignored to express pattern S3 but considered to express pattern S4.

Modeling pattern S2 was straightforward, while for pattern S1 we considered its specific use in the context of SBAs. It shall be used to specify the average response time of invocations made to a certain service over a certain time window. Since a service may provide multiple operations, we decided to include the possibility to specify which operations to consider when computing the aggregate response time, as well as the calling points within the workflow of a service composition from which the invocations originate. Moreover, every service invocation in the scope of an instance of pattern S1 is assumed to be synchronous and actually corresponding to a pair of events, the *start* and *end* one. These events corresponds to the start (end) of an invocation in a precise location of the workflow; a start (end) of an invocation to the same operation of a service but from a different location in the workflow is considered a distinct event. Under these premises, we assume that two subsequent occurrences of the same *start* or *end* event may not happen.

---

[2] Note that patterns S1–S4 express aggregate statistics, without assuming any underlying probabilistic model.

3 Service Compositions and Their Specifications at a Glance

We consider service compositions defined in terms of the BPEL [2] orchestration language. Very briefly, BPEL is a high-level XML-based language for the definition and execution of business processes, defined as workflows that compose external partner services. The definition of a workflow contains a set of variables; the business logic is expressed as a composition of *activities*. The main types of activities are primitives for communicating with other services (*receive, invoke, reply, pick*) and for executing assignments (*assign*) to variables, as well as control-flow structures like *sequence, while, switch* and parallel *flows*. Advanced control flow structures, like *event, fault,* and *compensation handlers* are also available. We assume that each variable defined in a BPEL process is of an XML simple type; variables that can hold a WSDL message or an XML schema element can be represented by flattening their multi-part structure as a sequence of XML simple type variables.

3.1 Examples of Properties of Service Compositions Interactions

Below we list some examples of properties expressed in natural language, which can be used to specify the interactions of a BPEL process. We assume that the process has an integer variable `foo`, an *invoke* activity named *invA* that takes and returns an integer, an *invoke* activity named *invB* with no input or output parameters, three *receive* activities named *recvP*, *recvQ*, and *recvR* and a reply activity *term* that takes no parameters. The detailed workflow structure of the process as well as the other variables are of no interest for the purpose of this section and are omitted for clarity. All properties are under the scope of an implicit universal temporal quantification as in *"In every process run, ... "*.

1. *"At the end of the execution of the activity* invA*, the value of variable* foo *should be equal to 42."*
2. *"The execution of activity* recvP *should alternate with the execution of activity* recvQ*, though other activities different from* recvQ *(respectively,* recvP*) can be executed in between."*
3. *"The response time of activity* invB *should not exceed 4 time units."*
4. *"If activity* invB *has been invoked 4 times in the past 16 units, than activity* recvR *will be executed within 32 time units."*
5. *"When activity* term *is executed, the average response time of all the invocations of activity* invB *completed in the past 720 time units should be less than 3 time units."*
6. *"When activity* term *is executed, the average number of invocations, in an interval of 60 time units, of activity* invB *during the past 720 time units should be less than 4".*
7. *"When activity* term *is executed, the maximum number of invocations, in an interval of 60 time units, of activity* invB *during the past 720 time units should be less than 5".*

4   SOLOIST

4.1   Preliminaries

A signature Σ is a tuple $\langle S; F; P \rangle$ where:

- S is a set of sort symbols, i.e., names representing various domains;
- F is a set of pairs $f \colon s_1 \times \ldots \times s_n \to w$ where $n \geq 0$, f is a function symbol, $s_1 \times \ldots \times s_n \to w$ is the type of f, and $s_1, \ldots, s_n, w \in S$;
- P is a set of pairs $p \colon s_1 \times \ldots \times s_n$ where $n \geq 0$, p is predicate symbol, $s_1 \times \ldots \times s_n$ is the type of p, and $s_1, \ldots, s_n \in S$.

The sets S, F, P of Σ are denoted by $Sort(\Sigma), Func(\Sigma), Pred(\Sigma)$. Notice that constants are modeled as nullary functions of the form $c \colon \to w$.

Let Σ be a signature. For each sort $s \in Sort(\Sigma)$, we assume a set V_s of variables of sort s disjoint from the constants in $Func(\Sigma)$. Also, for each sort $s \in S$, we define the set of terms of sort s by induction:

- a variable $x \in V_s$ of sort s is a term of type s;
- if $f \colon s_1 \times \ldots \times s_n \to w \in Func(\Sigma)$ and $t_1, \ldots, t_n$ are terms of type $s_1, \ldots, s_n$ respectively, than $f(t_1, \ldots, t_n)$ is a term of type w.

An atom has the form $p(t_1, \ldots, t_n)$, with $p(s_1, \ldots, s_n) \in Pred(\Sigma)$ and terms $t_1, \ldots, t_n$ of type $s_1, \ldots, s_n$.

4.2   Syntax

A SOLOIST formula over Σ is defined inductively by:

- if $t_1, \ldots, t_n$ are terms of type $s_1, \ldots, s_n$ and $p(s_1, \ldots, s_n) \in Pred(\Sigma)$ is a predicate symbol, then $p(t_1, \ldots, t_n)$ is a formula;
- if ϕ and ψ are formulae and x is a variable, then $\neg\phi$, $\phi \wedge \psi$, $\exists x \colon \phi$ are formulae;
- if ϕ and ψ are formulae and I is a nonempty interval over $\mathbb{N}$, then $\phi \mathsf{U}_I \psi$ and $\phi \mathsf{S}_I \psi$ are formulae;
- if $n, K \in \mathbb{N}$, $\bowtie \in \{<, \leq, \geq, >, =\}$, ϕ is a formula of the form $p(t_1, \ldots, t_n)$, with $p(s_1, \ldots, s_n) \in Pred(\Sigma)$ and terms $t_1, \ldots, t_n$ of type $s_1, \ldots, s_n$, then $\mathsf{C}^K_{\bowtie n}(\phi)$ is a formula;
- if $n, K, h \in \mathbb{N}$, $\bowtie \in \{<, \leq, \geq, >, =\}$, ϕ is a formula of the form $p(t_1, \ldots, t_n)$, with $p(s_1, \ldots, s_n) \in Pred(\Sigma)$ and terms $t_1, \ldots, t_n$ of type $s_1, \ldots, s_n$, then $\mathsf{V}^{K,h}_{\bowtie n}(\phi)$ and $\mathsf{M}^{K,h}_{\bowtie n}(\phi)$ are formulae;
- if $n, K \in \mathbb{N}$, $\bowtie \in \{<, \leq, \geq, >, =\}$, $\phi_1, \ldots, \phi_m, \psi_1, \ldots, \psi_m$ are formulae of the form $p(t_1, \ldots, t_n)$—with $p(s_1, \ldots, s_n) \in Pred(\Sigma)$ and terms $t_1, \ldots, t_n$ of type $s_1, \ldots, s_n$—where for all $i, 1 \leq i \leq n, \phi_i \neq \psi_i$, then $\mathsf{D}^K_{\bowtie n}\{(\phi_1, \psi_1), \ldots, (\phi_m, \psi_m)\}$ is a formula.

Additional temporal modalities can be defined from the U_I and S_I modalities using the usual conventions. Note that the arguments of modalities $\mathsf{C}, \mathsf{V}, \mathsf{M}, \mathsf{D}$ can only be atoms, i.e., positive literals; this reflects the fact that they represent the occurrences of certain events, which are then aggregated as prescribed by the modality.

4.3   SOLOIST at Work

In this section we show how SOLOIST can be used to specify properties related to the interactions of a service composition described in BPEL.

Let $\mathcal{A}$ be the set of activities defined in a BPEL process[3]; $\mathcal{A} = \mathcal{A}_{start-inv} \cup \mathcal{A}_{end-inv} \cup \mathcal{A}_{recv} \cup \mathcal{A}_{pick} \cup \mathcal{A}_{reply} \cup \mathcal{A}_{hdlr} \cup \mathcal{A}_{other}$ where:

- $\mathcal{A}_{start-inv}$ $(\mathcal{A}_{end-inv})$ is the set of *start* (*end*) events of all *invoke* activities[4];
- $\mathcal{A}_{recv}$ is the set of all *receive* activities;
- $\mathcal{A}_{pick}$ is the set of all *pick* activities;
- $\mathcal{A}_{reply}$ is the set of all *reply* activities;
- $\mathcal{A}_{hdlr}$ is the set of events associated with all kinds of *handlers*;
- $\mathcal{A}_{other}$ is the set of activities that are not an *invoke*, a *receive*, a *pick*, a *reply*, or related to a handler (e.g., an *assign*, a control structure activity).

Let $\mathcal{A}_{msg} = \mathcal{A} \setminus \mathcal{A}_{other}$ be the set of activities that involve a data exchange, i.e., that have either an input message or an output message attached with them. Each $\mu \in \mathcal{A}_{msg}$ has an arity corresponding to the sum of the simple type variables by which its input and output messages can be represented; each $\mu \in \mathcal{A}_{other}$ is nullary.

A signature Σ to specify the interactions of a BPEL process with partner services by means of SOLOIST can be defined as follows:

- S is the set of XML simple types (e.g., integer, character, string);
- F is the set of functions defined by the scripting language used within the process (e.g., XPath functions on integers and strings);
- $P = \mathcal{A}$. A predicate may correspond to the execution of an activity; its arity and type are then those of the corresponding activity. The usage of the equality predicate between terms of the same XML type is also allowed.

Following the definitions in Sect. 4, the variables of a BPEL process are partitioned into various domains V_s, with $s \in Sort(\Sigma)$.

Below we list the translations into SOLOIST of the formulae presented in Sect. 3, each one with the corresponding item number:

1. $\mathsf{G}(\forall x, y: invA_{end}(x, y) \to \mathtt{foo} = 42)$
2. $\mathsf{G}((recvP \to \neg recvP\mathsf{U}_{(0,\infty)} recvQ) \wedge (recvQ \to \neg recvQ\mathsf{U}_{(0,\infty)} recvP))$
3. $\mathsf{G}(invB_{start} \to \mathsf{F}_{[0,4]} invB_{end})$
4. $\mathsf{G}(\mathsf{C}^{16}_{=4} invB \to \mathsf{F}_{[0,32]} recvR)$
5. $\mathsf{G}(term_{end} \to \mathsf{D}^{720}_{\leq 3}(invB_{start}, invB_{end}))$
6. $\mathsf{G}(term_{end} \to \mathsf{V}^{720,60}_{\leq 4}(invB_{start}))$
7. $\mathsf{G}(term_{end} \to \mathsf{M}^{720,60}_{\leq 5}(invB_{start}))$

---

[3] Activities of a BPEL process can be uniquely identified by means of an XPath expression.

[4] A synchronous *invoke* is characterized both by a *start* event and by an *end* event; an asynchronous *invoke* is characterized only by a *start* event.

4.4   Informal Semantics

The informal semantics of SOLOIST is based on a sequence of time-stamped predicates. A predicate corresponds to an event, which models the execution of an activity defined within a service composition; its arguments are the parameters possibly associated with the activity, such as the input message of a service invocation.

The S_I and U_I modalities have the usual meaning in temporal logics ("*Until*" and "*Since*")[5].

The $C^K_{\bowtie n}(\phi)$ modality, evaluated in a certain time instant, states a bound on the number of occurrences of an event ϕ, counted over a time window K; it expresses pattern S2.

The $V^{K,h}_{\bowtie n}(\phi)$ modality, evaluated at a certain time instant τ_i, is used to express a bound on the average number (with respect to an observation interval h, open to left and closed to the right) of occurrences of an event ϕ, occurred within a time window K; this corresponds to pattern S3. As discussed in Sect. 2, since K may not be an exact multiple of h, the actual time window over which occurrences of event ϕ are counted is bounded by $\tau_i - \lfloor \frac{K}{h} \rfloor h$ on the left and τ_i on the right; similarly, the number of observation intervals taken into account to compute the average is $\lfloor \frac{K}{h} \rfloor$. Consider, for example, the sequence of events depicted in Fig. 1, where black circles correspond to occurrences of the ϕ event. Assuming $\tau_i = 42$, $K = 35$, and $h = 6$ (values expressed as time units), $\lfloor \frac{K}{h} \rfloor = \lfloor \frac{35}{6} \rfloor = 5$. The evaluation of the formula $V^{35,6}_{\bowtie n}(\phi)$ at time instant 42 is then $\frac{2+1+2+4+1}{5} \bowtie n$, where the numerator of the fraction to the left of $\bowtie$ is the number of event occurrences in the window bounded by τ_i and $\tau_i - 5h$.

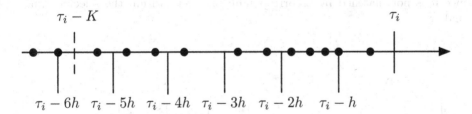

Fig. 1. Sequence of events over a time window K, with observation interval h (semantics of the V and M modalities)

The $M^{K,h}_{\bowtie n}(\phi)$ modality, evaluated in a certain time instant τ_i, is used to express a bound on the maximum number (with respect to an observation interval h, open to left and closed to the right) of occurrences of an event ϕ, occurred within a time window K; this corresponds to pattern S4. Differently from the V modality described above, this modality takes also into account the events occurring in a tail interval, even if its length is shorter than the one of the

---

[5] A strict semantics is assumed for the U_I and S_I modalities.

observation interval h. With reference to Fig. 1 and assuming the same values as above for τ_i, K, and h, the tail interval bounded by $\tau_i - K$ on the left and $\tau_i - \lfloor\frac{K}{h}\rfloor h = \tau_i - 5h$ on the right is also considered for computing the aggregate value. This leads to a final evaluation for the formula equivalent to $\max(\{1\}\cup\{4\}\cup\{2\}\cup\{1\}\cup\{2\}\cup\{1\}) \bowtie n = 4 \bowtie n$, where the i-th singleton set in the argument of the aggregate operator corresponds to the number of event occurrences in the i-th observation interval within the time window.

The D modality, evaluated in a certain time window τ_i, expresses a bound on the average time elapsed between pairs of specific adjacent events, occurred within a time window K; it can be used to express pattern S1. Consider, for example, the sequence of events depicted in Fig. 2, where capital letters in the lower part of the timeline correspond to events, and numbers in the upper part of the timeline indicate time-stamps; assume that the current time instant is $\tau_i = 18$ and that $K = 12$. To express a bound for the average distance between each occurrence of an event A and the first subsequent occurrence of an event B, as well as for the pair of events (C, D), for the previous 12 time units, one writes a formula like $\mathsf{D}^{12}_{\bowtie n}\{(A, B), (C, D)\}$, for some $\bowtie$ and n. With respect to $\tau_i = 18$, the time window of length $K = 12$ includes the events (with their respective time-stamp) $(A, 7)$, $(B, 8)$, $(C, 10)$, $(A, 12)$, $(D, 14)$, $(B, 16)$, $(A, 17)$, enclosed in the rectangle in Fig. 2. The average time distance is then computed by summing the differences between the time-stamps of each (A, B) and (C, D) pair (each pair of events is denoted by a different kind of arrow in Fig. 2), and dividing the result for the number of the selected events pairs (3 in the example). Finally, the D modality compares this result with value n, according to the relation defined by $\bowtie$; i.e., the evaluation of $\mathsf{D}^{12}_{\bowtie n}\{(A, B), (C, D)\}$ is $\frac{(8-7)+(16-12)+(14-10)}{3} \bowtie n$. Note that the event $(A, 17)$ is ignored for computing the (average) distance, since it is not matched by a corresponding B event within the selected time window.

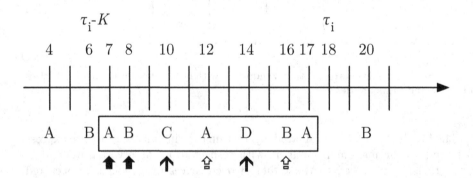

Fig. 2. Sequence of pairs of events over a time window K (semantics of the D modality)

4.5   Formal Semantics

A Σ-structure associates appropriate values to the elements of a signature Σ. A Σ-structure $\mathcal{D}$ consists of:

- a non-empty set $s^{\mathcal{D}}$ for each sort $s \in Sort(\Sigma)$;
- a function $f^{\mathcal{D}} \colon s_1^{\mathcal{D}} \times \ldots \times s_n^{\mathcal{D}} \to w^{\mathcal{D}}$ for each function symbol $f \colon s_1 \times \ldots \times s_n \to w \in Func(\Sigma)$;
- a relation $p^{\mathcal{D}} \subseteq s_1^{\mathcal{D}} \times \ldots \times s_n^{\mathcal{D}}$ for each predicate symbol $p \colon s_1 \times \ldots \times s_n \in Pred(\Sigma)$;

A *temporal first-order* structure over Σ is a pair $(\bar{\mathcal{D}}, \bar{\tau})$, where $\bar{\mathcal{D}} = \mathcal{D}_0, \mathcal{D}_1, \ldots$ is a sequence of Σ-structures and $\bar{\tau} = \tau_0, \tau_1, \ldots$ is a sequence of natural numbers (i.e., time-stamps), where:

- the sequence $\bar{\tau}$ is monotonically increasing (i.e., $\tau_i < \tau_{i+1}$, for all $i \geq 0$);
- for each $\mathcal{D}_i$ in $\bar{\mathcal{D}}$, with $i \geq 0$, for each $s \in Sort(\Sigma)$, $s^{\mathcal{D}_i} = s^{\mathcal{D}_{i+1}}$;
- for each $\mathcal{D}_i$ in $\bar{\mathcal{D}}$, with $i \geq 0$, for each function symbol $f \in Func(\Sigma)$, $f^{\mathcal{D}_i} = f^{\mathcal{D}_{i+1}}$.

A variable assignment σ is a $Sort(\Sigma)$-indexed family of functions $\sigma_s \colon V_s \to s^{\mathcal{D}}$ that maps every variable $x \in V_s$ of sort s to an element $\sigma_s(x) \in s^{\mathcal{D}}$. Notation $\sigma[x/d]$ denotes the variable assignment that maps x to d and maps all other variables as σ does.

The valuation function $[\![t]\!]_\sigma^{\mathcal{D}}$ of term t for a Σ-structure $\mathcal{D}$ is defined inductively as follows:

- if t is a variable $x \in V_s$, then $[\![t]\!]_\sigma^{\mathcal{D}} = \sigma_s(x)$;
- if t is a term $f(t_1, \ldots, t_n)$ then $[\![t]\!]_\sigma^{\mathcal{D}} = f^{\mathcal{D}}([\![t_1]\!]_\sigma^{\mathcal{D}}, \ldots, [\![t_n]\!]_\sigma^{\mathcal{D}})$.

For the sake of readability, we drop the superscript $\mathcal{D}$ and the subscript σ from the valuation function $[\![\cdot]\!]$ when they are clear from the context.

Given a temporal structure $(\bar{\mathcal{D}}, \bar{\tau})$ over Σ, a variable assignment σ, symbols $i, n, K, h \in \mathbb{N}$, $\bowtie \in \{<, \leq, \geq, >, =\}$, we define the satisfiability relation $(\bar{\mathcal{D}}, \bar{\tau}, \sigma, i) \models \phi$ for SOLOIST formulae as depicted in Fig. 3.

5   Translation to Linear Temporal Logic

In this section we show how SOLOIST can be translated into linear temporal logic. This translation guarantees the decidability of SOLOIST based on well-known results in temporal logic, allowing for its use with established verification techniques and tools. The translation presented here has not been designed to guarantee efficiency in verification but rather to be comprehensible.

SOLOIST is translated into a variant of linear temporal logic called MPLTL (Metric Linear Temporal Logic with Past) [31], which is a syntactically-sugared version of classical PLTL [21], defined over a mono-infinite discrete model of time represented by ω-words. For simplicity, we assume that the logic underlying SOLOIST is single-sorted; no expressiveness is lost, since it is well-known that

$(\bar{\mathcal{D}}, \bar{\tau}, \sigma, i) \models p(t_1, \ldots, t_n)$ iff $(\llbracket t_1 \rrbracket, \ldots, \llbracket t_n \rrbracket) \in p^{\mathcal{D}_i}$

$(\bar{\mathcal{D}}, \bar{\tau}, \sigma, i) \models \neg\phi$ iff $(\bar{\mathcal{D}}, \bar{\tau}, \sigma, i) \not\models \phi$

$(\bar{\mathcal{D}}, \bar{\tau}, \sigma, i) \models \phi \wedge \psi$ iff $(\bar{\mathcal{D}}, \bar{\tau}, \sigma, i) \models \phi \wedge (\bar{\mathcal{D}}, \bar{\tau}, \sigma, i) \models \psi$

$(\bar{\mathcal{D}}, \bar{\tau}, \sigma, i) \models \exists x \colon \phi$ iff $(\bar{\mathcal{D}}, \bar{\tau}, \sigma[x/d], i) \models \phi$
for some $d \in s^{\mathcal{D}}$ (with x of sort s)

$(\bar{\mathcal{D}}, \bar{\tau}, \sigma, i) \models \phi \mathsf{S}_I \psi$ iff for some $j < i, \tau_i - \tau_j \in I, (\bar{\mathcal{D}}, \bar{\tau}, \sigma, j) \models \psi$
and for all $k, j < k < i, (\bar{\mathcal{D}}, \bar{\tau}, \sigma, k) \models \phi$

$(\bar{\mathcal{D}}, \bar{\tau}, \sigma, i) \models \phi \mathsf{U}_I \psi$ iff for some $j > i, \tau_j - \tau_i \in I, (\bar{\mathcal{D}}, \bar{\tau}, \sigma, j) \models \psi$
and for all $k, i < k < j, (\bar{\mathcal{D}}, \bar{\tau}, \sigma, k) \models \phi$

$(\bar{\mathcal{D}}, \bar{\tau}, \sigma, i) \models \mathsf{C}^K_{\bowtie n}(\phi)$ iff $c(\tau_i - K, \tau_i, \phi) \bowtie n$ and $\tau_i \geq K$

$(\bar{\mathcal{D}}, \bar{\tau}, \sigma, i) \models \mathsf{V}^{K,h}_{\bowtie n}(\phi)$ iff $\dfrac{c(\tau_i - \lfloor \frac{K}{h} \rfloor h, \tau_i, \phi)}{\lfloor \frac{K}{h} \rfloor} \bowtie n$ and $\tau_i \geq K$

$(\bar{\mathcal{D}}, \bar{\tau}, \sigma, i) \models \mathsf{M}^{K,h}_{\bowtie n}(\phi)$ iff $\max \left\{ \bigcup_{m=0}^{\lfloor \frac{K}{h} \rfloor} \{c(lb(m), rb(m), \phi)\} \right\} \bowtie n$
given $lb(m) = \max\{\tau_i - K, \tau_i - (m+1)h\}$
and $rb(m) = \tau_i - mh$, with $\tau_i \geq K$

$(\bar{\mathcal{D}}, \bar{\tau}, \sigma, i) \models \mathsf{D}^K_{\bowtie n}\{(\phi_1, \psi_1), \ldots, (\phi_m, \psi_m)\}$ iff $\dfrac{\sum_{j=1}^m \sum_{(s,t) \in d(\phi_j, \psi_j, \tau_i, K)} (\tau_t - \tau_s)}{\sum_{j=1}^m |d(\phi_j, \psi_j, \tau_i, K)|} \bowtie n$
with $\tau_i \geq K$

where $c(\tau_a, \tau_b, \phi) = |\{s \mid \tau_a < \tau_s \leq \tau_b \text{ and } (\bar{\mathcal{D}}, \bar{\tau}, \sigma, s) \models \phi\}|$,
and $d(\phi, \psi, \tau_i, K) =$
$\{(s,t) \mid \tau_i - K < \tau_s \leq \tau_i \text{ and } (\bar{\mathcal{D}}, \bar{\tau}, \sigma, s) \models \phi, t = \min\{u \mid \tau_s < \tau_u \leq \tau_i, (\bar{\mathcal{D}}, \bar{\tau}, \sigma, u) \models \psi\}\}$.

Fig. 3. Formal semantics of SOLOIST

many-sorted first-order logic (on which SOLOIST is based) can be reduced to single-sorted first-order logic when the number of sorts is finite. Moreover, since we assume that the domains corresponding to sorts are finite, we can drop the first-order quantification and convert each quantifier into a conjunction or a disjunction of atomic propositions. Similarly, n-ary predicate symbols (with $n \geq 1$) are converted into atomic propositions. For example, a formula of the form $\exists x \colon P(x)$, with x ranging over the finite domain $\{1, 2, 3\}$, is translated into the formula $\bigvee_{x \in \{1,2,3\}} P_x$, where P_1, P_2, P_3 are atomic propositions. We denote with Π the finite set of atomic propositions used in formulae obtained as described above.

These simplifications allow us to replace the temporal first-order structure $(\bar{\mathcal{D}}, \bar{\tau})$ and the variable assignment σ used in the definition of the satisfiability relation of SOLOIST with *timed* ω-words, i.e., ω-words over $2^\Pi \times \mathbb{N}$. For a timed ω-word $z = z_0, z_1, \ldots$, every element $z_k = (\sigma_k, \delta_k)$ contains the set σ_k of atomic propositions that are true at the natural time-stamp denoted by $\tau_k = \sum_{i=0}^k \delta_i$ (with $\delta_i > 0$ for all $i > 0$). The satisfiability relation for SOLOIST can then be defined over timed ω-words, and it is denoted by $z, i \overset{\tau}{\models} \phi$, with z being a timed ω-word and $i \in \mathbb{N}$; we omit its definition since it can be derived with straightforward transformations from the one illustrated in Fig. 3.

Furthermore, we introduce a normal form where negations may only occur on atoms (see, for example, [31]). First, we extend the syntax of the language by introducing a dual version for each operator in the original syntax, except for the $C_{\bowtie n}^{K}, V_{\bowtie n}^{K,h}, M_{\bowtie n}^{K,h}, D_{\bowtie n}^{K}$ modalities[6]: the dual of $\wedge$ is $\vee$; the dual of U_I is "*Release*" R_I: $\phi R_I \psi \equiv \neg(\neg\phi U_I \neg\psi)$; the dual of S_I is "*Trigger*" T_I: $\phi T_I \psi \equiv \neg(\neg\phi S_I \neg\psi)$. For the sake of brevity, we do not explicitly report the semantics of these dual operators; it can be derived straightforwardly from the above definitions. A formula is in *positive normal form* if its alphabet is $\{\wedge, \vee, U_I, R_I, S_I, T_I, C_{\bowtie n}^{K}, V_{\bowtie n}^{K,h}, M_{\bowtie n}^{K,h}, D_{\bowtie n}^{K}\} \cup \Pi \cup \bar{\Pi}$, where $\bar{\Pi}$ is the set of formulae of the form $\neg p$ for $p \in \Pi$. For the rest of this section, we assume that SOLOIST formulae have been transformed into equivalent formulae in positive normal form.

Under these assumptions, the translation of SOLOIST to MPLTL boils down to expressing the temporal modalities $R_I, T_I, U_I, S_I, C_{\bowtie n}^{K}, V_{\bowtie n}^{K,h}, M_{\bowtie n}^{K,h}, D_{\bowtie n}^{K}$ in MPLTL, preserving their semantics.

First of all, we should remark that while in the semantics of SOLOIST the temporal information is denoted by a natural time-stamp, in MPLTL the temporal information is implicitly defined by the integer position in an ω-word. However, the model based on timed ω-words and the one based on ω-words can be transformed into each other. Given an ω-word w such that $w, i \models \phi$ (where $w, i \models \phi$ denotes the satisfiability relation over ω-words), it is possible to define a timed ω-word $z = z_0, z_1, \ldots$, with $z_0 = (w_0, 0)$ and $z_k = (w_k, 1)$ for $k > 0$, such that $z, i \models^{\tau} \phi$. Conversely, given a SOLOIST timed ω-word z, we need to pinpoint in an MPLTL ω-word w the positions that correspond to time-stamps in the z timed ω-word where an event occurred. We add to the set Π a special propositional symbol e, which is true in each position corresponding to a "valid" time-stamp in the z timed ω-word. In the MPLTL semantics, an ω-word w over $\Pi \cup \{e\}$ is defined as follows: $w_k = \sigma_k \cup \{e\}$ whenever τ_k is defined, and $w_k = \emptyset$ otherwise. We then define a mapping ρ from SOLOIST dual normal form formulae into MPLTL formulae, such that we can state that $z, i \models^{\tau} \phi$ iff $w, \tau_i \models \rho(\phi)$. The mapping ρ is defined by induction as follows:

1. $\rho(p(t_1, \ldots, t_n)) = p(t_1, \ldots, t_n)$.
2. $\rho(\neg p(t_1, \ldots, t_n)) = \neg p(t_1, \ldots, t_n)$.
3. If ϕ and ψ are formulae and x is a variable, then

$$\rho(\phi \wedge \psi) = \rho(\phi) \wedge \rho(\psi);$$
$$\rho(\phi \vee \psi) = \rho(\phi) \vee \rho(\psi);$$
$$\rho(\exists x \colon \phi) = \exists x \colon \rho(\phi);$$
$$\rho(\forall x \colon \phi) = \forall x \colon \rho(\phi).$$

4. If ϕ and ψ are formulae and I is a nonempty interval over $\mathbb{N}$, then

$$\rho(\phi U_I \psi) = (\neg e \vee \rho(\phi)) U_I (e \wedge \rho(\psi));$$
$$\rho(\phi S_I \psi) = (\neg e \vee \rho(\phi)) S_I (e \wedge \rho(\psi));$$
$$\rho(\phi R_I \psi) = (e \wedge \rho(\phi)) R_I (\neg e \vee \rho(\psi));$$
$$\rho(\phi T_I \psi) = (e \wedge \rho(\phi)) T_I (\neg e \vee \rho(\psi)).$$

---

[6] A negation in front of one of the $C_{\bowtie n}^{K}, V_{\bowtie n}^{K,h}, M_{\bowtie n}^{K,h}, D_{\bowtie n}^{K}$ modalities becomes a negation of the relation denoted by the $\bowtie$ symbol, hence no dual version is needed for them.

5. For $C^K_{\bowtie n}$, we consider only the case $C^K_{>n}$, since the other possible relations used for $\bowtie$ can be modeled with the following equivalences: $C^K_{\leq n} \equiv \neg C^K_{>n}$; $C^K_{\geq n} \equiv C^K_{>n-1}$; $C^K_{<n} \equiv \neg C^K_{>n-1}$; $C^K_{=n} \equiv C^K_{>n-1} \wedge \neg C^K_{>n}$.

$$\rho(C^K_{>n}(\phi)) = \bigvee_{0 \leq i_1 < ... < i_{n+1} < K} (Y^{i_1}(e \wedge \phi) \wedge ... \wedge Y^{i_{n+1}}(e \wedge \phi))$$

where the MPLTL modality Y ("$yesterday$") is the past version of "$next$" and refers to the previous time instant. Intuitively, the above MPLTL formula states that in the previous K time instants there have been at least $n+1$ occurrences of the event corresponding to $(e \wedge \phi)$; such a situation satisfies the constraint associated with the original formula defined in SOLOIST.

6. The mapping for the $V^{K,h}_{\bowtie n}$ modality is defined in terms of the C modality:

$$\rho(V^{K,h}_{\bowtie n}\phi) = \rho(C^{\lfloor \frac{K}{h} \rfloor \cdot h}_{\bowtie n \cdot \lfloor \frac{K}{h} \rfloor}\phi)$$

7. For the modality $M^{K,h}_{\bowtie n}$, we include only the two cases $M^{K,h}_{<n}$ and $M^{K,h}_{>n}$, as the others can be derived by properly combining instances of these two:

$$\rho(M^{K,h}_{<n}\phi) = \left(\bigwedge_{m=0}^{\lfloor \frac{K}{h} \rfloor - 1} Y^{m \cdot h}\left(\rho\left(C^h_{<n}\phi\right)\right) \right) \wedge \left(Y^{\lfloor \frac{K}{h} \rfloor \cdot h}\left(\rho\left(C^{(K \bmod h)}_{<n}\phi\right)\right) \right)$$

$$\rho(M^{K,h}_{>n}\phi) = \left(\bigvee_{m=0}^{\lfloor \frac{K}{h} \rfloor - 1} Y^{m \cdot h}\left(\rho\left(C^h_{>n}\phi\right)\right) \right) \vee \left(Y^{\lfloor \frac{K}{h} \rfloor \cdot h}\left(\rho\left(C^{(K \bmod h)}_{>n}\phi\right)\right) \right)$$

The formulae above decompose the computation of the maximum number of occurrences of the event $(e \wedge \phi)$ by suitably combining constraints on the number of occurrences of the event in each observation interval within the time window.

8. For the $D^K_{\bowtie n}$ modality, $\rho(D^K_{\bowtie n}(\phi, \psi))$ is defined[7] as follows:

$$\bigvee_{0 < h \leq \lfloor \frac{K}{2} \rfloor} \left(\bigvee_{\substack{0 \leq i_1 < j_1 < ... i_h < j_h < K \\ \text{and} \\ (\sum_{m=1}^{h} \frac{j_m - i_m}{h}) \bowtie n}} \left(\begin{array}{c} Y^{i_1}(e \wedge \phi) \wedge Y^{j_1}(e \wedge \psi) \wedge \\ \cdots \\ \wedge Y^{i_h}(e \wedge \phi) \wedge Y^{j_h}(e \wedge \psi) \wedge \\ \neg \left(\bigvee_{\substack{0 \leq s < t < K \\ s \notin \{i_1,...,i_h\} \\ t \notin \{j_1,...,j_h\}}} \left(Y^s(e \wedge \phi) \wedge Y^t(e \wedge \psi) \right) \right) \end{array} \right) \right)$$

The above formula considers all possible h occurrences (with h up to $\lfloor \frac{K}{2} \rfloor$, as indicated in the outer "or") of pairs of events corresponding to $(e \wedge \phi)$ and $(e \wedge \psi)$. The inner "or" considers a sequence of h pairs of time instants $(i_1, j_1), \ldots (i_h, j_h)$, constrained by the bound represented by $\bowtie n$. The top, right-hand part of the formula imposes that every pair of time instants actually corresponds to the

---

[7] For the sake of simplicity, we consider the case of only one pair of events (ϕ, ψ), but the formula can be generalized to the case of multiple pairs (ϕ_i, ψ_i).

occurrence of a pair of events; the bottom, right-hand part excludes the case that some pairs of events may occur at time instants which are not in the above sequence.

The complexity of a formula resulting from the translation may be exponential in the size of the constants occurring in the aggregate operators. Without aggregate operators, the translation is linear in the size of the original formula. The only relevant cases for aggregate operators are $C^K_{>n}$ and $D^K_{\bowtie n}$, since the other modalities can easily be defined in terms of these two. The mapping for $C^K_{>n}\phi$ considers all subsets of $n+1$ integers of the set $\{0,\dots,K-1\}$. Hence, it may require an MPLTL formula of size proportional to $(n+1)\binom{K}{n+1}$, which in the worst case, corresponding to $n+1 = \frac{K}{2}$, is $O(K \cdot 2^K)$. The mapping of $D^K_{\bowtie n}(\phi,\psi)$ essentially requires, in the worst case, to select all possible subsets of set $\{0,\dots,K-1\}$, i.e., 2^K subsets. Hence, again this may require an MPLTL formula of size $O(K \cdot 2^K)$. As remarked at the beginning of this section, the translation presented above has been designed to show the possibility of reducing SOLOIST to a linear temporal logic; nevertheless, future work will address efficiency in the verification of SOLOIST formulae.

6   Related Work

While performing the field study described in [8], we noticed that the three main formal languages used by researchers in the field of SBAs to specify and verify properties related to service interactions are LTL (Linear Temporal Logic), CTL (Computational Tree Logic), and Event Calculus [24]. While the first two are mainly used to describe untimed temporal relations between events, Event Calculus has been the basis to develop more expressive languages, such as EC-Assertion [27], which can express service guarantees terms such as those captured by patterns S1 and S2. However, it requires to introduce additional constructs in a formula, such as explicit variables to track response time or event counters, as well additional support formulae, like the ones used to maintain a list of variables which are used to compute an aggregate value.

In [8] we also noticed a recurring presence of extensions of temporal logics with support for first-order quantification, namely LTL-FO, CTL-FO [11], LTL-FO+ [17], and CTL-FO+ [18], which enrich the underlying logic to express *data-aware* properties, captured by pattern S7.

In the realm of SBAs there have also been several proposals of languages for specifying service level agreements, mainly targeting quality-of-service (QoS) attributes such as response time and throughput; among them, we mention WSLA [22] and a timeliness-related extension of WS-Agreement [28]. These languages usually do not have any formal or mathematical grounding, but in most cases they define an XML schema containing the definition of the main QoS attributes and their data types. One exception is SLAng, which—besides being defined on the top of standard modeling languages like EMOF and OCL, to guarantee precision and understandability—has been mapped to timed automata, to enable efficient run-time monitoring [34].

The fragment of SOLOIST corresponding to many-sorted metric first-order temporal logic is very similar to the work defined in [6], where a similar fragment is used to define system policies, which are then monitored; however, this fragment, without the other temporal operators introduced in SOLOIST, would have been inadeguate to express the service provisioning patterns.

In the field of (temporal) logics, there have been several proposals to express properties related or similar to the one captured by the service provisioning patterns identified in [8]. For example, references [26] and [25] propose, respectively, Counting CTL and Counting LTL, which extend the temporal modalities of the underlying (non-metric) logic with the ability to constrain the number of states satisfying certain sub-formulae along paths. In [7], a first-order policy specification language is introduced; the language, based on past time linear temporal logic with first-order quantifier, includes also a counting quantifier, used to express that a policy depends on the number of times another policy was satisfied in the past. Rabinovich [33] presents TLC, the metric temporal logic with counting modalities over continuous time, where a counting modality $C_k(X)$ states that X is true at least at k points in the unit interval ahead.

Aggregate operators have been studied in the context of mathematical logic, for database query languages [19] and logic programming [30]. More recently, they have also been considered in temporal logics, to express quantitative atomic assertions related to accumulative values of variables along a computation [9]. de Alfaro [1] introduces an operator to express bounds on the average time between events (conceptually similar to the D operator of SOLOIST) in the context of probabilistic temporal logic, to specify and verify performance and reliability properties of discrete-time probabilistic systems. Extensions of specification formalism with statistical operators have also been proposed in the context of run-time verification. In [13], LTL is extended with operators that evaluate aggregate statistics over an execution trace. Reference [14] presents the LARVA verification tool, based on *Dynamic Automata with Timers and Events*, which is able to evaluate statistical measures over dynamic intervals, like the ones identified with the C, V, M, D modalities of SOLOIST; however, the report does not provide enough details on the language used to specify the properties to monitor.

7   Conclusion and Future Work

Service-based applications demand rethinking the way software is designed, specified and verified. In this paper we focus on the specification aspect and, in particular, we propose a new language, called SOLOIST, that can be used to specify properties of service compositions interactions. The language has been designed from scratch, after capturing and reasoning on the most common property specification patterns used by practitioners in the field of SBAs. Based on a many-sorted first-order metric temporal logic, SOLOIST includes new temporal modalities that have been tailored to express properties that refer to aggregate operations for events occurring in a certain time window. We also show how SOLOIST can be translated into linear temporal logic, allowing for its use with established techniques and tools for both design-time and run-time verification.

Indeed, our next steps with SOLOIST will focus on its efficient verification based on the Zot toolkit [32], developed[8] within our group, by defining an efficient SMT-based encoding of the language. Although Zot has been used so far for design-time verification, we also want to experiment to embed it and its SOLOIST plug-in within a Web service monitoring architecture (such as Dynamo [15]), to enable support also for run-time verification.

Acknowledgments. This work has been partially supported by the European Community under the the the IDEAS-ERC grant agreement no. 227977-SMScom; by the Swiss NSF under the grant agreement no. 135051-CLAVOS; by the National Research Fund, Luxembourg (FNR/P10/03). The authors wish to thank Udi Boker, Srđan Krstić, and Franco Raimondi for their feedback on earlier drafts of this paper.

References

1. de Alfaro, L.: Temporal Logics for the Specification of Performance and Reliability. In: Reischuk, R., Morvan, M. (eds.) STACS 1997. LNCS, vol. 1200, pp. 165–176. Springer, Heidelberg (1997)
2. Andrews, T., et al.: Business Process Execution Language for Web Services, Version 1.1 (2003)
3. Baresi, L., Bianculli, D., Ghezzi, C., Guinea, S., Spoletini, P.: Validation of web service compositions. IET Softw. 1(6), 219–232 (2007)
4. Baresi, L., Di Nitto, E. (eds.): Test and Analysis of Web Services. Springer (2007)
5. Baresi, L., Di Nitto, E., Ghezzi, C.: Toward open-world software: Issue and challenges. IEEE Computer 39(10), 36–43 (2006)
6. Basin, D., Klaedtke, F., Müller, S.: Policy Monitoring in First-Order Temporal Logic. In: Touili, T., Cook, B., Jackson, P. (eds.) CAV 2010. LNCS, vol. 6174, pp. 1–18. Springer, Heidelberg (2010)
7. Bauer, A., Goré, R., Tiu, A.: A First-Order Policy Language for History-Based Transaction Monitoring. In: Leucker, M., Morgan, C. (eds.) ICTAC 2009. LNCS, vol. 5684, pp. 96–111. Springer, Heidelberg (2009)
8. Bianculli, D., Ghezzi, C., Pautasso, C., Senti, P.: Specification patterns from research to industry: a case study in service-based applications. In: Proc. of ICSE 2012, pp. 968–976. IEEE Computer Society (2012)
9. Boker, U., Chatterjee, K., Henzinger, T.A., Kupferman, O.: Temporal specifications with accumulative values. In: Proc. of LICS 2011, pp. 43–52. IEEE Computer Society (2011)
10. Canfora, G., Di Penta, M.: Service-Oriented Architectures Testing: A Survey. In: De Lucia, A., Ferrucci, F. (eds.) ISSSE 2006-2008. LNCS, vol. 5413, pp. 78–105. Springer, Heidelberg (2009)
11. Deutsch, A., Sui, L., Vianu, V.: Specification and verification of data-driven web applications. J. Comput. Syst. Sci. 73(3), 442–474 (2007)
12. Dwyer, M.B., Avrunin, G.S., Corbett, J.C.: Property specification patterns for finite-state verification. In: Proc. of FMSP 1998, pp. 7–15. ACM (1998)
13. Finkbeiner, B., Sankaranarayanan, S., Sipma, H.: Collecting statistics over runtime executions. Formal Methods in System Design 27, 253–274 (2005)

---

[8] http://code.google.com/p/zot/

14. Gauci, A., Pace, G.J., Colombo, C.: Statistics and runtime verification. Tech. rep., University of Malta (2010)
15. Ghezzi, C., Guinea, S.: Run-time monitoring in service-oriented architectures. In: Baresi, Di Nitto [4] pp. 237–264
16. Gruhn, V., Laue, R.: Patterns for timed property specifications. Electron. Notes Theor. Comput. Sci. 153(2), 117–133 (2006)
17. Hallé, S., Villemaire, R.: Runtime monitoring of message-based workflows with data. In: Proc. of EDOC 2008, pp. 63–72. IEEE Computer Society (2008)
18. Hallé, S., Villemaire, R., Cherkaoui, O.: Specifying and validating data-aware temporal web service properties. IEEE Trans. Softw. Eng. 35(5), 669–683 (2009)
19. Hella, L., Libkin, L., Nurmonen, J., Wong, L.: Logics with aggregate operators. J. ACM 48, 880–907 (2001)
20. Josuttis, N.: SOA in Practice: The Art of Distributed System Design. O'Reilly Media, Inc. (2007)
21. Kamp, H.W.: Tense Logic and the Theory of Linear Order. PhD thesis, University of California at Los Angeles, USA (1968)
22. Keller, A., Ludwig, H.: The WSLA framework: specifying and monitoring service level agreement for web services. J. Netw. Syst. Manage. 11(1) (2003)
23. Konrad, S., Cheng, B.H.C.: Real-time specification patterns. In: Proc. of ICSE 2005, pp. 372–381. ACM (2005)
24. Kowalski, R., Sergot, M.: A logic-based calculus of events. New Gen. Comput. 4, 67–95 (1986)
25. Laroussinie, F., Meyer, A., Petonnet, E.: Counting LTL. In: Proc. of TIME 2010, pp. 51–58. IEEE (2010)
26. Laroussinie, F., Meyer, A., Petonnet, E.: Counting CTL. In: Ong, L. (ed.) FOSSACS 2010. LNCS, vol. 6014, pp. 206–220. Springer, Heidelberg (2010)
27. Mahbub, K., Spanoudakis, G.: Monitoring WS-Agreements: An event calculus-based approach. In: Baresi, Di Nitto [4], pp. 265–306
28. Müller, C., Martín-Díaz, O., Ruiz-Cortés, A., Resinas, M., Fernández, P.: Improving Temporal-Awareness of WS-Agreement. In: Krämer, B.J., Lin, K.-J., Narasimhan, P. (eds.) ICSOC 2007. LNCS, vol. 4749, pp. 193–206. Springer, Heidelberg (2007)
29. Papazoglou, M.P.: The Challenges of Service Evolution. In: Bellahsène, Z., Léonard, M. (eds.) CAiSE 2008. LNCS, vol. 5074, pp. 1–15. Springer, Heidelberg (2008)
30. Pelov, N., Denecker, M., Bruynooghe, M.: Well-founded and stable semantics of logic programs with aggregates. Theory and Practice of Logic Programming 7(3), 301–353 (2007)
31. Pradella, M., Morzenti, A., San Pietro, P.: The symmetry of the past and of the future: bi-infinite time in the verification of temporal properties. In: Proc. of ESEC-FSE 2007, pp. 312–320. ACM (2007)
32. Pradella, M., Morzenti, A., San Pietro, P.: A Metric Encoding for Bounded Model Checking. In: Cavalcanti, A., Dams, D.R. (eds.) FM 2009. LNCS, vol. 5850, pp. 741–756. Springer, Heidelberg (2009)
33. Rabinovich, A.: Complexity of Metric Temporal Logics with Counting and the Pnueli Modalities. In: Cassez, F., Jard, C. (eds.) FORMATS 2008. LNCS, vol. 5215, pp. 93–108. Springer, Heidelberg (2008)
34. Raimondi, F., Skene, J., Emmerich, W.: Efficient online monitoring of web-service slas. In: Proc. of SIGSOFT 2008/FSE-16, pp. 170–180. ACM, New York (2008)
35. Salaün, G.: Analysis and verification of service interaction protocols - a brief survey. In: Proc. of TAV-WEB 2010. EPTCS, vol. 35, pp. 75–86 (2010)

A Categorical Approach to Structuring and Promoting Z Specifications

Pablo F. Castro[1,3], Nazareno Aguirre[1,3],
Carlos Gustavo López Pombo[2,3], and Tom Maibaum[4]

[1] Departamento de Computación, FCEFQyN, Universidad Nacional de Río Cuarto,
Río Cuarto, Córdoba, Argentina
{pcastro,naguirre}@dc.exa.unrc.edu.ar
[2] Departamento de Computación, FCEyN, Universidad de Buenos Aires,
Buenos Aires, Argentina
clpombo@dc.uba.ar
[3] Consejo Nacional de Investigaciones Científicas y Técnicas (CONICET), Argentina
[4] Department of Computing & Software, McMaster University, Hamilton (ON),
Canada
tom@maibaum.org

Abstract. In this paper, we study a formalisation of specification structuring mechanisms used in Z. These mechanisms are traditionally understood as syntactic transformations. In contrast, we present a characterisation of Z structuring mechanisms which takes into account the semantic counterpart of their typical syntactic descriptions, based on category theory. Our formal foundation for Z employs well established abstract notions of logical systems. This setting has a degree of abstraction that enables us to understand what is the precise semantic relationship between schemas obtained from a schema operator and the schemas it is applied to, in particular with respect to property preservation.

Our formalisation is a powerful setting for capturing structuring mechanisms, even enabling us to formalise *promotion*. Also, its abstract nature provides the rigour and flexibility needed to characterise extensions of Z and related languages, in particular the heterogeneous ones.

1 Introduction

The intrinsic preciseness of formal specification languages usually lead to very detailed, large descriptions of software systems. Therefore, appropriate mechanisms for structuring specifications are essential in contributing to the scalability of formal specification, and the usefulness of a formal method. This has been acknowledged by formal method developers, and many formal notations, e.g. B, Z and related languages, put a strong emphasis in structuring [1,25]. In the case of Z, there exist several mechanisms for structuring specifications, called *schema operations*, since they operate on schemas, the basic modularisation units of a Z specification. Traditionally, structuring mechanisms in Z are captured *syntactically*, i.e., their semantics are understood as syntactic transformations over the

C.S. Păsăreanu and G. Salaün (Eds.): FACS 2012, LNCS 7684, pp. 73–91, 2013.
© Springer-Verlag Berlin Heidelberg 2013

composed specifications [25]. This approach, although sound, makes it difficult to understand the precise relationship between the composite specifications and their components. Indeed, understanding how the properties of a specification are involved in properties of another specification including it, is an issue that generally needs to be analysed in an ad-hoc way in every concrete structuring situation, due to the syntactic semantics of the structuring mechanisms employed. This is particularly the case with *promotion*, a Z specification structuring technique. Promotion is typically used in order to compose specifications, and in particular to incorporate multiple instances of a component into a global system state. Since the use of promotion usually involves mapping a "local state" into a "global state" where multiple local states are subsumed, understanding the relationship between the local and global states is particularly difficult.

In this work, we study a formalisation of Z structuring mechanisms, including *promotion*, which in contrast to the syntactic approach to structuring mechanisms semantics, provides strong ties to the semantic counterpart of these mechanisms' syntactic description. This formalisation is based on category theory, and consists of a mathematical foundation for Z and its usual schema operators, making use of institutions and institution representations. This setting has a degree of abstraction that enables us to understand what is the precise semantic relationship between schemas obtained from a schema operator and the schemas it is applied to (in the case of promotion, between basic and promoted schemas), in particular with respect to property preservation. Our formalisation is targeted to Z. A main reason for this is that Z is a mature and widely known formal notation, used in many industrial projects, and supported by analysis tools. Moreover, Z has been used as the basis for other formalisms, such as B, Z++ and Object-Z. In these languages, structuring mechanisms based on or inspired by promotion are also present, and also syntactically captured (in particular, the mechanisms for characterising the notion of class in the object oriented extensions of Z). By basing our formalisation on Z, we make our results also relevant to these other languages.

Our formal foundation for structuring in Z has practical advantages. It leads to explicit semantic relationships between component schemas and the composite schemas they are part of, which can be exploited to *promote* reasoning. Furthermore, if a schema is restricted to a particular "simpler" logic (e.g., a decidable fragment of the Z notation), then one can reason in this simpler setting (perhaps via some automated tool) and then promote the obtained properties to the larger, composite specification in which the schema is involved, and where more expressive constructs may be used. Also, our foundations for promotion require dealing with schemas as types; our semantics of this facility, interpreted as a manipulation of the logical theories that schemas represent, makes it non dependent on higher order logic (as opposed to schema types as treated in [17]), constituting a potential benefit for automated reasoning. Finally, the abstract nature of our characterisation, at a level of abstraction that allows for a view of logical systems as building blocks, provides the rigour and flexibility needed to characterise not only Z but also its related languages and extensions, in particular the heterogeneous ones. It then provides the formal foundations for correctly composing Z with other formalisms, and a setting where one is able to formallly reason about the resulting heterogeneous specifications.

2 A Brief Overview of Z

Z is a formal notation based on mathematical logic and set theory. It is often regarded as being *model based*, since specifications in the language describe systems behaviour via *models*, typically involving data domains and operations on these domains [25]. Such models are expressed in terms of well defined types, including a rich set of built-in types such as the typical numerical domains, sets, sequences, tuples, relations and functions, etc. Z specifications are structured around the notion of *schema* [25]. Essentially, a schema defines a set of typed variables, whose values might be constrained. A schema has a *declaration* section, and a *constraint* (or predicate) section. This extremely simple notion is powerful and convenient for defining data domains and operations on these, as formal models of systems. As a first example, suppose that we need to specify a game similar to Risk, consisting of players whose goal is to conquer territories in a map. For simplicity, let us suppose that territories are labelled by natural numbers, identifying each territory. We might start by defining players, indicating the territories they own. In Z, this is achieved by the following schema:

$$
\begin{array}{|l}
\hline
\_Player _____ \\
owns : \mathbb{P}\,\mathbb{N} \\
\hline
\end{array}
$$

This is a very simple schema, that has an empty predicate part (no special constraints on the variables). Basic operations for a player are settling in a territory, and leaving an occupied territory. In Z, operations are also captured by schemas; schemas characterising the settle and leave operations are the following:

$$
\begin{array}{|l}
\hline
\_Settle _____ \\
\Delta Player \\
t : \mathbb{N} \\
\hline
t \notin owns \\
owns' = owns \cup \{t\} \\
\hline
\end{array}
\qquad
\begin{array}{|l}
\hline
\_Leave _____ \\
\Delta Player \\
t : \mathbb{N} \\
\hline
t \in owns \\
owns' = owns \setminus \{t\} \\
\hline
\end{array}
$$

In these schemas, $\Delta Player$ indicates that two copies of the schema *Player* are incorporated into *Settle* and *Leave*, one exact copy of *Player* and the other with its variables renamed by priming. This is done in order to capture the effect of settling (resp. leaving) as a relation between "pre" states of the player (the unprimed variables) and the "post" states of the player, resulting from settling on (resp. leaving from) a territory. Additional variables, in this case representing parameters of the operations, are incorporated and constrained in the predicate part of the schemas. When defining a schema in terms of another one, constraints from the used schema are made part of the constraints of the using schema; for instance, constraints from *Player* and *Player'* (coming from $\Delta Player$) are part of the *Settle* schema (although in this case no actual constraints are incorporated, because the used schemas had no constraints). According to the denotational semantics of Z, a model for a schema is an assignment, that provides values in the corresponding types for the variables in the schema, and satisfies the predicate part of the schema [21]. That is, a model provides actual values for the variables in a schema. Notice for instance that, for the case of *Player*, all possible models of the schema capture the "state space" for the player.

Z also features schema structuring operations, that is, operations that enable one to define schemas based on other existing schemas. A rather simple one is *schema composition*. Suppose that we would like to define an operation to capture the situation in which a player exchanges one territory for another one, i.e., it leaves a territory and settles in another one. Such an operation can be defined using schemas *Leave* and *Settle*, via a simple composition:

$$Exchange \mathrel{\widehat=} Leave[t_1/t] \mathbin{\text{\tiny ^{9}}} Settle[t_2/t]$$

This composition (slightly complicated with the renamings necessary for the composition to distinguish the t variables in the two schemas) captures the state change produced by applying the second operation to the state resulting of the application of the first operation.

Promotion is another structuring mechanism of Z. It enables one to *promote* definitions given in terms of "local states", to definitions of a "global state", often composed of various instances of the local state [25]. As an example, suppose that we define the game state, using our previously defined *Player* schema:

$Game$ ———————————————————
$ps : \mathbb{P}\, Player$
$ts : \mathbb{P}\,\mathbb{N}$
———
$ts \neq \emptyset$
$\forall\, p : ps \bullet p.owns \subseteq ts$
$\forall\, p_1, p_2 : ps \bullet p_1 \neq p_2 \Rightarrow p_1.owns \cap p_2.owns = \emptyset$

This schema explicitly indicates who are the players of the game (ps), and the territories composing the map (ts); it also constrains the valid states of the game to nonempty sets of territories, and prevents players from sharing the occupation of a territory. We have already defined game related operations *Settle* and *Leave*, but we have done so for *Player*. We would like to be able to *promote* these "local" operations to the "global" state characterised by *Game*, instead of having to redevelop them as operations on *Game*. In order to do so, one needs to define a *promotion schema*, i.e., a schema relating the local and global states:

$PromotePlayer$ ———————————————————
$\Delta Game$
$\Delta Player$
$p : Player$
———
$p = \theta Player \wedge p \in ps$
$ts = ts'$
$ps' = ps \setminus \{p\} \cup \{\theta Player'\}$

Notice that this schema indicates how a state change of a single player is embedded into a state change for the global state of the game. Now, one can promote the *Settle* operation to the system level, as follows:

$$GameSettle \mathrel{\hat{=}} \exists \, \Delta Player \bullet Settle \wedge PromotePlayer$$

The existential quantification in this definition has the purpose of hiding the "local state", which by the restrictions in the *PromotePlayer* schema is already embedded into the state of the game. This makes *GameSettle* an operation exclusively on the state of the game.

3   A Categorical View of Z

Let us recall some basic definitions of category theory. A category is a mathematical structure composed of two collections: the collection of objects: $a, b, c, \ldots$ and the collection of arrows (or morphisms): $f, g, h, \ldots$ between them. An arrow has a domain and a codomain, and we write $f : a \to b$ to indicate that a (resp. b) is the domain (resp. codomain) of f. We have two basic operations involving arrows: the *identity*, that given an object a produces an arrow $id_a : a \to a$, and the *composition*, which given arrows $f : a \to b$ and $g : b \to c$, returns an arrow $f \, ; \, g : a \to c$. Identity arrows satisfy: $f \, ; \, id_b = f$ and $id_a \, ; \, f = f$, for every $f : a \to b$. The composition of arrows is associative. A *functor* is essentially a homomorphism between categories. The most natural example of a category is **Set**, made up of the collection of sets and the collection of functions between sets. We refer the interested reader to [2], for an introduction to category theory. We will assume throughout the paper that the reader has some basic knowledge of category theory.

As we already discussed, a schema defines a set of typed variables, and provides constraints on these variables. Formally, a schema corresponds to a tuple $\langle N, T, \Sigma, \Phi \rangle$ composed of a name N, a set of given types T, a signature Σ (the set of typed variables declared in the schema) and a set Φ of formulas, constraining these variables [22]. For the sake of simplicity, we omit the name and the set T of types when no confusion is possible. The formulas of the predicate part Φ of a schema are higher-order formulas (since Z includes recursive datatypes, lambda expressions, quantification over relations and other elements that go beyond first-order logic's expressiveness) defined over the variables in the declaration part of the schema.

In order to study Z structuring, we need to look at the way schemas relate to each other. A *morphism* between two schema signatures $\tau : \Sigma \to \Sigma'$ is a mapping between symbols that preserves types. Examples of signature morphisms are symbol substitutions (renaming variables in a signature), and embeddings of a signature into another one. Signatures and signature morphisms constitute a category.

Theorem 1. *The structure* **Zign** $= \langle S, M \rangle$, *where S is the set of Z signatures and M is the set of signature morphisms, is a category.*

Signature morphisms can be straightforwardly extended to schema morphisms:

Definition 1. *A schema morphism* $\tau : \langle \Sigma, \Phi \rangle \to \langle \Sigma', \Phi' \rangle$ *is a signature morphism* $\sigma : \Sigma \to \Sigma'$ *that satisfies the following condition:*

$$\forall \phi \in \Phi \bullet \Phi' \vdash \sigma^*(\phi)$$

where σ^* *is the inductive extension of* σ *to formulas, obtained by preserving logical symbols, and* $\Phi \vdash \phi$ *expresses that* ϕ *can be proven from* Φ *using the deductive machinery of Z.*

Essentially, a schema morphism is a mapping between logical theories [11]. Using schemas and schema morphisms, a category can be defined:

Theorem 2. *The structure* **Zchem** $= \langle Sch, Tr \rangle$*, where Sch is the set of Z schemas and Tr is the set of schema morphisms, is a category.*

The category **Zchem** enables us to capture the way in which Z schemas relate to each other, and in particular how these are connected in the definition of a structured specification.

In order to clarify the above view of signatures and schemas as objects in a category, consider the diagram in Figure 1. This diagram involves two simple schemas, one of them being our previous *Game* schema, and the other being a simple schema defining a nonempty set of natural numbers. The schema morphism in this diagram shows that the simpler schema is embedded, after translation, into the schema *Game*. Notice that, for this morphism to be correct, one must be able to prove that the translation of $\#ns > 0$ (i.e., $\#ts > 0$) is a consequence of the constraints in the *Game* schema, which is trivial. After this simple example, the reader familiar with Z may notice that schema morphisms subsume the notion of schema strengthening. Models complement the picture of schemas and schema morphisms. An interpretation for a given signature is a valuation of its variables (a function which maps variables to values). For instance, an interpretation for the signature of *Numbers* is simply a nonempty set of natural numbers. Now, given a signature, a model of it is a nonempty collection of interpretations for its variables. In some sense, this enables a *loose* semantics for schemas: each schema denotes a collection of interpretations, in contrast to the more usual *tight* semantics, where a schema denotes only one interpretation. This semantics will be in particular useful for formalising promotion (see section 4). An example of a model for *Numbers* is shown below it in Fig. 1, using a notation borrowed from [25]. This model maps *ns* to the sets $\{0, 1\}$ and $\{2, 3\}$. Given a schema morphism $\tau : S_1 \to S_2$, this morphism induces a mapping $()_{|\tau} : Mod(\Sigma') \to Mod(\Sigma)$ between models of S_2 and models of S_1 [15]. This mapping builds *reducts* [10], i.e., given a model of the "larger" schema, it removes from the model all the parts that are unnecessary to interpret symbols originating in S_1, obtaining a model of the smaller schema. An example of a reduct, obtained from a model of the schema *Game*, is also shown in Figure 1. Given an interpretation I, we say $I \vDash \phi$ if I satisfies the property ϕ; and given a model M and a collection of formulas Φ, we say $M \vDash \Phi$, if for every $I \in M$

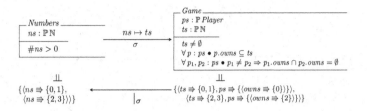

Fig. 1. An example involving schemas, schema models, a schema morphism and the corresponding model reduct

and $\phi \in \Phi$, we have $I \vDash \phi$. Models of schemas are those satisfying the predicate part of the schema. As usual, we will use the notation $M \vDash \Sigma$ (resp. $M \vDash S$) to express that M is a model of a signature Σ (resp. of a schema S). It is worth remarking the following property, which relates signature morphisms with models and formulas:

$$M_{|\sigma} \vDash \phi \Leftrightarrow M \vDash \sigma^*(\phi),$$

where $\sigma : \Sigma_1 \to \Sigma_2$ is a signature morphism, M is a model of Σ_2 and $M_{|\sigma}$ is the reduct of M to the syntax of Σ_1. This property expresses that syntactic changes of formulas via signature morphisms do not affect the notion of truth. This is a main characteristic of an *Institution* [15]. Indeed, regarding Z, we have the following theorem.

Theorem 3. *The structure* **Z** *composed of: (i) the category* **Zign**, *(ii) the functor sen :* **Zign** $\to$ **Sen**, *that sends each signature to its set of formulas, (iii) the functor Mod :* **Zign**^{op} $\to$ **Cat**, *that sends each signature to the category of its models[1], and (iv) the collection of relations* $\vDash_\Sigma$ *(satisfaction relations relating models of a signature to formulas of the signature), is an* Institution.

Let us continue with our categorical characterisation of Z concepts. The main mechanism for putting two Z schemas together is *schema conjunction*. In a categorical setting, the corresponding way of combining two schemas is captured by a categorical operation called *pushout*. The diagram in Figure 2 depicts what a pushout is, and how it captures schema conjunction. In this diagram, W is the common part of S and T, i and j are identity arrows, and $S \wedge T$ is obtained by putting S and T together, keeping only once the common part (exactly what schema conjunction does [25]). The pushout is *minimal*, in the sense that for any other schema U such that we have arrows from S, T to it, we can obtain a unique arrow from $S \wedge T$ to U such that the diagram shown in Figure 2 commutes.

Another useful operation over schemas is symbol renaming, in particular renaming by *priming*. Categorically, this schema operation corresponds to an *endofunctor* $(-)'$: **Zchem** $\to$ **Zchem**, the straightforward extension to schemas of the endofunctor $(-)'$: **Zign** $\to$ **Zign** which maps every symbol in a signature to its primed version.

---

[1] **Zign**^{op} denotes the dual category of **Zign**, obtained by reversing arrows. This is needed since reducts and morphisms go in different directions.

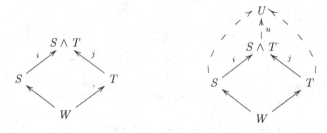

Fig. 2. Schema conjunction as a pushout

As we explained in the previous section, in a Z specification one usually defines operations via particular schemas, relating other schemas describing domains. In our categorical view of Z, operations correspond to a particular class of diagrams, of the form shown in Figure 3 (a), where A and B are the related "domain" schemas, and C is the operation schema. Such a diagram is indeed a categorical diagram in the category **Zchem**, called a *cospan*. In particular, an operation for a system S (captured as a schema) is typically specified as a schema over ΔS, i.e., over the conjunction of S and S', where S' represents the "post" state of S, i.e., the state after the operation has been executed. Such an operation is also a cospan, and has the form shown in Figure 3 (b).

Let us more precisely formalise the concept of operations.

Definition 2. *An operation is a cospan in* **Zchem** *of the following form:*

$$S \to Op \leftarrow S'$$

We use the notation $Op : S \Rightarrow S'$ to express the above diagram.

Operations modifying the state S of a system (captured as a schema) are usually defined over ΔS. ΔS can also be captured categorically:

Definition 3. *Given a schema S, we denote by ΔS the coproduct of S and S', where S' is the result of applying the priming functor to schema S.*

The coproduct is a pushout of two schemas S_1 and S_2 with no common part (i.e., in the figure above we set $W = \langle \emptyset, \emptyset \rangle$); that is, for any other schema combining S_1 and S_2 (meaning that we have schema morphisms from S_1 and S_2 to the combined schema), there exists a unique schema morphism u from the coproduct to this combined schema that makes the diagram involving these schemas and the

Fig. 3. Cospans, and Z operations as cospans

Fig. 4. Categorical definition of ΔS as a coproduct

schema morphisms corresponding to the combinations commute. This situation is described in Figure 4, for the case of ΔS, the coproduct of S and S'.

We have used an arrow notation for cospans, in our characterisation of Z operations. In fact, cospans can be thought of as arrows (or morphisms), which are composed by applying pushouts [4]. This is the way schema composition is categorically captured.

Definition 4. *Given two operations* $Op_1 : S \Rightarrow S'$ *and* $Op_2 : S \Rightarrow S'$ *we define the operation* $Op_1 \,\S\, Op_2$ *as follows:*

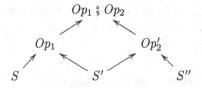

where the tip of the diagram is obtained by means of pushouts, and Op'_2 *is built up by applying the functor* $(-)'$ *to* Op_2.

Another useful construction in Z is the ΞS operation. This operator on schemas denotes a *skip* operation. That is, it is a special case of ΔS, in which S and S' are identical. This schema operator can also be defined (up to isomorphism) in a categorical way.

Definition 5. $\Xi S : S \Rightarrow S'$ *is a schema that satisfies:* $\Xi S \,\S\, Op \cong Op \,\S\, \Xi S \cong Op$, *for every operation* Op, *where* $S \cong S'$ *expresses that there is an isomorphism between the corresponding schemas.*

Given schemas S and S', we have a category $OP(S, S')$ where the objects are the operations between S and S' and the morphisms are the schema morphisms between the corresponding cospans. This construction is called a *bicategory* [4]. An important point is that we can think of our category of schemas as having two different kinds of arrows, one representing schema morphisms (schema embeddings after translation), and another one capturing Z operations (as cospans), with $\S$ working as the composition for the latter.

Definition 6. *Zpec is the* bicategory of Z specifications, *defined as the structure composed of:*

- *The set of schemas as its set of objects.*

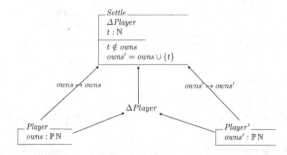

Fig. 5. A Z specification as a categorical diagram in **Zpec**

- *For each pair of schemas S, S', the category $OP(S, S')$ of cospans between S and S' (called 1-cells), and morphisms between cospans (called 2-cells).*
- *The composition between 2-cells is defined as usual by using the composition (i.e., pushouts) of cospans (denoted by $\fatsemi$).*

Summarising, a Z specification is a collection of schemas $S_0, \ldots, S_n$ together with a set of cospans $Op_i : S_i \Rightarrow S'_i$, all "living" in the bicategory of Z specifications. An example illustrating schemas and operations, and their relationships, is shown in Figure 5, as a diagram in **Zpec**.

4   Schemas as Types and Promotion

Let us now concentrate on analysing *promotion*. A key feature of Z, that facilitates promotion, is the use of schemas as types. In order to do this, we need to spice up our categorical framework with some additional machinery. Basically, we introduce the concept of schema manager, which conveys the idea of schema instances. Essentially, a manager of a component C is a component that intuitively provides the behaviour of various instances of C, and usually enables the manipulation of these instances. We will deal with the possibility of interpreting schemas as types in a way that differs from the established mechanism to do so, presented in [25]. Our approach consists of building a manager specification. Consider the schemas in Figure 6; the one on the left represents an arbitrary schema, involving $v_0 : T_0, \ldots, v_n : T_n$ as its typed variables. The schema on the right represents the *manager* for the previous schema, where ϕ^P is obtained from ϕ by adding the parameter s of type S to each variable. For the schema on the right, S does not represent the schema on the left; instead, it is simply a fresh *given type*, although for simplicity we maintain for this given type the same name as for the schema it represents.

An example of the use of managers is shown is Figure 10. In this figure, $Numbers^P$, the manager of $Numbers$, is used to provide semantics to the use of schema $Numbers$ as a type (to be explained later on).

We can define a similar transformation over operations. Consider the schemas in Figure 7; the schema on the left is the definition of an operation, where

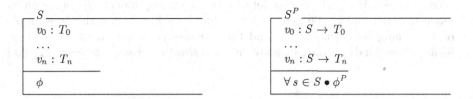

Fig. 6. A schema and its manager construction

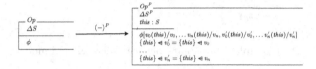

Fig. 7. Operation promotion using managers

$v_0, \ldots, v_n, v_0', \ldots, v_n'$ are the variables of S and S', respectively. We introduce the schema on the right; that is, we add a parameter, in this case named *this*, representing the instance to which the operation is applied. This situation is graphically depicted as a categorical diagram in Figure 8. Therein, the dashed arrows denote the application of the transformation described above. The translation $(-)^P : \textbf{Zpec} \to \textbf{Zpec}$ is a functor, which maps schemas to promoted schemas, and operations to promoted operations. We can define it in three parts:

- A functor $(-)^P : \textbf{Zign} \to \textbf{Zign}$, which translates signatures in the way described above.
- A functor $(-)^P : OP(S, S') \to OP(S^P, (S^P)')$, that translates operations to promoted operations. (For the sake of simplicity we use $(-)^P$ for naming these two functors.)
- The canonical extension of $(-)^P$ to formulas, as explained above.

The following theorem can be proven by resorting to the definition of $(-)^P$.

Theorem 4. $(-)^P : \textbf{Zpec} \to \textbf{Zpec}$ *is a lax functor.*

Lax functors are morphisms between bicategories; this means that promotion is coherent with respect to identities and composition of operations. Moreover,

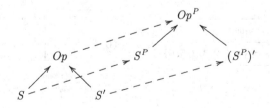

Fig. 8. Categorical diagram depicting operation promotion

given a model M of Σ^P we can define a corresponding model M_D (a degraded model), which forgets the new sort introduced. In Figure 9, a simple example of a mapping between schemas and their models is shown, to illustrate these ideas. These kinds of mappings are called *institution representations* [23], and

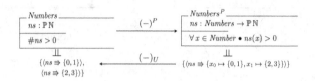

Fig. 9. Example of mappings between schemas and models

are mappings between logical systems. Intuitively, a collection of schemas and the relations between them conform a logical system. An institution representation allows us to move inside the same system but adding certain useful features, while keeping the basic properties of these schemas.

The operation of using a schema as a type can be understood as a kind of schema inclusion. Consider for instance the schema given in Figure 10 (a); it defines the end state of a game where the player needs to conquer territories 0 to 6. Notice that the actual semantics of this schema can be defined using the schema manager $Numbers^P$ introduced above, simply by including $Numbers^P$ in the schema. This has a self evident categorical interpretation, and the existence of an arrow between $Numbers$ and $EndGame$ relates them both syntactically and semantically. This resulting diagram is shown in Figure 10 (b), where $result.ns$ is just syntactic sugar for $ns(result)$.

This simple approach based on managers allows us to deal with schemas as types. We just dealt with "single instances", but the approach is also suitable for dealing with indexed instances of a schema, as is usual when using promotion. For instance, consider a game where we have various players, each player with its own set of territories. A schema illustrating this situation, with a promoted operation and showing the role of managers, is shown in Figure 11.

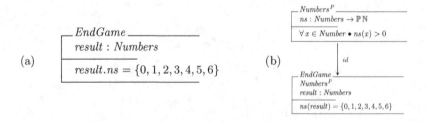

Fig. 10. Using managers as types

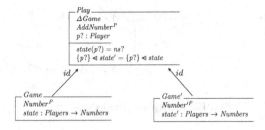

Fig. 11. Using managers for promoting an operation

4.1 Promotion as an Institution Representation

Institution representations were introduced informally above, where we argued about their need for capturing promotion. As institutions are an abstract characterisation of logical systems, institution representations capture the notion of embedding of a logical system into another one [23]. The logical machinery of Z used for describing states and operations constitutes an institution, and the operation of promoting schemas corresponds to an institution representation from this institution to itself. The key elements involved in the promotion process are:

- The definition of a mapping (functor) $(-)^P$: **Zign** $\to$ **Zign**, mapping a signature to its promoted signature.
- The definition of a mapping (natural transformation) $(-)_D$: $Mod\,; (-)^P \to Mod$, mapping models of promoted signatures to models of the original signature.
- The definition of a mapping (natural transformation) $(-)^P$: **Sen** $\to$ **Sen**; $(-)^P$ mapping formulas of the original signature to formulas of the promoted signature.

These mappings satisfy the property $M \vDash \phi^P \Leftrightarrow M_D \vDash \phi$. That is, a model of a promoted signature satisfies a promoted property if and only if the degraded model satisfies the original property. A graphical representation of this situation is shown in Figure 12. To clarify this diagram, suppose that we have a translation from one schema signature to another schema signature (named σ). Notice that reducts move in the opposite direction of translations (this explains the $(-)^{op}$ in the definition of institutions). Then, if we take a reduct of a promoted schema, and so we take the degraded model (the right path of the diagram), we obtain the same model as if we take the degraded model first and then take the reduct (the left path in the diagram). This ensures the coherence between the operations of strengthening and promotion in Z, which is guaranteed by the following theorem.

Theorem 5. $(-)^P$ and $(-)_D$ are institution representations.

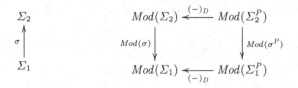

$$\Sigma_2 \qquad\qquad Mod(\Sigma_2) \xleftarrow{(-)_D} Mod(\Sigma_2^P)$$

Fig. 12. Institution representations

5   Heterogeneous Z Specifications and Structuring

Following the recent trend in Software Engineering that favours a "multiple
views" approach to specification and design, the Z notation has been extended
in various ways, in combination with other notations. Some of these extensions
are Z-CSP [14] (Z plus the process algebra CSP), and Z plus statecharts [24].
These *heterogeneous* specifications pose new challenges, e.g., for defining appropriate formal semantics for the composite languages, and for providing effective
mechanisms to reason about their specifications.

A consequence of the abstract nature of our formalisation of Z, and its structuring mechanisms, is that we can deal with these extensions in a systematic way.
Basically, individual formalisms for specifying software systems can be viewed
as institutions; indeed, first-order logics [15], temporal logics [15], modal logics
[15], Unity-like languages [13] and process algebras [19], all constitute institutions. Our formalisation of Z in an institutional setting, and the wide toolset
available from the theory of Institutions, enables us to flexibly combine Z with
other formalisms, obtaining extensions of Z with appropriate, well structured
semantics[2]. In order to illustrate this nice characteristic of our formalisation, we
briefly describe in this section the combination of Z with CSP (structured CSP, as
introduced in [19]). The obtained combination is, in essence, similar to the framework Z-CSP, with a well defined structured semantics, that makes the semantic
relationships between different (heterogeneous) components of a specification
explicit. We make use of the **CSP** (structured CSP) institution. The interested
reader can find the details of this formalism in [19]. Signatures in this institution
are pairs $\langle A, P \rangle$, where A is an alphabet (used for the communication of processes), and P is a collection of process names. Elements of both A and P have
an associated list of typed parameters. A morphism $\langle f, g \rangle : \langle A, P \rangle \to \langle A', P' \rangle$
between two **CSP** signatures consists of an injective function $f : A \to A'$, map-
ping members of A to members of A' preserving parameters and their types[3],
and a function $g : P \to P'$, mapping process names to process names, preserving parameters and their types. The category of **CSP** signatures is called
CSPSig [19]. A **CSP** theory is a tuple $\langle \Sigma, \pi \rangle$, where Σ is a **CSP** signature,
and π is a set of processes in the CSP notation. A model of a theory is given
by a set of traces corresponding to the processes of the theory. For the sake of

---

[2] The combination of institutions is well studied; see for instance [18].

[3] The use of injective mappings introduces some subtle technical problems when combining specifications. A way of avoiding these problems is described in [19].

$$\begin{array}{ll} \{\langle\rangle, \langle coin\rangle, & A = \{coin, choc\} \\ \langle coin, choc\rangle, & \\ \langle coin, choc, coin\rangle & \vDash P = \{VM\} \\ \ldots\} & \pi = \{VM = coin \rightarrow choc \rightarrow VM\} \end{array}$$

Fig. 13. A theory in Structured CSP, and a model of it

simplicity, we employ a finite trace semantics (as introduced in [19]), although also the failure-divergence semantics is supported in this institution. We have a morphism between models $M_1 \rightarrow M_2$ iff $M_2 \sqsubseteq M_1$ (i.e., M_2 is a refinement of M_1). A simple example of a vending machine is described as a **CSP** theory in Fig. 13. Neither communication letters nor processes have parameters in this example. A model of the theory accompanies the example as well.

A new institution **CZP** can be defined using the institutions **CSP** and **Z**. Essentially, we want specifications to have a data part, given in Z with its corresponding operations, and a process part, with each atomic process being associated with an operation as described in the Z part of the specification.

The category **SignCZP** of **CZP** signatures is composed of: *(i)* tuples $\Sigma = \langle \Sigma_{CSP}, \Sigma_Z \rangle$ as signatures, where Σ_{CSP} and Σ_Z are CSP and Z signatures, respectively; *(ii)* a morphism $\sigma : \Sigma \rightarrow \Sigma'$ is a tuple of morphisms $\langle f : \Sigma_{CSP} \rightarrow \Sigma'_{CSP}, g : \Sigma_Z \rightarrow \Sigma'_Z \rangle$. The functor sen_{CZP} is defined as follows:

$$sen_{CZP}(\langle \Sigma_{CSP}, \Sigma_Z \rangle) = \langle sen_{CSP}(\Sigma_{CSP}), sen_Z(\Sigma_Z) \rangle.$$

The functor Mod_{CZP} is defined as follows: *(i)* Given $\Sigma = \langle \Sigma_{CSP}, \Sigma_Z \rangle$, we define:

$$Mod(\Sigma) = \{\langle \langle a_1, \ldots, a_n \rangle, s \rangle \mid \exists M \in Mod(\Sigma_{CSP}) : \langle a_1, \ldots, a_n \rangle \in M \wedge s \in Mod(\Sigma_{Op})\},$$

where Σ_{Op} is the signature of the operation $event(a_1)\;\; \cdots \;\; event(a_n)$. That is, models are execution traces, together with models of the corresponding operation. *(ii)* Given a morphism $\sigma : \langle A, N \rangle \rightarrow \langle A', N' \rangle$, the morphism $Mod(\sigma)$ is defined pointwise, using reducts of traces as defined in [19], and reducts of schema valuations as defined in Section 3.

The relation $\vDash_{CZP}$ is also defined resorting to $\vDash_{CSP}$ and $\vDash_Z$ as follows:

$$M \vDash \langle \pi, \phi \rangle \text{ iff } \pi_1(M) \vDash \pi \text{ and for every } s \in \pi_2(M) \text{ we have } s \vDash \varphi.$$

A theory in **CZP** is a tuple $\langle \Sigma_{CSP}, \Sigma_Z, S, Ops, events, \pi \rangle$, where *(i)* $\Sigma_{CSP} = \langle A, N \rangle$ is a signature in **CSP**, *(ii)* Σ_Z is a signature in **Z**, *(iii)* S is a schema $\langle S, \Phi \rangle$, *(iv)* $Ops = \{op_0 : S \Rightarrow S', \ldots, op_n : S \Rightarrow S'\}$ is a collection of operations over the state S, *(v)* $event : A \rightarrow Ops$ is a function mapping events to operations, and *(vi)* π is a set of CSP processes. Morphisms between **CZP** theories are straightforwardly defined pointwise.

The relation $\vDash$ is extended to theories: $M \vDash \langle \Sigma_{CSP}, \Sigma_Z, S, Ops, event, \pi \rangle$ iff for every $\langle \langle a_1, \ldots, a_n \rangle, \langle s_i, \ldots, s_n \rangle \rangle \in M$ we have that $\pi_1(M) \vDash \pi$, and $\pi_2(M) \vDash event(a_1)\;\; \cdots \;\; event(a_n)$. Figure 15 shows an example of a **CZP** theory.

Promotion can be easily extended to this new institution. We define functor $(-)^P : \textbf{CZPSign} \rightarrow \textbf{CZPSign}$, mapping signatures to signatures, as follows.

$(skip)^P \stackrel{\text{def}}{=} skip$

$(stop)^P \stackrel{\text{def}}{=} stop$

$(a \rightarrow Proc)^P \stackrel{\text{def}}{=} a?x : X \rightarrow Proc^P$

$(?y{:}T \rightarrow Proc)^P \stackrel{\text{def}}{=} ?x{:}X?y{:}T \rightarrow Proc^P$

$(S \Box Q)^P \stackrel{\text{def}}{=} S^P \Box S^P$

$(S \sqcap Q)^P \stackrel{\text{def}}{=} S^P \sqcap Q^P$

$(S \parallel Q)^P \stackrel{\text{def}}{=} S^P \parallel Q^P$

$(P \interleave Q)^P \stackrel{\text{def}}{=} S^P \interleave S^P$

$M_D \stackrel{\text{def}}{=} \bigcup_{x \in S}\{\sigma_x \mid \sigma \in M\}$

where σ_x is obtained by deleting the events in the trace where x is not present, similarly for the corresponding interpretation of schemas.

Fig. 14. Promoting basic CSP operators, and degrading traces

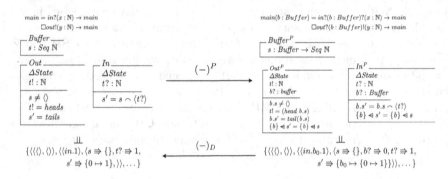

Fig. 15. Promoting CZP specifications

Given a signature $\langle \Sigma_{CSP}, \Sigma_Z \rangle$, Σ_Z is translated to Σ_Z^P, and Σ_{CSP} is mapped to the following **CSP** signature:

  – If $a \in A$, then $a^P = a?(x : S)$, being S the new type introduced in Σ_Z^P,
  – If $n \in N$, then $n(x_1 : T_1, \ldots, x_n : T_n)^P = n(x : S, x_1 : T_1, \ldots, x_n : T_n)$.

This functor is extended to sentences in **CZP**: the translation of a process is defined inductively as in Fig. 14, and the translation of Z formulas is defined as in Section 3. Furthermore, we define the mapping $(-)_D$ between models as in Fig. 14. This extension of promotion is also an institution representation:

Theorem 6. *Mappings $(-)^P$ and $(-)_D$ are institution representations.*

Figure 15 shows, using a simple example, how promotion works in this new setting. In this case, we have a standard specification of a buffer with its corresponding process specification. The schemas and the CSP process on the left are promoted to the the corresponding on the right. Via promotion, we obtain a specification with various buffers whose executions interleave.

6   Related Work and Conclusions

We proposed a mathematical foundation for Z and its structuring mechanisms, which makes use of well established abstract notions of logical systems.

Indeed, the notions that we used in this formalisation have been employed to structure concurrent system specification languages, algebraic specification languages, and other formalisms [13,12]. Several alternative approaches to provide a formal semantics to Z can be found in the literature. One of these is the one presented in [21], where schemas are interpreted as axiomatic theories (signatures plus predicates), and the semantics of these axiomatic theories is given by means of varieties; in that work, no semantics is proposed for promotion and the use of schemas as types. In [3], institutions are used for providing semantics to Z specifications; in that work, schemas are captured as logical sentences in an institution, and therefore a Z specification is viewed as an unstructured set of expressions. In contrast, our approach makes use of theories and morphisms between them in formalising Z designs, thus leading to a well structured categorical semantics of designs. In [7], category theory is used in the definition of a relational semantic framework to interpret Z as well as other specification languages. As in our case, the approach allows for heterogeneous specification; however, the work uses Z simply as an example of a language based on the "state & operations" viewpoint, but it does not show how to deal with Z's structuring mechanisms. In [6], the authors propose a set of rules to manipulate Z schemas; as opposed to our work, these rules are motivated as a means for refactoring specifications. In [16], the authors propose to interpret schemas as types; they build a logical machinery in order to deal with these types. These ideas were adopted in the international ISO standard of Z [17]. Some issues are, in our opinion, not dealt with adequately in that approach; for instance, schema priming is difficult to explain in this context, since a schema and its primed version correspond to different unrelated types. We believe that our approach fits better with the original motivations for Z's schema operators, where priming denotes a purely syntactical operation, an operation also extensively used in other logics for program specification (e.g., in TLA). The interpretation of priming (and related operators) as categorical operations over logical theories provides a simple understanding of Z constructions, with a good separation of concerns between the interpretation of schemas and schema operators, dealing even with promotion, a sophisticated, and widely used, specification structuring mechanism. Moreover, our approach maintains the structure of specifications when providing semantics to them, leading to explicit semantic relationships between component schemas and the composite schemas they are part of, which can be exploited to *promote* reasoning, and with potential benefits for automated reasoning. Finally, our formalisation is at a level of abstraction that allows for a view of logical systems as building blocks. This provides the rigour and flexibility needed to characterise not only Z but also its related languages and extensions, in particular the heterogeneous ones. We have illustrated this point via a formal, well structured, combination of Z with CSP, resulting in a formalism in essence equivalent to the Z-CSP formal method, and "inheriting" the structuring of the composed languages, in particular promotion.

Acknowledgements. The authors would like to thank the anonymous referees for their helpful comments. This work was partially supported by the Argentinian Agency for Scientific and Technological Promotion (ANPCyT), through grants PICT PAE 2007 No. 2772, PICT 2010 No. 1690 and PICT 2010 No. 2611, and by the MEALS project (EU FP7 programme, grant agreement No. 295261).

References

1. Abrial, J.-R.: The B-Book, Assigning Programs to Meanings. Cambridge University Press (1996)
2. Barr, M., Wells, C.: Category Theory for Computer Science, Centre de Recherches Mathématiques, Université de Montréal (1999)
3. Baumeister, H.: Relating Abstract Datatypes and Z-Schemata. In: Bert, D., Choppy, C., Mosses, P.D. (eds.) WADT 1999. LNCS, vol. 1827, pp. 366–382. Springer, Heidelberg (2000)
4. Bérnabou, J.: Introduction to bicategories. In: Complementary Definitions of Programming Language Semantics. LNM, vol. 42. Springer (1967)
5. Borceux, F.: Handbook of Categorical Algebra: Volume 1: Basic Category Theory. Enc. of Mathematics and its Applications. Cambridge University Press (1994)
6. Brien, S.M., Martin, A.P.: A Calculus for Schemas in Z. Journal of Symbolic Computation 30(1) (2000)
7. Bujorianu, M.C.: Integration of Specification Languages Using Viewpoints. In: Boiten, E.A., Derrick, J., Smith, G.P. (eds.) IFM 2004. LNCS, vol. 2999, pp. 421–440. Springer, Heidelberg (2004)
8. Burstall, R., Goguen, J.: Putting Theories together to make Specifications. In: Proc. of Intl. Joint Conference on Artificial Intelligence (1977)
9. Castro, P.F., Aguirre, N.M., López Pombo, C.G., Maibaum, T.S.E.: Towards Managing Dynamic Reconfiguration of Software Systems in a Categorical Setting. In: Cavalcanti, A., Deharbe, D., Gaudel, M.-C., Woodcock, J. (eds.) ICTAC 2010. LNCS, vol. 6255, pp. 306–321. Springer, Heidelberg (2010)
10. Chang, C.C., Keisler, H.J.: Model Theory, 3rd edn. North-Holland (1990)
11. Enderton, H.: A Mathematical Introduction to Logic, 2nd edn. Academic Press (2001)
12. Fiadeiro, J.: Categories for Software Engineering. Springer (2004)
13. Fiadeiro, J., Maibaum, T.: Temporal Theories as Modularisation Units for Concurrent System Specification. Formal Aspects of Computing 4(3) (1992)
14. Fischer, C.: Combining CSP and Z, Technical Report, University of Oldenburg (1997)
15. Goguen, J., Burstall, R.: Institutions: Abstract Model Theory for Specification and Programming. Journal of the ACM, 39(1) (1992)
16. Henson, M., Reeves, S.: Revising Z: Part I - Logic and Semantics. Formal Aspects of Computing 11(4) (1999)
17. Nicholls, J.: Z Notation: Version 1.2, Z Standards Panel (1995)
18. Mossakowski, T., Tarlecki, A., Pawlowski, W.: Combining and Representing Logical Systems. In: Moggi, E., Rosolini, G. (eds.) CTCS 1997. LNCS, vol. 1290, pp. 177–196. Springer, Heidelberg (1997)
19. Mossakowski, T., Roggenbach, M.: Structured CSP – A Process Algebra as an Institution. In: Fiadeiro, J.L., Schobbens, P.-Y. (eds.) WADT 2006. LNCS, vol. 4409, pp. 92–110. Springer, Heidelberg (2007)

20. Smith, G.: The Object Z Specification Language. Advances in Formal Methods Series. Kluwer Academic Publishers (2000)
21. Spivey, J.M.: Understanding Z: A Specification Language and its Formal Semantics. Cambridge Tracts in Theoretical Computer Science (1988)
22. Spivey, J.M.: The Z Notation: A Reference Manual. Prentice Hall (1992)
23. Tarlecki, A.: Moving Between Logical Systems. In: Haveraaen, M., Dahl, O.-J., Owe, O. (eds.) ADT 1995 & COMPASS 1995. LNCS, vol. 1130, pp. 478–502. Springer, Heidelberg (1996)
24. Webber, M.: Combining Statecharts and Z for the Design of Safety-Critical Control Systems. In: Gaudel, M.-C., Wing, J.M. (eds.) FME 1996. LNCS, vol. 1051, pp. 307–326. Springer, Heidelberg (1996)
25. Woodcock, J., Davies, J.: Using Z: Specification, Refinement, and Proof. Prentice Hall (1996)

Assume-Guarantee Reasoning
for Safe Component Behaviours

Chris Chilton[1], Bengt Jonsson[2], and Marta Kwiatkowska[1]

[1] Department of Computer Science, University of Oxford, UK
[2] Department of Information Technology, Uppsala University, Sweden

Abstract. We formulate a sound and complete assume-guarantee framework for reasoning compositionally about safety properties of component behaviours. The specification of a component, which constrains the temporal ordering of input and output interactions with the environment, is expressed in terms of two prefix-closed sets of traces: an assumption and guarantee. The framework supports dynamic reasoning about components and specifications, and includes rules for parallel composition, logical conjunction corresponding to independent development, and quotient for incremental synthesis. Practical applicability of the framework is demonstrated by considering a simple printing example.

Keywords: assume-guarantee, specification theory, components, compositionality, parallel, conjunction, quotient.

1 Introduction

Component-based design methodologies enable both design- and run-time assembly of software systems from heterogeneous components, thus facilitating component reuse, incremental development and independent implementability. To improve the reliability and predictability of such systems, specification theories have been proposed that permit the mixing of specifications and implementations, and allow for the construction of new components from existing ones by means of compositional operators [1,2,3]. A specification should make explicit the *assumptions* that a component can make about the environment, and the corresponding *guarantees* that it will provide about its own behaviour. This allows for the use of compositional assume-guarantee (AG) reasoning, in order to combat issues of complexity and state space explosion during system development and verification.

In earlier work [4], we introduced a component-based specification theory, in which components communicate by synchronisation of I/O actions, with the understanding that inputs are controlled by the environment, while outputs (which are non-blocking) are under the control of the component. The component-model is conceptually similar to the interface automata of de Alfaro and Henzinger [5], except that our refinement is based on classical sets of traces, as opposed to alternating simulation, and that we allow explicit specification of inconsistent traces, which can model underspecification and errors, etc. With both trace-based and

C.S. Păsăreanu and G. Salaün (Eds.): FACS 2012, LNCS 7684, pp. 92–109, 2013.
© Springer-Verlag Berlin Heidelberg 2013

operational representations for components, a distinguishing feature of our theory is the inclusion of conjunction and quotient operators (which generalise those of [2,6]) for supporting independent and incremental development, respectively. Logical disjunction and hiding can also be added. The theory enjoys strong algebraic properties with all the operators being compositional under refinement, and we prove full abstraction with respect to a simple testing framework.

In [4] and [5], the assumptions and guarantees of components are merged into one behavioural representation. In many cases, this avoids duplication of common information, although there are situations in which it is desirable to manipulate the assumptions and guarantees separately. For instance, we may want to express a simple guarantee (such as "no failure will occur") without having to weave it into a complex assumption. Another advantage of separation is specification reuse, in that the same guarantees (or assumptions) can be used for several related interfaces, each representing different versions of a component.

Contributions. In this paper, we present a complete specification theory for reasoning about AG specifications of components (as modelled in [4]). Assumptions and guarantees are prefix-closed sets of traces, meaning our framework facilitates reasoning about safety behaviours, and differs from (arguably) more complex approaches based on modal specifications and alternating simulation. Building upon the theory in [4], we define the operators of parallel, conjunction and quotient directly on AG specifications (the last being the first such definition), and prove their compositionality. By treating AG specifications as first-class citizens, the theory supports flexible development and verification of component-based systems using AG principles. A component can be characterised by its weakest AG specification, and, in the opposite direction, we can infer the least refined component satisfying a given specification. From this, a notion of refinement corresponding to implementation containment is defined. In relating implementations with AG specifications by means of satisfaction, we formulate a collection of sound and complete AG reasoning rules for the preservation of safety properties under the operations and refinement preorder of the specification theory. These rules are inspired by the Compositionality Principle of [7,8] for parallel composition, which we generalise to the operations of conjunction and quotient. The rules allow us to infer properties of compositions for both AG specifications and components, thus enabling designers to deduce whether it is safe to substitute a component, for example one synthesised at run-time by means of the quotient operator, with another.

Related Work. Compositional AG reasoning has been extensively studied in the literature, where traditionally the work was concerned with compositional reasoning for processes, components and properties expressed in temporal logics [9,10,11]. A variety of rule formats have been proposed, although Maier demonstrates through a set-theoretic setting in [12] that compositional circular AG rules for parallel composition (corresponding to intersection) cannot both be sound and complete. This seems to contradict the work of Namjoshi and

Trefler [13], although the discrepancy is attributed to the fact that the sound and complete circular rule presented in [13] is non-compositional.

Compositional reasoning about AG specifications in the form of AG pairs, similar to what we consider in this paper, is discussed in [7] for the generic setting of state-based processes. The authors formulate a Compositionality Principle for parallel composition, and observe that this is sound for safety properties. A logical formulation for specifications is then discussed in [8], where intuitionistic and linear logic approaches are put forward. The main difference with our approach is that we consider an action-based component model and have a richer set of composition operators, including conjunction and quotient. We also prove completeness, by relying on the convention that an output is controlled by at most one component, which can be used to break circularity.

More recent proposals focus on compositional verification for interface theories [14,15], namely interface and I/O automata, which are closest to our work. In [14], Emmi *et al.* extend a learning-based compositional AG method to interface automata. They only consider the much more limited asymmetric rules for safety properties, which are shown to be both sound and complete. The rules are supplied for the original subset of operators and relations defined in [5], namely compatibility, parallel composition and refinement based on alternating simulation. Thus, no consideration is given to conjunction or quotient. Other notable work concerning compositional reasoning for interface theories is the AG framework defined by Larsen *et al.* in [15] for I/O automata, where assumptions and guarantees are themselves specified as I/O automata. The authors consider a parallel composition operator on AG specifications that is the weakest specification for composed components respecting independent implementability, for which they present a sound and complete rule. Our work allows a more general component model that does not require input-enabledness, and allows for specifications to have non-identical interfaces to their implementations. We go beyond [15] by defining conjunction and quotient operations directly on AG specifications, thus providing a significantly richer basis for AG based reasoning and development, and we do not require input-enabledness of guarantees.

A compositional specification theory based on modal specifications has been developed in [3], which includes all the operations we consider in this paper, but for systems without I/O distinction. Larsen *et al.* consider a cross between modal specifications and interface automata [1], where refinement is given in terms of alternating simulation/modal refinement (which is stronger than our trace containment), and no operations for conjunction and quotient are given. Surveying [16], Bauer *et al.* provide a generic construction for obtaining a contract framework based on AG pairs from a component-based specification theory. The abstract ideas share similarity with our framework, and it is interesting to note how parallel composition of contracts is defined in terms of the conjunction and quotient operators of the specification theory. Our work differs in that we define both of these operators directly on contracts. A definition of conjunction on contracts is provided in [17], but this is for a simplified contract framework, as witnessed by the definition of parallel composition on contracts.

Outline. In Section 2 we summarise the compositional specification theory of [4], which serves as a basis for our AG reasoning framework. Section 3 introduces the main definitions of the AG framework, and presents a number of sound and complete compositional rules for the operators of the specification theory. An application of our framework is illustrated in Section 4, while Section 5 concludes our work and suggests possible extensions. Proofs of our results are made available as the technical report [18].

2   Compositional Specification Theory

In this section, we briefly survey the essential features of our compositional specification theory presented in [4]. In that paper, we present two notations for modelling components: a trace-based formalism and an operational representation. Here we focus on the trace-based models, since operational models can be mapped to semantically equivalent trace-based ones.

A component comes equipped with an interface, together with a set of behaviours over the interface. The interface is represented by a set of input actions and a set of output actions, which are necessarily disjoint, while the behaviour is characterised by sets of traces.

Definition 1 (Components). *A component $\mathcal{P}$ is a tuple $\langle \mathcal{A}_\mathcal{P}^I, \mathcal{A}_\mathcal{P}^O, T_\mathcal{P}, F_\mathcal{P} \rangle$ in which $\mathcal{A}_\mathcal{P}^I$ and $\mathcal{A}_\mathcal{P}^O$ are disjoint sets referred to as inputs and outputs respectively (the union of which is denoted by $\mathcal{A}_\mathcal{P}$), $T_\mathcal{P} \subseteq \mathcal{A}_\mathcal{P}^*$ is a non-empty set of permissible traces, and $F_\mathcal{P} \subseteq \mathcal{A}_\mathcal{P}^*$ is a set of inconsistent traces. The trace sets must satisfy the constraints:*

1. *$F_\mathcal{P} \subseteq T_\mathcal{P}$*
2. *If $t \in T_\mathcal{P}$ and $i \in \mathcal{A}_\mathcal{P}^I$, then $ti \in T_\mathcal{P}$*
3. *$T_\mathcal{P}$ is prefix closed*
4. *If $t \in F_\mathcal{P}$ and $t' \in \mathcal{A}_\mathcal{P}^*$, then $tt' \in F_\mathcal{P}$.*

The permissible traces contain all possible interaction sequences between the component and the environment; they are thus receptive to all inputs, as these are under the control of the environment. If on some interaction sequence an error arises in the component, or the environment issues a non-enabled input, the trace is said to be inconsistent. We adopt the convention that any inconsistent trace is suffix closed, meaning that, once the component becomes inconsistent, it behaves similarly to the process CHAOS in CSP.

From hereon let $\mathcal{P}$, $\mathcal{Q}$ and $\mathcal{R}$ be components with signatures $\langle \mathcal{A}_\mathcal{P}^I, \mathcal{A}_\mathcal{P}^O, T_\mathcal{P}, F_\mathcal{P} \rangle$, $\langle \mathcal{A}_\mathcal{Q}^I, \mathcal{A}_\mathcal{Q}^O, T_\mathcal{Q}, F_\mathcal{Q} \rangle$ and $\langle \mathcal{A}_\mathcal{R}^I, \mathcal{A}_\mathcal{R}^O, T_\mathcal{R}, F_\mathcal{R} \rangle$ respectively.

Notation. Let $\mathcal{A}$, $\mathcal{B}$ and $\mathcal{C}$ be sets of actions. For a trace t, write $t \upharpoonright \mathcal{A}$ for the projection of t onto $\mathcal{A}$. Now for $T \subseteq \mathcal{A}^*$, write $T \upharpoonright \mathcal{B}$ for $\{t \upharpoonright \mathcal{B} : t \in T\}$, $T \Uparrow \mathcal{B}$ for $\{t \in \mathcal{B}^* : t \upharpoonright \mathcal{A} \in T\}$, $T \Uparrow\Uparrow \mathcal{B}$ for $\epsilon + (T \Uparrow \mathcal{B})(\epsilon + \mathcal{A}^I)$, $T \uparrow \mathcal{B}$ for $T(\mathcal{B})(\mathcal{A} \cup \mathcal{B})^*$, $T \uparrow_\epsilon \mathcal{B}$ for $T \cup (T \uparrow \mathcal{B})$, $\overline{T}$ for $\mathcal{A}^* \setminus T$, and $\mathsf{pre}(T)$ for the largest prefix-closed set contained in T.

Refinement. In the specification theory, refinement corresponds to safe-substitutivity. This means that Q is a refinement of P if Q can be used safely in any environment that is safe for P. An environment is safe for a component if any interaction between the two cannot be extended by a sequence of output actions under the control of the component such that the resulting trace is inconsistent. We will thus need to consider the safe representation of a component, obtained by propagating inconsistencies backwards over outputs.

Definition 2 (Safe component). *Let P be a component. The most general safe representation for P is a component $\mathcal{E}(P) = \langle \mathcal{A}_P^I, \mathcal{A}_P^O, T_{\mathcal{E}(P)}, F_{\mathcal{E}(P)} \rangle$, where $T_{\mathcal{E}(P)} = T_P \cup F_{\mathcal{E}(P)}$ and $F_{\mathcal{E}(P)} = \{ tt' \in \mathcal{A}_P^* : t \in T_P \text{ and } \exists t'' \in (\mathcal{A}_P^O)^* \cdot tt'' \in F_P \}$.*

We can now give the formal definition of refinement. Intuitively, Q must be willing to accept any input that P can accept, but it must produce no more outputs than P, otherwise we could not be certain how the environment would respond to these additional outputs.

Definition 3 (Refinement). *For components P and Q, Q is said to be a refinement of P, written $Q \sqsubseteq_{imp} P$, iff:*

1. $\mathcal{A}_P^I \subseteq \mathcal{A}_Q^I$
2. $\mathcal{A}_Q^O \subseteq \mathcal{A}_P^O$
3. $T_{\mathcal{E}(Q)} \subseteq T_{\mathcal{E}(P)} \cup T_{\mathcal{E}(P)} \uparrow (\mathcal{A}_Q^I \setminus \mathcal{A}_P^I)$
4. $F_{\mathcal{E}(Q)} \subseteq F_{\mathcal{E}(P)} \cup T_{\mathcal{E}(P)} \uparrow (\mathcal{A}_Q^I \setminus \mathcal{A}_P^I)$.

The set $T_{\mathcal{E}(P)} \uparrow (\mathcal{A}_Q^I \setminus \mathcal{A}_P^I)$ represents the extension of P's interface to include all inputs in $\mathcal{A}_Q^I \setminus \mathcal{A}_P^I$. As these inputs are not ordinarily accepted by P, they are treated as bad inputs, hence the suffix closure with arbitrary behaviour.

Parallel Composition. The parallel composition of two components is obtained as the cross-product by synchronising on common actions and interleaving on independent actions. To support broadcasting, we make the assumption that inputs and outputs synchronise to produce outputs. Communication mismatches arising through non-input enabledness automatically appear as inconsistent traces in the product, on account of our component formulation. As the outputs of a component are controlled locally, we assume that the output actions of the components to be composed are disjoint.

Definition 4 (Parallel composition). *Let P and Q be components such that $\mathcal{A}_P^O \cap \mathcal{A}_Q^O = \emptyset$. Then $P \parallel Q$ is the component $\langle \mathcal{A}_{P\parallel Q}^I, \mathcal{A}_{P\parallel Q}^O, T_{P\parallel Q}, F_{P\parallel Q} \rangle$, where:*

- $\mathcal{A}_{P\parallel Q}^I = (\mathcal{A}_P^I \cup \mathcal{A}_Q^I) \setminus (\mathcal{A}_P^O \cup \mathcal{A}_Q^O)$
- $\mathcal{A}_{P\parallel Q}^O = \mathcal{A}_P^O \cup \mathcal{A}_Q^O$
- $T_{P\parallel Q} = [(T_P \Uparrow \mathcal{A}_{P\parallel Q}) \cap (T_Q \Uparrow \mathcal{A}_{P\parallel Q})] \cup F_{P\parallel Q}$
- $F_{P\parallel Q} = [(T_P \Uparrow \mathcal{A}_{P\parallel Q}) \cap (F_Q \Uparrow \mathcal{A}_{P\parallel Q})]\mathcal{A}_{P\parallel Q}^* \cup$
  $[(F_P \Uparrow \mathcal{A}_{P\parallel Q}) \cap (T_Q \Uparrow \mathcal{A}_{P\parallel Q})]\mathcal{A}_{P\parallel Q}^*.$

Informally, a trace is permissible in $\mathcal{P} \parallel \mathcal{Q}$ if its projection onto $\mathcal{A}_{\mathcal{P}}$ is a trace of $\mathcal{P}$ and its projection onto $\mathcal{A}_{\mathcal{Q}}$ is a trace of $\mathcal{Q}$. A trace is inconsistent if it has a prefix whose projection onto the alphabet of one of the components is inconsistent and the projection onto the alphabet of the other component is a permissible trace of that component.

Conjunction. The conjunction of components $\mathcal{P}$ and $\mathcal{Q}$ is the coarsest component that will work safely in any environment that $\mathcal{P}$ or $\mathcal{Q}$ can work safely in. It can be thought of as finding a common implementation for a number of specifications. Thus, conjunction is essentially the meet operator on the refinement preorder. Consequently, the conjunction of two components is only defined when the union of their inputs is disjoint from the union of their outputs.

Definition 5 (Conjunction). *Let $\mathcal{P}$ and $\mathcal{Q}$ be components such that $\mathcal{A}_{\mathcal{P}}^I \cup \mathcal{A}_{\mathcal{Q}}^I$ and $\mathcal{A}_{\mathcal{P}}^O \cup \mathcal{A}_{\mathcal{Q}}^O$ are disjoint. Then $\mathcal{P} \wedge \mathcal{Q}$ is the component $\langle \mathcal{A}_{\mathcal{P} \wedge \mathcal{Q}}^I, \mathcal{A}_{\mathcal{P} \wedge \mathcal{Q}}^O, T_{\mathcal{P} \wedge \mathcal{Q}},$ $F_{\mathcal{P} \wedge \mathcal{Q}} \rangle$, where:*

- $\mathcal{A}_{\mathcal{P} \wedge \mathcal{Q}}^I = \mathcal{A}_{\mathcal{P}}^I \cup \mathcal{A}_{\mathcal{Q}}^I$
- $\mathcal{A}_{\mathcal{P} \wedge \mathcal{Q}}^O = \mathcal{A}_{\mathcal{P}}^O \cap \mathcal{A}_{\mathcal{Q}}^O$
- $T_{\mathcal{P} \wedge \mathcal{Q}} = [(T_{\mathcal{P}} \cup T_{\mathcal{P}} \uparrow (\mathcal{A}_{\mathcal{Q}}^I \setminus \mathcal{A}_{\mathcal{P}}^I)) \cap (T_{\mathcal{Q}} \cup T_{\mathcal{Q}} \uparrow (\mathcal{A}_{\mathcal{P}}^I \setminus \mathcal{A}_{\mathcal{Q}}^I))] \cap \mathcal{A}_{\mathcal{P} \wedge \mathcal{Q}}^*$
- $F_{\mathcal{P} \wedge \mathcal{Q}} = [(F_{\mathcal{P}} \cup T_{\mathcal{P}} \uparrow (\mathcal{A}_{\mathcal{Q}}^I \setminus \mathcal{A}_{\mathcal{P}}^I)) \cap (F_{\mathcal{Q}} \cup T_{\mathcal{Q}} \uparrow (\mathcal{A}_{\mathcal{P}}^I \setminus \mathcal{A}_{\mathcal{Q}}^I))] \cap \mathcal{A}_{\mathcal{P} \wedge \mathcal{Q}}^*.$

Intuitively, after any trace of $\mathcal{P} \wedge \mathcal{Q}$, the conjunction must accept any input offered by either $\mathcal{P}$ or $\mathcal{Q}$, but can only issue an output if both $\mathcal{P}$ and $\mathcal{Q}$ are willing to offer it. Once $\mathcal{P}$ becomes inconsistent, or an input is seen that is not an input of $\mathcal{P}$, the conjunction behaves like $\mathcal{Q}$ (and vice-versa).

Quotient. In [4], we introduced a quotient operator acting on components. Given a component $\mathcal{R}$, together with a component $\mathcal{P}$ implementing part of $\mathcal{R}$, the quotient $\mathcal{R}/\mathcal{P}$ yields the coarsest component for the remaining part of $\mathcal{R}$ to be implemented. Thus, the quotient satisfies the property: there exists $\mathcal{Q}$ such that $\mathcal{P} \parallel \mathcal{Q} \sqsubseteq_{imp} \mathcal{R}$ iff $\mathcal{P} \parallel (\mathcal{R}/\mathcal{P}) \sqsubseteq_{imp} \mathcal{R}$ and $\mathcal{Q} \sqsubseteq_{imp} (\mathcal{R}/\mathcal{P})$. Whether the quotient exists depends on the extent to which $\mathcal{P}$ is a sub-component of $\mathcal{R}$.

For the development in this paper, we will not use quotient on components, and refer to [4]. Instead, we will define a quotient operator that acts on AG specifications. Thus, the quotient of two AG specifications yields an AG specification characterising a set of component implementations.

3   Assume-Guarantee Framework for Safety Properties

To support reasoning about components, we introduce the concept of an AG specification, which consists of two prefix-closed sets of traces referred to as the *assumption* and *guarantee*. The assumption specifies the environment's allowable interaction sequences, while the guarantee is a constraint on the component's behaviour. As assumptions and guarantees are prefix-closed, our theory ensures that components preserve (not necessarily regular) safety properties[1].

Definition 6 (AG specification). *An AG specification $\mathcal{S}$ is a tuple $\langle \mathcal{A}_\mathcal{S}^I, \mathcal{A}_\mathcal{S}^O, \mathcal{R}_\mathcal{S}, \mathcal{G}_\mathcal{S} \rangle$, in which $\mathcal{A}_\mathcal{S}^I$ and $\mathcal{A}_\mathcal{S}^O$ are disjoint sets, referred to as the inputs and outputs respectively, and $\mathcal{R}_\mathcal{S}$ and $\mathcal{G}_\mathcal{S}$ are prefix closed subsets of $(\mathcal{A}_\mathcal{S}^I \cup \mathcal{A}_\mathcal{S}^O)^*$, referred to as the assumption and guarantee respectively, such that $t \in \mathcal{R}_\mathcal{S}$ and $t' \in (\mathcal{A}_\mathcal{S}^O)^*$ implies $tt' \in \mathcal{R}_\mathcal{S}$.*

Since outputs are under the control of a component, we insist that assumptions are closed under output-extensions. On the other hand, we need not insist that the guarantee is closed under input-extensions, since the assumption can select inputs under which the guarantee is given.

Given an AG specification $\mathcal{S}$, we want to be able to say whether a component $\mathcal{P}$ satisfies $\mathcal{S}$. Informally, $\mathcal{P}$ satisfies $\mathcal{S}$ if for any interaction between $\mathcal{P}$ and the environment characterised by a trace t, if $t \in \mathcal{R}_\mathcal{S}$, then $t \in \mathcal{G}_\mathcal{S}$ and t cannot become inconsistent in $\mathcal{P}$ without further stimulation from the environment. Components can thus be thought of as implementations of AG specifications.

Before defining satisfaction, we need to introduce a notion of compatibility between AG specifications and components, meaning that they do not disagree on what are inputs or outputs.

Definition 7 (Compatibility). *Let $\mathcal{P}$ be a component, and let $\mathcal{S}$ and $\mathcal{T}$ be AG-specifications. Then $\mathcal{P}$ is compatible with $\mathcal{S}$, written $\mathcal{P} \sim \mathcal{S}$, iff $\mathcal{A}_\mathcal{P}^I \cap \mathcal{A}_\mathcal{S}^O = \emptyset = \mathcal{A}_\mathcal{P}^O \cap \mathcal{A}_\mathcal{S}^I$. Similarly, $\mathcal{S}$ is compatible with $\mathcal{T}$, written $\mathcal{S} \sim \mathcal{T}$, iff $\mathcal{A}_\mathcal{S}^I \cap \mathcal{A}_\mathcal{T}^O = \emptyset = \mathcal{A}_\mathcal{S}^O \cap \mathcal{A}_\mathcal{T}^I$.*

We can now give the formal definition for satisfaction of an AG specification by a component.

Definition 8 (AG satisfaction). *A component $\mathcal{P}$ satisfies the AG specification $\mathcal{S}$, written $\mathcal{P} \models \mathcal{S}$, iff:*

S1. $\mathcal{P} \sim \mathcal{S}$
S2. $\mathcal{A}_\mathcal{S}^I \subseteq \mathcal{A}_\mathcal{P}^I$
S3. $\mathcal{A}_\mathcal{P}^O \subseteq \mathcal{A}_\mathcal{S}^O$
S4. $\mathcal{R}_\mathcal{S} \cap T_\mathcal{P} \subseteq \mathcal{G}_\mathcal{S} \cap \overline{F_\mathcal{P}}$.

By output-extension closure of assumptions, condition S4 is equivalent to checking $\mathcal{R}_\mathcal{S} \cap T_\mathcal{P} \subseteq \mathcal{G}_\mathcal{S} \cap \overline{F_{\mathcal{E}(\mathcal{P})}}$, which involves the most general safe representation $\mathcal{E}(\mathcal{P})$ of $\mathcal{P}$ (see Definition 2). The following lemma shows that this definition of satisfaction is preserved under the component-based refinement corresponding to safe-substitutivity, subject to compatibility.

Lemma 1. *Let $\mathcal{P}$ and $\mathcal{Q}$ be components, and let $\mathcal{S}$ be an AG specification. If $\mathcal{P} \models \mathcal{S}$, $\mathcal{Q} \sqsubseteq_{imp} \mathcal{P}$ and $\mathcal{Q} \sim \mathcal{S}$, then $\mathcal{Q} \models \mathcal{S}$.*

---

[1] Model-checking components against AG specifications would force us to restrict the properties we can encode and check. In this setting, we would naturally restrict to the regular safety properties, which can be encoded by finite-state automata.

3.1 Refinement

There is a natural hierarchy on AG specifications respecting the satisfaction rule defined in Definition 8. From this we can define a refinement relation on AG specifications that corresponds to implementation containment. But first, we introduce the shorthand: $\text{violations}(X) \triangleq \{t \in \mathcal{A}_X^* : t(\mathcal{A}_X^I)^* \in \mathcal{R}_X \cap \overline{\mathcal{G}_X}\}\mathcal{A}_X^*$.

Definition 9 (AG refinement). *Let $\mathcal{S}$ and $\mathcal{T}$ be AG specifications. $\mathcal{S}$ is said to be a refinement of $\mathcal{T}$, written $\mathcal{S} \sqsubseteq \mathcal{T}$, iff:*

R1. $\mathcal{S} \sim \mathcal{T}$
R2. $\mathcal{A}_{\mathcal{T}}^I \subseteq \mathcal{A}_{\mathcal{S}}^I$
R3. $\mathcal{A}_{\mathcal{S}}^O \subseteq \mathcal{A}_{\mathcal{T}}^O$
R4. $\text{violations}(\mathcal{T}) \cap \mathcal{A}_{\mathcal{S}}^* \subseteq \text{violations}(\mathcal{S})$
R5. $\mathcal{R}_{\mathcal{T}} \cap \mathcal{A}_{\mathcal{S}}^* \subseteq \mathcal{R}_{\mathcal{S}} \cup \text{violations}(\mathcal{S})$.

It is our intention that $\mathcal{S} \sqsubseteq \mathcal{T}$ iff the implementations of $\mathcal{S}$ are contained within the implementations of $\mathcal{T}$ (subject to compatibility). Conditions R1-R3 are the bare minimum to uphold this principle. For condition R4, any component having a trace $t \in \text{violations}(\mathcal{T}) \cap \mathcal{A}_{\mathcal{S}}^*$ cannot be an implementation of $\mathcal{T}$, so it should not be an implementation of $\mathcal{S}$. For this to be the case, the component must violate the guarantee on $\mathcal{S}$, i.e., $t \in \text{violations}(\mathcal{S})$. Condition R5 deals with inconsistent traces. If a component has an inconsistent trace $t \in \mathcal{R}_{\mathcal{T}} \cap \mathcal{A}_{\mathcal{S}}^*$, then this cannot be an implementation of $\mathcal{T}$. Consequently, the component must not be an implementation of $\mathcal{S}$, so either t must violate the guarantee of $\mathcal{S}$, i.e., $t \in \text{violations}(\mathcal{S})$, or t must be in $\mathcal{R}_{\mathcal{S}}$, so that the component cannot satisfy $\mathcal{S}$.

Lemma 2. *Refinement respects implementation containment:*

$$\mathcal{S} \sqsubseteq \mathcal{T} \iff \{\mathcal{P} : \mathcal{P} \models \mathcal{S} \text{ and } \mathcal{P} \sim \mathcal{T}\} \subseteq \{\mathcal{P} : \mathcal{P} \models \mathcal{T}\}.$$

In [15], Larsen *et al.* give a sound and complete characterisation of their refinement relation (which corresponds to implementation containment, as for us) by means of conformance tests. The definition assumes equality of interfaces, so does not need to deal with issues of compatibility or the complexities of both covariant and contravariant inclusion of inputs and outputs respectively (i.e., conditions R1-R3). Thus, their definition largely corresponds to condition R4. Condition R5 is not necessary in that setting, as implementation models are required to be input-enabled.

Refinement can be shown to be a preorder, provided that we add the minor technical condition that compatibility of components is maintained, as the next lemma shows.

Lemma 3 (Weak transitivity). *For AG specifications $\mathcal{S}$, $\mathcal{T}$ and $\mathcal{U}$, if $\mathcal{S} \sqsubseteq \mathcal{T}$, $\mathcal{T} \sqsubseteq \mathcal{U}$ and $\mathcal{S} \sim \mathcal{U}$, then $\mathcal{S} \sqsubseteq \mathcal{U}$.*

As an aside, component-based refinement $\sqsubseteq_{imp}$ is a preorder because, in refining a component $\mathcal{P}$ to a component $\mathcal{Q}$, it is possible to transform some of $\mathcal{P}$'s outputs into inputs of $\mathcal{Q}$, as this preserves safe-substitutivity. However, this transformation of action types does not make sense with AG specifications, which talk explicitly about the behaviour of the environment.

3.2   Inferring Components from AG Specifications

Given a specification for a component, we require a way for developers to construct an actual component that satisfies the requirements of the specification. In the following definition, we show how to infer the least refined component that satisfies a given specification.

Definition 10 (Inferred component). *Let $\mathcal{S}$ be an AG specification. Then the least refined implementation of $\mathcal{S}$ is the component $\mathcal{I}(\mathcal{S}) = \langle \mathcal{A}_{\mathcal{S}}^{I}, \mathcal{A}_{\mathcal{S}}^{O}, T_{\mathcal{I}(\mathcal{S})}, F_{\mathcal{I}(\mathcal{S})} \rangle$, defined only when $\epsilon \in T_{\mathcal{I}(\mathcal{S})}$, where:*

- $T_{\mathcal{I}(\mathcal{S})} = \mathsf{pre}(\{t \in \mathcal{R}_{\mathcal{S}} \cap \mathcal{G}_{\mathcal{S}} : \forall t' \in (\mathcal{A}_{\mathcal{S}}^{I})^{*} \cdot tt' \in \overline{\mathcal{R}_{\mathcal{S}}} \cup \mathcal{G}_{\mathcal{S}}\}) \cup F_{\mathcal{I}(\mathcal{S})}$
- $F_{\mathcal{I}(\mathcal{S})} = \{tit' : t \in \mathcal{R}_{\mathcal{S}} \cap \mathcal{G}_{\mathcal{S}}, i \in \mathcal{A}_{\mathcal{S}}^{I} \text{ and } ti \notin \mathcal{R}_{\mathcal{S}}\} \cup \{t \in \mathcal{A}_{\mathcal{S}}^{*} : \epsilon \notin \mathcal{R}_{\mathcal{S}}\}$.

The following lemma shows that the obtained component model really is least refined with respect to the refinement preorder $\sqsubseteq_{imp}$ on implementations.

Lemma 4. *Let $\mathcal{S}$ be an AG specification, and let $\mathcal{P}$ be a component. Then:*

- $\epsilon \notin T_{\mathcal{I}(\mathcal{S})}$ *implies $\mathcal{S}$ is non-implementable;*
- $\epsilon \in T_{\mathcal{I}(\mathcal{S})}$ *implies $\mathcal{I}(\mathcal{S}) \models \mathcal{S}$; and*
- $\mathcal{P} \models \mathcal{S}$ *iff $\mathcal{P} \sqsubseteq_{imp} \mathcal{I}(\mathcal{S})$.*

3.3   Characteristic AG Specification of a Component

One may be interested in the most general AG specification that satisfies a component, which we refer to as the characteristic AG specification of the component. This can be found by examining the component's safe traces.

Definition 11 (Characteristic AG specification). *The characteristic AG specification for the component $\mathcal{P}$ is an AG specification $\mathcal{AG}(\mathcal{P}) = \langle \mathcal{A}_{\mathcal{P}}^{I}, \mathcal{A}_{\mathcal{P}}^{O}, \mathcal{R}_{\mathcal{AG}(\mathcal{P})}, \mathcal{G}_{\mathcal{AG}(\mathcal{P})} \rangle$, where $\mathcal{R}_{\mathcal{AG}(\mathcal{P})} = \mathcal{A}_{\mathcal{P}}^{*} \setminus F_{\mathcal{E}(\mathcal{P})}$ and $\mathcal{G}_{\mathcal{AG}(\mathcal{P})} = T_{\mathcal{P}} \setminus F_{\mathcal{E}(\mathcal{P})}$.*

The largest assumption safe for component $\mathcal{P}$ is the set of all non-inconsistent traces, while the guarantee is the set of traces of $\mathcal{E}(\mathcal{P})$ that are non-inconsistent. As the following lemma demonstrates, the characteristic AG specification satisfies the desired properties.

Lemma 5. *Let $\mathcal{P}$ be a component and let $\mathcal{S}$ be an AG specification. Then:*

- $\mathcal{P} \models \mathcal{AG}(\mathcal{P})$; *and*
- $\mathcal{P} \models \mathcal{S}$ *iff $\mathcal{AG}(\mathcal{P}) \sqsubseteq \mathcal{S}$.*

The final point in the previous lemma shows that satisfaction of a specification by a component is equivalent to checking whether the characteristic AG specification of the component is a refinement of the specification. This means that implementability of specifications built up compositionally follows immediately from compositionality results on AG specifications, as we will see in the subsequent sections.

We are now in a position to present sound and complete AG rules for inferring properties of composite systems from the properties of their sub-components.

3.4 Parallel Composition

The AG rule for parallel composition is based on the well-established theorem of Abadi and Lamport [7], which has appeared in several forms [19,20,21]. Intuitively, the guarantee of any component must not be allowed to violate the assumptions of the other components. Such reasoning seems circular, but the circularity can be broken up in our setting as a safety property cannot be simultaneously violated by two or more components. This is due to an output being under the control of at most one component.

Notation. To assist in our definition, we introduce the following shorthands:

- $\mathcal{R}(\mathcal{S}_\mathcal{P}, \mathcal{S}_\mathcal{Q}) \triangleq (\mathcal{R}_{\mathcal{S}_\mathcal{P}} \Uparrow \mathcal{A}_{\mathcal{S}_\mathcal{P} || \mathcal{S}_\mathcal{Q}}) \cap (\mathcal{R}_{\mathcal{S}_\mathcal{Q}} \Uparrow \mathcal{A}_{\mathcal{S}_\mathcal{P} || \mathcal{S}_\mathcal{Q}})$
- $\mathcal{G}(\mathcal{S}_\mathcal{P}, \mathcal{S}_\mathcal{Q}) \triangleq (\mathcal{G}_{\mathcal{S}_\mathcal{P}} \Uparrow \mathcal{A}_{\mathcal{S}_\mathcal{P} || \mathcal{S}_\mathcal{Q}}) \cap (\mathcal{G}_{\mathcal{S}_\mathcal{Q}} \Uparrow \mathcal{A}_{\mathcal{S}_\mathcal{P} || \mathcal{S}_\mathcal{Q}})$
- $\mathcal{G}^+(\mathcal{S}_\mathcal{P}, \mathcal{S}_\mathcal{Q}) \triangleq (\mathcal{G}_{\mathcal{S}_\mathcal{P}} \Uparrow\!\uparrow \mathcal{A}_{\mathcal{S}_\mathcal{P} || \mathcal{S}_\mathcal{Q}}) \cap (\mathcal{G}_{\mathcal{S}_\mathcal{Q}} \Uparrow\!\uparrow \mathcal{A}_{\mathcal{S}_\mathcal{P} || \mathcal{S}_\mathcal{Q}})$.

Definition 12. *Let $\mathcal{S}_\mathcal{P}$ and $\mathcal{S}_\mathcal{Q}$ be AG specifications such that $\mathcal{A}^O_{\mathcal{S}_\mathcal{P}} \cap \mathcal{A}^O_{\mathcal{S}_\mathcal{Q}} = \emptyset$. If $\mathcal{S}_\mathcal{P}$ and $\mathcal{S}_\mathcal{Q}$ are both implementable, then $\mathcal{S}_\mathcal{P} \parallel \mathcal{S}_\mathcal{Q}$ is an AG specification $\langle \mathcal{A}^I_{\mathcal{S}_\mathcal{P} || \mathcal{S}_\mathcal{Q}}, \mathcal{A}^O_{\mathcal{S}_\mathcal{P} || \mathcal{S}_\mathcal{Q}}, \mathcal{R}_{\mathcal{S}_\mathcal{P} || \mathcal{S}_\mathcal{Q}}, \mathcal{G}_{\mathcal{S}_\mathcal{P} || \mathcal{S}_\mathcal{Q}} \rangle$ defined by:*

- $\mathcal{A}^I_{\mathcal{S}_\mathcal{P} || \mathcal{S}_\mathcal{Q}} = (\mathcal{A}^I_{\mathcal{S}_\mathcal{P}} \cup \mathcal{A}^I_{\mathcal{S}_\mathcal{Q}}) \setminus (\mathcal{A}^O_{\mathcal{S}_\mathcal{P}} \cup \mathcal{A}^O_{\mathcal{S}_\mathcal{Q}})$
- $\mathcal{A}^O_{\mathcal{S}_\mathcal{P} || \mathcal{S}_\mathcal{Q}} = \mathcal{A}^O_{\mathcal{S}_\mathcal{P}} \cup \mathcal{A}^O_{\mathcal{S}_\mathcal{Q}}$
- $\mathcal{R}_{\mathcal{S}_\mathcal{P} || \mathcal{S}_\mathcal{Q}} \subseteq \mathcal{A}^*_{\mathcal{S}_\mathcal{P} || \mathcal{S}_\mathcal{Q}}$ *is the largest prefix closed set satisfying*
  $\mathcal{R}_{\mathcal{S}_\mathcal{P} || \mathcal{S}_\mathcal{Q}} (\mathcal{A}^O_{\mathcal{S}_\mathcal{P} || \mathcal{S}_\mathcal{Q}})^* \cap \mathcal{G}^+(\mathcal{S}_\mathcal{P}, \mathcal{S}_\mathcal{Q}) \subseteq \mathcal{R}(\mathcal{S}_\mathcal{P}, \mathcal{S}_\mathcal{Q})$
- $\mathcal{G}_{\mathcal{S}_\mathcal{P} || \mathcal{S}_\mathcal{Q}} = \mathcal{R}_{\mathcal{S}_\mathcal{P} || \mathcal{S}_\mathcal{Q}} \cap \mathcal{G}(\mathcal{S}_\mathcal{P}, \mathcal{S}_\mathcal{Q})$.

If at least one of $\mathcal{S}_\mathcal{P}$ or $\mathcal{S}_\mathcal{Q}$ is non-implementable, then $\mathcal{S}_\mathcal{P} \parallel \mathcal{S}_\mathcal{Q} = \langle \mathcal{A}^I_{\mathcal{S}_\mathcal{P} || \mathcal{S}_\mathcal{Q}}, \mathcal{A}^O_{\mathcal{S}_\mathcal{P} || \mathcal{S}_\mathcal{Q}}, \mathcal{A}^*_{\mathcal{S}_\mathcal{P} || \mathcal{S}_\mathcal{Q}}, \emptyset \rangle$

$\mathcal{S}_\mathcal{P} \parallel \mathcal{S}_\mathcal{Q}$ yields the strongest specification satisfiable by the parallel composition of any two components that satisfy $\mathcal{S}_\mathcal{P}$ and $\mathcal{S}_\mathcal{Q}$. The specification only guarantees what can be assured by both $\mathcal{S}_\mathcal{P}$ and $\mathcal{S}_\mathcal{Q}$, thus it is the strongest composition. The assumption is the largest collection of environmental behaviours that cannot violate either of the guarantees $\mathcal{G}_{\mathcal{S}_\mathcal{P}}$ or $\mathcal{G}_{\mathcal{S}_\mathcal{Q}}$, and moreover does not permit a component implementing one of the specifications to violate the other specification's assumption. Ignoring differences in alphabets, this can loosely be phrased as $\mathcal{R}_{\mathcal{S}_\mathcal{P} || \mathcal{S}_\mathcal{Q}} \cap \mathcal{G}_{\mathcal{S}_\mathcal{P}} \subseteq \mathcal{R}_{\mathcal{S}_\mathcal{Q}}$ and $\mathcal{R}_{\mathcal{S}_\mathcal{P} || \mathcal{S}_\mathcal{Q}} \cap \mathcal{G}_{\mathcal{S}_\mathcal{Q}} \subseteq \mathcal{R}_{\mathcal{S}_\mathcal{P}}$, which is akin to the presentation in [7]. However, as implementations are not required to be input-enabled, this must be reformulated as $\mathcal{R}_{\mathcal{S}_\mathcal{P} || \mathcal{S}_\mathcal{Q}} \cap \mathcal{G}^+(\mathcal{S}_\mathcal{P}, \mathcal{S}_\mathcal{Q}) \subseteq \mathcal{R}(\mathcal{S}_\mathcal{P}, \mathcal{S}_\mathcal{Q})$.

The set $\mathcal{G}^+(\mathcal{S}_\mathcal{P}, \mathcal{S}_\mathcal{Q})$ extends $\mathcal{G}(\mathcal{S}_\mathcal{P}, \mathcal{S}_\mathcal{Q})$ by a single input on each of $\mathcal{G}_{\mathcal{S}_\mathcal{P}}$ and $\mathcal{G}_{\mathcal{S}_\mathcal{Q}}$, and also includes ϵ. This has the effect of ensuring that, if $t \in \mathcal{G}^+(\mathcal{S}_\mathcal{P}, \mathcal{S}_\mathcal{Q}) \cap \mathcal{R}(\mathcal{S}_\mathcal{P}, \mathcal{S}_\mathcal{Q})$ and $ta \notin \mathcal{G}^+(\mathcal{S}_\mathcal{P}, \mathcal{S}_\mathcal{Q})$, then whatever the action type of a, wlog $t \upharpoonright \mathcal{A}_{\mathcal{S}_\mathcal{P}} \in \mathcal{R}_{\mathcal{S}_\mathcal{P}} \cap \mathcal{G}_{\mathcal{S}_\mathcal{P}}$ or $ta \upharpoonright \mathcal{A}_{\mathcal{S}_\mathcal{P}} \in \mathcal{R}_{\mathcal{S}_\mathcal{P}} \cap \overline{\mathcal{G}_{\mathcal{S}_\mathcal{P}}}$. Thus, any implementation of $\mathcal{S}_\mathcal{P}$ must have suppressed an output at some stage along the trace $ta \upharpoonright \mathcal{A}_{\mathcal{S}_\mathcal{P}}$, implying the parallel composition of any two implementations of $\mathcal{S}_\mathcal{P}$ and $\mathcal{S}_\mathcal{Q}$ will suppress an output along ta. Thus, $\mathcal{R}_{\mathcal{S}_\mathcal{P} || \mathcal{S}_\mathcal{Q}}$ contains only traces within $\mathcal{G}_{\mathcal{S}_\mathcal{P} || \mathcal{S}_\mathcal{Q}}$ and traces not reachable by any pair of implementations of $\mathcal{S}_\mathcal{P}$ and $\mathcal{S}_\mathcal{Q}$.

Subject to suitable constraints on the alphabets of AG specifications, it can be shown that the parallel composition operator on AG specifications is compositional under the AG refinement relation, as the following theorem demonstrates.

Theorem 1. *Let $S_{\mathcal{P}}$, $S'_{\mathcal{P}}$, $S_{\mathcal{Q}}$ and $S'_{\mathcal{Q}}$ be AG specifications such that $\mathcal{A}^O_{S_{\mathcal{P}}} \cap \mathcal{A}^O_{S_{\mathcal{Q}}} = \emptyset$, $S'_{\mathcal{P}} \parallel S'_{\mathcal{Q}} \sim S_{\mathcal{P}} \parallel S_{\mathcal{Q}}$, $\mathcal{A}^I_{S'_{\mathcal{P}}} \cap \mathcal{A}^O_{S'_{\mathcal{Q}}} \subseteq \mathcal{A}^I_{S_{\mathcal{P}}} \cap \mathcal{A}^O_{S_{\mathcal{Q}}}$, $\mathcal{A}^O_{S'_{\mathcal{P}}} \cap \mathcal{A}^I_{S'_{\mathcal{Q}}} \subseteq \mathcal{A}^O_{S_{\mathcal{P}}} \cap \mathcal{A}^I_{S_{\mathcal{Q}}}$ and $\mathcal{A}^I_{S'_{\mathcal{P}}} \cap \mathcal{A}^I_{S'_{\mathcal{Q}}} \cap \mathcal{A}^I_{S_{\mathcal{P}} \parallel S_{\mathcal{Q}}} \subseteq \mathcal{A}^I_{S_{\mathcal{P}}} \cap \mathcal{A}^I_{S_{\mathcal{Q}}}$. If $S'_{\mathcal{P}} \sqsubseteq S_{\mathcal{P}}$ and $S'_{\mathcal{Q}} \sqsubseteq S_{\mathcal{Q}}$, then $S'_{\mathcal{P}} \parallel S'_{\mathcal{Q}} \sqsubseteq S_{\mathcal{P}} \parallel S_{\mathcal{Q}}$.*

The condition $\mathcal{A}^O_{S_{\mathcal{P}}} \cap \mathcal{A}^O_{S_{\mathcal{Q}}} = \emptyset$ ensures that the parallel composition of the AG specifications is defined, while $S'_{\mathcal{P}} \parallel S'_{\mathcal{Q}} \sim S_{\mathcal{P}} \parallel S_{\mathcal{Q}}$ means $S'_{\mathcal{P}} \parallel S'_{\mathcal{Q}}$ and $S_{\mathcal{P}} \parallel S_{\mathcal{Q}}$ are comparable under refinement. The remaining three conditions are standard for compositionality of parallel composition. From this compositionality result, it is easy to give a sound and complete AG rule.

Theorem 2. *Let $\mathcal{P}$ and $\mathcal{Q}$ be components, and let $S_{\mathcal{P}}$, $S_{\mathcal{Q}}$ and S be AG specifications such that $\mathcal{P} \parallel \mathcal{Q} \sim S$, $\mathcal{A}^I_{\mathcal{P}} \cap \mathcal{A}^O_{\mathcal{Q}} \subseteq \mathcal{A}^I_{S_{\mathcal{P}}} \cap \mathcal{A}^O_{S_{\mathcal{Q}}}$, $\mathcal{A}^O_{\mathcal{P}} \cap \mathcal{A}^I_{\mathcal{Q}} \subseteq \mathcal{A}^O_{S_{\mathcal{P}}} \cap \mathcal{A}^I_{S_{\mathcal{Q}}}$ and $\mathcal{A}^I_{\mathcal{P}} \cap \mathcal{A}^I_{\mathcal{Q}} \cap \mathcal{A}^I_{S_{\mathcal{P}} \parallel S_{\mathcal{Q}}} \subseteq \mathcal{A}^I_{S_{\mathcal{P}}} \cap \mathcal{A}^I_{S_{\mathcal{Q}}}$. Then the following AG rule is both sound and complete:*

$$\text{PARALLEL} \frac{\mathcal{P} \models S_{\mathcal{P}} \qquad \mathcal{Q} \models S_{\mathcal{Q}} \qquad S_{\mathcal{P}} \parallel S_{\mathcal{Q}} \sqsubseteq S}{\mathcal{P} \parallel \mathcal{Q} \models S}.$$

3.5 Conjunction

In this section we define a conjunctive operator on AG specifications for combining independently developed requirements. From this we show that the operator is both compositional and corresponds to the meet operation on the refinement relation. This allows us to formulate a sound and complete AG rule.

The conjunction of AG specifications $S_{\mathcal{P}}$ and $S_{\mathcal{Q}}$ is only defined when $\mathcal{A}^I_{S_{\mathcal{P}}} \cup \mathcal{A}^I_{S_{\mathcal{Q}}}$ is disjoint from $\mathcal{A}^O_{S_{\mathcal{P}}} \cup \mathcal{A}^O_{S_{\mathcal{Q}}}$, in which case we say $S_{\mathcal{P}}$ and $S_{\mathcal{Q}}$ are composable. The composability constraint is necessary, as otherwise it is not possible to find an interface that can refine both $S_{\mathcal{P}}$ and $S_{\mathcal{Q}}$.

Definition 13. *Let $S_{\mathcal{P}}$ and $S_{\mathcal{Q}}$ be AG specifications composable for conjunction. Then $S_{\mathcal{P}} \wedge S_{\mathcal{Q}}$ is an AG specification $\langle \mathcal{A}^I_{S_{\mathcal{P}} \wedge S_{\mathcal{Q}}}, \mathcal{A}^O_{S_{\mathcal{P}} \wedge S_{\mathcal{Q}}}, \mathcal{R}_{S_{\mathcal{P}} \wedge S_{\mathcal{Q}}}, \mathcal{G}_{S_{\mathcal{P}} \wedge S_{\mathcal{Q}}} \rangle$ defined by:*

- $\mathcal{A}^I_{S_{\mathcal{P}} \wedge S_{\mathcal{Q}}} = \mathcal{A}^I_{S_{\mathcal{P}}} \cup \mathcal{A}^I_{S_{\mathcal{Q}}}$
- $\mathcal{A}^O_{S_{\mathcal{P}} \wedge S_{\mathcal{Q}}} = \mathcal{A}^O_{S_{\mathcal{P}}} \cap \mathcal{A}^O_{S_{\mathcal{Q}}}$
- $\mathcal{R}_{S_{\mathcal{P}} \wedge S_{\mathcal{Q}}} = (\mathcal{R}_{S_{\mathcal{P}}} \cup \mathcal{R}_{S_{\mathcal{Q}}}) \cap \mathcal{A}^*_{S_{\mathcal{P}} \wedge S_{\mathcal{Q}}}$
- $\mathcal{G}_{S_{\mathcal{P}} \wedge S_{\mathcal{Q}}}$ *is the intersection of the following sets:*
  - $\mathcal{R}_{S_{\mathcal{P}} \wedge S_{\mathcal{Q}}} \cap (\mathcal{G}_{S_{\mathcal{P}}} \cup \mathcal{G}_{S_{\mathcal{Q}}})$
  - $\text{pre}(\overline{\mathcal{R}_{S_{\mathcal{P}}}} \cup \mathcal{G}_{S_{\mathcal{P}}}) \uparrow_\epsilon (\mathcal{A}^I_{S_{\mathcal{Q}}} \setminus \mathcal{A}^I_{S_{\mathcal{P}}})$
  - $\text{pre}(\overline{\mathcal{R}_{S_{\mathcal{Q}}}} \cup \mathcal{G}_{S_{\mathcal{Q}}}) \uparrow_\epsilon (\mathcal{A}^I_{S_{\mathcal{P}}} \setminus \mathcal{A}^I_{S_{\mathcal{Q}}}).$

The assumption $\mathcal{R}_{\mathcal{S_P} \wedge \mathcal{S_Q}}$ is constrained to be within at least one of $\mathcal{R}_{\mathcal{S_P}}$ or $\mathcal{R}_{\mathcal{S_Q}}$. On the other hand, the guarantee $\mathcal{G}_{\mathcal{S_P} \wedge \mathcal{S_Q}}$ must be within at least one of $\mathcal{G}_{\mathcal{S_P}}$ or $\mathcal{G}_{\mathcal{S_Q}}$, and must ensure that, if the assumption for one of the specifications is satisfied, then the corresponding guarantee cannot have been violated.

The next two theorems show that our definition of conjunction corresponds to the meet operator on the refinement relation, and is compositional under refinement. Consequently, the set of implementations for $\mathcal{S_P} \wedge \mathcal{S_Q}$ is the intersection of the implementation sets for $\mathcal{S_P}$ and $\mathcal{S_Q}$.

Theorem 3. *Let $\mathcal{S_P}$ and $\mathcal{S_Q}$ be AG specifications such that $\mathcal{S_P}$ and $\mathcal{S_Q}$ are composable for conjunction. Then:*

- $\mathcal{S_P} \wedge \mathcal{S_Q} \sqsubseteq \mathcal{S_P}$
- $\mathcal{S_P} \wedge \mathcal{S_Q} \sqsubseteq \mathcal{S_Q}$
- $\mathcal{S_R} \sqsubseteq \mathcal{S_P}$ and $\mathcal{S_R} \sqsubseteq \mathcal{S_Q}$ implies $\mathcal{S_R} \sqsubseteq \mathcal{S_P} \wedge \mathcal{S_Q}$.

Theorem 4. *Let $\mathcal{S_P}$, $\mathcal{S_Q}$, $\mathcal{S'_P}$ and $\mathcal{S'_Q}$ be AG specifications such that $\mathcal{S'_P}$ and $\mathcal{S'_Q}$ are composable for conjunction, $\mathcal{S'_P} \sim \mathcal{S_Q}$ and $\mathcal{S'_Q} \sim \mathcal{S_P}$. If $\mathcal{S'_P} \sqsubseteq \mathcal{S_P}$ and $\mathcal{S'_Q} \sqsubseteq \mathcal{S_Q}$, then $\mathcal{S'_P} \wedge \mathcal{S'_Q} \sqsubseteq \mathcal{S_P} \wedge \mathcal{S_Q}$.*

From these strong algebraic properties, we can formulate an AG rule for conjunction that is both sound and complete.

Theorem 5. *Let $\mathcal{P}$ and $\mathcal{Q}$ be components composable for conjunction, and let $\mathcal{S_P}$ and $\mathcal{S_Q}$ be AG specifications such that $\mathcal{P} \sim \mathcal{S_Q}$, $\mathcal{Q} \sim \mathcal{S_P}$ and $\mathcal{P} \wedge \mathcal{Q} \sim \mathcal{S}$. Then the following AG rule is both sound and complete:*

$$\text{CONJUNCTION} \frac{\mathcal{P} \models \mathcal{S_P} \qquad \mathcal{Q} \models \mathcal{S_Q} \qquad \mathcal{S_P} \wedge \mathcal{S_Q} \sqsubseteq \mathcal{S}}{\mathcal{P} \wedge \mathcal{Q} \models \mathcal{S}}.$$

3.6 Quotient

The AG rule for parallel composition in Theorem 2 makes use of the composition $\mathcal{S_P} \parallel \mathcal{S_Q}$. To support incremental development, we need a way of decomposing the composition to find $\mathcal{S_Q}$ given $\mathcal{S_P}$. We can do this using a quotient operator.

Definition 14. *Let $\mathcal{S_P}$ and $\mathcal{S_W}$ be AG specifications. Then the quotient $\mathcal{S_W}/\mathcal{S_P}$ is an AG specification $\langle A^I_{\mathcal{S_W}/\mathcal{S_P}}, A^O_{\mathcal{S_W}/\mathcal{S_P}}, \mathcal{R}_{\mathcal{S_W}/\mathcal{S_P}}, \mathcal{G}_{\mathcal{S_W}/\mathcal{S_P}} \rangle$, defined only when $A^O_{\mathcal{S_P}} \subseteq A^O_{\mathcal{S_W}}$, where $A^I_{\mathcal{S_W}/\mathcal{S_P}} = A^I_{\mathcal{S_W}} \setminus A^I_{\mathcal{S_P}}$, $A^O_{\mathcal{S_W}/\mathcal{S_P}} = A^O_{\mathcal{S_W}} \setminus A^O_{\mathcal{S_P}}$ and:*

- *If $\mathcal{S_P}$ is implementable, and $\epsilon \in \mathcal{R}_{\mathcal{S_W}}$ implies $\epsilon \in \mathcal{R}_{\mathcal{S_P}}$, then:*
  - $\mathcal{R}_{\mathcal{S_W}/\mathcal{S_P}} = [\mathcal{R}_{\mathcal{S_W}} \cap (\mathcal{G}_{\mathcal{S_P}} \Uparrow A_{\mathcal{S_W}})(A^O_{\mathcal{S_W}})^*] \upharpoonright A_{\mathcal{S_W}/\mathcal{S_P}}$
  - $\mathcal{G}_{\mathcal{S_W}/\mathcal{S_P}} = \mathcal{R}_{\mathcal{S_W}/\mathcal{S_P}} \cap (X \upharpoonright A_{\mathcal{S_W}/\mathcal{S_P}})$, *where X is the largest prefix closed set satisfying* $X(A^I_{\mathcal{S_P}})^* \cap \mathcal{R}_{\mathcal{S_W}} \subseteq \mathsf{pre}(\mathcal{G}_{\mathcal{S_W}} \cup \overline{\mathcal{G}_{\mathcal{S_P}}} \Uparrow A_{\mathcal{S_W}}) \cap$
    $\mathsf{pre}((\mathcal{R}_{\mathcal{S_P}}) \Uparrow A_{\mathcal{S_W}}) \cup \overline{\mathcal{G}_{\mathcal{S_P}}} \Uparrow A_{\mathcal{S_W}})$.
- *If $\mathcal{S_P}$ is implementable and $\epsilon \in \mathcal{R}_{\mathcal{S_W}} \cap \overline{\mathcal{R}_{\mathcal{S_P}}}$, then $\mathcal{R}_{\mathcal{S_W}/\mathcal{S_P}} = A^*_{\mathcal{S_W}/\mathcal{S_P}}$ and $\mathcal{G}_{\mathcal{S_W}/\mathcal{S_P}} = \emptyset$.*
- *If $\mathcal{S_P}$ is non-implementable, then $\mathcal{R}_{\mathcal{S_W}/\mathcal{S_P}} = \mathcal{G}_{\mathcal{S_W}/\mathcal{S_P}} = \emptyset$.*

Although not immediately obvious, the assumption in the previous definition is closed under output-extensions. Before explaining the definition, we introduce the following theorem, which shows that the quotient operator on AG specifications yields the weakest decomposition of the parallel composition.

Theorem 6. *Let $\mathcal{S}_\mathcal{P}$ and $\mathcal{S}_\mathcal{W}$ be AG specifications. Then there exists an AG specification $\mathcal{S}_\mathcal{Q}$ such that $\mathcal{S}_\mathcal{P} \parallel \mathcal{S}_\mathcal{Q} \sqsubseteq \mathcal{S}_\mathcal{W}$ iff the following properties hold:*

- *The quotient $\mathcal{S}_\mathcal{W}/\mathcal{S}_\mathcal{P}$ is defined*
- $\mathcal{S}_\mathcal{P} \parallel (\mathcal{S}_\mathcal{W}/\mathcal{S}_\mathcal{P}) \sqsubseteq \mathcal{S}_\mathcal{W}$
- $\mathcal{S}_\mathcal{Q} \sqsubseteq \mathcal{S}_\mathcal{W}/\mathcal{S}_\mathcal{P}.$

To make sense of the definition for quotient (in the difficult case of $\mathcal{S}_\mathcal{P}$ being implementable and $\epsilon \in \mathcal{R}_{\mathcal{S}_\mathcal{W}}$ implies $\epsilon \in \mathcal{R}_{\mathcal{S}_\mathcal{P}}$), it is necessary to consider the final two results in Theorem 6. For these, we need to show that: (i) $\mathcal{R}_{\mathcal{S}_\mathcal{W}} \subseteq \mathcal{R}_{\mathcal{S}_\mathcal{P} \parallel (\mathcal{S}_\mathcal{W}/\mathcal{S}_\mathcal{P})}$; and (ii) $\mathcal{R}_{\mathcal{S}_\mathcal{W}} \cap \overline{\mathcal{G}_{\mathcal{S}_\mathcal{W}}} \subseteq$ violations$(\mathcal{S}_\mathcal{P} \parallel (\mathcal{S}_\mathcal{W}/\mathcal{S}_\mathcal{P}))$. Clause (i) amounts to showing $\mathcal{R}_{\mathcal{S}_\mathcal{W}} \cap \mathcal{G}^+(\mathcal{S}_\mathcal{P}, \mathcal{S}_\mathcal{W}/\mathcal{S}_\mathcal{P}) \subseteq \mathcal{R}(\mathcal{S}_\mathcal{P}, \mathcal{S}_\mathcal{W}/\mathcal{S}_\mathcal{P})$, i.e., the condition for parallel composition. Thus, the assumption $\mathcal{R}_{\mathcal{S}_\mathcal{W}/\mathcal{S}_\mathcal{P}}$ is the smallest output-closed set such that $t \in \mathcal{R}_{\mathcal{S}_\mathcal{W}}$ and $t \in \mathcal{G}_{\mathcal{S}_\mathcal{P}} \Uparrow \mathcal{A}_{\mathcal{S}_\mathcal{W}}$ implies $t \in \mathcal{R}_{\mathcal{S}_\mathcal{W}/\mathcal{S}_\mathcal{P}} \Uparrow \mathcal{A}_{\mathcal{S}_\mathcal{W}}$. The cases of $t \notin \mathcal{R}_{\mathcal{S}_\mathcal{P}} \Uparrow \mathcal{A}_{\mathcal{S}_\mathcal{W}}$ or $t \notin \mathcal{G}_{\mathcal{S}_\mathcal{W}/\mathcal{S}_\mathcal{P}} \Uparrow \mathcal{A}_{\mathcal{S}_\mathcal{W}}$ are handled by $\mathcal{G}_{\mathcal{S}_\mathcal{W}/\mathcal{S}_\mathcal{P}}$.

Considering the guarantee $\mathcal{G}_{\mathcal{S}_\mathcal{W}/\mathcal{S}_\mathcal{P}}$, it is obvious that it need only be contained within the assumption $\mathcal{R}_{\mathcal{S}_\mathcal{W}/\mathcal{S}_\mathcal{P}}$. Moreover, it is safe to have $t \in \mathcal{G}_{\mathcal{S}_\mathcal{W}/\mathcal{S}_\mathcal{P}} \Uparrow \mathcal{A}_{\mathcal{S}_\mathcal{W}}$ if $t \notin \mathcal{G}_{\mathcal{S}_\mathcal{P}} \Uparrow \mathcal{A}_{\mathcal{S}_\mathcal{W}}$ or $t \in \mathcal{R}_{\mathcal{S}_\mathcal{P}} \Uparrow_{\mathcal{A}_{\mathcal{S}_\mathcal{P}}} \mathcal{A}_{\mathcal{S}_\mathcal{W}}$; this is equivalent to requiring $t \in \mathsf{pre}((\mathcal{R}_{\mathcal{S}_\mathcal{P}} \Uparrow \mathcal{A}_{\mathcal{S}_\mathcal{W}}) \cup \overline{\mathcal{G}_{\mathcal{S}_\mathcal{P}} \Uparrow \mathcal{A}_{\mathcal{S}_\mathcal{W}}})$. For requirement (ii), if $t \in \mathcal{G}_{\mathcal{S}_\mathcal{W}/\mathcal{S}_\mathcal{P}} \Uparrow \mathcal{A}_{\mathcal{S}_\mathcal{W}}$, then it must be the case that $t \notin \mathcal{G}_{\mathcal{S}_\mathcal{W}}$ implies $t \notin \mathcal{G}_{\mathcal{S}_\mathcal{P}} \Uparrow \mathcal{A}_{\mathcal{S}_\mathcal{W}}$. This is equivalent to requiring $t \in \mathsf{pre}(\mathcal{G}_{\mathcal{S}_\mathcal{W}} \cup \overline{\mathcal{G}_{\mathcal{S}_\mathcal{P}} \Uparrow \mathcal{A}_{\mathcal{S}_\mathcal{W}}})$. Piecing these conditions together yields a definition of quotient that is correct by construction.

Theorem 7. *Let $\mathcal{S}_\mathcal{P}$ and $\mathcal{S}_\mathcal{W}$ be AG specifications such that $\mathcal{P}$ ranges over components having the same interface as $\mathcal{S}_\mathcal{P}$, and $\mathcal{Q}$ is a component having the same interface as $\mathcal{S}_\mathcal{W}/\mathcal{S}_\mathcal{P}$. If $\mathcal{S}_\mathcal{W}/\mathcal{S}_\mathcal{P}$ is defined (i.e., $\mathcal{A}^\mathcal{O}_{\mathcal{S}_\mathcal{P}} \subseteq \mathcal{A}^\mathcal{O}_{\mathcal{S}_\mathcal{W}}$), then the following AG rule is sound and complete:*

$$\text{QUOTIENT} \frac{\forall \mathcal{P} \cdot \mathcal{P} \models \mathcal{S}_\mathcal{P} \text{ implies } \mathcal{P} \parallel \mathcal{Q} \models \mathcal{S}_\mathcal{W}}{\mathcal{Q} \models \mathcal{S}_\mathcal{W}/\mathcal{S}_\mathcal{P}}.$$

The restriction on $\mathcal{P}$ and $\mathcal{S}_\mathcal{P}$ having the same interface, and $\mathcal{Q}$ and $\mathcal{S}_\mathcal{W}/\mathcal{S}_\mathcal{P}$ having the same interface, is necessary, because the parallel operator is only compositional under certain restrictions on the interfaces (cf Theorem 1).

3.7 Decomposing Parallel Composition

The following corollary shows how we can revise the AG rule for parallel composition so that it makes use of quotient on AG specifications when we know the global specification $\mathcal{S}$. This is useful for system development, as we will often have the specification of a global system, rather than the specifications of the systems to be composed.

Corollary 1. *Let $\mathcal{P}$ and $\mathcal{Q}$ be components such that $\mathcal{A}_\mathcal{P}^I \cap \mathcal{A}_\mathcal{Q}^I = \emptyset$, and let $\mathcal{S}_\mathcal{P}$, $\mathcal{S}_\mathcal{Q}$ and $\mathcal{S}$ be AG specifications. If $\mathcal{A}_{\mathcal{S}_\mathcal{P}}^O \cap \mathcal{A}_{\mathcal{S}_\mathcal{Q}}^O = \emptyset$, $\mathcal{P} \parallel \mathcal{Q} \sim \mathcal{S}$, $\mathcal{A}_\mathcal{P}^I \cap \mathcal{A}_\mathcal{Q}^O \subseteq \mathcal{A}_{\mathcal{S}_\mathcal{P}}^I \cap \mathcal{A}_{\mathcal{S}_\mathcal{Q}}^O$ and $\mathcal{A}_\mathcal{P}^O \cap \mathcal{A}_\mathcal{Q}^I \subseteq \mathcal{A}_{\mathcal{S}_\mathcal{P}}^O \cap \mathcal{A}_{\mathcal{S}_\mathcal{Q}}^I$, then the following rule is both sound and complete:*

$$\text{PARALLEL-DECOMPOSE} \frac{\mathcal{P} \models \mathcal{S}_\mathcal{P} \qquad \mathcal{Q} \models \mathcal{S}_\mathcal{Q} \qquad \mathcal{S}_\mathcal{Q} \sqsubseteq \mathcal{S}/\mathcal{S}_\mathcal{P}}{\mathcal{P} \parallel \mathcal{Q} \models \mathcal{S}}.$$

This rule, based on Theorem 2, differs in having the premise $\mathcal{S}_\mathcal{Q} \sqsubseteq \mathcal{S}/\mathcal{S}_\mathcal{P}$ in place of $\mathcal{S}_\mathcal{P} \parallel \mathcal{S}_\mathcal{Q} \sqsubseteq \mathcal{S}$. This substitution is permitted by the results of Theorem 6. The condition $\mathcal{A}_\mathcal{P}^I \cap \mathcal{A}_\mathcal{Q}^I = \emptyset$ is necessary in order to show that $\mathcal{S}_\mathcal{P} \parallel \mathcal{S}_\mathcal{Q} \sqsubseteq \mathcal{S}_\mathcal{P} \parallel (\mathcal{S}/\mathcal{S}_\mathcal{P})$, given the constraints on parallel compositionality, and the fact that $\mathcal{A}_{\mathcal{S}_\mathcal{P}}^I$ and $\mathcal{A}_{\mathcal{S}/\mathcal{S}_\mathcal{P}}^I$ are always disjoint.

4   A Printing Example

We illustrate our assume-guarantee framework on a simple example of component-based design for a system concerned with printing a document. The system as a whole is composed of a job scheduler, a printer controller and the physical printer itself. Intuitively, the scheduler decides when a print job can *start*, and expects to be informed when the job has *finished*. The controller, on the other hand, waits for the *start* signal from the scheduler, after which it instructs the printer to *print* the document, and awaits confirmation from the printer that the document has *printed*. At this stage, the controller will signal to the scheduler that the job has *finished*. The printer accepts a *print* command, after which it will start to print the document, and will signify when the document is *printed*.

We iteratively derive a design by successively applying AG rules and constructions. We start by making use of two specifications for the combined effect of the scheduler and printer controller:

1. Spec1: If the number of jobs sent to *print* is equal to or one greater than the number of jobs *printed*, then the number of job *starts* must be equal to or one greater than the number of requests sent to *print*.
2. Spec2: If the number of jobs sent to *print* is equal to or one greater than the number of jobs *printed*, then the number of *printed* documents must be equal to or one greater than the number of jobs *finished*.

Spec1 and Spec2 can be represented by the AG specifications $\langle \mathcal{R}_{\text{Spec}}, \mathcal{G}_{\text{Spec1}} \rangle$ and $\langle \mathcal{R}_{\text{Spec}}, \mathcal{G}_{\text{Spec2}} \rangle$ respectively, where the assumptions and guarantees are depicted in Figure 1. For simplicity, we represent sets of traces by means of finite automata, and annotate states with an F to indicate that a trace becomes inconsistent. The combined effect of Spec1 and Spec2 is given by the conjunctive specification Spec1 $\wedge$ Spec2 $= \langle \mathcal{R}_{\text{Spec}}, \mathcal{G}_{\text{Spec1} \wedge \text{Spec2}} \rangle$, the guarantee of which is presented in Figure 2.

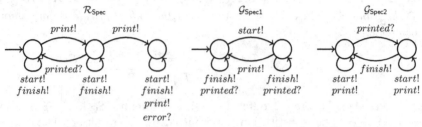

Fig. 1. Assumption and guarantees for Spec1 and Spec2

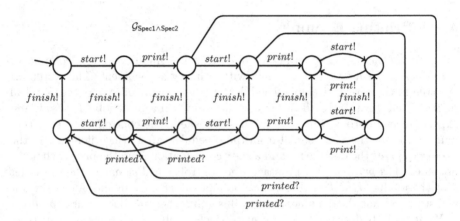

Fig. 2. The guarantee for Spec1 ∧ Spec2

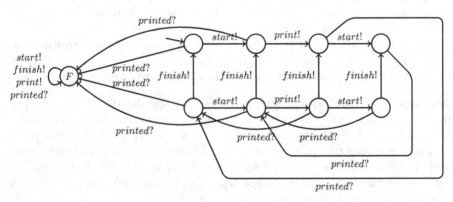

Fig. 3. The most general implementation of Spec1 ∧ Spec2

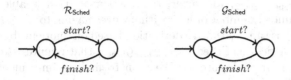

Fig. 4. Specification of a scheduling constraint Sched

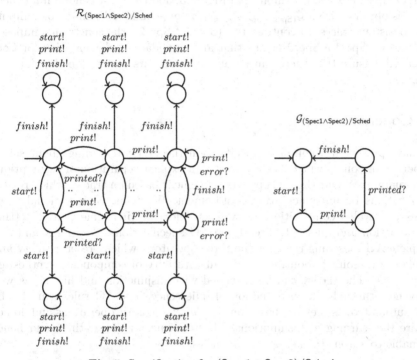

Fig. 5. Specification for (Spec1 ∧ Spec2)/Sched

To demonstrate compositional AG reasoning, by Definition 10 we can find implementations $\mathcal{I}(\mathsf{Spec1})$ and $\mathcal{I}(\mathsf{Spec2})$ of Spec1 and Spec2 respectively, which by Theorem 5 allows us to derive $\mathcal{I}(\mathsf{Spec1}) \wedge \mathcal{I}(\mathsf{Spec2}) \models \mathsf{Spec1} \wedge \mathsf{Spec2}$. According to Lemma 4, this means that $\mathcal{I}(\mathsf{Spec1}) \wedge \mathcal{I}(\mathsf{Spec2}) \sqsubseteq_{imp} \mathcal{I}(\mathsf{Spec1} \wedge \mathsf{Spec2})$. Now by Theorem 3, we know $\mathsf{Spec1} \wedge \mathsf{Spec2} \sqsubseteq \mathsf{Spec1}$, so from Lemma 2 we obtain $\mathcal{I}(\mathsf{Spec1} \wedge \mathsf{Spec2}) \models \mathsf{Spec1}$, and from Lemma 4 we derive $\mathcal{I}(\mathsf{Spec1} \wedge \mathsf{Spec2}) \sqsubseteq_{imp} \mathcal{I}(\mathsf{Spec1})$. By similar reasoning it can be shown that $\mathcal{I}(\mathsf{Spec1} \wedge \mathsf{Spec2}) \sqsubseteq_{imp} \mathcal{I}(\mathsf{Spec2})$, hence by Theorem 2 of [4] we acquire $\mathcal{I}(\mathsf{Spec1} \wedge \mathsf{Spec2}) \sqsubseteq_{imp} \mathcal{I}(\mathsf{Spec1}) \wedge \mathcal{I}(\mathsf{Spec2})$. Mutual refinement of components in our framework corresponds to equality of models, so $\mathcal{I}(\mathsf{Spec1} \wedge \mathsf{Spec2}) = \mathcal{I}(\mathsf{Spec1}) \wedge \mathcal{I}(\mathsf{Spec2})$. Such an implementation is shown in Figure 3. Note how this component is unwilling to *print* after encountering two *start* requests not separated by a job being *printed*. This is because $\mathcal{R}_{\mathsf{Spec}}$ can issue an *error* after such an occurrence, but this is not accepted by $\mathcal{G}_{\mathsf{Spec1} \wedge \mathsf{Spec2}}$. Moreover, this implementation is able to *start* and *print* an unbounded number of jobs without ever having to *finish* one of them.

We now propose an alternative derivation based on quotient, by making use of a constraint specification $\mathsf{Sched} = \langle \mathcal{R}_{\mathsf{Sched}}, \mathcal{G}_{\mathsf{Sched}} \rangle$ that requires *start* and *finish* to alternate (shown in Figure 4). We wish to find an implementation for the printer controller, let it be called Controller, such that Controller is an implementation of Spec1 $\wedge$ Spec2 subject to the constraints imposed by Sched. This is equivalent to requiring Controller $\models$ (Spec1 $\wedge$ Spec2)/Sched. The specification (Spec1 $\wedge$ Spec2)/Sched is exhibited in Figure 5, and the most general implementation is obtained from $\mathcal{G}_{(\mathsf{Spec1} \wedge \mathsf{Spec2})/\mathsf{Sched}}$ by appending all non-enabled inputs as inconsistent traces. In contrast to $\mathcal{I}(\mathsf{Spec1} \wedge \mathsf{Spec2})$, the constraints imposed by Sched on Spec1 $\wedge$ Spec2 means that any candidate implementation for Controller will ensure that there can be at most one outstanding job that has not *finish*ed.

5   Conclusion

We have presented a complete specification theory for reasoning about safety properties of component behaviours with an explicit separation of assumptions from guarantees. Our theory supports refinement based on traces, which relates specifications by implementation containment. We define compositional operations of parallel composition, as well as – for the first time in this setting – conjunction and quotient, directly on AG specifications. We give sound and complete AG reasoning rules for the three operators, which preserve safety and enable the reasoning about, e.g., safe substitutivity of components synthesised at run-time. The theory can be extended with disjunction and hiding, as well as liveness through the introduction of quiescence. The AG rules can also be fully automated, as they are based on simple set-theoretic operations and do not require the learning of assumptions. The refinement is linear-time, and hence amenable to automata-theoretic approaches.

Acknowledgments. The authors are supported by EU FP7 project CONNECT and ERC Advanced Grant VERIWARE.

References

1. Larsen, K.G., Nyman, U., Wąsowski, A.: Modal I/O Automata for Interface and Product Line Theories. In: De Nicola, R. (ed.) ESOP 2007. LNCS, vol. 4421, pp. 64–79. Springer, Heidelberg (2007)
2. Doyen, L., Henzinger, T.A., Jobstmann, B., Petrov, T.: Interface theories with component reuse. In: Proc. 8th ACM International Conference on Embedded Software, EMSOFT 2008, pp. 79–88. ACM (2008)
3. Raclet, J.-B., Badouel, E., Benveniste, A., Caillaud, B., Legay, A., Passerone, R.: A modal interface theory for component-based design. Fundam. Inform. 108, 119–149 (2011)

4. Chen, T., Chilton, C., Jonsson, B., Kwiatkowska, M.: A Compositional Specification Theory for Component Behaviours. In: Seidl, H. (ed.) ESOP 2012. LNCS, vol. 7211, pp. 148–168. Springer, Heidelberg (2012)
5. de Alfaro, L., Henzinger, T.A.: Interface automata. SIGSOFT Softw. Eng. Notes 26, 109–120 (2001)
6. Bhaduri, P., Ramesh, S.: Interface synthesis and protocol conversion. Form. Asp. Comput. 20, 205–224 (2008)
7. Abadi, M., Lamport, L.: Composing specifications. ACM Transactions on Programming Languages and Systems 15, 73–132 (1993)
8. Abadi, M., Plotkin, G.: A logical view of composition. Theoretical Computer Science 114, 3–30 (1993)
9. Pnueli, A.: Logics and models of concurrent systems, pp. 123–144. Springer (1985)
10. Clarke, E., Long, D., McMillan, K.: Compositional model checking. In: Proc. 4th Annual Symposium on Logic in Computer Science, pp. 353–362. IEEE Press (1989)
11. Grumberg, O., Long, D.E.: Model checking and modular verification. ACM Transactions on Programming Languages and Systems 16 (1991)
12. Maier, P.: A Set-Theoretic Framework for Assume-Guarantee Reasoning. In: Orejas, F., Spirakis, P.G., Leeuwen, J. (eds.) ICALP 2001. LNCS, vol. 2076, pp. 821–834. Springer, Heidelberg (2001)
13. Namjoshi, K.S., Trefler, R.J.: On the completeness of compositional reasoning methods. ACM Trans. Comput. Logic 11, 16:1–16:22 (2010)
14. Emmi, M., Giannakopoulou, D., Păsăreanu, C.S.: Assume-Guarantee Verification for Interface Automata. In: Cuellar, J., Maibaum, T., Sere, K. (eds.) FM 2008. LNCS, vol. 5014, pp. 116–131. Springer, Heidelberg (2008)
15. Larsen, K.G., Nyman, U., Wąsowski, A.: Interface Input/Output Automata. In: Misra, J., Nipkow, T., Sekerinski, E. (eds.) FM 2006. LNCS, vol. 4085, pp. 82–97. Springer, Heidelberg (2006)
16. Bauer, S.S., David, A., Hennicker, R., Larsen, K.G., Legay, A., Nyman, U., Wąsowski, A.: Moving from Specifications to Contracts in Component-Based Design. In: de Lara, J., Zisman, A. (eds.) FASE 2012. LNCS, vol. 7212, pp. 43–58. Springer, Heidelberg (2012)
17. Delahaye, B., Caillaud, B., Legay, A.: Probabilistic contracts: a compositional reasoning methodology for the design of systems with stochastic and/or non-deterministic aspects. FMSD 38, 1–32 (2011)
18. Chilton, C., Jonsson, B., Kwiatkowska, M.: Assume-Guarantee Reasoning for Safe Component Behaviours. Technical Report CS-RR-12-07, Department of Computer Science, University of Oxford (2012)
19. Collette, P.: Application of the Composition Principle to Unity-Like Specifications. In: Gaudel, M.-C., Jouannaud, J.-P. (eds.) CAAP 1993, FASE 1993, and TAPSOFT 1993. LNCS, vol. 668, pp. 230–242. Springer, Heidelberg (1993)
20. Abadi, M., Lamport, L.: Conjoining specifications. ACM Transactions on Programming Languages and Systems 17, 507–534 (1995)
21. Jonsson, B., Tsay, Y.K.: Assumption/guarantee specifications in linear-time temporal logic. Theoretical Computer Science 167, 47–72 (1996)

A Petri Net Based Analysis of Deadlocks for Active Objects and Futures*

Frank S. de Boer[1], Mario Bravetti[2], Immo Grabe[1],
Matias Lee[3], Martin Steffen[4], and Gianluigi Zavattaro[3]

[1] CWI, Amsterdam, The Netherlands
[2] University of Bologna, Focus Team INRIA, Italy
[3] University of Córdoba, Argentina
[4] University of Oslo, Norway

Abstract. We give two different notions of deadlock for systems based on active objects and futures. One is based on blocked objects and conforms with the classical definition of deadlock by Coffman, Jr. et al. The other one is an extended notion of deadlock based on blocked processes which is more general than the classical one. We introduce a technique to prove deadlock freedom of systems of active objects. To check deadlock freedom an abstract version of the program is translated into Petri nets. Extended deadlocks, and then also classical deadlock, can be detected via checking reachability of a distinct marking. Absence of deadlocks in the Petri net constitutes deadlock freedom of the concrete system.

1 Introduction

The increasing importance of distributed systems demands flexible communication between distributed components. In programming languages like Erlang [3] and Scala [13] asynchronous method calls by active objects have successfully been introduced to better combine object-orientation with distributed programming, with a looser coupling between a caller and a callee than in the tightly synchronized (remote) method invocation model. In [5] so-called futures are used to manage return values from asynchronous calls. Futures can be accessed by means of either a *get* or a *claim* primitive: the first one blocks the object until the return value is available, while the second one is not blocking as the control is released. The combination of blocking and non-blocking mechanisms to access to futures may give rise to complex deadlock situations which require a rigorous formal analysis. In this paper we give two different notions of deadlock for systems based on active objects and futures. One is based on blocked objects and conforms with the classical definition of deadlock by Coffman, Jr. et al [8]. The other one is an extended notion of deadlock based on blocked processes which is

---

* Part of this work has been supported by the EU-project FP7-231620 HATS (Highly Adaptable and Trustworthy Software using Formal Methods), Eramus Mundus Action 2 Lot 13A EU Mobility Programme 2010-2401/001-001-EMA2 and EU 7FP grant agreement 295261 (MEALS).

C.S. Păsăreanu and G. Salaün (Eds.): FACS 2012, LNCS 7684, pp. 110–127, 2013.
© Springer-Verlag Berlin Heidelberg 2013

more general than the classical one. We introduce a technique to prove deadlock freedom of models of active objects by a translation of an abstraction of the model into Petri nets. Extended deadlocks, and then also classical deadlock, can be detected via checking reachability of a distinct marking. Absence of deadlocks in the Petri net constitutes deadlock freedom of the concrete system.

The formally defined language that we consider is Creol [15] (Concurrent Reflective Object-oriented Language). It is an object oriented modeling language designed for specifying distributed systems. A Creol object provides a high-level abstraction of a dedicated processor and thus encapsulates an execution thread. Different objects communicate only by asynchronous method calls, i.e., similar to message passing in Actor models [12]; however in Creol, the caller can poll or wait for return values which are stored in future variables. An initial configuration is started by executing a *run* method (which is not associated to any class). The active objects in the systems communicate by means of method calls. When receiving a method call a new process is created to execute the method. Methods can have processor release points which define interleaving points explicitly. When a process is executing, it is not interrupted until it finishes or reaches a release point. Release points can be conditional: if the guard at a release point evaluates to true, the process keeps the control, otherwise, it releases the processor and becomes disabled as long as the guard is not true. Whenever the processor is free, an enabled process is *nondeterministically* selected for execution, i.e., scheduling is left unspecified in Creol in favor of more abstract modeling.

In order to define an appropriate notion of deadlock for Creol, we start by considering the most popular definition of deadlock that goes back to an example titled *deadly embrace* given by Dijkstra [7] and the formalization and generalization of this example given by Coffman Jr. et al.[8]. Their characterization describes a deadlock as a situation in a program execution where different processes block each other by denial of resources while at the same time requesting resources. Such a deadlock can not be resolved by the program itself and keeps the involved processes from making any progress.

A more general characterization by Holt [14] focuses on the processes and not on the resources. According to Hold a process is deadlocked if it is blocked forever. This characterization subsumes Coffman Jr.'s definition. A process waiting for a resource held by another process in the circle will be blocked forever. In addition to these deadlocks Holt's definition also covers deadlocks due to infinite waiting for messages that do not arrive or conditions, e.g. on the state of an object, that are never fulfilled.

We now explain our notions of deadlock by means of an example. Consider two objects o_1 and o_2 belonging to classes c_1 and c_2, respectively, with c_1 defining methods m_1 and m_3 and c_2 defining method m_2. Such methods, plus the method *run*, are defined as follows:

- $run() ::= o_1.m_1()$
- $m_1() ::= \text{let } x_1 = o_2.m_2() \text{ in get@}(x_1, self); ret$
- $m_2() ::= \text{let } x_2 = o_1.m_3() \text{ in get@}(x_2, self); ret$
- $m_3() ::= ret$

The variables x_1 and x_2 are futures, accessed (in this case) with the blocking *get* statement. This program clearly originates a deadlock because the execution of m_1 blocks the object o_1 and the execution of m_2 blocks the object o_2. In particular, the call to m_3 cannot proceed because the object o_1 is being blocked by m_1 waiting on its *get*. We call *classical* deadlocks these cases in which there are groups of objects such that each object in the group is blocked by a *get* on a future related to a call to another object in the group.

Consider now the case in which the method m_2 is defined as follows:

– $m_2() ::= \text{let}\, x_2 = o_1.m_3()\, \text{in claim@}(x_2, self);\, ret$

In this case, object o_2 is not blocked because m_2 releases the control by performing a *claim* instead of a *get*. Nevertheless, the process executing m_2 will remain blocked forever. We call *extended* deadlock this case of deadlock at the level of processes.

After formalization of the notions of *classical* and *extended* deadlock, we prove that the latter includes the former. Moreover, as our main technical contribution, we show a way for proving extended deadlock freedom. The idea is to consider an abstract semantics of Creol expressed in terms of Petri nets. In order to reduce to Petri nets, we abstract away several details of Creol, in particular, we represent futures as quadruples composed of the invoking object, the invoking method, the invoked object, and the invoked method. For instance, the above future x_1 is abstractly represented by $o_1.m_1@o_2.m_2$.

Due to this abstraction, in the abstract semantics a process could access a wrong future simply because it has the same abstract name. Consider, for instance, the following example:

– $run() ::= o_1.m_1()$
– $m_1() ::= \text{let}\, x_1 = o_2.m_2(1)\, \text{in}$
    $\text{let}\, x_2 = o_2.m_2(2)\, \text{in}$
        $\text{get@}(x_2, self);\, \text{claim@}(x_1, self);\, ret$
– $m_2(x_1) ::= \text{if}\, x_1 = 1\, \text{then}\, ret\, \text{else let}\, x_2 = o_1.m_3()\, \text{in claim@}(x_2, self);\, ret$
– $m_3() ::= ret$

Both the futures x_1 and x_2 will be represented by the same abstract name $o_1.m_1@o_2.m_2$. For this reason, even if this program originates a deadlock when *get* is performed on x_2, according to the abstract semantics the system could not deadlock. In fact, the return value of the first call could unblock the *get* as the two futures have the same name in the abstract semantics. To overcome this limitation, we add in the abstract semantics marked versions of the methods: when a method m is invoked, the abstract semantics nondeterministically selects either the standard version of m or its marked version denoted with $m?$. Both method versions have the same behavior, but the return value will be stored in two futures with two distinct abstract names. For instance, in the example above, if we consider that the first call to m_2 actually activates the standard version m_2 while the second one activates the marked version $m_2?$, there will be no confusion between the two futures as their abstract names will be $o_1.m_1@o_2.m_2$

and $o_1.m_1@o_2.m_2$?, respectively. In this case, the system will deadlock also under the abstract semantics.

To apply this technique internal choice is an obstacle. We explain this with more details in Section 4. To overcome this problem we move all internal choices up front. During the transformation we make a data abstraction, remove superfluous internal steps and duplicated choices from the program to reduce the size of the Petri net. This transformation can add spurious deadlock but it cannot remove them because the new abstract model is an overapproximation of the original system.

The Petri net based abstract semantics allow us to obtain a decidable way for proving extended deadlock freedom. In fact, reachability problems are decidable in Petri nets, and we show how to reduce extended deadlock to a reachability problem in the abstract Petri net semantics.

Outline. In Section 2 we report the definition of Creol. We present the two notions of deadlock in Section 3. In Section 4 we present the translation into Petri nets. In Section 5 we present the main result of the paper: if in the Petri net associated to a program a particular marking cannot be reached then the program is deadlock free, and we show that such reachability problem is decidable for Petri nets. Section 6 concludes the paper.

Extended version of the paper. Due the lack of space, neither the translation to Petri net nor the complete proof of our main result, Theorem 1, is presented in detail in this paper. These ones can be found in [6]

2   A Calculus for Active Objects

In this section we present a calculus with active objects communicating via *futures*, based on *Creol*. The calculus is a slight simplification of the object calculus as given in e.g. [2], and can be seen as an active-object variant of the concurrent object calculus from [11]. Specific to the variant of the language here and the problem of deadlock detection are the following key ingredients of the communication model:

Futures. Futures are a well-known mechanism to hold a "forthcoming" result, calculated in a separate thread. In Creol, the communication model is based on futures for the results of method calls which results in a communication model based of asynchronously communicating active object. In this paper we do not allow references to futures to be passed around, i.e. the futures in this paper are not first-class constructs. This restriction is enforced (easily) by the type system.

Obtaining the Results and Cooperative Scheduling. Method calls are done asynchronously and the caller obtains the result back when needed, querying the future reference. The model here support two variants of that querying operation: the non-blocking claim-statement, which allows reschedule of the querying code in case the result of not yet there, and the blocking

Table 1. Abstract syntax

$$
\begin{array}{lll}
C ::= \mathbf{0} \mid C \parallel C \mid n\langle\!\langle O \rangle\!\rangle \mid n[n, F, L] \mid \underline{n\langle t \rangle} & & \text{component} \\
O ::= F, M & & \text{object} \\
M ::= l = m, \ldots, l = m & & \text{method suite} \\
F ::= l = f, \ldots, l = f & & \text{fields} \\
m ::= \varsigma(n{:}T).\lambda(x{:}T, \ldots, x{:}T).t & & \text{method} \\
f ::= v & & \text{field} \\
t ::= v \mid \mathsf{stop} \mid \mathsf{let}\, x{:}T = e\, \mathsf{in}\, t & & \text{thread} \\
e ::= t \mid \mathsf{if}\, e\, \mathsf{then}\, e\, \mathsf{else}\, e \mid n.l(\vec{v}) \mid v.l \mid v.l := v & & \text{expr.} \\
\quad\ \mid\ \mathsf{claim@}(n, n) \mid \mathsf{get@}(n, n) \mid \underline{\mathsf{get@}n} & & \\
\quad\ \mid\ \mathsf{suspend}(n) \mid \underline{\mathsf{grab}(n)} \mid \underline{\mathsf{release}(n)} & & \\
v ::= x \mid n & & \text{values} \\
L ::= \perp \mid \top & & \text{lock status}
\end{array}
$$

get-statement, which insist on getting the result without a re-scheduling point. In [2], we did not consider the latter as part of the user syntax.

Statically Fixed Number of Objects. In this paper we omit object creation to facilitate the translation to Petri nets.

The type system and properties of the calculus, e.g. subject reduction and absence of (certain) run-time errors, presented in [2] still apply. For brevity we only present explanation for language constructs relevant to the development of deadlocks. Missing details with respect to other language constructs, formalizations and proofs of the mentioned (and further) properties of the calculus can be found in [2].

2.1 Syntax

The abstract syntax is given in Table 1, distinguishing between *user* syntax and *run-time* syntax, the latter underlined. The user syntax contains the phrases in which programs are written; the run-time syntax contains syntactic constituents additionally needed to express the behavior of the executing program in the operational semantics.

The basic syntactic category of names n, represents references to classes, to objects, and to futures/thread identifiers. To facilitate reading, we write o and its syntactic variants for names referring to objects, c for classes, and n for threads/futures, resp. when being unspecific. Technically, the disambiguation between the different roles of the names is done by the type system. x stands for variables, i.e., local variables and formal parameters, but not instance variables. Besides names and variables x, we assume standard data types (such as booleans, integers, etc) and their values without showing them in the syntax of the core calculus. They are unproblematic for the deadlock analysis, which, using data abstraction, concentrates on the analysis of the communication behavior.

A *configuration* C is a collection of classes, objects, and (named) threads, with 0 representing the empty configuration. The sub-entities of a configuration are composed using the parallel-construct $\|$ (which is commutative and associative, as usual). The entities executing in parallel are the named threads $n\langle t\rangle$, where t is the code being executed and n the name of the thread. Threads are identified with futures, and their name is the reference under which the future result value of t will be available. A class $c[\![O]\!]$ carries a name c and defines its methods and fields in O. An object $o[c, F, L]$ with identity o keeps a reference to the class c it instantiates, stores the current value F of its fields, and maintains a *binary lock* L. The symbols $\top$, resp., $\bot$, indicate that the lock is taken, resp., free. The *initial* configuration consists of a number of classes, one initial thread, and a number of objects (with their locks free); under our restriction that we do not allow object instantiation, and we assume that their identities are known to the initial thread. By convention, the initial thread is assumed to be the body of a (unique) method named *run*.

Besides configurations, the grammar specifies the lower level syntactic constructs, in particular, methods, expressions, and (unnamed) threads, which are basically sequences of expressions, written using the let-construct. The stop-construct denotes termination, so the evaluation of a thread terminates by evaluating to a value or terminating with stop. A method $\varsigma(s{:}T).\lambda(\vec{x}{:}\vec{T}).t$ provides the method body t abstracted over the ς-bound "self" parameter s the formal parameters $\vec{x}$ —the ς-binder is borrowed from the well-known object-calculus of Abadi and Cardelli [1]. Note that the methods are stored in the classes but the fields are kept in the objects.

Methods are called asynchronously, i.e., executing $o.l(\vec{v})$ creates a new thread to execute the method body with the formal parameters appropriately replaced by the actual ones; the corresponding thread identity at the same time plays the role of a future reference, used by the caller to obtain, upon need, the eventual result of the method. The further expressions claim, get, suspend, grab, and release deal with communication and synchronization. As mentioned, objects come equipped with binary locks which assures mutual exclusion. The operations for lock acquisition and release (grab and release) are run-time syntax and inserted before and at the end of each method body code when invoking a method. Besides that, lock-handling is involved also when futures are claimed, using claim or get. The get@(n, o) operation is easier: it blocks object o (it executes in) if the result of future n is not (yet) available, i.e., if the thread n is not of the form of $n\langle v\rangle$. The claim@(n, o), is a more "cooperative" version of get: if the value is not yet available, it releases the lock of the object o (it executes in) to try again later, meanwhile giving other threads the chance to execute in that object. By convention, user-syntax commands only refer to the self-parameter *self*, (i.e., the ς-bound variable) in their object-argument, i.e., they are written claim@$(n, self)$, get@$(n, self)$, and suspend$(self)$. We also include a variant get@n of the get-operation as part of the run-time syntax, for consumption of the return value also when a lock is not held (it is needed to define the semantics of claim). As usual we use sequential composition $t_1; t_2$ as syntactic sugar for $\mathsf{let}\,x{:}T = t_1\,\mathsf{in}\,t_2$, when x does not occur free in t_2. We refer to [2] for further details on the language constructs, a type system for the language and a comparison with the multi-threading model of *Java*.

2.2 Operational Semantics

Relevant reduction steps of the operational semantics are shown in Table 2, distinguishing between confluent steps $\rightsquigarrow$ and other transitions $\overset{\tau}{\rightarrow}$. The $\rightsquigarrow$-steps, on the one hand, do not access the instance state of the objects. The $\overset{\tau}{\rightarrow}$-steps, on the other hand, access the instance state, either by reading or by writing it, and may thus lead to race conditions. When not differentiating between the two kinds of transitions, then we replace both symbol by $\rightarrow$. An execution is a sequence of configurations, $C_0, \ldots, C_n$ such that C_{i+1} is obtained from C_i by applying a reduction step. We denote this execution by $C_0 \rightarrow \ldots \rightarrow C_n$.

We omit reduction rules dealing with the basic constructs like substitution, sequential composition (let), conditionals, field access, and lock handling. These rules are straightforward (cf. [2]). For deadlock detection later, most of these constructs will be subject to data abstraction.

Table 2. Operational semantics

$$c[\![(F', M)]\!] \;\|\; o[c, F, L] \;\|\; n_1\langle\mathsf{let}\,x{:}T = o.l(\vec{v})\,\mathsf{in}\,t_1\rangle \overset{\tau}{\rightarrow}$$
$$c[\![(F', M)]\!] \;\|\; o[c, F, L] \;\|\; n_1\langle\mathsf{let}\,x{:}T = n_2\,\mathsf{in}\,t_1\rangle \qquad \textsc{Fut}_i$$
$$\|\; n_2\langle\mathsf{let}\,x{:}T_2 = \mathsf{grab}(o); M.l(o)(\vec{v})\,\mathsf{in}\,\mathsf{release}(o); x\rangle$$

$$n_1\langle v\rangle \;\|\; n_2\langle\mathsf{let}\,x : T = \mathsf{claim@}(n_1, o)\,\mathsf{in}\,t\rangle \rightsquigarrow n_1\langle v\rangle \;\|\; n_2\langle\mathsf{let}\,x : T = v\,\mathsf{in}\,t\rangle \qquad \textsc{Claim}_i^1$$

$$\frac{t_2 \neq v}{n_2\langle t_2\rangle \;\|\; n_1\langle\mathsf{let}\,x : T = \mathsf{claim@}(n_2, o)\,\mathsf{in}\,t_1'\rangle \rightsquigarrow} \qquad \textsc{Claim}_i^2$$
$$n_2\langle t_2\rangle \;\|\; n_1\langle\mathsf{let}\,x : T = \mathsf{release}(o); \mathsf{get@}n_2\,\mathsf{in}\,\mathsf{grab}(o); t_1'\rangle$$

$$n_1\langle v\rangle \;\|\; n_2\langle\mathsf{let}\,x : T = \mathsf{get@}(n_1, o)\,\mathsf{in}\,t\rangle \rightsquigarrow n_1\langle v\rangle \;\|\; n_2\langle\mathsf{let}\,x : T = v\,\mathsf{in}\,t\rangle \qquad \textsc{Get}_i^1$$

$$n_1\langle v\rangle \;\|\; n_2\langle\mathsf{let}\,x : T = \mathsf{get@}n_1\,\mathsf{in}\,t\rangle \rightsquigarrow n_1\langle v\rangle \;\|\; n_2\langle\mathsf{let}\,x : T = v\,\mathsf{in}\,t\rangle \qquad \textsc{Get}_i^2$$

$$n\langle\mathsf{suspend}(o); t\rangle \rightsquigarrow n\langle\mathsf{release}(o); \mathsf{grab}(o); t\rangle \qquad \textsc{Suspend}$$

Invoking a method (cf. rule $\textsc{Fut}_i$) creates a new future reference and a corresponding thread is added to the configuration. In the configuration after the reduction step, the meta-mathematical notation $M.l(o)(\vec{v})$ stands for $t[o/s][\vec{v}/\vec{x}]$, when the method suite $[M]$ equals $[\ldots, l = \varsigma(s{:}T).\lambda(\vec{x}{:}\vec{T}).t, \ldots]$. Upon termination, the result is available via the claim- and the get-syntax (cf. the Claim- and Get-rules), but not before the lock of the object is given back again using $\mathsf{release}(o)$. If the thread is not yet terminated, in the case of claim statement, the requesting thread suspends itself, thereby giving up the lock. The rule Suspend releases the lock to allow for interleaving. To continue, the thread has to reacquire the lock.

The above reduction relations are used modulo structural congruence, which captures the algebraic properties of especially parallel composition.

3   Deadlock

We give two different notions of deadlock in Creol. The first one follows [8]. In this case not only processes are blocked but also the objects hosting them.

The second notion resembles the definition of deadlock by Holt [14]. Instead of looking at blocked objects we look at blocked processes. A blocked process does not necessarily block the object hosting it.

To facilitate the definition of deadlock we introduce two notions of the location and state of a process. The notion of a *waiting* process links a process to another process or to an object. In the first case, it is waiting to read a future that the other process has to calculate. In the second case, the process is waiting to obtain the lock of the object.

Definition 1 (Waiting Process). *A process* $n_1\langle t\rangle$ *is waiting for:*

1. n_2 *iff* $\langle t\rangle$ *is of the form* $\langle \text{let } x{:}T = \text{claim@}(n_2,o) \text{ in } t'\rangle$, $\langle \text{let } x{:}T = \text{get@}(n_2,o) \text{ in } t'\rangle$, *or* $\langle \text{let } x{:}T = \text{get@}n_2 \text{ in } t'\rangle$;
2. o *iff* $\langle t\rangle$ *is of the form* $\langle \text{let } x{:}T = \text{grab}(o) \text{ in } t'\rangle$

The notion of a *blocking* process links a process that is waiting for a future while holding the lock of the object.

Definition 2 (Blocking Process). *A process* $n_1\langle t\rangle$ *blocks object* o *iff* $\langle t\rangle$ *is of the form* $\langle \text{let } x : T = \text{get@}(n_2,o) \text{ in } t'\rangle$.

Note that a process needs to hold the object lock and execute a blocking statement, i.e. get-statement, to block an object. Furthermore note that the process can at most acquire one lock, i.e. the lock of its hosting object.

Our notion of a classical deadlock follows the definition of deadlock by Coffman Jr. et al.[8]. The resource of interest is the exclusive access to an object represented by the object lock. In opposite to the multithreaded setting, e.g. like in Java, where a thread can collect a number of these exclusive right, a process in the active object setting can at most acquire the lock of the object hosting it. But by calling a method on another object and requesting the result of that call it requests access to that object indirectly. Or to be more precise a process can derive the information, that the process created to handle its call and access to the callee, by the availability of the result in terms of the future.

Definition 3 (Classical Deadlock). *A configuration* Θ *is deadlocked iff there exists a set of objects* O *such that, for all* $o \in O$, o *is blocked by a process* n_1 *which is waiting for a process* n_2 *which is waiting for* $o' \in O$.

Note that the definition of "waiting for" plays a crucial role here, because the process is waiting, the process does not finish its computation. Being blocked by a process, another process can only gain access to the object after the blocking process has made progress. Since each process blocking an object in O is waiting for another process blocking an object in O we have a classical deadlock situation. Note that a blocking process does not necessarily directly wait for another blocking process but can also wait for a process which is waiting to get access to an object in O. But this process can only proceed if the process blocking the object proceeds.

The second notion resembles the definition of deadlock by Holt [14]. Instead of looking at blocked objects we look at blocked processes. A process can be blocked due to the execution of either a get–statement or a claim–statement. In the first case the object is blocked via the active process, in the second case only the process is blocked. Processes that are blocked on a claim–statement are not part of a deadlock according to the first definition since they are not holding any resources. Yet they can be part of a circular dependency that prevents them from making any progress.

Definition 4 (Extended Deadlock). *A configuration Θ is deadlocked iff there exists a finite set of processes N such that, for all $n_1 \in N$, n_1 is waiting for $n_2 \in N$, or waiting for o which is blocked by $n_2 \in N$.*

We require the set of processes to be finite in order to guarantee circularity. This notion of deadlock is more general than the classical one.

Corollary 1. *Every classical deadlock is an extended deadlock.*

4   Translation into Petri Nets

We translate Creol programs into Petri nets in such a way that extended deadlocks in a Creol program can be detected by analyzing the reachability of a given class of markings (that we will call *extended deadlock markings*) in the corresponding Petri net.

We first recall the definition of Petri nets. A Petri net is a tuple $\langle P, T, \vec{m_0} \rangle$ such that P is a finite set of places, T is a finite set of transitions, and $\vec{m_0}$ is a marking, i.e. a mapping from P to $\mathbb{N}$ that defines the initial number of tokens in each place of the net. A transition $t \in T$ is defined by a mapping $^\bullet t$ (preset) from P to $\mathbb{N}$, and a mapping $t^\bullet$ (postset). A configuration is a marking $\vec{m}$. Transition t is enabled at marking $\vec{m}$ iff $^\bullet t(p) \leq \vec{m}(p)$ for each $p \in P$. Firing t at $\vec{m}$ leads to a new marking $\vec{m}'$ defined as $\vec{m}'(p) = \vec{m}(p) - {^\bullet t}(p) + t^\bullet(p)$, for every $p \in P$. A marking $\vec{m}$ is reachable from $\vec{m_0}$ if it is possible to produce it after firing finitely many times transitions in T.

During this translation we apply abstraction with respect to the futures. In Creol a fresh unique label is created for each method invocation; instead, we use abstract labels for the futures only identifying a tuple of caller, calling method, callee, and called method. The reason for this abstraction is to get a Petri nets with finite places. Yet we still allow for an unbounded number of method invocations, i.e. an unbounded number of processes.

In the Petri net, we will have two kinds of places: those representing a method code to be executed by a given object, and those representing object locks. In order to keep the Petri net finite, we assume that only boundedly many objects will be present in a Creol configuration (otherwise we will have to consider unboundedly many places for the object locks). Moreover, in the places representing the method code to be executed, we abstract away from the data that could influence such method (like, e.g., the object fields) otherwise we would need infinitely many places.

Due to the abstraction with respect to the labels of futures, the abstract Petri net semantics could have the following *token confusion* problem. Namely, if there are two concurrent invocations between the same two methods of the same two objects, in the Petri net it could happen that one caller could read the reply generated by the method actually called by the other one. To avoid at least the propagation of the *token confusion* problem, in the Petri net, as soon a caller accesses to a return value in a future, such value is consumed. In this way, we assign the future to a concrete caller and consuming the future prevents it from being claimed by two different processes. To apply this technique in a sound way we have to transform the program. Removing the future upon first claim implies that it is not available for consecutive claims (in opposite to the concrete case). On the other hand consecutive claims do not provide any new information with respect to deadlock detection. Once a future has been claimed in the concrete case all consecutive claims pass. We model this by removing consecutive claims from the program.

But this approach only allows to avoid the token confusion for sequential identical abstract processes. In the case of concurrent identical abstract processes this is not enough. To address this problem each future creation can be marked or not. The Petri net will be defined in such a way that token confusion will not occur between a marked and non-marked call. The deadlock analysis will be done only over the marked processes: if only the method calls directly involved in the deadlock are marked, then there will be no token confusion between the method executions which are involved in the deadlock and those which are not.

Internal choice is an obstacle with respect to this approach. In a sequence of internal choices the kind of a claim (first or consecutive) depends on the choices taken so far and can vary depending on them. To overcome this problem we move all internal choices up front.

During the transformations we remove superfluous internal steps and duplicated choices from the program to reduce the size of the Petri net. For the technical details of the transformations we refer the reader to [6]. We now describe the Petri net construction more in details.

4.1 Places and Tokens

The resulting Petri net contains two kinds of places:

Locks. Places identifying the locks of the objects. Each object has its designated lock place labeled by the unique name of the object. A token in such a place represents the lock of the corresponding object being available. There is at most one token in such a place.

Process. Places identifying a particular process in execution or the future as a result of the execution of a process. These places are labeled with $l\langle t \rangle$ where l is an abstract label identifying the call and t is abstract method code to be "executed". A token in this place represents one instance of such a process in execution or a future. In case of a future, the token is consumed if the future is claimed.

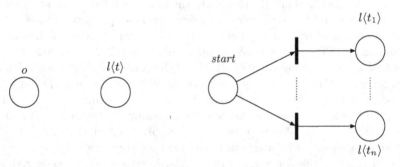

(a) Places for objects and abstract processes

(b) Transition from the initial place *start*: t_i's are the abstract traces of the initial process *run*

Fig. 1. Places and Initial transitions

4.2   Code Abstractions

In [6] the code abstraction is defined in detail, here we give a quick description. The syntactical transformation is composed of five functions:

Step One s_1. It applies data abstraction.

Step Two s_2. It removes choices. If t is the code of a method, $s_2(s_1(t))$ is a set of sequential code without branching. We will call these also "traces", as they represent possible (abstract) executions of the method.

Step Three s_3^F. It removes the redundant claims of a future, i.e. the claims that are after the first one with respect to particular future. Notice that this function is applied over traces, then, it can be checked when a future is claimed. It also replaces claim–statement by a sequence of release, get and grab statements. We justify this decision below, when we define the transition associated to the claim–statement. The function also replaces suspend–statement by a release and a grab. F is a set used to keep track of the already claimed futures.

Step Four s_4. The function takes a trace and returns a set of traces. The set is constructed such that each trace in the set is the received trace with at most one of the future claims marked. In this way, the function takes into account every claim for deadlock analysis (if a deadlock exists, the corresponding trace will be included among the possible non-deterministic ones considered). Notice that a trace without mark, i.e. the received trace, is also included.

Step Five s_5. It applies the abstraction on the futures replacing them with the tuple calling object, calling method, called object, and called method.

Functions s_3^F, s_4 and s_5 are lifted to support sets of traces. Then the code transformation is defined as the composition of all the functions $ST ::= s_5 \circ s_4 \circ s_3^0 \circ s_2 \circ s_1$ and it is applied to the method definitions. Suppose m is the method code in a class definition, i.e. in the configuration there is a method suite $[M]$ equals to $[\ldots, l = \varsigma(s{:}T).\lambda(\vec{x}{:}\vec{T}).m, \ldots]$. Then, $ST(m)$ is a set of traces where each trace represents a possible abstract execution of the method l. A trace in $ST(m)$ is a sequence of abstract statements of the following form: let $x{:}T = o.l$, claim@(n, n'), get@(n, n'), get@n, suspend(n), release(n), grab(n), stop, claim@$(n?, n')$, get@$(n?, n')$ and get@$n?$. Notice that the last three statements include marked calls. Each trace will have at most one marked claim.

4.3   Transitions

The transitions of the Petri net are determined by the translation of the semantic steps. For each object and each method a path for all pairs of caller and calling method is created. We give the translation for the individual execution steps according to the operational semantics in Section 2.2. In case the syntactical transformation affects the operational step we briefly discuss the consequences of the transformation.

Initial Transitions. A Creol program is defined by an initial configuration C_0 composed of a set of classes, a set of objects and an initial thread. We denote the initial thread *run*. This one is the main process in the program, then it is not called by another thread, does not belong to any object, nor class. The code associated to this thread has to be also translated using ST. The election of the trace for the main process is done by the initial transition depicted in Fig. 1(b), to do this we have included an auxiliary place *start*. This place will be the initial place of the Petri net.

Method Calls. We present the Petri net transitions for a method call in Fig. 2. A process place in the Petri net is labeled with a tuple $o_1.l_1$@$o_2.l_2$ where o_1 denotes the caller, l_1 the calling method, o_2 the callee, and l_2 the called method. We abbreviate parts of the label by c@$o.l$ resp. $o.l$@c or the whole label by l if details are not needed. Depending on whether the result of the call will be assumed to be part of a deadlock the created process is marked (see Fig. 2(a), notice the symbol "?") or is not (see Fig. 2(b)). The method body of the called process t' is in both cases of the form grab$(o); t_{o.l};$ release(o) where $t_{o.l}$ is an abstract trace execution of the method l of the object o according to the definitions in the associated class. At this point, the abstract execution unifies all the internal choices into one general internal choice that is resolved when the method is called.

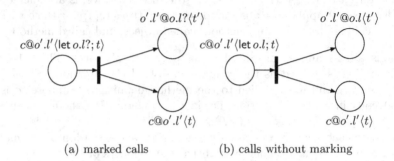

(a) marked calls   (b) calls without marking

Fig. 2. Transitions for method calls

Lock Handling. To execute the grab(o) statement the object lock of object o must be available. When releasing the lock of an object o by release(o) a token is added to the place representing the object lock. (Fig. 3)

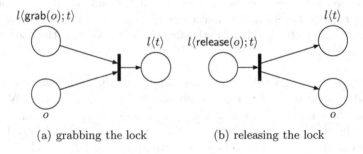

(a) grabbing the lock   (b) releasing the lock

Fig. 3. Transitions for lock handling

Claiming Results. We present the Petri net transitions for claiming the result of a method call in Fig. 4. The notations "$o.l^+$" or "$o.l^*$" denote that $o.l$ can be marked or not: formally, $+$ and $*$ are meta-variables that can be either the empty string or ?. As was explained before, to avoid the token confusion of sequential calls, the tokens are consumed. Notice that removing the result is not problematic with respect to multiple claims of a value because subsequent claims are removed in the syntactical transformation.

Rescheduling. In Creol semantics there are two different kinds of rescheduling. Unconditional rescheduling, using keyword suspend(o), which is translated to release(o); grab(o) and covered by the transition rules for lock handling (Fig. 3).

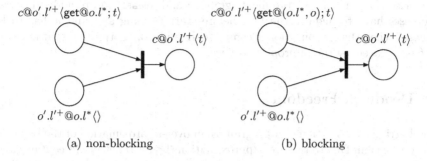

Fig. 4. Translation of a claim of a result

The translation of conditional rescheduling on the other hand deviates from the operational semantics of the claim statement. In opposite to the concrete case the object lock is always released upon reaching the claim statement. The statement claim@(n, o) is translated to the sequence release(o); get@n; grab(o) (by function s_3). In the concrete case the lock is only released if the result, that the process is waiting for, is not available. In case the result is available the process continues its execution without rescheduling.

This deviation is justified by the syntactical transformation. In the concrete case the rules for the operational semantics have to cover both the first claim of a result and the subsequent claims. In case of a subsequent result the claim statement has to be executed without rescheduling since the existence of the result has been proven by the previous claim. In the abstract semantics, consecutive claims have been removed, i.e. each claim in the abstract case is the first claim of the result. This justifies the deviation from the operational semantics.

4.4 Petri Net Construction for *Creol* Programs

We complete the definition of the Petri net associated to an initial configuration.

Definition 5. *Given an initial configuration*

$$C_0 = c_0[(F_0, M_0)] \parallel \ldots \parallel o_0[c_{o_0}, F_0, L_0] \parallel \ldots \parallel o_n[c_{o_n}, F_n, L_n] \parallel run\langle t \rangle$$

the corresponding Petri net P_{C_0} has one starting place start, the lock places $o_0, \ldots, o_n$, and the places $n\langle t' \rangle$ with:

1. *$n = run$@run or $n = run$@$o_i.l_j$ or $n = o_{i'}.l_{j'}$@$o_i.l_j$ with l_j and $l_{j'}$ methods of the classes c_j and $c_{j'}$, respectively. Same condition holds for abstract names containing the marker ?;*
2. *if $n = run$@run then t' is a suffix of one of the traces in $ST(t)$;*
3. *if $n = c$@$o_i.l_j$ then t' is a suffix of one of the traces in $ST(\text{grab}(o_i); m[o_i/\text{self}]; \text{release}(o_i))$, where m is the method definition of l_j, namely, given the class c_i of o_i and $c_i[(F_i, M_i)]$, we have $[M_i] = [\ldots, l_j = \varsigma(self{:}T_0).\lambda(\vec{x}_0{:}\vec{T}_0).m, \ldots]$.*

The initial marking of P_{C_0} has one token in the places start, $o_0, \ldots, o_n$. The transitions are defined as already described in Section 4.3.

Notice that in item 3, statements $\mathsf{grab}(o_i)$ and $\mathsf{release}(o_i)$ are added because processes have to acquire the lock before start running and and it has to be released when the computation is complete. In addition, notice also that keyword *self* is replaced by the appropiate object.

5 Deadlock Freedom

The Petri net translation of a program is an over-approximation of the behavior of the program. Due to the over-approximation the Petri net might contain more deadlocks than the concrete program. By proving the Petri net to be deadlock free we prove the concrete program to be deadlock free.

We give a Petri net representation of the notion of extended deadlock in terms of marking of the Petri net. These markings can be detected by reachability analysis. By proving the absence of the deadlock markings in the Petri net we prove deadlock freedom of the program.

When speaking about a Petri net, we implicitly assume that the Petri net was derived from a program by the above mentioned translation. We only focus in the extended deadlock because it subsumes the classical one (Corollary 1).

5.1 Extended Deadlock Marking

An extended deadlock in the Petri net can be characterized in terms of a marking. This particular marking is just the mapping of Definition 4 to the Petri net context more some extra conditions that we explain after definition.

Definition 6 (Extended Deadlock Marking). *A marking m in a Petri net is an* extended deadlock marking *iff the set of places in the Petri net can be divided in three disjoint sets P_1, P_2 and P_3 such that*

1. *P_1 is a set of places of the form $o.l^+@o'.l'^*\langle\mathsf{get}@(o'.l'?,o);t\rangle$, $o.l^+@o'.l'^*\langle\mathsf{get}@o'.l'?;t\rangle$ or $o.l^+@o'.l'^*\langle\mathsf{grab}(o);t\rangle$ such that*
   (a) *if $+ = ?$ then there is $p \in P_1$ in the form $c@c'\langle\mathsf{get}@(o.l?,o');t'\rangle$ or $c@c'\langle\mathsf{get}@o.l?;t'\rangle$;*
   (b) *if $* = ?$ then there is $p \in P_1$ in the form $c@c'\langle\mathsf{get}@(o'.l'?,o');t'\rangle$ or $c@c'\langle\mathsf{get}@o'.l'?;t'\rangle$;*
   (c) *if $t = \mathsf{grab}(o);t'$ then t' does not contain a claim with a question mark and there is $p \in P_1$ with the form $c@c'\langle\mathsf{get}@(o'.l'?,o);t''\rangle$.*
   All the places of P_1 have at least one token in m.
2. *P_2 is a set of places $c@c'\langle t\rangle$ such that one of the following holds*
   (a) *c, c' and t do not contain question marks;*
   (b) *c' and t do not contain question marks and if $c = o.l?$ then there is $c''@o.l?\langle t'\rangle \in P_1$.*
   All the places of P_2 have zero or more tokens in m.
3. *All the remaining places, composing the set P_3, have zero tokens in m.*

Conditions in item (1) are the condition defined in Definition 4 adapted to the Petri net context. In addition extra conditions are added to ensure the consistency between the marked calls and the marked abstract names. Conditions in (2) refer to the places that can be used to represent an active process that does do not belong to the deadlock and cannot produce the token confusion. This is evident in condition (2a), because there are no marks. On the other hand, condition (2b) is the abstract representation of a process that was called by another process that belongs to the deadlock. Notice that this process cannot create a token confusion because t has not a marked claim, then it could not do a marked call. Condition (3) is imposed to avoid the token confusion in the marked calls. Notice that P_3 are the places with a question mark that do not belong to P_1 or P_2. Not allowing tokens in these places guarantees that token confusion is not possible.

Theorem 1 (Inclusion of Extended Deadlock). *Given a Creol program, if it has an extended deadlock which is reachable, then the corresponding Petri net has a reachable extended deadlock marking.*

To prove Theorem 1 we define a mapping from both a *Creol* configuration and the *Creol* execution that reaches this configuration, to a set of markings in the Petri net. We prove that the mapping is sound, i.e. if C is a *Creol* configuration reached with an execution α and it reaches *Creol* configuration C' with a step of the operational semantics, then all markings associated to C' are reachable from at least one marking associated to C. Finally, we apply this mapping to a *Creol* execution that reaches a deadlock and we show that there is a marking in the set of reachable markings in the Petri net that satisfies the conditions in Definition 6. The definition of the mapping and the proofs are in [6].

Due to the connection between the extended deadlock in the *Creol* configuration and the extended deadlock marking in the Petri net, we can conclude freedom of extended deadlock of the program from freedom of extended deadlock markings of the Petri net.

As a final remark, we observe that the reachability of an extended deadlock marking is decidable in a Petri net. This is a consequence of the decidability of the *target reachability* problem for Petri nets [4]. Such a problem consists in checking whether a marking is reachable which satisfies some given lower bounds (possibly 0) and upper bounds (possibly 0 or ∞) associated to the places.

Notice that it is not possible to reduce our reachability problem to a coverability problem because we need to check the "absence" of tokens. In particular, we need to check the absence of return values or active methods which are computing the marked return value.

6 Conclusion

In this paper we presented a technique based on Petri net translation and Petri net reachability analysis to detect deadlock in systems made of asynchronously communicating active objects where futures are used to handle return values which can be retrieved via a lock detaining get primitive or a lock releasing claim primitive. We showed soundness of our analysis with respect to extended deadlocks (which encompass also blocked processes in addition to blocked objects considered in the classical notion of deadlock), i.e. if the analysis does not detect any deadlock then we are guaranteed that the original system is deadlock free.

Concerning the other direction, we claim our technique to be complete apart from false positives due to abstraction from data values, i.e. transformation of "if" primitives into non-deterministic choices (which obviously leads to new behavioral possibilities, hence deadlocks, with respect to the original system).

We now make some remark concerning related and future work.

We would like to mention the work in [9,10]. The authors deal with a similar language but use a different technique to discover deadlock: an abstract global system behaviour representation is statically devised from the program code in the form of a transition system whose states are labeled with set of dependencies (basically pairs of objects representing an invocation from an object to another one). The system is, then, deadlock free if no circular dependency is found. With respect to [9,10] our analysis is somehow more precise in that it is process based (i.e. also detecting extended deadlocks) and not just object based. An example of a false positive detected by the [9,10] approach, taken from [10] itself (and translated to our language), follows.

Consider the program consisting of two objects o_1 and o_2 belonging to classes c_1 and c_2, respectively, with c_1 defining methods m_1 and m_3 and c_2 defining method m_2. Such methods, plus the (static) initial method run are defined as:

- $run() ::= o_1.m_1()$
- $m_1() ::= \text{let } x = o_2.m_2() \text{ in}$
      $\text{claim@}(x, self); ret$
- $m_2() ::= \text{let } x = o_1.m_3() \text{ in}$
      $\text{get@}(x_2, self); ret$
- $m_3() ::= ret$

This program would originate a deadlock if we had a get instead of a claim in method m_1. This because method m_1 would call method m_2, which in turn would call m_3 which would not be able to proceed because the lock on object o_1 would be kept by m_1 waiting on the get. Differently from [9,10], our analysis correctly detects that the system is deadlock free in that method m_1 is waiting on a claim instead of a get.

Concerning language expressivity, [9,10] additionally considers, with respect to our language, a (finitely bound) "new" primitive for object creation and the capability of accounting for (a finite set of) objects used as values (e.g. passed as parameters or stored in fields) in the analysis. Concerning the former, only objects within a finite set of object names can be created (if invocations to the "new" primitive exceed the amount of available object names, as in the case of recursive object creation, old objects are returned), thus such primitive can be easily encoded in our approach by considering all the objects in the set of object names to be present since the beginning (and then "activated"). Concerning the latter, we can quite easily extend the language abstraction considered in our analysis by considering objects, out of a finite set, passed to methods (by considering object names as part of the method name). Dealing with objects stored in fields would however require an extension of the encoding into the Petri net, where a different place is considered for each possible object to be stored. We plan to do such extensions and to prove our claim about completeness as a future work.

References

1. Abadi, M., Cardelli, L.: A Theory of Objects. Monographs in Computer Science. Springer (1996)
2. Ábrahám, E., Grabe, I., Grüner, A., Steffen, M.: Behavioral interface description of an object-oriented language with futures and promises. Journal of Logic and Algebraic Programming 78(7), 491–518 (2009)
3. Armstrong, J.: Erlang. Communications of ACM 53(9), 68–75 (2010)
4. Busi, N., Zavattaro, G.: Deciding reachability problems in turing-complete fragments of mobile ambients. Mathematical Structures in Computer Science 19(6), 1223–1263 (2009)
5. Caromel, D., Henrio, L., Serpette, B.P.: Asynchronous and deterministic objects. SIGPLAN Not. 39(1), 123–134 (2004)
6. de Boer, F.S., Bravetti, M., Grabe, I., Lee, M., Steffen, M., Zavattaro, G.: A petri net based analysis of deadlocks for active objects and futures, extended version (2012), http://cs.famaf.unc.edu.ar/~lee/publications/facs12_complete.pdf
7. Dijkstra, E.W.: Cooperating sequential processes. In: Genuys, F. (ed.) Programming Languages: NATO Advanced Study Institute, pp. 43–112. Academic Press (1968)
8. Edward, J., Coffman, G., Elphick, M.J., Shoshani, A.: System deadlocks. ACM Computing Surveys 3(2), 67–78 (1971)
9. Giachino, E., Laneve, C.: Analysis of Deadlocks in Object Groups. In: Bruni, R., Dingel, J. (eds.) FMOODS/FORTE 2011. LNCS, vol. 6722, pp. 168–182. Springer, Heidelberg (2011)
10. Giachino, E., Laneve, C., Lascu, T.: Deadlock and livelock analysis in concurrent objects with futures. Technical report, University of Bologna (December 2011), http://www.cs.unibo.it/~laneve/publications.html
11. Gordon, A.D., Hankin, P.D.: A concurrent object calculus: Reduction and typing. In: Nestmann, U., Pierce, B.C. (eds.) Proceedings of HLCL 1998. Electronic Notes in Theoretical Computer Science, vol. 16.3, Elsevier Science Publishers (1998)
12. Smith, S.F., Agha, G.A., Mason, I.A., Talcott, C.L.: A foundation for actor computation. Journal of Functional Programming (1997)
13. Haller, P., Odersky, M.: Scala actors: Unifying thread-based and event-based programming. Theoretical Computer Science 410(2-3), 202–220 (2009)
14. Holt, R.C.: Some deadlock properties of computer systems. ACM Computing Surveys 4(3), 179–196 (1972)
15. Johnsen, E.B., Owe, O.: An Asynchronous Communication Model for Distributed Concurrent Objects. Software and Systems Modeling (2007)

Run-Time Verification of Black-Box Components Using Behavioral Specifications: An Experience Report on Tool Development*

Frank S. de Boer[1,2] and Stijn de Gouw[1,2]

[1] CWI, Amsterdam, The Netherlands
[2] Leiden University, The Netherlands

Abstract. We introduce a generic component-based design of a run-time checker, identify its components and their requirements, and evaluate existing state of the art tools instantiating each component.

1 Introduction

Run-time assertion checking is one of the most useful techniques for detecting faults, and can be applied during any program execution context, including debugging, testing, and production [3]. Compared to program logics, assertion checking emphasizes *executable specifications*. Whereas program logics statically cover all possible execution paths, run-time assertion checking is fully automated, and applies on demand to the actual runs of the program.

By their very nature, assertions are state-based in that they describe properties of the program variables (fields of classes and local variables of methods). In general, assertions expressed in languages supporting design by contract (like the Java Modeling Language (JML) [1]) cannot be used to specify the *interaction protocol* between objects or components, in contrast to other formalisms such as message sequence charts and UML sequence diagrams. Nor can state-based assertions be used to specify component interfaces since such interfaces do not have a state[1].

This paper reports on an integrated tool environment which provides a smooth integration of the specification and run-time checking of both data- and protocol-oriented properties of component interfaces. The basic idea underlying our framework is the representation of message sequences as words of a language generated by a grammar. The formalism of *attribute grammars* allows the high-level specification of user-defined abstractions of message sequences in terms of attributes of grammars describing these sequences. We introduce a generic component-based

---

* This research is partly funded by the EU project FP7-231620 HATS: Highly Adaptable and Trustworthy Software using Formal Models (http://www.hats-project.eu/).

[1] JML uses model variables for interface specifications. However, a separate *represents* clause is needed for a full specification, and such clauses can only be defined once an implementation has been given (and is not implementation independent).

C.S. Păsăreanu and G. Salaün (Eds.): FACS 2012, LNCS 7684, pp. 128–133, 2013.
© Springer-Verlag Berlin Heidelberg 2013

design which supports run-time checking of assertions about these attributes, which involves parsing the generated sequences of messages. We identify the components and their requirements, and evaluate existing state of the art tools which instantiate the components of the generic tool architecture.

Related Work. A preliminary version describing a prototype of an instantiation of our tool architecture was presented at the workshop "Formal Techniques for Java-Like Programs 2010" and appeared in its *informal* proceedings[2]. This prototype was based on state of the art tools. However, for industrial usage we need a component-based design (as described above), and an experience report on various instantiations of the generic tool design.

There exist many other interesting approaches to run-time verification and monitoring of message sequences which however do not address its integration with the general context of run-time assertion checking, e.g. JML: PQL, Tracematches, JmSeq, LARVA, Jass and JavaMOP. Due to space limitations we do not further discuss these approaches individually.

2 The Modeling Framework

Abstracting from implementation details (such as field values of objects), an execution of a Java program can be represented by its *global communication history*: the sequence of messages corresponding to the invocation and completion of (possibly static) methods. Similarly, the execution of a single object can be represented by its *local communication history*, which consists of all messages sent and received by that object. The *behavior* of a program (or object) can then be defined as the set of its allowed histories. Whether a history is allowed depends in general both on data (the contents of the messages, e.g. parameter and return values of method calls) and protocol (the order between messages). The question arises how such allowed sets of histories can be defined conveniently. In this section we show how attribute grammars provide a powerful and declarative way to define such sets. We will use the interface of the Java `BufferedReader` (Figure 1) as a running example to explain the basic modeling concepts.

```
interface BufferedReader {
    void close();
    int read();
}
```

$$S ::= \text{open } C_1 \text{ assert open.caller != null}$$
$$\qquad ==> \text{open.caller} == C_1.\text{caller};$$
$$| \quad \epsilon$$
$$C ::= \text{read } C_1 \quad C.\text{caller} = C_1.\text{caller};$$
$$| \quad \text{close } S_1 \quad C.\text{caller} = \text{close.caller};$$
$$| \quad \epsilon \qquad C.\text{caller} = \text{null};$$

Fig. 1. Relevant methods of the BufferedReader Interface

Fig. 2. Extended Attribute Grammar modeling the behavior of a BufferedReader

---

[2] Available in the ACM Digital Library with the title "Prototyping a tool environment for run-time assertion checking in JML with communication histories", authored by Frank S. de Boer, Stijn de Gouw and Jurgen Vinju.

To each method m in the interface we associate two *communication events*: 'call-m' and 'return-m'. The *observable* communication history of an object of a class implementing the above interface consists of sequences of communication events.

Context-free grammars provide a declarative way to define the allowed histories of an object. The context-free grammar underlying the attribute grammar in Figure 2 generates the valid histories for BufferedReader, describing the *prefix closure* of sequences of the terminals call-BufferedReader', 'call-read' and 'call-close' as given by the regular expression (call-BufferedReader call-read* call-close). Note that since grammars specify *invariant* properties of the ongoing behavior of an object, they must be prefix-closed. In general, communication events form the terminal symbols of the grammar, and non-terminal symbols specify the valid sequences of communication events.

While context-free grammars provide a convenient way to specify the *protocol structure* of the valid histories, they do not take data such as parameters and return values of method calls and returns into account. Thus the question arises how to specify the *data-flow* of the valid histories. To that end, we extend the grammar with attributes. A terminal symbol 'call-m' has *built-in* attributes 'caller', 'callee' and the parameter names for respectively the actual parameters and object identities of the caller and callee. A terminal 'return-m' additionally has an attribute result referring to the return value. Non-terminals have *user-defined* attributes to define data properties of sequences of events. However the attributes themselves do not alter the language generated by the attribute grammar, they only *define* properties of data-flow of the history. We extend the attribute grammar with assertions to specify properties of attributes. For example, in the attribute grammar in Figure 2 a user-defined attribute 'caller' for the non-terminal 'C' is defined storing the identity of the object which closed the BufferedReader (and is null if the reader was not closed yet). The assertion allows only those histories in which the object which opened (created) the reader also closed it.

Assertions can be placed at any position in a production rule and are evaluated there. Note that assertions appearing directly before a terminal can be seen as a precondition of a terminal, whereas post-conditions are placed directly after the terminal. This is in fact a generalization of traditional pre- and post-conditions for methods as used in design-by-contract: a single terminal 'call-m' can appear in multiple productions, each of which followed by a different assertion. Hence different preconditions (or postconditions) can be used for the same method, depending on the context (grammar production) in which the call was made.

3   Generic Tool Architecture

Given a Java interface specified with an attribute grammar, we would like to test whether an object implementing the interface satisfies the properties defined in the grammar at every point in its lifetime. In this section we describe a generic tool architecture which achieves this. Four different components are combined: a state-based assertion checker, a parser generator, a debugger and a general tool for meta-programming. Traditionally these tools are used for very diverse purposes and don't need to interact with each other. We therefore investigate requirements needed to achieve a seamless integration of these components, motivated by describing the workflow of the run-time checker.

Suppose that during execution of a Java program, a method of a class (subsequently referred to as CUT, the 'class under test') which implements an interface specified by an attribute grammar is called. The new history of the object on which the method was called should be updated to reflect the addition of the method call. To represent the history of an object of CUT, the **Meta-Programming** tool generates for each method m in CUT two classes call-m and return-m. These classes contain the following fields: the object identity of the *callee*, the identity of the *caller* and the actual parameters. Additionally return-m contains a field result containing the return value. A Java List containing instances of call-m and return-m then stores the history of an object of CUT.

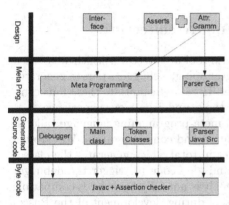

Fig. 3. Generic Tool Architecture

The meta-programming tool further generates code for a wrapper class which replaces the original main class. This wrapper class contains a field H, a Java map containing pairs (id, h) of an object identity id and its local history h. The new main class executes the original program inside the **Debugger**. The Debugger is responsible for monitoring execution of the program. It must be capable of temporarily 'pausing' the program whenever a call or return occurs, and execute user-defined code to update H appropriately . Moreover the Debugger must be able to read the identity of the callee, caller and parameters/return-value.

After the history is updated the run-time checker must decide whether it still satisfies the specification (the attribute grammar). Observe that a communication history can be seen as a sequence of tokens (in our setting: communication events). Since the attribute grammar together with the assertions generate the language of all valid histories, checking whether a history satisfies the specification reduces to deciding whether the history can be parsed by a parser for the attribute grammar, where moreover during parsing the assertions must evaluate to true. Therefore the **Parser Generator** creates a parser for the given attribute grammar. Since the history is a heterogenous list of call-m and return-m objects, the parser must support parsing streams of tokens with user-defined types. Assertions in general describe properties of Java objects, and the grammar contains assertions over attributes, the attributes must be normal Java variables. Consequently the parser generator must allow arbitrary user-defined java code (to set the attribute value) in rule actions. The use of Java code ensures the attribute values are computable. Since assertions are allowed in-between any two (non)-terminals, the parser generator should support user-defined actions between arbitrary grammar symbols. At run-time, the parser is triggered whenever the history of an object is updated. The result is either a parse error, which indicates that the current communication history has violated the protocol structure specified by the attribute grammar, or a parse tree with new attribute values. During parsing, the **Assertion Checker** evaluates the assertions in the grammar on the newly computed attribute values. To avoid parsing the whole history of a given object each time a new call or return is appended, ideally the parser should support incremental parsing [4]. An incremental parser computes a parse tree for the new history based on the parse trees for prefixes of the history. In our setting, the attribute grammar specifies invariant properties of the ongoing behavior. Hence the parser constructs a new parse tree after each call/return, consequently parse trees for all prefixes of the current history can be exploited for incremental parsing.

4   Instantiating the Generic Tool Architecture

The previous section introduced the generic tool architecture, which was based on four different components: meta-programming, debugger, parser generator and state-based run-time assertion checker. Here we instantiate these four components with particular (state of the art) tools, and report our experiences.

Rascal [5] is a powerful tool-supported meta-programming language tailored for program analysis, program transformation and code generation. We wrote a Rascal program of approximately 600 lines in total which generates the classes `call-m`, `return-m`, the new main class, and glue code to trigger the debugger and parser. Rascal is still in an alpha stage, it is not fully backwards compatible and we discovered numerous bugs in Rascal during development of the Rascal program. However overall our experience was quite positive. All bugs were fixed quickly by the Rascal team, and its powerful parsing, pattern matching and transforming concrete syntax features proved indispensable.

We evaluated Sun's implementation of the Java Debugging Interface for the debugger component. It is part of the standard Java Development Kit, hence maintenance of the debugger is practically guaranteed. The Sun debugger starts the original user program in a virtual machine which is monitored for occurences of `MethodEntryEvent` (method calls) and `MethodExitEvent` (method returns). It allows defining event handlers which are executed whenever such events occur. It also allows retrieving the caller, callee, parameters values and return value of events using `StackFrames`. The Sun debugger meets all requirements for the debugger stated above. As the main disadvantage, we found that the current implementation of the debugger is very slow. In fact it was responsible for the majority of the overhead of the run-time checker. This is not necessarily problematic: as testing is done during development, the debugger will typically not be present in performance critical production code. Moreover, one usually wants to test only up to a certain bound (for instance, in time, or in the number of events), and report on results once the bound is exceeded. Nonetheless, for testing up to huge bounds, a different implementation for the debugger is needed.

We instantiated the parser generator component with ANTLR, a state of the art parser generator. It generates fast recursive descent parsers for Java and allows grammar actions and custom token streams. It even supports *conditional productions*: such productions are only chosen during parsing whenever an associated Boolean expression (the condition) is true. Attribute grammars with conditional productions express protocols that depend on data which are typically not context-free. ANTLR can only handle LL(*) grammars[3], and it lacks support for incremental parsing, though this is planned by the ANTLR developers. We could not find any Java parser generator which supports general context-free grammars and incremental parsing of attribute grammars.

We tested two state-based assertion languages: standard Java assertions and the Java Modeling Language (JML). Both languages suffice for our purposes. JML is far more expressive than the standard Java assertions, though its tool support is not ready for industrial usage. In particular, the last stable version of the JML run-time assertion checker dates back over 8 years, when for instance generics were not supported yet. The main reason is that JML's run-time assertion checker only works with a proprietary implementation of the Java compiler, and unsurprisingly it is costly to update the proprietary compiler each time the standard compiler is updated. This problem is recognized by the JML developers [2]. OpenJML, a new pre-alpha version of the JML run-time assertion checker integrates into the standard Java compiler, and initial tests with it provided many valuable input for real industrial size applications. See the Sourceforge tracker for the kind of issues we have encountered when using OpenJML.

A (variant of) the above tool suite can be obtained from http://www.cwi.nl/~cdegouw. It was applied successfully to an industrial size case study of the eCommerce software company Fredhopper.

References

1. Burdy, L., Cheon, Y., Cok, D.R., Ernst, M.D., Kiniry, J.R., Leavens, G.T., Leino, K.R.M., Poll, E.: An overview of JML tools and applications. International Journal on Software Tools for Technology Transfer 7(3), 212–232 (2005)
2. Chalin, P., James, P.R., Karabotsos, G.: Jml4: Towards an industrial grade ive for java and next generation research platform for jml. In: VSTTE, pp. 70–83 (2008)
3. Clarke, L.A., Rosenblum, D.S.: A historical perspective on runtime assertion checking in software development. ACM SIGSOFT Software Engineering Notes 31(3), 25–37 (2006)
4. Hedin, G.: Incremental Attribute Evaluation with Side-effects. In: Hammer, D. (ed.) CCHSC 1988. LNCS, vol. 371, pp. 175–189. Springer, Heidelberg (1989)
5. Klint, P., van der Storm, T., Vinju, J.: Rascal: a domain specific language for source code analysis and manipulation. In: Walenstein, A., Schupp, S. (eds.) SCAM 2009, pp. 168–177 (2009)

---

[3] A strict subset of the context-free grammars. Left-recursive grammars are not LL(*).

Symbolic Counterexample Generation for Discrete-Time Markov Chains*

Nils Jansen[1], Erika Ábrahám[1], Barna Zajzon[1], Ralf Wimmer[2],
Johann Schuster[3], Joost-Pieter Katoen[1], and Bernd Becker[2]

[1] RWTH Aachen University, Germany
[2] Albert-Ludwigs-University Freiburg, Germany
[3] University of the Federal Armed Forces Munich, Germany

Abstract. In this paper we investigate the generation of *counterexamples* for discrete-time Markov chains (DTMCs) and PCTL properties. Whereas most available methods use explicit representations for at least some intermediate results, our aim is to develop *fully symbolic* algorithms. As in most related work, our counterexample computations are based on *path search*. We first adapt *bounded model checking* as a path search algorithm and extend it with a novel *SAT-solving heuristics* to prefer paths with higher probabilities. As a second approach, we use *symbolic graph algorithms* to find counterexamples. Experiments show that our approaches, in contrast to other existing techniques, are applicable to very large systems with millions of states.

1 Introduction

Model checking is a very successful technique to automatically analyze the correctness of a system. During the last two decades, a lot of work has been done to develop model checking techniques for different kinds of systems like digital circuits, hybrid and probabilistic systems.

One feature which made model checking for digital circuits a standard technology in industry is the ability to deliver a *counterexample* if a desired property is violated. Counterexamples, which provide an explanation for the violation, are indispensable for reproducing and fixing errors in the design. They are also crucial for so-called CEGAR frameworks [1,2], in which the system is abstracted for verification. In case the abstraction is too coarse, verification might yield a spurious counterexample, which is used to refine the abstraction accordingly.

This paper addresses counterexample generation for probabilistic systems modeled as *discrete-time Markov chains (DTMCs)* and properties formalized in the logic *PCTL* [3]. Standard model checking algorithms for PCTL properties of DTMCs are based on probabilistic reachability analysis: they compute

---

* This work was partly supported by the German Research Council (DFG) as part of the research project CEBug (AB 461/1-1), the Transregional Collaborative Research Center AVACS (SFB/TR 14) and by the Netherlands Organisation for Scientific Research (NWO) as part of the DFG/NWO Bilateral Research Programme ROCKS.

C.S. Păsăreanu and G. Salaün (Eds.): FACS 2012, LNCS 7684, pp. 134–151, 2013.
© Springer-Verlag Berlin Heidelberg 2013

the probability of reaching a given set of states by solving a linear equation system [4]. However, if a PCTL property is violated, e. g., if the probability to reach a set of unsafe states is larger than a certain value, these model checking algorithms are not able to return any information about the reason of the violation.

Therefore, in the last few years intensive research was carried out to develop methods which allow to generate *counterexamples* for PCTL properties of DTMCs. For digital circuits a single execution that leads from an initial state to a safety-critical state suffices as a counterexample, for DTMCs a *set* of such executions is required whose cumulated probability mass exceeds the maximally tolerated value. While some of the available counterexample generation methods [5,6,7,8] represent counterexamples as such sets of paths, other methods use alternative representations: Counterexamples are represented as regular expressions in [8] and as winning strategies for probabilistic games in [9,10]. In [11], abstractions of strongly connected components of DTMCs are used. Most relevant for our work is the representation of counterexamples as paths of a *subsystem* of the given DTMC [12,13,14]. In [13] we proposed two methods to build such subsystems. The *global* search starts with an empty subsystem, searches incrementally for paths to be included and extends the subsystem with the states along the paths and all induced transitions until the subsystem is large enough to violate the given property. The *local* search not only finds further violating paths but also path fragments which connect parts of already included paths.

Practically relevant systems are often too large to be represented explicitly, i. e., by enumerating all the states and transitions. To overcome this problem, large DTMCs can be represented *symbolically* by *binary decision diagrams (BDDs)* [15,16]. Sets of states and transitions are encoded by acyclic graphs, with the elements in the set being represented by paths in the graph. Symbolic representations are often smaller by orders of magnitude than explicit ones.

Symbolic model checking has been successfully established for DTMCs [17,18]. However, there is still a lack of symbolic algorithms for counterexample generation. In order to take full advantage of efficient representations of DTMCs and path sets, the applied path search methods should work on symbolic representations without using any explicit representations for intermediate results. In [5,6] approaches for symbolic counterexamples are presented, but all paths forming a counterexample are enumerated explicitly. For very large systems, this approach is not scalable, as (1) a counterexample may consist of a very large or even infinite number of paths. Their explicit representation has to be computed which may consist of a very large number of states. An alternative symbolic path search algorithm was introduced in [7]. This algorithm calculates the k most probable paths of a symbolically represented DTMC. Although this algorithm is well-suited for fully symbolic counterexample generation, due to some auxiliary data structures, the memory requirements increase strongly with increasing k.

As mentioned above, most of the available counterexample generation approaches for DTMCs apply *path search algorithms* (e. g., k shortest paths search [8] or heuristic search [12]). A suitable path search method which works on symbolic system representations is *bounded model checking*, encoding paths of a given length from the initial state of a DTMC to a target state by a formula such that each satisfying solution corresponds to such a path. In [5,6], counterexamples are generated by searching for solutions until enough paths have been found to form a counterexample. The method in [5] encodes paths without their probabilities in propositional logic and uses SAT-solving to find satisfying solutions. A disadvantage of this method is that it finds paths with fewer steps first, in contrast to more probable ones. The approach [6] uses SMT-solving to search for paths having at least a given minimal probability, which leads to longer running times while more probable paths are found earlier.

In this paper we first adapt SAT-based bounded model checking to support the ideas of local and global search from [13] and suggest a heuristic for SAT-solving that allows to influence the SAT search to find more probable paths first, without the need to invoke SMT-solving. Furthermore, we do not restrict the search to paths of a fixed length as suggested by standard bounded model checking, but search for paths whose length is between a given lower and upper bound.

As a second approach, we propose in this paper novel fully symbolic methods based on BDDs for the generation of counterexamples for DTMCs and PCTL properties. Our methods take as input a DTMC which is symbolically represented by BDDs. The counterexample computation uses the algorithm from [7] to find most probable paths of a DTMC. In our first BDD-based method, we combine the symbolic k-shortest path search with the idea of global search from [13] to compute a symbolically represented subsystem of the original DTMC, whose paths form a counterexample. However, this suffers from very high memory consumption, while by not enumerating the paths some computation time can be saved. As our best approach, we adapt the idea for local search, also presented in [13] which is applicable to systems with up to $1.2 \cdot 10^8$ states.

The contribution of this paper is the development of *fully symbolic* algorithms, which overcome the main disadvantages of previous approaches:

- No explicit representation of states is needed during the counterexample generation. This is crucial for handling large systems.
- In comparison to other approaches we are now able to generate counterexamples for systems with millions of states.
- As in [12,13] the counterexample is not represented by an enumeration of paths which yields a counterexample that is smaller by orders of magnitude.

In the next section we briefly introduce some theoretical foundations. Section 3 describes the general framework of our symbolic methods for counterexample generation. The usage of SAT-based path search is described in Section 4 and the application of BDD-based graph search algorithms in Section 5. These methods are evaluated experimentally on some case studies in Section 6. We conclude our work and discuss future work in Section 7.

2 Preliminaries

We introduce the basic definitions and concepts used in this paper. For more details we refer to [4].

2.1 Discrete-Time Markov Chains and Critical Subsystems

Definition 1. *A* discrete-time Markov chain (DTMC) *is a tuple* $M = (S, I, P, L)$ *with S being a finite set of states, $I : S \to [0,1] \subseteq \mathbb{R}$ with $\sum_{s \in S} I(s) \leq 1$ an initial distribution, $P : S \times S \to [0,1] \subseteq \mathbb{R}$ a matrix of transition probabilities such that $\sum_{s' \in S} P(s, s') \leq 1$ for all $s \in S$, and L a labeling function with $L : S \to 2^{AP}$ with AP a denumerable set of atomic propositions.*

Please note that we allow *sub-stochastic* distributions $\sum_{s \in S} I(s) \leq 1$ and $\sum_{s' \in S} P(s, s') \leq 1$ for all $s \in S$. Usually, these sums of probabilities are required to be exactly 1. This can be obtained by defining $M' = (S \cup \{s_\perp\}, I', P', L')$ with $s_\perp$ a fresh sink state such that for all $s, s' \in S$ we have $I'(s) = I(s)$ and $I'(s_\perp) = 1 - \sum_{s \in S} I(s)$, $P'(s, s') = P(s, s')$, $P'(s, s_\perp) = 1 - \sum_{s' \in S} P(s, s')$, $P'(s_\perp, s_\perp) = 1$ and $P'(s_\perp, s) = 0$, and finally $L'(s) = L(s)$ and $L'(s_\perp) = \emptyset$.

For simplicity, in the following we restrict ourselves to DTMCs (S, I, P, L) having a *single initial state* $s_I \in S$ with $I(s_I) = 1$ and use the notation (S, s_I, P, L). Note that every DTMC having an arbitrary initial distribution can be transformed to this form by adding a fresh unique initial state.

Assume in the following a DTMC $M = (S, s_I, P, L)$. We say that there is a *transition* (s, s') from a state $s \in S$ to a state $s' \in S$ iff $P(s, s') > 0$. A *path* of M is a finite or infinite sequence $\pi = s_0 s_1 \ldots$ of states $s_i \in S$ such that $P(s_i, s_{i+1}) > 0$ for all i. We call the transitions (s_i, s_{i+1}) to be *contained* in the path π, written $(s_i, s_{i+1}) \in \pi$. We write π^i for the ith state on path π; its position is called *depth*. The *length* of a finite path $\pi = s_0 \ldots s_n$ is the number n of its transitions.

We write $Paths^M_{inf}$ for the set of all infinite paths of M, and $Paths^M_{inf}(s)$ for those starting in $s \in S$. Analogously, $Paths^M_{fin}$ is the set of all finite paths of M, $Paths^M_{fin}(s)$ of those starting in $s \in S$, and $Paths^M_{fin}(s, t)$ of those starting in $s \in S$ and ending in $t \in S$. A state $t \in S$ is called *reachable* from another state $s \in S$ iff $Paths^M_{fin}(s, t) \neq \emptyset$.

The *cylinder set* of a finite path π of M is defined as $Cyl(\pi) = \{\pi' \in Paths^M_{inf} \mid \pi \text{ is a prefix of } \pi'\}$. To each state $s \in S$ of M we associate the smallest σ-algebra that contains all cylinder sets of all finite paths in $Paths^M_{fin}(s)$. This yields a unique probability measure Pr^M_s (or short Pr) on the σ-algebra where the probabilities of the cylinder sets are given by

$$Pr\big(Cyl(s_0 \ldots s_n)\big) = \prod_{i=0}^{n-1} P(s_i, s_{i+1}) \, .$$

For finite paths π we set $Pr_{fin}(\pi) = Pr\big(Cyl(\pi)\big)$. For sets of finite paths $R \subseteq Paths^M_{fin}(s)$ we define $Pr_{fin}(R) = \sum_{\pi \in R'} Pr_{fin}(\pi)$ with $R' = \{\pi \in R \mid \forall \pi' \in R. \ \pi' \text{ is not a prefix of } \pi\}$.

The syntax of *probabilistic computation tree logic (PCTL)* [19] is given by[1]

$$\varphi ::= p \mid \neg\varphi \mid \varphi \wedge \varphi \mid \mathbb{P}_{\sim\lambda}(\varphi \, U \, \varphi)$$

for (state) formulae with $p \in AP$, $\lambda \in [0,1] \subseteq \mathbb{R}$, and $\sim \, \in \{<, \leq, \geq, >\}$. We define the "finally"-operator $\Diamond$ and the "globally"-operator $\Box$ in the usual way.

For a property $\mathbb{P}_{\leq\lambda}(\varphi_1 \, U \, \varphi_2)$ refuted by M, a *counterexample* is a set $C \subseteq Paths_{fin}^M(s_I)$ of finite paths starting in the initial state and *satisfying* $\varphi_1 \, U \, \varphi_2$ such that $Pr_{fin}(C) > \lambda$. For $\mathbb{P}_{<\lambda}(\varphi_1 \, U \, \varphi_2)$, the probability mass has to be at least λ. We consider only upper probability bounds; see [8] for the reduction of lower bounds to this case.

The model checking and counterexample generation problems for $\mathbb{P}_{\leq\lambda}(\varphi_1 \, U \, \varphi_2)$ can be recursively reduced to a reachability problem as follows: We transform the DTMC $M = (S, s_I, P, L)$ to a DTMC $M' = (S, s_I, P', L)$ by removing all outgoing transitions from states satisfying $\neg\varphi_1 \vee \varphi_2$, i. e., $P'(s, s') = 0$ if s satisfies $\neg\varphi_1 \vee \varphi_2$ and $P'(s, s') = P(s, s')$ otherwise. Then M satisfies $\mathbb{P}_{\leq\lambda}(\varphi_1 \, U \, \varphi_2)$ iff M' satisfies $\mathbb{P}_{\leq\lambda}(\Diamond\,\varphi_2)$. In the following we concentrate on this reduced problem.

Consider a DTMC $M = (S, s_I, P, L)$, a set of target states $T \subseteq S$ and an upper bound $\lambda \in [0, 1]$ on the allowed probability to reach one of these target states from the initial state s_I. For notational convenience we write $\mathcal{P}_{\leq\lambda}(\Diamond T)$ for the property that the probability of reaching a target state from the initial state is less or equal λ. We assume this property to be violated, i. e., the actual probability of reaching T exceeds λ.

In [13] we proposed to represent counterexamples as so-called *critical subsystems* instead of large, possibly infinite sets of paths. Intuitively, a critical subsystem is a part of the original system in which the given probability bound is already exceeded.

Definition 2. *A subsystem of a DTMC $M = (S, s_I, P, L)$ is a DTMC $M' = (S', s_I, P', L')$ such that $S' \subseteq S$, $s_I \in S'$, $P'(s, s') \in \{P(s, s'), 0\}$ and $L'(s) = L(s)$ for all $s, s' \in S'$. We call such a subsystem M' of M critical for $T \subseteq S$ and $\lambda \in [0,1] \subseteq \mathbb{R}$ iff $S' \cap T \neq \emptyset$ and the probability to reach a state in $S' \cap T$ from s_I in M' is larger than λ.*

Note that the set of all paths leading from the initial state s_I to the set of target states T inside the critical subsystem forms a counterexample.

2.2   Symbolic Representation of DTMCs

In this paper we use symbolic representations of DTMCs and generate symbolic critical subsystems. *Explicit* means that the transition probabilities are represented as a sparse matrix, which contains one entry per transition with non-zero probability. This representation is used, e. g., by the probabilistic model checker MRMC [20]. A *symbolic* DTMC representation encodes state and transition sets, e. g., as paths in a graph or as solutions of a certain formula. Symbolic representations are often smaller by orders of magnitude than the explicit ones and

---

[1] In this paper we only consider unbounded properties.

allow to reduce not only the memory consumption but also the computational costs for operations on the data structures.

As a symbolic data structure for the representation of DTMCs we choose *binary decision diagrams* [15] and *multi-terminal binary decision diagrams* [16].

Definition 3. *Let Var be a set of Boolean variables. A* binary decision diagram *(BDD) over Var is a rooted, acyclic, directed graph* $B = (V, n_{\text{root}}, E)$ *with a finite set V of* nodes, *a* root node $n_{\text{root}} \in V$ *and* edges $E \subseteq V \times V$. *Each node is either an* inner *node or a* leaf *node.* Leaf nodes $n \in V$ *have no outgoing edges and are labeled with $label(n) \in \{0, 1\}$.* Inner nodes $n \in V$ *have exactly two successor nodes, denoted by $hi(n)$ and $lo(n)$, and are labeled with a variable $label(n) \in Var$.*

A multi-terminal binary decision diagram *(MTBDD) is like a BDD but it labels leaf nodes $n \in V$ with real values $label(n) \in \mathbb{R}$.*

Let B be a BDD over *Var* and $\mathcal{V}(Var) = \{\nu : Var \to \{0, 1\}\}$ the set of all variable valuations. Each $\nu \in \mathcal{V}(Var)$ induces a unique path in B from the root to a leaf node by moving from each inner node n to $hi(n)$ if $\nu(label(n)) = 1$ and to $lo(n)$ otherwise. A BDD B represents a function $f_B : \mathcal{V}(Var) \to \{0, 1\}$ assigning to each $\nu \in \mathcal{V}(Var)$ the label of the leaf node reached in B by the path induced by ν. We often identify B with f_B and write $B(\nu)$ instead of $f_B(\nu)$. Analogously, each MTBDD B represents a function $f_B : \mathcal{V}(Var) \to \mathbb{R}$.

An (MT)BDD is *ordered* if there is a linear order $< \subseteq Var \times Var$ on the variables such that for all inner nodes n either $hi(n)$ is a leaf node or $label(n) < label(hi(n))$, and the same for $lo(n)$. An (MT)BDD is *reduced* if all functions rooted at the different nodes of the (MT)BDD are different. For a fixed variable order, they are canonical data structures for representing functions $f : \mathcal{V}(Var) \to \{0, 1\}$ resp. $f : \mathcal{V}(Var) \to \mathbb{R}$ [15]. In the following we assume all (MT)BDDs to be reduced and ordered with respect to a fixed variable order.

By *Var'* we denote the variable set *Var* with each variable $x \in Var$ renamed to some $x' \in Var'$ such that $Var \cap Var' = \emptyset$. Our algorithms use the standard (MT)BDD operations union $B_1 \cup B_2$, intersection $B_1 \cap B_2$, variable renaming $B[x \to x']$, and existential quantification $\exists x.\ B$ for $x \in Var$, $x' \in Var'$.

BDDs and MTBDDs can be used to represent DTMCs symbolically as follows: Let $M = (S, s_I, P, L)$ be a DTMC and *Var* a set of Boolean variables such that for each $s \in S$ there is a unique binary encoding $\nu_s : Var \to \{0, 1\}$ with $\nu_s \neq \nu_{s'}$ for all $s, s' \in S$, $s \neq s'$. For $s, s' \in S$ we also define $\nu_{s,s'} : Var \cup Var' \to \mathbb{R}$ with $\nu_{s,s'}(x) = \nu_s(x)$ and $\nu_{s,s'}(x') = \nu_{s'}(x)$ for $x \in Var$, $x' \in Var'$. A target state set $T \subseteq S$ is represented by a BDD $\hat{T}$ over *Var* such that $\hat{T}(\nu_s) = 1$ iff $s \in T$. Similarly for the initial state, $\hat{I}(\nu_s) = 1$ iff $s = s_I$. The probability matrix $P : S \times S \to [0, 1] \subseteq \mathbb{R}$ is represented by an MTBDD $\hat{P}$ over $Var \cup Var'$ such that $\hat{P}(\nu_{s,s'}) = P(s, s')$ for all $s, s' \in S$. For an MTBDD B over *Var* we use B_{bool} to denote the BDD over *Var* with $B_{bool}(\nu) = 1$ iff $B(\nu) > 0$ for all valuations ν.

This formalism is used, e.g., by the stochastic model checker PRISM [21], whose benchmark set [22] is standard for DTMCs. These test-cases are modeled in a guarded command language describing system *components*; the global state space and the transition probabilities are generated by parallel composition. The transition matrices are usually sparse and well-structured with relatively few different probabilities; therefore the symbolic MTBDD representation is in many cases more compact by several orders of magnitude than explicit representations. For more details we refer to documentation of PRISM.

3   Symbolic Counterexample Generation Framework

In this section we present our framework for the generation of probabilistic counterexamples with symbolic data structures. We give an algorithm that computes, for a symbolically represented DTMC as input, a critical subsystem, which is again symbolically represented. As the most significant ingredient, this algorithm needs a *symbolic path search* method, which returns paths of the input DTMC. The critical subsystem is initially empty and is incrementally extended with the states along found paths and with transitions between them. Implementations of the path search method will be described in Sections 4 and 5.

Algorithm 1. Finding a critical subsystem

FindCriticalSubsystem(MTBDD $\hat{P}$, BDD $\hat{I}$, BDD $\hat{T}$, double λ)
begin
    BDD *States* $= \emptyset$; BDD *NewStates* $= \emptyset$; MTBDD *SubSys* $= \emptyset$;   (1)
    if (`ModelCheck`$(\hat{P}, \hat{I}, \hat{T}) > \lambda$)   (2)
      while (`ModelCheck`(*SubSys*$, \hat{I}, \hat{T}) \leq \lambda$)   (3)
        NewStates $:=$ `FindNextPath`$(\hat{P}, \hat{I}, \hat{T}, SubSys)$;   (4)
        if (*NewStates* $\neq \emptyset$)   (5)
          States $:=$ *States* $\cup$ *NewStates*;   (6)
          SubSys $:=$ `ToTransitionBDD`(*States*)$\cap \hat{P}$ (7)
      end if   (8)
    end while   (9)
    end if   (10)
    return *SubSys*   (11)
end

The algorithm for finding a symbolic counterexample is depicted in Algorithm 1. The parameters specify the input DTMC symbolically by the MTBDD $\hat{P}$ for the transition probabilities, the BDD $\hat{I}$ for the initial state and the BDD $\hat{T}$ for the target states, as well as a probability bound λ which shall be exceeded by the resulting critical subsystem. The local variable *States* is used to symbolically represent the set of states which are part of the current subsystem, while *NewStates* is used to store the states occurring on a path which shall extend the current subsystem. The MTBDD *SubSys* stores the transition MTBDD of the current subsystem. The algorithm uses the following methods:

ModelCheck(MTBDD $\hat{P}$, BDD $\hat{I}$, BDD $\hat{T}$) performs symbolic probabilistic model checking [17,18] and returns the probability of reaching states in $\hat{T}$ from states in $\hat{I}$ via transitions from $\hat{P}$.

FindNextPath(MTBDD $\hat{P}$, BDD $\hat{I}$, BDD $\hat{T}$, MTBDD *SubSys*) computes a path leading through the DTMC induced by the transition MTBDD $\hat{P}$, the initial state $\hat{I}$, and the set of target states $\hat{T}$. Which path is found next depends on the current subsystem *SubSys* and therefore on the set of previously found paths. Implementations of this method will be discussed in Sections 4 and 5.

ToTransitionBDD(BDD *States*) computes first the BDD *States'* by renaming each variable $x \in Var$ occurring in *States* to $x' \in Var'$ and returns the transition BDD *States* ∩ *States'* in which there is a transition between all pairs of states occurring in *States*, i. e., $(States \cap States')(\nu_{s_1,s_2}) = 1$ iff $States(\nu_{s_1}) = States(\nu_{s_2}) = 1$.

The algorithm proceeds as follows. First, the three empty objects *States*, *NewStates*, and *SubSys* are created in line (1). If ModelCheck($\hat{P}, \hat{I}, \hat{T}$) in line (2) reveals that λ is exceeded then the reachability property is violated and the search for a counterexample starts. Otherwise the algorithm just terminates. The condition of the while-loop in line (3) invokes model checking for the current subsystem described by *SubSys* and the original initial states and target states. The loop runs until ModelCheck(*SubSys*, $\hat{I}, \hat{T}$) returns a value which is greater than λ. In this case, the current subsystem is *critical*. Please note, that in our implementation we do not invoke model checking in every iteration. Depending on the input system, we search for a certain number of paths until we invoke this method. In every iteration, first the method FindNextPath($\hat{P}, \hat{I}, \hat{T}, SubSys$) in line (4) returns a set of states which occur on a path through the system. If this set is not empty, the current set of states is extended by these new states in line (6). Afterwards, the current subsystem is extended in line (7): ToTransitionBDD(*States*) generates a transition relation between all states found so far. The intersection of the resulting BDD and the original transition MTBDD $\hat{P}$ represents a probability matrix $P' \subseteq P$ which is restricted to transitions between the states in *States*. These induced transitions define the updated subsystem *SubSys*.

4   Searching Paths Using SAT Solving

In this section we present two implementations for the path searching method (Algorithm 1) using bounded model checking and SAT solving. First, an existing method which searches paths with certain lengths is adapted to our symbolic framework. Second, we present a new method which searches for path fragments that extend the subsystem. Finally, we describe a new SAT-solving heuristic which guides the SAT solver to prefer more probable path fragments.

4.1   Adapting Bounded Model Checking for Global Search

In [5], a bounded model checking (BMC) approach for DTMCs was developed. Starting with a symbolic representation of a DTMC by an MTBDD $\hat{P}$ and

BDDs $\hat{I}$ and $\hat{T}$ as described before, first Tseitin's transformation [23] is applied to generate formulae in conjunctive normal form (CNF) from the BDDs. We will denote the resulting CNF predicates by $\check{P}$, $\check{I}$, and $\check{T}$, respectively.

The BMC formula built from the symbolic representation of a DTMC is parameterized in $k \in \mathbb{N}$ and has the following structure:

$$BMC(k) = \check{I}(Var_0) \wedge \bigwedge_{i=0}^{k-1} \check{P}(Var_i, Var_{i+1}) \wedge \check{T}(Var_k) \tag{1}$$

where k is the length of the paths considered.

This formula depends on sets $Var_i = \{\sigma_{i,1}, \ldots, \sigma_{i,m}\}$ of Boolean variables which encode the ith state of a path of length k through the DTMC starting in an initial state and ending in a target state. Each satisfying assignment ν of formula (1) corresponds to such a path. If there is no satisfying assignment, there is no such path with length k. We identify the assignment $(\nu(\sigma_{i,1}), \ldots, \nu(\sigma_{i,m}))$ with the state s_i of the DTMC.

Since usually multiple paths need to be found in order to form a counterexample, the solver has to enumerate satisfying solutions for $BMC(k)$, $k = 0, 1, \ldots$, until enough probability mass has been accumulated. To exclude an already found solution from further search, new clauses are added to the SAT solver's clause database. Consider a path $\pi_j = s_0 \ldots s_k$ that was found in the jth iteration of the search process. Let $\nu : \bigcup_{i=0}^{k} Var_i \to \{0, 1\}$ be the corresponding satisfying assignment. The path π_j is uniquely described by the following formula:

$$\bigwedge_{i=0}^{k} \sigma_{i,1}^{\nu(\sigma_{i,1})} \wedge \sigma_{i,2}^{\nu(\sigma_{i,2})} \wedge \cdots \wedge \sigma_{i,m}^{\nu(\sigma_{i,m})} , \tag{2}$$

where $\sigma_{i,j}^1 = \sigma_{i,j}$ and $\sigma_{i,j}^0 = \neg\sigma_{i,j}$. To exclude π_j from the solution space of $BMC(k)$, its negation is built and added to the solver's clause database:

$$\bigvee_{i=0}^{k} \bigvee_{j=1}^{m} \sigma_{i,j}^{1-\nu(\sigma_{i,j})} . \tag{3}$$

This ensures that for a new path at least one state variable has to be differently assigned than for path π_j.

Every time the SAT solver returns a new satisfying assignment, the probability of the underlying path is computed and the path is saved. This proceeds until the probability of all paths found exceeds the bound λ. The resulting counterexample is therefore a set of explicitly represented paths whose cumulated probability mass exceeds the probability bound. If no further satisfying assignment can be found, the path length k is increased by one and the search process gets restarted.

We adopt this procedure for our framework for generating a symbolically represented critical subsystem. Instead of computing the probability of single paths, the BDD state representation of each new path is computed and returned to Algorithm 1. This is done in form of a callback, as we do not want to restart the solver after each iteration. If model checking reports that the probability mass of the generated subsystem is high enough, the procedure stops.

In general, termination is guaranteed as the SAT solver finds all possible paths of length k. Eventually, the subsystem will consist of all states that are part of paths from initial to target states. This subsystem induces the whole probability mass of reaching a target state in the original system. As the algorithm only starts if the probability bound is exceeded, the probability mass of this system will also exceed the bound. Therefore, the algorithm always terminates.

4.2 Adapting Bounded Model Checking for Fragment Search

The previously described approach of using the SAT solver to find paths leading from the initial state of the DTMC to the target states is now extended according to the *local search* approach described in [13]. We aim at finding *path fragments* that extend the already found system iteratively.

The intuition is as follows: In the first search iteration, the CNF formula given to the SAT solver is satisfied if and only if the assignment corresponds to a path of *maximal* length n through the input DTMC leading from the initial state s_I to a target state $t \in T$. This path induces the initial subsystem. Subsequently, this system is extended by paths whose first and last states are included in the current subsystem, while all states in between are fresh states.

For this we need to consider already found states for all possible depths $0 \leq d \leq n$. For a state s let $\nu_s^d : Var_d \to \{0,1\}$ be the unique assignment of Var_d corresponding to state s.

We introduce a flag f_s^d for each state s and each depth d. This flag is assigned 1 if and only if the assignment of the state variables at depth d corresponds to the state s:

$$f_s^d \leftrightarrow (\sigma_{d,1}^{\nu_s^d(\sigma_{d,1})} \wedge \cdots \wedge \sigma_{d,m}^{\nu_s^d(\sigma_{d,m})}) . \tag{4}$$

The next variable K_j^d describes the whole set of states which have been found in the iterations $0, 1, \ldots, j$ of the search process (again in terms of the variables Var_d for depth d). Note, that these are exactly the states of the current subsystem *SubSys* after iteration j. We set $K_{-1}^d := $ false. Assume that in iteration j of the search process path $\pi_j = s_0 s_1 \ldots s_n$ is found. We then define

$$K_j^d \leftrightarrow \left(K_{j-1}^d \vee \bigvee_{i=1}^n f_{s_i}^d\right) . \tag{5}$$

In the first search iteration we need a formula which is true iff the variable assignment corresponds to a path of maximal length n leading from the initial state to a target state of the DTMC:

$$\check{I}(Var_0) \wedge \bigvee_{i=0}^n \check{T}(Var_i) \wedge \tag{6a}$$

$$\bigwedge_{i=0}^{n-1} \left[(\neg \check{T}(Var_i) \to \check{P}(Var_i, Var_{i+1})) \wedge (\check{T}(Var_i) \to (Var_i = Var_{i+1}))\right]. \tag{6b}$$

Assume that ν is an assignment corresponding to the path $\pi = s_0 s_1 \ldots s_n$. Formula (6a) states, that the first state s_0 is the initial state and that one of the states $s_0, \ldots s_n$ is a target state. Formula (6b) ensures, that if a state s_i is not a target state, a transition will be taken to the next state. Contrary, if s_i is a target state, all following state variables will be assigned s_i which creates an implicit self loop on this state. In the context of the original system, this path ends with a target state s_n.

For the following iterations $j > 1$, we need the previously defined variables K_d^j:

$$K_{j-1}^0 \wedge \check{P}(Var_0, Var_1) \wedge \neg K_{j-1}^1 \wedge \bigvee_{d=2}^{n} K_{j-1}^d \tag{7a}$$

$$\wedge \bigwedge_{d=1}^{n-1} \left[(\neg K_{j-1}^d \rightarrow \check{P}(Var_i, Var_{i+1})) \wedge (K_{j-1}^d \rightarrow Var_i = Var_{i+1}) \right] . \tag{7b}$$

Formula (7a) ensures that the first state s_0 of a solution path $\pi_j = s_0 \ldots s_n$ is contained in the set K_{j-1}^0 of previously found states, that a transition is taken from this state to a not yet found state s_1 and that one of the following states s_d, $d \geq 2$, is again contained in K_{j-1}^d. Formula (7b) enforces transitions from all not yet found states s_i to s_{i+1}. If s_i was already included in previous paths then all following states are assigned as s_i.

Termination is guaranteed, as the length of the paths is bounded by n. If no further satisfying assignments are found, this number has to be increased. However, the diameter, i. e., the longest cycle-free path of the underlying graph, is an upper bound on the length of loop-free paths from s_{init} to target states. Therefore, n needs to be increased only finitely many times, such that a critical subsystem is always determined in finite time.

4.3   SAT Heuristic for Finding More Probable Paths

A drawback of the SAT-based search strategies is that paths are found without considering their probability beforehand. If paths or transitions with higher probabilities are preferred, the process can be accelerated. We therefore try to modify the variable selection of the SAT solver.

SAT solvers have efficient variable selection strategies, i. e., strategies to decide which variable should be assigned next during the search process. We adjust the choice of the *value* the solver assigns to the selected variable, in order to prefer paths with higher probabilities.

The decision how to assign a variable is based on the transition probabilities. If a variable $\sigma_{i+1,j}$ is to be assigned at depth $0 < i + 1 \leq n$, its value partly determines s_{i+1}, being the target state of a transition from s_i. We choose the value for $\sigma_{i+1,j}$ which corresponds to the state s_{i+1} to which the transition with the highest probability can be taken (under the current assignment).

Example 1. Assume the following DTMC:

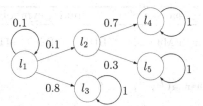

Let the states of the DTMC be encoded by three propositional variables and assume that the solver partially assigned the state variables for the ith and the $(i+1)$th time instance as follows:

	$\sigma_{j,1}$	$\sigma_{j,2}$	$\sigma_{j,3}$
l_1	0	0	0
l_2	0	0	1
l_3	0	1	0
l_4	0	1	1
l_5	1	0	0

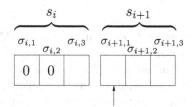

The ith state s_i is determined to be l_1 or l_2. For s_{i+1} still all states are possible. The first bit of the $(i+1)$th state, as indicated by the arrow, should be assigned next. We would choose to set the bit to 0, because in this way we do not exclude the most probable eligible transition from l_1 to l_3.

5   Searching Paths Symbolically

In this section we use symbolic graph algorithms to implement the path search (Algorithm 1) by which a critical subsystem of a DTMC is built. We first recall how one can find the k most probable paths through a symbolically represented DTMC. We call this the *symbolic global search* as the most probable paths through the whole system are found. We embed this procedure into our symbolic counterexample search. Afterwards we present a new search method which symbolically searches for the most probable path fragments that extend the current subsystem. We call this approach the *symbolic fragment search*.

5.1   Symbolic Global Search

The goal of this procedure is to find paths leading from the initial state to a target state ordered by their probability, starting with the most probable path. As usually classical graph algorithms are used, this is also referred to as the k shortest path search, although this corresponds to the k most probable paths. Utilized for a counterexample search, the value of k is not fixed beforehand but the search terminates if enough probability mass is accumulated [8].

In [7], a symbolic version of the k shortest path search was presented. The core components are the calculation of the actual shortest path and a transformation of the DTMC such that the shortest path in the altered system corresponds to the second shortest path in the original system. We adapt this method for

---

Algorithm 2. The global search algorithm for symbolic DTMCs

SymbolicGlobalSearch(MTBDD $\hat{P}$, BDD $\hat{I}$, BDD $\hat{T}$, MTBDD SP)
begin
    if ($SP \neq \emptyset$)   (1)
        ($\hat{P}$, $\hat{I}$, $\hat{T}$) := Change($\hat{P}$, $\hat{I}$, $\hat{T}$, SP);   (2)
    endif (3)
      SP := ShortestPath($\hat{P}$, $\hat{I}$, $\hat{T}$); (4)
    return SP; (5)
end

---

symbolic counterexample computation for DTMCs. The resulting algorithm is depicted in Algorithm 2.

Parameters are as usual $\hat{P}$, $\hat{I}$ and $\hat{T}$ as well as an MTBDD SP to store the path computed in the last iteration. The following methods are used (for details on the MTBDD operations we refer to the appendix of [7]):

ShortestPath(MTBDD $\hat{P}$, BDD $\hat{I}$, BDD $\hat{T}$) computes the most probable path leading from a state of $\hat{I}$ to a state of $\hat{T}$ via transitions from $\hat{P}$ and returns the MTBDD representation SP of this path. For this method, a set-theoretic variant of Dijkstra's algorithm is used.

Change(MTBDD $\hat{P}$, BDD $\hat{I}$, BDD $\hat{T}$, MTBDD SP) changes the DTMC $(\hat{P},\hat{I},\hat{T})$ to a new one such that the shortest path in the new DTMC corresponds to the second shortest path of the original DTMC(for the basic algorithm cf. [24]). The core idea of the symbolic implementation is to add an additional state variable that indicates a copy (when set to 1) or the original state (when set to 0). The MTBDD $\hat{P}$ is therefore extended by two variables: One for the source and one for the target state.

The original algorithm works with a fixed number k of search iterations. We modified this method to be incremental, i.e., the resulting $\hat{P}$ and SP after an iteration step are input for the next iteration. If the SP parameter is empty, the first shortest path is computed (line 4). Otherwise, the system is modified to exclude the previously found path (line 2). On the modified system, a new search is performed, yielding the next shortest path (line 4).

As in our framework the termination condition lies inside the symbolic counterexample algorithm (see Algorithm 1), we call Algorithm 2 as often as needed to form a counterexample. We use the MTBDD SP as a parameter in order to determine, what the *next* shortest path is. Note that in this case Algorithm 1 has to call the search method with the last shortest path instead of the current subsystem and it also has to transform the resulting shortest path MTBDD SP to a state set BDD (see the method **ToStateBDD**($\cdot$) on page 147).

Finally, this procedure yields a critical subsystem induced by a finite number k of paths. The paths are ordered w.r.t. to their probability. Note that the MTBDD resulting from the iterative application of the **Change()**-method grows rapidly and renders this method not applicable to systems which require a large number of paths, as our test cases will show.

5.2 Symbolic Fragment Search

In contrast to the previous approach, where we search for whole paths through the system, we aim now at finding most probable *path fragments*. Intuitively, first a *base path* is found being the most probable path from the initial state to one of the target states of the input system. This path forms the initial subsystem. Afterwards, the subsystem is incrementally extended by finding the most probable path fragment that connects states from the current subsystem. This approach was successfully implemented for explicit graph representations [13] and is now adapted to symbolic representations. The algorithm is depicted in Algorithm 3.

Algorithm 3. The fragment search for symbolic DTMCs

SymbolicFragmentSearch(MTBDD $\hat{P}$, BDD $\hat{I}$, BDD $\hat{T}$, MTBDD $SubSys$)
begin
    MTBDD SP;   (1)
    BDD $SubSysStates$;   (2)
    if ($SubSys = \emptyset$)   (3)
      $SP :=$ **ShortestPath**($\hat{P}$, $\hat{I}$, $\hat{T}$);   (4)
    else   (5)
      $SubSysStates :=$ **ToStateBDD**($SubSys$);   (6)
      $SP :=$ **ShortestPath**($\hat{P} \setminus SubSys$, $SubSysStates$, $SubSysStates$);   (7)
    end if   (8)
    return ToStateBDD(SP)   (9)
end

We need an MTBDD SP to store the path which is computed and a BDD $SubSysStates$ which stores the states of the current subsystem. The following methods are used:

ShortestPath(MTBDD $\hat{P}$, BDD $\hat{I}$, BDD $\hat{T}$) uses a set-theoretic variant of Dijkstra's algorithm as in Section 5.1.

ToStateBDD(MTBDD $SubSys$) computes for the transition MTBDD $SubSys$ a BDD describing all states that occur as source state or target state for one of the transitions of $SubSys$. When $SubSys$ is defined over the variables $Var = \{x_1, \ldots, x_n\}$ and $Var' = \{x'_1, \ldots, x'_n\}$, this is done by first building the set $OUT := \exists x'_1, \ldots, x'_n. SubSys_{bool}$ of all states with an outgoing transition. Afterwards, the set $IN' := \exists x_1, \ldots, x_n. SubSys_{bool}$ of states with ingoing transitions is built. These resulting BDDs have to be defined over the same variable set, therefore we perform a variable renaming for the set of states with ingoing transitions: $IN := IN'[x'_1 \to x_1] \ldots [x'_n \to x_n]$. Building the union $IN \cup OUT$ yields the needed BDD.

The symbolic fragment search checks whether the parameter *SubSys* is empty, which means, whether this is the first search iteration. If this is the case then the base path leading from the initial state $s_I \in \hat{I}$ to one of the target states $t \in \hat{T}$ is computed by invoking the shortest path search. The resulting path, stored in the BDD *SP*, is transformed into a state BDD and returned to the symbolic model checking framework (see Algorithm 1). If *SubSys* is not empty then a part of the subsystem has already been determined. In this case, we compute the state BDD *SubSysStates* by invoking `ToStateBDD(`*SubSys*`)`. The shortest path algorithm is called to find the most probable path from a state in *SubSysStates* to a state in *SubSysStates* inside the DTMC induced by $\hat{P}$ without using direct transitions from *SubSysStates* to *SubSysStates*. Note that, since we seach for the most probable such path, this path will not contain any *SubSysStates* states between the starting and ending ones.

6   Case Studies

We developed prototypes in C++ for all approaches described in this paper using the BDD package CUDD [25] and the SAT solver MiniSat [26]. All experiments were performed on a QuadCore Intel CPU (2.66 GHz) with 8 GB RAM. We present results for the Probabilistic Contract Signing protocol [27] and the CROWDS protocol [28]. We used the PRISM models [22] of both protocols.

Probabilistic Contract Signing is a network protocol targeting the *fair* exchange of critical information between two parties A and B. In particular, whenever B has obtained A's commitment to a *contract*, B shall not be able to prevent A from getting B's commitment. The PCTL property $\mathbb{P}_{\leq 0.5}(\lozenge [knowA \wedge \neg knowB])$ we are investigating describes an unfair situation where A knows B's secrets while B doesn't know A's secrets. The target states in our model carry corresponding labels. The model size is scaled by the

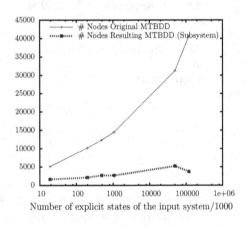

Fig. 1. BDD sizes

number of data pieces to exchange and the size of each data piece.

The CROWDS protocol aims at anonymous communication in networks, where a crowd of n users is divided in *good members* and *bad members*. A good member delivers a message to its destination with probability $1 - p_f$ and forwards it to another member, randomly chosen, with probability p_f. This guarantees that no bad member knows the original sender of the message. Each *session* describes the delivery of a message to a sender. If a user is identified twice by a bad member, anonymity is no longer guaranteed. This is called *positively identified* (*Pos*).

		Crowds protocol					Contract Signing protocol		
# states		18817	198199	485941	1058353	50445495	33790	156670	737278
model checking		0.426153	0.716089	0.807731	0.871703	0.85054	0.515625	0.515625	0.503906
probability threshold		0.25	0.35	0.4	0.4	0.2	0.5	0.5	0.5
Symb global	# states	630	622	622	622	1013	**6804**	24006	13222
	# paths	1019	978	977	979	738	**512**	326	733
	prob.	0.149138	0.14843	0.14843	0.14843	0.117311	**0.5**	0.318359	0.0447388
	time (s)	TO	TO	TO	TO	TO	**1871.82**	TO	TO
Symb fragment	# states	**600**	**1611**	**2415**	**2884**	**10239**	**6927**	**38247**	**139980**
	# paths	**201**	**1359**	**555**	**835**	**2641**	**521**	**521**	**8192**
	prob.	**0.25659**	**0.350066**	**0.401258**	**0.400333**	**0.201197**	**0.508789**	**0.508789**	**0.5**
	time (s)	**12.18**	**169.93**	**276.41**	**413.15**	**2830.55**	**26.61**	**740.15**	**972.57**
BMC classic	# states	1241	1205	1241	1241	1558	**6684**	**37464**	**139302**
	# paths	140822	127845	126318	129960	43250	**513**	**513**	**8193**
	prob.	0.175123	0.173481	0.173651	0.1746	0.0994408	**0.500977**	**0.500977**	**0.500061**
	time (s)	TO	TO	TO	TO	TO	**20.17**	**410.61**	**367.1**
SAT global	# states	**908**	997	997	997	1583	**6825**	**38025**	**139302**
	# paths	**231359**	295240	258860	253733	238894	**520**	**520**	**8193**
	prob.	**0.250057**	0.261859	0.26189	0.261859	0.179294	**0.507812**	**0.507812**	**0.500061**
	time (s)	**3492.98**	TO	TO	TO	TO	**23.1**	**449.1**	**411.42**
SAT fragment	# states	**6757**	9079	8581	16038	10158	**6684**	9131	11875
	# paths	**1973**	2446	2211	4434	2728	**3074**	1956	604
	prob.	**0.250548**	0.165949	0.0764908	0.0866818	0.0653038	**0.500977**	0.0715447	0.0378418
	time (s)	**805.68**	TO	TO	TO	TO	**3584.47**	TO	TO
SAT fragment + H	# states	**2489**	**7535**	19132	19662	5898	**6684**	8254	7009
	# paths	**700**	**2166**	5573	5556	1704	**3073**	1807	537
	prob.	**0.2858817**	**0.350044**	0.0971835	0.0648511	0.0562423	**0.500977**	0.092741	0.038967
	time (s)	**192.33**	**4172.44**	TO	TO	TO	**5152.11**	TO	TO

Fig. 2. Results for crowds and contract signing (TO > 2h)

The PCTL property we consider is $\mathbb{P}_{\leq p}(\Diamond Pos)$. The models are parameterized in their size by the number of sessions and the size of the crowd.

In Figure 2 we have collected a number of results we achieved on different instances of the described case studies. For the input data, we list the number of states (# states), the actual model checking result of reaching target states (model checking) and the probability threshold. We tested the methods for symbolic counterexample generation described in this paper as well as the bounded model checking approach, which computes a set of paths [5]:

- Symb global: The symbolic global search approach, Section 5.1
- Symb fragment: The symbolic fragment search approach, Section 5.2
- BMC classic: The standard bounded model checking approach for DTMCs as described in [5]
- SAT global: The global search approach using SAT solvers, Section 4.1
- SAT fragment: The fragment search approach using SAT solvers, Section 4.2
- SAT fragment + H: The SAT-based fragment search approach together with the SAT heuristic preferring more probable paths, Section 4.3.

For the resulting critical subsystems we present the number of states, the number of performed path searches (# paths), the probability of this system (prob), and the computing time in seconds (time (s)). The timeout (TO) was defined as 2 hours. All results which were finished within this time are printed in **boldface**. For unfinished cases we give the results that were achieved so far. Note that the probability for these unfinished benchmarks lies under the probability threshold.

In Figure 1 we present the number of MTBDD nodes for original instances of the CROWDS-protocol w. r. t. the number of explicit nodes presented by these MTBDDs. The figure shows, that the number of nodes highly increases while the number of nodes for the subsystems stay relatively constant.

The results show that the symbolic fragment search outperforms all other approaches by far on our benchmarks sets. We can compute critical subsystems for benchmarks consisting of millions of states. A result could still be computed for a system having over $1.2 \cdot 10^8$ states in about 3 hours. The explicit counterexample algorithms described in [13,29] were faster on small benchmarks but explicit approaches are not applicable to benchmarks as large as presented here.

7 Conclusion and Future Work

In this paper we presented a new framework for the generation of probabilistic counterexamples for symbolic DTMC representations. We suggested several methods, while the symbolic fragment search turned out to be the best alternative. Our experiments showed that using our framework the size of possible input systems for counterexample generation is increased by orders of magnitude.

In the future we want to integrate this symbolic framework into the COMICS tool [29] for counterexample generation for DTMCs. The adaption of the hierarchical abstraction techniques presented in [13] would increase the usability of counterexamples even for very large systems. It would also be interesting to see if using an SMT solver instead of a SAT solver would accelerate the search process.

References

1. Hermanns, H., Wachter, B., Zhang, L.: Probabilistic CEGAR. In: Gupta, A., Malik, S. (eds.) CAV 2008. LNCS, vol. 5123, pp. 162–175. Springer, Heidelberg (2008)
2. Chadha, R., Viswanathan, M.: A counterexample-guided abstraction-refinement framework for Markov decision processes. ACM TOCL 12(1), 1–45 (2010)
3. Hansson, H., Jonsson, B.: A logic for reasoning about time and reliability. Formal Aspects of Computing 6(5), 512–535 (1994)
4. Baier, C., Katoen, J.P.: Principles of Model Checking. The MIT Press (2008)
5. Wimmer, R., Braitling, B., Becker, B.: Counterexample Generation for Discrete-Time Markov Chains Using Bounded Model Checking. In: Jones, N.D., Müller-Olm, M. (eds.) VMCAI 2009. LNCS, vol. 5403, pp. 366–380. Springer, Heidelberg (2009)
6. Braitling, B., Wimmer, R., Becker, B., Jansen, N., Ábrahám, E.: Counterexample Generation for Markov Chains Using SMT-Based Bounded Model Checking. In: Bruni, R., Dingel, J. (eds.) FMOODS/FORTE 2011. LNCS, vol. 6722, pp. 75–89. Springer, Heidelberg (2011)
7. Günther, M., Schuster, J., Siegle, M.: Symbolic calculation of k-shortest paths and related measures with the stochastic process algebra tool CASPA. In: Proc. of DYADEM-FTS 2010, pp. 13–18. ACM Press (2010)
8. Han, T., Katoen, J.P., Damman, B.: Counterexample generation in probabilistic model checking. IEEE Trans. on Software Engineering 35(2), 241–257 (2009)
9. Kattenbelt, M., Huth, M.: Verification and refutation of probabilistic specifications via games. In: Proc. of FSTTCS 2009. LIPIcs, vol. 4, pp. 251–262. Schloss Dagstuhl – Leibniz-Zentrum für Informatik (2009)

10. Fecher, H., Huth, M., Piterman, N., Wagner, D.: PCTL model checking of Markov chains: Truth and falsity as winning strategies in games. Performance Evaluation 67(9), 858–872 (2010)
11. Andrés, M.E., D'Argenio, P., van Rossum, P.: Significant Diagnostic Counterexamples in Probabilistic Model Checking. In: Chockler, H., Hu, A.J. (eds.) HVC 2008. LNCS, vol. 5394, pp. 129–148. Springer, Heidelberg (2009)
12. Aljazzar, H., Leue, S.: Directed explicit state-space search in the generation of counterexamples for stochastic model checking. IEEE Trans. on Software Engineering 36(1), 37–60 (2010)
13. Jansen, N., Ábrahám, E., Katelaan, J., Wimmer, R., Katoen, J.-P., Becker, B.: Hierarchical Counterexamples for Discrete-Time Markov Chains. In: Bultan, T., Hsiung, P.-A. (eds.) ATVA 2011. LNCS, vol. 6996, pp. 443–452. Springer, Heidelberg (2011)
14. Wimmer, R., Jansen, N., Ábrahám, E., Becker, B., Katoen, J.-P.: Minimal Critical Subsystems for Discrete-Time Markov Models. In: Flanagan, C., König, B. (eds.) TACAS 2012. LNCS, vol. 7214, pp. 299–314. Springer, Heidelberg (2012)
15. Bryant, R.E.: Graph-based algorithms for boolean function manipulation. IEEE Trans. Computers 35(8), 677–691 (1986)
16. Fujita, M., McGeer, P.C., Yang, J.C.Y.: Multi-terminal binary decision diagrams: An efficient data structure for matrix representation. Formal Methods in System Design 10(2/3), 149–169 (1997)
17. Baier, C., Clarke, E.M., Hartonas-Garmhausen, V., Kwiatkowska, M.Z., Ryan, M.: Symbolic Model Checking for Probabilistic Processes. In: Degano, P., Gorrieri, R., Marchetti-Spaccamela, A. (eds.) ICALP 1997. LNCS, vol. 1256, pp. 430–440. Springer, Heidelberg (1997)
18. Parker, D.: Implementation of Symbolic Model Checking for Probabilistic Systems. PhD thesis, University of Birmingham (2002)
19. Hansson, H., Jonsson, B.: A logic for reasoning about time and reliability. Formal Aspects of Computing 6(5), 512–535 (1994)
20. Katoen, J.P., Zapreev, I.S., Hahn, E.M., Hermanns, H., Jansen, D.N.: The ins and outs of the probabilistic model checker MRMC. Performance Evaluation 68(2), 90–104 (2011)
21. Kwiatkowska, M., Norman, G., Parker, D.: PRISM 4.0: Verification of Probabilistic Real-Time Systems. In: Gopalakrishnan, G., Qadeer, S. (eds.) CAV 2011. LNCS, vol. 6806, pp. 585–591. Springer, Heidelberg (2011)
22. Kwiatkowska, M., Norman, G., Parker, D.: The PRISM benchmark suite. In: Proc. of QEST. IEEE CS (September 2012)
23. Tseitin, G.S.: On the complexity of derivations in the propositional calculus. Studies in Mathematics and Mathematical Logic (Part II), 115–125 (1968)
24. Schmid, W.: Berechnung kürzester Wege in Straßennetzen mit Wegeverboten. PhD thesis, Universität Stuttgart, Fakultät für Bauingenieur- und Vermessungswesen (2000)
25. Somenzi, F.: Cudd: Cu decision diagram package release 2.4.1 (2005)
26. Eén, N., Sörensson, N.: An extensible SAT-solver. In: Giunchiglia, E., Tacchella, A. (eds.) SAT 2003. LNCS, vol. 2919, pp. 502–518. Springer, Heidelberg (2004)
27. Norman, G., Shmatikov, V.: Analysis of probabilistic contract signing. Journal of Computer Security 14(6), 561–589 (2006)
28. Reiter, M.K., Rubin, A.D.: Crowds: Anonymity for web transactions. ACM Trans. on Information and System Security 1(1), 66–92 (1998)
29. Jansen, N., Ábrahám, E., Volk, M., Wimmer, R., Katoen, J.-P., Becker, B.: The COMICS Tool – Computing Minimal Counterexamples for DTMCs. In: Chakraborty, S., Mukund, M. (eds.) ATVA 2012. LNCS, vol. 7561, pp. 349–353. Springer, Heidelberg (2012)

XCD – Modular, Realizable Software Architectures *

Christos Kloukinas and Mert Ozkaya

School of Informatics
City University London
London EC1V 0HB, U.K.
{c.kloukinas,mert.ozkaya.1}@city.ac.uk

Abstract. Connector-Centric Design (XCD) is centred around a new formal architectural description language, focusing mainly on *complex connectors*. Inspired by Wright and BIP, XCD aims to cleanly separate in a *modular* manner the high-level *functional, interaction*, and *control* system behaviours. This can aid in both increasing the understandability of architectural specifications and the reusability of components and connectors themselves. Through the independent specification of control behaviours, XCD allows designers to experiment more easily with different design decisions early on, without having to modify the functional behaviour specifications (components) or the interaction ones (connectors).

At the same time XCD attempts to ease the architectural specification by following (and extending) a Design-by-Contract approach, which is more familiar to software developers than process algebras like CSP or languages like BIP that are closer to synchronous/hardware specification languages. XCD extends Design-by-Contract *(i)* by separating component contracts into functional and interaction sub-contracts, and *(ii)* by allowing service consumers to specify their own contractual clauses. XCD connector specifications are completely decentralized, foregoing Wright's connector glue, to ensure their realizability by construction.

Keywords: Software architecture, Modular specifications, Separation of functional interaction and control behaviours, Design by contract, Connector realizability.

1 Introduction

Architectural descriptions of systems are extremely valuable for communicating high-level system design aspects and the different solutions that have been evaluated for meeting system-wide, non-functional properties. The need for components and connectors to be first-class architectural entities has been advocated from the very beginning [15, 30]. However, support for complex connectors is minimal in languages used more widely by practitioners currently, e.g., AADL [13], SysML [6]. These rely mostly on simple interconnection mechanisms like procedure-calls and provide no support for specifying complex connectors, focusing their attention mostly upon components. The end result is that architectures end up more like low-level designs [11].

---

* This work has been partially supported by the EU project FP7-257367 IoT@Work.

C.S. Păsăreanu and G. Salaün (Eds.): FACS 2012, LNCS 7684, pp. 152–169, 2013.
© Springer-Verlag Berlin Heidelberg 2013

With minimal support for connectors, components have to incorporate specific interaction protocols, thus reducing their reusability. Worse yet, when component specifications omit to specify explicitly which protocols they have been designed for, we have the problem of "architectural mismatch" [14], i.e., the inability to compose seemingly compatible components, due to the (undocumented) assumptions these make on their interaction with their environment. In quite a few cases designers are supposed to use specific components that act as connectors in order to represent complex connectors. This hinders analysis, as it is not possible to identify automatically which components represent components and which ones represent connectors. It also places a lot of responsibility upon designers for ensuring that the architectural abstraction constraints are respected. It is similar to trying to encode some O-O features by hand in C – possible but very difficult to get (and keep...) correct. In our view the main value of software architectures is to enable early formal system analysis and not to be used for code generation alone. As such, an ADL needs to cleanly represent the various entities, in order to aid the automation of architectural analysis.

The Connector-Centric Design (XCD) approach attempts to apply Wirth's equation *"Algorithms + Data Structures = Programs"* [35] at an architectural level. We advocate that *"Connectors + Components = Systems"*, with connectors being essentially decentralized algorithms and components the equivalent to data structures [22]. *This means that the main active elements in an architecture are its connectors, not its components.* XCD focuses on improving the modularity of architectural specifications, so to aid their development, their formal analysis, and the experimentation with different design solutions. Complex connectors are at the very centre of XCD, since it is them that are responsible for meeting system-wide, non-functional requirements that no component can meet, such as reliability, performance, etc. In the following we shortly introduce the reasons behind the three orthogonal goals of XCD, namely support for complex connectors, support for external control strategies, and specification through a Design by Contract approach.

Complex Connectors for Architectural Analysis. Herein we use an example from electrical engineering to demonstrate the importance of complex connectors for analyzing system architectures. Let us consider k concrete electrical resistors, $r_1, \cdots, r_k$, i.e., the system components. When using a sequential connector ($\rightarrow$), the overall resistance is computed as $R^{\rightarrow}(N, \{R_i\}_{i=1}^{N}) = \sum_{i=1}^{N} R_i$, where N, R_i are variables (R_i correspond to connector roles), to be assigned eventually some concrete values k, r_j. If using a parallel connector ($\|$) instead, it is computed as $R^{\|}(N, \{R_i\}_{i=1}^{N}) = 1/\sum_{i=1}^{N} 1/R_i$. So the interaction protocol (connector) used is the one that gives us the formula we need to use to analyze it – if it does not do so, then we are probably using the wrong connector abstraction. The components (r_j) are simply providing some numerical values to use in the formula, while the system configuration tells us which specific value (k, r_j) we should assign to each variable (N, R_i) of the connector-derived formula. By simply enumerating the wires between resistors, as AADL and SysML do, we miss the forest for the trees. Analysis becomes difficult and architectural errors can go undetected until later development phases. Indeed, we are essentially forced to reverse-engineer the architect's intention in order to analyze our system – after all, the architect did not select the specific wire connections by chance but because they form a specific complex connector. The current situation is similarly to coding with labels and go-to statements and expecting our compilers to identify the higher-level looping and procedural constructs within our code so as to analyse and optimize it.

Connector Role Strategies for Control/Design Decisions. A cleaner separation of functional and interaction behaviour aids in increasing the reusability of both components and connectors. However, one can go even further, e.g., as in BIP [8], and attempt to separate the control behaviour as well. XCD supports this through modular *connector role strategies*, which are specified *externally* to connectors, and so can be replaced and modified easily. These are used to specify *different design solutions* for various issues that basic role specifications do not address (on purpose) so as to be as reusable as possible. In fact, such role strategies are already being used in good designs implicitly. Consider a simple call in C: foo(i, ++i), where i=1. According to the C language specification this call is undefined since the second parameter expression (++i) may potentially change the value of the first one (i). So we can obtain either foo(1,2) or foo(2,2). The C language specification does not specify a specific order for evaluating parameters either in the caller or the callee role, instead *under-specifying* the procedure-call connector specification on purpose. If compilers have multiple cores at their disposal they are allowed to evaluate parameters in parallel, instead of having to evaluate each one in a specific sequential order. The C language specification allows compilers to apply different evaluation strategies on the caller role by delaying this design decision until the optimal choice can be made, based on the call context and the implementation costs of the available strategies.

Design by Contract. JML [9] seems to be gaining popularity among developers, as they use it for "test-driven development". XCD attempts to follow this trend so as to maximize adoption by practitioners. Thus, it departs from Wright's [1] use of a process algebra (Hoare's CSP [18]) and follows a Design by Contract (DbC) [28] approach like JML instead, specifying systems through simple *pairs of method pre-/post-conditions*, based upon Hoare's logic [17]. In fact, XCD extends DbC in two ways. First, it *separates* the component *functional behaviour* from its *minimal interaction requirements*. Second, it allows *service consumers* to specify their own *contractual clauses*.

1.1 Running Example – The Dining Philosophers

We present XCD through the classic *Dining Philosophers* problem, since one needs a complex enough system to demonstrate the need for the different aspects of the approach. This system can be designed with either decentralized or centralized control (i.e., a butler), and for each of these general architectural solutions, there are different specific design solutions for controlling the system in particular ways (e.g., for deadlock-freedom). In the dining philosophers problem a set of *n* philosophers occasionally sit on seats at a round table, sharing a fork at their right and left. Each philosopher needs both forks to be able to eat but if all philosophers get one fork then there is a deadlock, since no philosophers put down a fork until they have finished eating.

We show how designers can specify the system architecture and experiment with different control policies, without changing the specifications of either the connectors

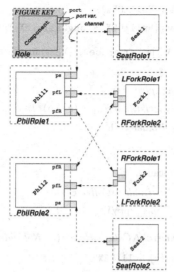

Philosopher ports are named (ps, pfL, pfR) as they are mirrored.

Fig. 1. Dining Philosophers System configuration for decentralized control

Component	Connector
Data, Predicates	Roles
Socket|Plug Ports	Data, Predicates
Methods	Socket|Plug Port Variables
Interaction Constraints	Methods
Functional Constraints	Interaction Constraints
	Channels (connecting role port variables)
Role Strategy	
Data	Configuration
Predicates	Component Instances
Socket|Plug Port Variables	Connector Instances
Methods	Role Strategy Instances
Interaction Constraints	Component/Role/Strategy Instance Bindings

Fig. 2. XCD language top-level structure

or components. Fig. 1 shows a possible configuration of the dining philosophers case study, for two philosophers. Some of the elements there (ports, port variables, etc.) are explained later, though Fig. 2 presents a quick summary of the main language structure. All constraints in XCD's elements in Fig. 2 are expressed as pre/post-conditions. Strategies may introduce their own data, predicates, and constraints but can refer only to methods of port variables defined in a role. Designers are expected to start an architectural description by the components, then derive connectors for them, and finally specify appropriate strategies. Connector roles are defined over component interface fragments, as is done in generic programming [10,29]. For example, C++'s STL defines algorithm

```
void sit(ID caller)   throws (NullIDEX);
void arise(ID caller) throws (NullIDEX, WrongCallerEX, InteractionEX);
```

Fig. 3. The `sit`/`arise` (i_{SA}) Seat interface

$$<D = \begin{bmatrix} ID\ h := \bot \end{bmatrix}, preds = \begin{bmatrix} Occupied = (h \neq \bot), & NullCaller(c) = (c = \bot), \\ CallerIsHolder(c) = (c = h), & HolderIsCaller(c) = (h' = c), \\ NoHolder = (h' = \bot), & \end{bmatrix},$$

$$P^s = \{p_s^{i_{SA}}\}, P^p = \emptyset, \phi, \chi >$$

(a) Seat top-level specification

$$\begin{bmatrix} s_1^\phi = (p_s, \texttt{sit(c)}, \neg NullCaller(c), HolderIsCaller(c)) \\ s_2^\phi = (p_s, \texttt{sit(c)}, NullCaller(c), \texttt{NullIDEX}) \end{bmatrix}$$

$$\begin{bmatrix} a_1^\phi = (p_s, \texttt{arise(c)}, \neg NullCaller(c) \wedge CallerIsHolder(c), NoHolder) \\ a_2^\phi = (p_s, \texttt{arise(c)}, NullCaller(c), \texttt{NullIDEX}) \\ a_3^\phi = (p_s, \texttt{arise(c)}, \neg CallerIsHolder(c), \texttt{WrongCallerEX}) \end{bmatrix}$$

(b) Seat functional constraints (ϕ)

$$\begin{bmatrix} s_1^\chi = \begin{pmatrix} p_s, \texttt{sit(c)}, \\ \textbf{when}(\neg Occupied), T \end{pmatrix} \end{bmatrix} \begin{bmatrix} a_1^\chi = (p_s, \texttt{arise(c)}, Occupied, T) \\ a_2^\chi = (p_s, \texttt{arise(c)}, \neg Occupied, \texttt{InteractionEX}) \end{bmatrix}$$

(c) Seat interaction constraints (χ)

Fig. 4. Seat component specification

sort on a sequence of elements of type T, using T's less-than, assignment, and copy constructor operations.

1.2 Paper Structure

We consider first component specifications in XCD, concentrating then on connectors – their specification in a decentralized manner that facilitates their implementation and analysis, and the fundamental properties that a connector should provide. We then consider role strategies for expressing control and other design decisions, and present an evaluation of the approach before discussing related work and concluding.

2 XCD Components

Fig. 3 shows the i_{SA} interface implemented by Seat components; the `get`/`put` one implemented by Forks (i_{GP}) is exactly the same. Method `sit` throws a `NullIDEX` exception, while `arise` also throws `WrongCallerEX` when the Seat is occupied by someone that is not the caller. However, `arise` throws yet another exception – the enigmatic

$$pre(s_1^\chi) \to \wedge \begin{pmatrix} pre(s_1^\phi) \to post(s_1^\phi) \\ pre(s_2^\phi) \to post(s_2^\phi) \end{pmatrix}, pre(a_1^\chi) \to \wedge \begin{pmatrix} pre(a_1^\phi) \to post(a_1^\phi) \\ pre(a_2^\phi) \to post(a_2^\phi) \\ pre(a_3^\phi) \to post(a_3^\phi) \end{pmatrix}, pre(a_2^\chi) \to post(a_2^\chi)$$

Fig. 5. Constraint composition semantics

InteractionEX. Components "throw" this special exception when their *minimal interaction constraints* (rather than functional ones) have been violated, to denote subsequent chaotic behaviour. If one opens the door of a washing machine while it is washing, subsequent behaviours include everything, even electrocution.

2.1 Extending DbC – Different Contract Types

Fig. 4a shows the Seat component specification. It defines its *data* variable set (D) and some helper *predicates* (*preds*). Then it defines two sets of *ports*, (P^s, P^p), for the "*socket*" and "*plug*" ports (empty set) respectively, i.e., the ones *providing* some interface and these *using* some interface – what in CORBA are *facets* and *receptacles*. Finally, it defines *functional* (ϕ) and *interaction* (χ) constraints, as in Fig. 4b and 4c.

All constraints use the syntax (*port-expr.*, *method*, *pre-condition*, *post-condition*). They are grouped ([]) by the (*port-expr.*, *method*) pair they apply to. They are labelled here for easy reference as $(s|a)^{(\phi|\chi)}$ – for sit/arise ($s|a$) and for functional/interaction ($\phi|\chi$). So in s_1^ϕ, p_s's sit pre-condition is ¬*NullCaller*(c) and *HolderIsCaller*(c) its post-condition, where c is sit's parameter. This is a JML "normal_behaviour", unlike s_2^ϕ that throws a NullIDEX if the pre-condition *NullCaller*(c) is true. Constraints a_1^ϕ, a_2^ϕ are similar ones for arise, while a_3^ϕ covers the case when the pre-condition is ¬*CallerIsHolder*(c). In that case, the post-condition throws a WrongCallerEX.

This last constraint a_3^ϕ introduces the difference between functional and (minimal) interaction constraints. Method arise accepts calls where the caller is not the current seat holder and throws an exception, while sit does not specify anything about this. According to s_1^ϕ it seems it simply replaces Seat's holder with the caller. However, this is captured in Fig. 4c, through Seat's *minimal interaction constraints*. Constraint s_1^χ asks that sit be delayed until *Occupied* is false. This is expressed using the "**when**" keyword as in JML's extension for multi-threaded programming [33], though in XCD functional constraints are not allowed to use it. To relate it to JML, one can think of it as a "normal" interaction behaviour, describing a method's acceptable concurrent behaviours. For all "normal" interaction constraints of components, the post-condition is always **T**. Fig. 4c also specifies the minimal interaction constraints of arise. Constraint a_1^χ states that calling arise on an occupied Seat is acceptable. Constraint a_2^χ, however, states that calling arise on an unoccupied Seat, results in an InteractionEX exception (which functional constraints cannot use). This is a situation that Seat does not know how to deal with, like calling a method on a component without having initialized it first. An InteractionEX exception leads to *undefined/chaotic* component behaviour.

Interaction constraints *take precedence* over functional ones and if both can throw an exception then the exception thrown is InteractionEX. With *pre*(ϕ) and *post*(ϕ)

standing for the pre-condition and the post-condition respectively of a constraint ϕ, the real specification of the Seat constraints is shown in Fig. 5. As highlighted there for a_2^χ, when an interaction exception's precondition is true, then the functional constraints are ignored. Otherwise, when the pre-condition of a normal interaction constraint is satisfied, the functional constraints should also be satisfied.

If one specified contracts in the usual JML manner, they would need $F \times I$ cases in the worst case, combining F functional and I interaction constraints, e.g., for `arise`:

Case 1: $pre(a_1^\chi) \wedge pre(a_1^\phi) \rightarrow post(a_1^\phi)$ **Case 3:** $pre(a_1^\chi) \wedge pre(a_3^\phi) \rightarrow post(a_3^\phi)$

Case 2: $pre(a_1^\chi) \wedge pre(a_2^\phi) \rightarrow post(a_2^\phi)$ **Case 4:** $pre(a_2^\chi) \rightarrow post(a_2^\chi)$

Repeating "$pre(a_1^\chi)$" each time makes specifications more difficult to read than they need be and much easier to get wrong. The introduction of the (minimal) interaction constraints *imposes* a much cleaner and modular manner (and guides the specification of connectors as discussed later).

2.2 Extending DbC – Service Consumer Contracts

In DbC service providers specify pre-/post-conditions for their methods but service consumers cannot express their own contractual clauses on them. Indeed, most languages do not allow consumers to even declare the services/interfaces they use. However, in component models like CORBA one declares both the services it provides (our sockets) and those it consumes (our plugs). Here we *extend DbC further*, so that we can *specify contracts for consumed services* as well. This is done for the Philosopher in Fig. 6a. Philosopher has a Boolean variable *wte* ("want to eat"), and three more (*hs, hl, hr*) to state whether it has a Seat, a left and a right Fork respectively. These change their values according to its functional constraints in Fig. 6b, *which apply when a method does not throw an exception* – that is why we call them "normal". On exceptions components do not update their data. Keyword `self` denotes the ID of the component instance.

The Philosopher interaction constraints in Fig. 6c state *when services may be requested* from others. These constraints *specify no resource acquisition/release order*. Philosopher is free to acquire a Seat after both Forks or in between them. In fact, it can even acquire or release a resource multiple times. The constraints state that when it wants to eat it will need to acquire all three resources, without releasing any of them. When it does not want to eat, it will release all three resources (again in some unspecified order), without attempting to re-acquire any of them until all of them have been released. These constraints were added so that the system can deadlock. Otherwise, Philosopher can always release the resources it holds when those it needs are not available. It is exactly for this that we have introduced functional and interaction constraints to plug ports (required interfaces). They are needed to express the constraints under which the service providers must operate, i.e., the service's *"environment model"*.

2.3 Component Structure and Its Translation to FSP

XCD components have six components – Data, Predicates, Socket_Ports, Plug_Ports, Functional_Constraints, and Interaction_Constraints. We encode these into the FSP process algebra [26] by first creating a process for the Data component of each component C, that acts as the XCD component's internal memory.

$$<D = \begin{cases} \text{Bool } wte := \mathbf{T}, \text{Bool } hs := \mathbf{F}, \\ \text{Bool } hl := \mathbf{F}, \text{Bool } hr := \mathbf{F} \end{cases}, preds = \begin{bmatrix} Eat = (wte \wedge hs' \wedge hl' \wedge lr'), \\ Think = \neg(wte \vee hs' \vee hl' \vee lr') \end{bmatrix},$$

$$P^s = \emptyset, P^p = \{p_{p\_s}^{isA}, p_{p\_fR}^{iGP}, p_{p\_fL}^{iGP}\}, \phi, \chi >$$

(a) Philosopher top-level specification

$$[(p_{p\_s}, \text{sit(self)}, \mathbf{T}, hs' = \mathbf{T} \wedge wte' = \neg Eat)] \qquad [(p_{p\_s}, \text{arise(self)}, \mathbf{T}, hs' = \mathbf{F} \wedge wte' = Think)]$$

$$[(p_{p\_fL}, \text{get(self)}, \mathbf{T}, hl' = \mathbf{T} \wedge wte' = \neg Eat)] \qquad [(p_{p\_fL}, \text{put(self)}, \mathbf{T}, hl' = \mathbf{F} \wedge wte' = Think)]$$

$$[(p_{p\_fR}, \text{get(self)}, \mathbf{T}, hr' = \mathbf{T} \wedge wte' = \neg Eat)] \qquad [(p_{p\_fR}, \text{put(self)}, \mathbf{T}, hr' = \mathbf{F} \wedge wte' = Think)]$$

(b) *"Normal"* functional constraints (ϕ)

$$[(p_{p\_s}, \text{sit(self)}, \mathbf{when}(wte), \mathbf{T})] \qquad [(p_{p\_s}, \text{arise(self)}, \mathbf{when}(\neg wte), \mathbf{T})]$$

$$[(p_{p\_fL}, \text{get(self)}, \mathbf{when}(wte), \mathbf{T})] \qquad [(p_{p\_fL}, \text{put(self)}, \mathbf{when}(\neg wte), \mathbf{T})]$$

$$[(p_{p\_fR}, \text{get(self)}, \mathbf{when}(wte), \mathbf{T})] \qquad [(p_{p\_fR}, \text{put(self)}, \mathbf{when}(\neg wte), \mathbf{T})]$$

(c) Philosopher interaction constraints (χ)

Fig. 6. Philosopher component specification

```
1 C_Mem = D([InitialValue(V)])*,
2 D([Name(V):Type(V)])* = read([Name(V)])* -> D([Name(V)])*
3  | write([Name(V)_n:Type(V)])* -> D([Name(V)_n:Type(V)])*  .
```

That is, a state of the memory is indexed for each Data variable (V) and the initial state is selected according to the initializations in the Data component. Name/Type(V) produces the name, respectively type, of the variable and the star operator means zero or more occurrences of its operand. Our translator currently supports Boolean and bounded integer variables. For Philosopher, this produces:

```
1 Philosopher_Mem = D[True][False][False][False],
2 D[wte:Bool][hs:Bool][hl:Bool][hr:Bool]
3 = ( read[wte][hs][hl][hr] -> D[wte][hs][hl][hr]
4   | write[wten:Bool][hsn:Bool][hln:Bool][hrn:Bool]
5       -> D[wten][hsn][hln][hrn] )  .
```

Then each port P of a component C is encoded as an FSP process that locks the memory, reads its current state, and evaluates the interaction constraints of the port's methods.

```
1 C_P(ID=1) = Port,
2 Port = (lock -> read([Name(V):Type(V)])* -> P([Name(V)])*),
3 P([Name(V):Type(V)])* =
4 {forall(m : Method, i : Interaction_Constraint)
5 when(pre(interaction(m, i))) m([Name(arg):Type(arg)])*
6   -> internal_m([Name(arg)])* ([Name(V)])*
7   -> internal_m([Name(arg)])* ([Name(V)_n:Type(V)])*
8                   [r:RES][e:EX]
9  -> ( when (NoEXCEPTION != e) unlock
```

```
10         -> RES_m([Name(arg)])*[r][e]  ([Name(V)])*
11                                        ([Name(V)_n])*
12     | when (NoEXCEPTION == e) write([Name(V)_n])* -> unlock
13         -> RES_m([Name(arg)])*[r][e]  ([Name(V)])*
14                                        ([Name(V)_n])* )
15 ...
16 } // end of forall(m, i)
17 | when({forall(m,i) !pre(interaction(m, i))}) unlock->Port,
```

Here, when a method m's i^{th} interaction precondition is satisfied, a call to it is accepted (m([Name(arg):Type(arg)])*) and it is passed to another process through the internal_m action. The other process, which can be seen as m's "implementation", responds by an action internal_m which has the same values for the arguments and the new values for the Data variables, as well as the result (r) and exception (e) returned. When there is an exception the memory is unlocked and we pass control to sub-process "RES_m". When there is no exception we update the memory, unlock it and then pass control to RES_m. Here, RES_m is a sub-process of P (one per method m) responsible for checking m's functional constraints, using m's arguments (arg), return type (r), exception thrown (e), and values of the Data variables (V). Predicates are expanded wherever they are used.

Processes implementing a method m (those controlling the "internal_m" actions), follow this pattern, where C is the component name and P its port:

```
1 C_P_m(ID=1) = (
2 internal_m([Name(arg)]:Type(arg))* ([Name(V):Type(V)])*
3 -> ({forall(f : Functional_Constraint)
4       when (pre(functional(m,f)))
5       internal_m([Name(arg)])* ([V'])* [r'][e'] -> C_P_m }
6     | when !(CP2) incomplete_pre_conditions -> ERROR).
7 // where CP2 is {∨_f pre(functional(m,f))} -- see eq. (2) below
```

2.4   Testing Architectural Components

Following Fig. 5's constraint semantics, one needs to check that (CP_1) the interaction pre-conditions are *complete*; and that *whenever the normal interaction pre-conditions are satisfied* that (CP_2) the functional pre-conditions are *complete*; and (CP_3) the functional constraints are *consistent*.

$$CP_1 = \forall m. \bigvee_n pre(m_n^\chi) \tag{1}$$

$$CP_2 = \forall m. \bigwedge_k \left(pre(m_k^\chi) \to \bigvee_n pre(m_n^\phi) \right) \tag{2}$$

$$CP_3 = \forall m. \bigwedge_k \left(pre(m_k^\chi) \to \bigwedge_n [pre(m_n^\phi) \to post(m_n^\phi)] \right) \tag{3}$$

In equation (1) n ranges over both the normal and exceptional interaction constraints and the predicate **when**(ϕ) always evaluates to **T**. So for Seat's sit, we need to verify that $pre(s_1^\chi)$ holds. Being a **when** predicate, this is the case. For Seat's arise we can also verify that $(pre(a_1^\chi) \lor pre(a_2^\chi)) = (Occupied \lor \neg Occupied)$ holds. In equation (2) k ranges over the *normal* interaction constraints of method m and n ranges over all its functional constraints. Both here and in equation (3) the predicate **when** is evaluated as the *identity* function, i.e., **when**$(\phi) = \phi$. This is because we want to evaluate the completeness of the functional pre-conditions only when the method is eventually executed, in which case the **when** condition should hold.

The **CP$_3$** condition is effectively checked in our FSP models through the RES_m sub-processes of ports mentioned in the previous section:

```
1 RES_m([Name(arg):Type(arg)])*
2      [r:RES][e:EX] ([Name(V):Type(V)])* =
3 Let CP3={∧_f !pre(functional(m,f)) || post(functional(m,f))}
4   when ( CP3) m_ret([Name(arg)])* [r][e] -> Port
5 | when (! CP3) inconsistent_normal_conditions -> ERROR
```

3   XCD Connectors

We can now consider connectors, as Fork is similar to Seat. If we opt for something like procedure-call, event-bus, etc. then we are specifying our system at a very low level. The extra details obfuscate the design, making it difficult to identify the high-level interaction protocols, thanks to which the system achieves its non-functional requirements. This is why XCD focuses instead on *complex connectors*. These connectors consist of a set of *roles*, each one with a set of *port variables*. Role port variables are assumed by some component ports, as specified by the architectural configuration.

Glue-Less Connectors. XCD connectors differ from those of Wright [1], since XCD employs no "glue" element for coordinating role behaviours. The glue is problematic for a number of reasons. First, the *glue is a choreography*, so one needs to realize it as a set of individual services (i.e., role implementations) composed in parallel. But [2,3] have shown that the *choreography realization* problem is *undecidable* in general. Deciding realizability in certain cases is indeed possible, e.g., [7], and in some cases unrealizable choreographies can be repaired by extending the recipient set of messages [25]. However, this is the least of the problems introduced by glues. More importantly, if we need to consider multiple instances of some role, then we need to manually specify in the glue all the acceptable composed behaviours of these instances. For example, when considering a market system with one consumer and two merchants in [12], the glue describes all possible interactions of the three roles. This *does not scale* – it is impractical to specify a glue with five or more merchants and quasi-impossible to do so for N merchants. Finally, the glue hinders the architectural analysis for further non-functional requirements, such as reliability, performance, real-time behaviour, etc. It introduces an *artificial centralization point* in the connector, even if the protocol represented by the connector does not have such a centralization point, e.g., the procedure-call. This makes analysis more difficult, since now one has to consider the real centralization points (e.g., for reliability analysis), while ignoring the fictitious ones (the glue elements of the various connectors). It also makes the modelling more *difficult to validate*. For example, in [12] the authors perform a probabilistic analysis of a market system, assigning a rate

$$< R = \{r_p, r_s, r_{fL}, r_{fR}\}, Chan >$$

(a) Connector top-level specification

$$r_p = \begin{bmatrix} D = \begin{cases} \textbf{Bool } sitting := \textbf{F}, \\ \textbf{Bool } gotLF := \textbf{F}, \\ \textbf{Bool } gotRF := \textbf{F} \end{cases}, \\ preds = \emptyset, P_v^p = \begin{cases} pv_{p\_s}^{iSA}, pv_{p\_fL}^{iGP}, \\ pv_{p\_fR}^{iGP} \end{cases}, \\ P_v^s = \emptyset, \chi_p \end{bmatrix}$$

$$r_s = \begin{bmatrix} P_v^s = \left\{ pv_s^{iSA} \right\} \end{bmatrix}$$

$$r_{fL} = \begin{bmatrix} P_v^s = \left\{ pv_{fL}^{iGP} \right\} \end{bmatrix}$$

$$r_{fR} = \begin{bmatrix} P_v^s = \left\{ pv_{fR}^{iGP} \right\} \end{bmatrix}$$

(b) Role (R) definitions

$$[(pv_{p\_s}, \texttt{sit(self)}, \textbf{when}(\neg sitting), sitting' = \textbf{T})]$$

$$[(pv_{p\_s}, \texttt{arise(self)}, \textbf{when}(sitting), sitting' = \textbf{F})]$$

$$[(pv_{p\_fL}, \texttt{get(self)}, \textbf{when}(\neg gotLF), gotLF' = \textbf{T})]$$

$$[(pv_{p\_fL}, \texttt{put(self)}, \textbf{when}(gotLF), gotLF' = \textbf{F})]$$

$$[(pv_{p\_fR}, \texttt{get(self)}, \textbf{when}(\neg gotRF), gotRF' = \textbf{T})]$$

$$[(pv_{p\_fR}, \texttt{put(self)}, \textbf{when}(gotRF), gotRF' = \textbf{F})]$$

(c) Philosopher role constraints (χ_p)

$$c_{p,s}^{\rightleftharpoons} = (pv_{p\_s}, pv_s), c_{p,fl}^{\rightleftharpoons} = (pv_{p\_fL}, pv_{fL}),$$
$$c_{p,fr}^{\rightleftharpoons} = (pv_{p\_fR}, pv_{fR})$$

(d) Channels (*Chan*) connecting port-variables

Fig. 7. Dining philosophers decentralized control connector

R_1 to all transitions between the consumer role and the glue and a rate R_2 to all transitions among the glue and the merchant roles. However, transitions between the consumer and the glue represent in reality requests from the consumer to the merchants, as well as responses from the merchants to the consumer. The transitions among the glue and the merchants also represent the same requests and responses. We fail to see how these rate assignments can be justified – in our view, the glue complicates the situation so much that it is very easy to produce models that are difficult to understand, and, thus, difficult to ensure that they represent the real system faithfully.

Wrapper-Like Connectors. In [1], a component should implement the roles it assumes, $\mathcal{L}(Comp) \subseteq \mathcal{L}(Role)$, i.e., have the same set of behaviours as the role or a subset of that. This seems too constraining and limiting component reusability. Instead, XCD components focus on implementing just the minimum interaction constraints that they need to operate correctly. The roles they assume act as a sort of *wrapper*, controlling their behaviour so that it meets the expected role behaviours.

Another way of looking at it is to consider components as machines that (modulo their constraints) execute the script (constraints) specified by the connector roles they assume, just like human actors do.

3.1 Decentralized Control Connector

Fig. 7 shows the specification of a complex Decentralized Control connector for the dining philosophers. The connector defines a set of roles and interaction channels (Fig. 7a). The specifications of the roles are shown in Fig. 7b. Each of them has five constituent parts: a set of *role data variables* (D), a set of *predicates* (*preds*), a set of *plug port variables* (P_v^p), a set of *socket port variables* (P_v^s), and a set of *interaction constraints* (χ). Roles r_s, r_{fL}, and r_{fR}, have socket port variables only (rest omitted for brevity). Role r_p

uses variables to keep track of the state of resources and to control it through its constraints in Fig. 7c so that it only acquires resources when it does not hold them already and releases them when it does hold them. Constraints modify role variables only when the respective methods do not raise exceptions. Channels in Fig. 7d state which role port variables are linked to each other – all the channels we use are *rendez-vous* ones.

This connector does not describe the full system configuration. If there are n instances of the Philosopher, Seat, and Fork components in the system then there should be n instances of the Decentralized connector as well, since a single connector instance can only connect one Philosopher, with one Seat and two Forks.

3.2   FSP Encoding of XCD Connector Roles

Encoding connector role port variables is similar to encoding component ports. The only difference is that since roles do not have functional constraints, a request for a method "m([Name(arg):Type(arg)])*" is immediately followed by a response through its corresponding "m_ret" action (performed by some component's RES_m sub-process).

3.3   Fundamental Connector Properties

There is *only one fundamental property* for a connector to be complete: ($\mathbf{XP_1}$) *interaction exception-freedom*. ($\mathbf{XP_1}$) is a connector-level property. It requires that component socket ports never throw an interaction exception, no matter how the component plug ports behave. This can be checked by composing the connector with the corresponding components that assume its roles, *while setting all interaction pre-conditions of component plug ports to* $\mathbf{T}$ (i.e., those in Fig. 6c). Doing so allows us to explore all possible interaction patterns that the connector roles allow for the components and verify that interaction exceptions have been rendered impossible by it. However, a connector can be left incomplete on purpose and be completed later using role strategies.

It should be noted that a connector is not necessarily deadlock-free, not even at a local, role level. That is, a role may introduce such constraints that it renders its component's actions impossible after some point. XCD permits this as the designer may need it to essentially remove a component from a protocol at some point. If one wants to check that this is not the case, then they need to check local deadlock-freedom ($\mathbf{XP_2}$): $\mathscr{L}(Comp \parallel Role)@\Sigma^{Role} \subseteq \mathscr{L}(Role)$, where @ projects a language on an alphabet.

Even when a connector is complete and locally deadlock-free it is not necessarily deadlock-free as a whole. Nevertheless we do not view this as being problematic because we believe that connector-level deadlock-freedom is best met through external role strategies as discussed in section 4.

4   Role Strategies – Control/Design Decisions

XCD *advocates the underspecification of connectors* – additional interaction properties are to be imposed through *modular role strategies* [22]. These can enforce an action order, e.g., that Seat is acquired before the Forks, or render the system deadlock-free. Deadlock-freedom can usually be achieved through different techniques. Instead of

$[(pv_{p\_fL}, \texttt{get}(c), \textbf{when}(sitting), \textbf{T})]$ $[(pv_{p\_s}, \texttt{arise}(c), \textbf{when} \neg(gotLF \vee gotRF), \textbf{T})]$

$[(pv_{p\_fR}, \texttt{get}(c), \textbf{when}(sitting), \textbf{T})]$ **(b)** Resource release order

(a) Resource acquisition order

$[(pv_{p\_fL}, \texttt{get}(c), \textbf{when}(gotRF \vee c\%2 = 0), \textbf{T})]$

$[(pv_{p\_fR}, \texttt{get}(c), \textbf{when}(gotLF \vee c\%2 \neq 0), \textbf{T})]$

(c) Deadlock-avoidance by asymmetry – for even/odd c

$[(pv_{p\_fL}, \texttt{get}(c), \textbf{when}(gotRF \vee (r_{fL}.\texttt{ID} < r_{fR}.\texttt{ID})), \textbf{T})]$

$[(pv_{p\_fR}, \texttt{get}(c), \textbf{when}(gotLF \vee \neg(r_{fL}.\texttt{ID} < r_{fR}.\texttt{ID})), \textbf{T})]$

(d) Deadlock-avoidance by resource order – the fork with the least ID has priority

Fig. 8. Philosopher role strategies (their constraints)

hard-coding one in the connector, XCD allows designers to re-use the same connector specification and experiment with different strategies for it in a modular fashion.

Fig. 8 shows examples of such strategies for the Philosopher role. The strategy in Fig. 8a forces Seat to be acquired before the Forks, while that of Fig. 8b forces Forks to be released first. Then the asymmetry strategy in Fig. 8c avoids deadlocks by picking a different Fork when the ID of the caller c is odd or even. The strategy in Fig. 8d also avoids deadlocks but does so by always acquiring the Fork with the smallest ID first.

Strategies are encoded in FSP like roles are. Finally, configurations are encoded by a series of action prefixing, renaming, etc., that are too tortuous to describe in detail.

5   Evaluating XCD's Modular Specifications

We have encoded (first manually, then automatically) these architectural specifications in the FSP process algebra [26] and have verified them automatically. Our goal was to establish that our architectural specifications can be verified automatically indeed and to obtain some early results on the usefulness of modular specifications. In particular we wanted to evaluate the usefulness of control strategies and how these could aid designers when developing an architecture. In total, we considered 12 different configurations for the decentralized system, shown in Fig. 1 for two philosophers, using different combinations of strategies. In all these cases our models remained the same, with the only difference being the enabling/disabling of strategies. This cannot be stressed enough – without such a modular specification it would have been extremely difficult to encode in FSP the different models of connector/strategy combinations or, even worse, the different models of connector/strategy/component combinations if we were to use AADL-like simple connectors. Not having a compiler initially (a prototype one is available now) had forced us to increase the modularity of our language as much as possible. This modularity maximizes architectural exploration in practice – one can start with minimal component and connector specifications and test multiple strategies without having to modify any specifications.

The different role strategies defined in Fig. 8 allow designers to easily experiment with controlling their system and evaluating different design decisions early on. XCD

Table 1. Different decentralized control strategy combinations

(a) 2 Philosophers

Strategies	States	Red. (%)	Trans.	Red. (%)	Dead-lock
No strategies	505	0.00	1104	0.00	Yes
Acq(uisition)	303	40.00	628	43.12	Yes
Rel(ease)	345	31.68	732	33.70	Yes
As(ymmetry)	335	33.66	708	35.87	No
Acq./Rel.	179	64.55	352	68.12	Yes
Acq./As.	245	51.49	504	54.35	No
Rel./As.	205	59.41	412	62.68	No
Acq./Rel./As.	133	73.66	256	76.81	No
Res. Order (**RO**)	335	33.66	708	35.87	No
Acq./RO	245	51.49	504	54.35	No
Rel./RO	205	59.41	412	62.68	No
Acq./Rel./RO	133	73.66	256	76.81	No

(b) 3 Philosophers

Strategies	States	Red. (%)	Trans.	Red. (%)	Dead-lock
No strategies	12750	0.00	42060	0.00	Yes
Acq(uisition)	6381	49.95	20178	52.03	Yes
Rel(ease)	6615	48.12	21030	50.00	Yes
As(ymmetry)	7550	40.78	24320	42.18	No
Acq./Rel.	2532	80.14	7452	82.28	Yes
Acq./As.	4850	61.96	15278	63.68	No
Rel./As.	3260	74.43	9892	76.48	No
Acq./Rel./As.	1667	86.93	4804	88.58	No
Res. Order (**RO**)	7550	40.78	24320	42.18	No
Acq./RO	4850	61.96	15278	63.68	No
Rel./RO	3260	74.43	9892	76.48	No
Acq./Rel./RO	1667	86.93	4804	88.58	No

(c) 4 Philosophers

Strategies	States	Red. (%)	Trans.	Red. (%)	Dead-lock
No strategies	304325	0.00	1340320	0.00	Yes
Acq(uisition)	123327	59.48	521992	61.05	Yes
Rel(ease)	124545	59.08	527864	60.62	Yes
As(ymmetry)	146925	51.72	631480	52.89	No
Acq./Rel.	34775	88.57	136496	89.82	Yes
Acq./As.	85725	71.83	361960	72.99	No
Rel./As.	44455	85.39	178168	86.71	No
Acq./Rel./As.	19561	93.57	75136	94.39	No
Res. Order (**RO**)	156675	48.52	675680	49.59	No
Acq./RO	86925	71.44	366896	72.63	No
Rel./RO	50305	83.47	204108	84.77	No
Acq./Rel./RO	20173	93.37	77568	94.21	No

(d) 5 Philosophers

Strategies	States	Red. (%)	Trans.	Red. (%)	Dead-lock
No strategies	7178125	0.00	39529000	0.00	Yes
Acq(uisition)	2334189	67.48	12361790	68.73	Yes
Rel(ease)	2340375	67.40	12398970	68.63	Yes
As(ymmetry)	2996250	58.26	16129250	59.20	No
Acq./Rel.	475359	93.38	2332320	94.10	Yes
Acq./As.	1497825	79.13	7915260	79.98	No
Rel./As.	691550	90.37	3484630	91.18	No
Acq./Rel./As.	235655	96.72	1132228	97.14	No
Res. Order (**RO**)	3191250	55.54	17227750	56.42	No
Acq./RO	1518225	78.85	8020772	79.71	No
Rel./RO	773450	89.22	3929690	90.06	No
Acq./Rel./RO	242387	96.62	1165100	97.05	No

aids designers to decide on, and *explicitly document*, the relative importance of the various system properties and the specific solutions they have provided for each. XCD also makes it easier to experiment with different strategies and configurations of strategies, as these are represented explicitly and externally to connectors.

Table 1a shows results from combinations of the two ordering strategies of Fig. 8a and Fig. 8b with the asymmetry strategy of Fig. 8c and the resource order strategy of Fig. 8d, for a system with 2 philosophers. Table 1b, Table 1c, and Table 1d show results for 3, 4, and 5 philosophers respectively. We used LTSA v. 2.2 with 7000 MB of RAM. Surprisingly, we see that the best state space reduction (third column, headed "**Red.** (**%**)") for two strategies is obtained when combining the two strategies that constrain the acquisition (**Acq.**) and release order (**Rel.**) of resources (64%, 80%, 88%, and 93% respectively), even though these do not render the system deadlock-free. These reductions are almost the double of those achieved by the strategies for deadlock-freedom (**As.**, **RO**) on their own (33%, 40%, 51%, and 58% respectively).

As these results indicate, it is not necessarily true that a designer should choose to apply a deadlock-freedom strategy first. In fact, the results obtained by the two deadlock-freedom strategies for 2 and 3 philosophers in Table 1a and Table 1b give a reason for not doing so, since they are identical. So designers have to consider a larger system, with 4 philosophers and possibly with 5, to be able to choose one deadlock-freedom strategy over another. There the two strategies produce different results (a 51% versus 48% reduction and a 58% versus a 55% one respectively). However, checking a larger system is far more expensive and may lead to state-space explosion. So we can see that constraining first with some strategies that do not meet any critical properties, as with the acquisition and release ordering strategies, is a sensible step for reducing the overall state-space. It allows designers to explore larger instances of the system, which may potentially help identify further problems, opportunities for optimization, or simply provide evidence for choosing among alternative strategies for meeting a particular property, as it does here. Designers can then easily remove some of the non-critical strategies, if they need to use the extra degrees of freedom for meeting other critical properties, e.g., performance. This is made possible by the modular nature of the strategies – adding and removing them requires no modifications to either component or connector specifications.

A connector for centralized control (with a "Butler" role) and associated evaluation results is described in a separate technical report [23].

6   Related Work

Research in software architectures identified the need for first-class connectors from the very beginning [15, 30]. The problems created by the non-documentation of protocols was also identified early on in [14] and a formalization of connectors was presented in [1] shortly after that – a formalization that is still being used today, e.g., [19, 34]. Indeed, the connectors in CONNECT [19] follow the same general structure as Wright's (roles and glue), but seem to be specified in FSP instead of CSP. Compared to Wright [1], XCD adds the extra element of *role strategy*, and the additional constraint that connectors and strategies should *not have a glue*. As such XCD avoids the glue realizability problem – XCD connector roles are realizable by construction, as they only require access to local data (Booleans, integers, buffers, etc.). XCD also abandons the use of CSP for what we believe is a more developer-friendly approach.

Work which has been done at identifying different types of connectors [16, 27] has tended to focus at cataloguing and specifying basic interaction mechanisms, e.g., procedure calls, event buses, etc., especially since these were needed to base upon them more complex connectors. However, the use of basic interaction mechanisms as connectors in an architectural specification makes it difficult to understand what the real protocols in the system are and leads to system specifications that are at a very low level of abstraction, as is the case with AADL [11]. Indeed, designers are forced to incorporate the behaviour of the more complex connectors they wish to use into their components, decreasing their re-use potential and increasing the chance of architectural mismatch [14]. In fact, the presence of low-level connectors [16, 27] in a system architecture should alert designers that they have a potential problem. That is, they have *over-designed* the architectural description and/or have failed to describe the general protocols that are supposed to be used among their components in a way that is sufficiently abstract, and therefore understandable and analyzable. Blackboards, event buses, tuple spaces, etc., are low-level interconnection mechanisms that give precious little information on what interaction protocols a system uses and how these meet its non-functional requirements.

Languages used by practitioners suffer from this problem in particular. A connector in UML 2.0 is just a UML association, so architects must use modelling elements other than UML connectors to describe architectural connectors [20]. AADL [13] only supports certain specific, basic connector types and does not offer the possibility to define more complex connector types, while SysML [6] does not support architectural connectors at all (only UML ones).

Plasil et al.'s work [5, 31, 32] is somewhat similar to ours, in particular the need to describe component interactions as separate entities, albeit ones which still form part of the component. Instead, XCD cleanly separates component and connector behaviour, and further separates the control parts of the connectors through role strategies.

It should be noted here that the constraints introduced through strategies are orthogonal to architectural style constraints, such as those of ACME [21]. The latter are global constraints enforcing a style, while strategies are local constraints. So there are cases where the strategy constraints are met but the style ones are not, as in a pipe-and-filter style prohibiting cycles, something that cannot be enforced through role strategies.

Compared to BIP [8], XCD differs in the fact that it tries to support complex connectors as first class entities, while BIP only provides two basic connectors, for "rendezvous" and "atomic broadcast". We believe that latter can be misused very easily by designers who mistake it for "broadcast". At the same time, BIP offers a specification framework that is closer to synchronous/hardware description languages that XCD tries to avoid as we believe that languages like JML will prove much more popular with software developers.

Compared to Exogenous Connectors [24] and Reo [4], XCD differs by introducing role strategies and by not trying to remove interaction constraints from components entirely. We believe that components still need to be able to specify some interaction constraints so as to describe what they expect of their environment and how they plan to use it. Another difference is with the way a designer is expected to specify their system. XCD uses pre-/post-conditions to specify the behaviour of components, connectors, and strategies, while exogenous connectors uses a graphical representation, which to our eyes looks too much like hardware block diagrams. Reo also constructs complex connectors by the appropriate composition of simpler channel specifications, in a manner that again resembles a circuit design. We do not expect such languages to gain a significant follow up from the general software development community – they do not look like "code" enough. XCD does use some of Reo's basic connectors as channel types that link connector roles together.

7   Conclusions

XCD is a new connector-centric approach for designing systems, aimed at facilitating their formal analysis at an early stage. XCD views connectors as the most important architectural element and uses them to cleanly separate *functional behaviour* from *interaction behaviour*. XCD attempts to further modularize architectural specifications by separating *control behaviour* into external *controller role strategies* that can be easily combined and replaced, without having to modify the component or connector specifications. These structural characteristics of XCD mean that designers can experiment more easily with different combinations of components, connectors, and strategies, to formally evaluate the properties of their systems and the potential solutions that exist for meeting those, without having to modify the specifications of any of these elements.

Inspired by JML, XCD follows a *Design by Contract (DbC)* specification approach, through the use of *simple* pre-/post-conditions so that it is easier to use. XCD *extends DbC* in two ways. First XCD introduces a *new structure for contracts*, to distinguish between the different behaviour/contract types (functional/interaction) in a clean manner. Second, XCD extends DbC so that *service consumers can specify contractual terms too*, expressing their intended use of the services they are interested in, i.e., providing a *service "environment model"*. Finally, by foregoing the use of Wright's [1] connector glue element and instead expressing all constraints through local pre-/post-conditions, XCD ensures that *connectors can be realized by construction* and that *connectors can be easily specified even in the case where the number of roles is high (or a parameter)*.

Apart from improving tool support, we are currently considering extensions of XCD so that it can deal with events (i.e., asynchronous oneway calls), and different types of interaction channels (buffered, lossy, etc.).

Acknowledgements. This work has been partially supported by the EU project FP7-257367 IoT@Work – "Internet of Things at Work".

References

1. Allen, R., Garlan, D.: A formal basis for architectural connection. ACM TOSEM 6(3), 213–249 (1997)
2. Alur, R., Etessami, K., Yannakakis, M.: Inference of message sequence charts. IEEE Trans. Software Eng. 29(7), 623–633 (2003)
3. Alur, R., Etessami, K., Yannakakis, M.: Realizability and verification of MSC graphs. Theor. Comput. Sci. 331(1), 97–114 (2005)
4. Arbab, F.: Reo: A channel-based coordination model for component composition. Mathematical Structures in Computer Science 14(3), 329–366 (2004)
5. Bálek, D., Plasil, F.: Software connectors and their role in component deployment. In: IFIP Conf. Proc. vol. 198, pp. 69–84. Kluwer (2001)
6. Balmelli, L.: An overview of the systems modeling language for products and systems development. J. of Obj. Tech. 6(6), 149–177 (2007), www.sysml.org
7. Basu, S., Bultan, T., Ouederni, M.: Deciding choreography realizability. In: Field, J., Hicks, M. (eds.) POPL 2012, pp. 191–202. ACM (2012)
8. Bliudze, S., Sifakis, J.: The algebra of connectors – Structuring interaction in BIP. In: Em-Soft, pp. 11–20 (October 2007)
9. Chalin, P., Kiniry, J.R., Leavens, G.T., Poll, E.: Beyond Assertions: Advanced Specification and Verification with JML and ESC/Java2. In: de Boer, F.S., Bonsangue, M.M., Graf, S., de Roever, W.-P. (eds.) FMCO 2005. LNCS, vol. 4111, pp. 342–363. Springer, Heidelberg (2006)
10. Dehnert, J.C., Stepanov, A.A.: Fundamentals of Generic Programming. In: Jazayeri, M., Loos, R., Musser, D. (eds.) Generic Programming 1998. LNCS, vol. 1766, pp. 1–11. Springer, Heidelberg (2000)
11. Delanote, D., Van Baelen, S., Joosen, W., Berbers, Y.: Using AADL to model a protocol stack. In: ICECCS, pp. 277–281 (April 2008)

12. Di Giandomenico, F., Kwiatkowska, M., Martinucci, M., Masci, P., Qu, H.: Dependability Analysis and Verification for CONNECTed Systems. In: Margaria, T., Steffen, B. (eds.) ISoLA 2010, Part II. LNCS, vol. 6416, pp. 263–277. Springer, Heidelberg (2010)
13. Feiler, P.H., Lewis, B.A., Vestal, S.: The SAE architecture analysis & design language. In: IEEE Intl. Symp. on Intell. Control, pp. 1206–1211 (October 2006), http://www.aadl.info
14. Garlan, D., Allen, R., Ockerbloom, J.: Architectural mismatch or why it's hard to build systems out of existing parts. In: ICSE, pp. 179–185 (April 1995)
15. Garlan, D., Shaw, M.: An introduction to software architecture. In: Adv. in SW Eng. and Knowledge Eng., pp. 1–39. World Scientific Publishing Company, Singapore (1993)
16. Hirsch, D., Uchitel, S., Yankelevich, D.: Towards a Periodic Table of Connectors. In: Ciancarini, P., Wolf, A.L. (eds.) COORDINATION 1999. LNCS, vol. 1594, p. 418. Springer, Heidelberg (1999)
17. Hoare, C.A.R.: An axiomatic basis for computer programming. Commun. ACM 12(10), 576–580 (1969)
18. Hoare, C.A.R.: Communicating sequential processes. Commun. ACM 21(8), 666–677 (1978)
19. Issarny, V., Bennaceur, A., Bromberg, Y.-D.: Middleware-Layer Connector Synthesis: Beyond State of the Art in Middleware Interoperability. In: Bernardo, M., Issarny, V. (eds.) SFM 2011. LNCS, vol. 6659, pp. 217–255. Springer, Heidelberg (2011)
20. Ivers, J., Clements, P., Garlan, D., Nord, R., Schmerl, B., Silva, J.R.O.: Documenting component and connector views with UML 2.0. TR CMU/SEI-2004-TR-008 (2004)
21. Kim, J.S., Garlan, D.: Analyzing architectural styles with Alloy. In: ROSATEA (July 2006)
22. Kloukinas, C.: Better abstractions for reusable components & architectures. In: ICSE-NIER – ICSE Companion, pp. 199–202. IEEE Press, Vancouver (2009)
23. Kloukinas, C., Ozkaya, M.: Xcd – Simple, modular, formal software architectures. Tech. Rep. TR/2012/DOC/01, Department of Computing, School of Informatics, City University London, Northampton Square, London, EC1V 0HB, U.K. (May 2012), ISSN 1364–4009
24. Lau, K.K., Elizondo, P.V., Wang, Z.: Exogenous Connectors for Software Components. In: Heineman, G.T., Crnković, I., Schmidt, H.W., Stafford, J.A., Ren, X.-M., Wallnau, K. (eds.) CBSE 2005. LNCS, vol. 3489, pp. 90–106. Springer, Heidelberg (2005)
25. Lekeas, G., Kloukinas, C., Stathis, K.: Producing Enactable Protocols in Artificial Agent Societies. In: Kinny, D., Hsu, J.Y.-J., Governatori, G., Ghose, A.K. (eds.) PRIMA 2011. LNCS, vol. 7047, pp. 311–322. Springer, Heidelberg (2011)
26. Magee, J., Kramer, J.: Concurrency – state models and Java programs, 2nd edn. Wiley (2006)
27. Mehta, N.R., Medvidovic, N., Phadke, S.: Towards a taxonomy of SW connectors. In: ICSE, pp. 178–187 (2000)
28. Meyer, B.: Applying "Design by Contract". IEEE Computer 25(10), 40–51 (1992)
29. Musser, D.R., Stepanov, A.A.: Generic Programming. In: Gianni, P. (ed.) ISSAC 1988. LNCS, vol. 358, pp. 13–25. Springer, Heidelberg (1989)
30. Perry, D.E., Wolf, A.L.: Foundations for the study of software architecture. SIGSOFT Softw. Eng. Notes 17(4), 40–52 (1992)
31. Plasil, F., Besta, M., Visnovsky, S.: Bounding component behavior via protocols. In: TOOLS, vol. (30), pp. 387–398. IEEE (1999)
32. Plasil, F., Visnovsky, S.: Behavior protocols for software components. IEEE Trans. Software Eng. 28(11), 1056–1076 (2002)
33. Rodríguez, E., Dwyer, M.B., Flanagan, C., Hatcliff, J., Leavens, G.T., Robby: Extending JML for Modular Specification and Verification of Multi-threaded Programs. In: Gao, X.-X. (ed.) ECOOP 2005. LNCS, vol. 3586, pp. 551–576. Springer, Heidelberg (2005)
34. Taylor, R.N., Medvidovic, N., Dashofy, E.M.: Software Architecture: Foundations, Theory, and Practice. John Wiley & Sons (2010), ISBN-13: 978-0470167748
35. Wirth, N.: Algorithms + Data Structures = Programs. Prentice-Hall (1975)

LOVER: Light-Weight fOrmal Verification of adaptivE Systems at Run Time

Amir Molzam Sharifloo[1] and Paola Spoletini[2]

[1]Dipartimento di Elettronica e Informazione, Politecnico di Milano,
P.zza Leonardo da Vinci 32, 20133 Milano, Italy
[2]Università dell'Insubria
via Ravasi, 2, 21100 - Varese, Italy
molzam@elet.polimi.it, paola.spoletini@uninsubria.it

Abstract. Adaptive systems are able to modify their behaviors to respond to significant changes at run time such as component failures. In many cases, run-time adaptation is simply replacing a piece of system with a new one without interrupting the system operation. In terms of component-based systems, an adaptation may be defined as replacing a system component with a new version at run time. However, updating a system with new components requires the assurance that the new configuration will fully satisfy the expected requirements. Formal verification has been widely used to guarantee that a system specification satisfies a set of properties. However, applying verification techniques at run time for any potential change can be very expensive and sometimes unfeasible. In this paper, we present a methodology, called LOVER, for the lightweight verification of component-based adaptive systems. LOVER provides a new process model supported with formalisms, verification algorithms and tool to verify a significant subset of CTL properties.

1 Introduction

Adaptive systems have been deeply studied over the last decade as means for developing dependable software applications, always more flexible and dynamic [4]. Examples of such systems are service-oriented applications [10], active sensor networks [12] and smart grids [1]. Due to the increasingly use of such systems, a lot of research has been carried out to develop techniques that support adaptation [4,8]. Run-time adaptation is required if a system is not able to cope with the unpredicted changes occurring at run time. For example, a service hired from an external component fails during the system operation or stops supporting a set of requirements. To react to such failures, a new component, discovered at run time, may be plugged to the system. Similarly, new components with higher level of QoS may become available while the system is operating, which may be preferred to the currently used component. However, since there has been no information about the behavior of the new component at design time, it is necessary to reason about its impact and negative side effects on the overall system behavior at run time.

C.S. Păsăreanu and G. Salaün (Eds.): FACS 2012, LNCS 7684, pp. 170–187, 2013.
© Springer-Verlag Berlin Heidelberg 2013

To avoid any violations, it is necessary to guarantee that the overall system properties will be satisfied in case of applying an adaptation. This could be assured by formally verifying the new system specification, which is obtained by integrating the specification of the new component, against the properties. Intuitively, it is an extra work and overhead due to the fact that the major part of the specification does not change. Moreover, model checking a large specification at run time is quite difficult because of the time and resource limitations. If we could reuse the verification results of the invariant part for future verifications, this would significantly save the time and resource usage at run time.

The existing approaches to verifying adaptive systems mainly focus on the specification and verification of adaptation process [19,2]. These approaches assume that there is a complete knowledge about the system and environment behavior at design time, so they are able to reason about the properties of the whole interaction model. However, this is not the case in many realistic examples, in which the information about the behavior of some components and the environment are obtained only at run time. This is why run-time verification techniques come into play to monitor and check that the running system does not violate the specification and the properties [11,14]. Although these approaches are less expensive than model-checking techniques but still they are not complete, and do not guarantee the satisfaction of the properties.

The contribution of this paper is a methodology, called LOVER[1], to efficiently verify that a set of adaptations will lead to the satisfaction of the overall system properties. More specifically, our approach allows the designer to verify the system at design time, even if some components are unspecified. Our model checking algorithm then verifies if the requirements hold and produces a set of constraints for the unspecified components, if needed. Once the components are specified at runtime they can be verified in isolation against this new set of constraints, without checking again the entire system.

Our approach is different from the assume-guarantee approaches in which a set of assumptions on the environment of a component is made that guarantees the satisfaction of the desired properties [13,6,9]. Instead we address the run-time model checking of incomplete or changing specifications that comprise dynamic components evolving at run time. We focus on component-based adaptive systems represented by an extension of Labeled Transition Systems (LTS) and verification algorithms for *qualitative* Computational Tree Logic (qCTL), CTL without the next operator. Moreover, we provide a tool support for the verification algorithm, and a formalism to specify the constraints.

The remainder of the paper is organized as follows. Section 2 intuitively motivates the research problem through a running example. Section 3 presents LOVER process model, the formalisms, and the verification algorithms. Experimental results are reported in Section 4. Section 5 discusses the state of the art in verifying adaptive systems, and finally, Section 6 concludes the paper and gives some hints for the future work.

---

[1] Light-weight formal verification of adaptive systems at run time.

2 The Running Example

In this section, we introduce the running example that is used through the paper. *Secure Information Retrieval* (SIR) is an information system that receives requests, in form of questions, from the clients and responds to them via encrypted messages. The system behavior, in terms of the interactions among the components, is illustrated in Figure 1.

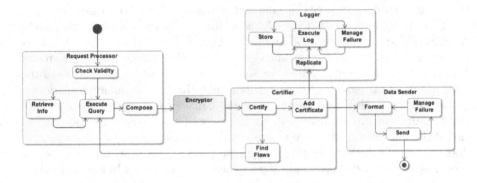

Fig. 1. The activity flow of the Secure Information Retrieval system

A request received from a client is processed by *Request Processor* component. First, the validity of the request is checked and then the requested information is retrieved by querying on different data centers. The results are composed as a message to be sent to the client. This message is encrypted by an *Encryptor* component. The system is designed in such a way that is able to dynamically change the encryption method depending on the level of the requested security and performance. Hence, Encryptor can be rebound to different components at run time with respect to the context. The encrypted message is checked against a set of security standards by a *Certifier* component. The certified message is logged and sent to the client. For security and reliability reasons, the following set of properties shall be guaranteed by the system.

Security Property: Any message shall be encrypted before being sent out over the network;

Reliability Property: The system shall recover from any failure.

Note that the satisfiability of these properties strongly depends on how the encryption is performed and the details of this module are unknown at design time. Indeed, even if an encryption module is selected and the verification is accomplished at design time, this binding may change for different reasons at run time and may require a new verification phase to re-assure the properties. The SIR system is only an example of many component-based systems whose properties depend on dynamic components, which may be bound or changed at run time. Such systems require a continuous verification process that should be as light-weight as possible to avoid intolerable overheads.

3   The LOVER Framework

Differently from traditional model checking approaches, LOVER deals with incomplete models, where a set of components are unspecified at design time and are known only at run time. Obviously, the classical techniques could be applied by checking the system every time the bindings (unspecified at design time) are resolved or changed. Indeed, the time and space required for the verification could be considerable, and since some bindings are resolved only while the system is operating, the total overhead in resolving them should be kept as small as possible.

To overcome these limitations, we propose LOVER, which is a two-phase approach, that allows the designer to verify the incomplete system specification at design time and generates a set of constraints for the unspecified components. Those constraints are verified at run time whenever the component specifications become available. An overall view of LOVER is given in Figure 2. At design time, the incomplete system is described as a particular kind of LTS, where some states are transparent w.r.t. the labels. This model is then checked against a desired qCTL property. The result of the verification could be "yes", "no" or "conditionally yes". The last option gives the set of constraints that has to be satisfied by the unspecified components such that the whole system satisfies the given property. These constraints are expressed in path-qCTL, an extension of qCTL that allows the specification of properties also over finite paths. The constraints are verified by a path-qCTL model checker, which can be obtained by a simple extension to any CTL model checker, such as NuSMV [5].

In this section, we first introduce the novel formalisms and briefly recall qCTL. Then we present the core of LOVER: the model checking algorithm for incomplete models, and a sketch the proof of its equivalence with the traditional solution. We then conclude by showing how to check path-qCTL properties on a component specification expressed as a variation of LTS.

3.1   Incompletely Labeled Transition System

An Incompletely Labeled Transition System (ILTS) is a labelled transition system (LTS) in which the set of states is partitioned in R, the set of *regular* states, and T, the set of *transparent* states, that are special states that can represent more complex components and are considered as unknown. Formally, an ILTS is specified as a tuple $\langle S, s_0, \rightarrow, L \rangle$ over the alphabet A of atomic propositions, where

- S is a set of states, which is partitioned in two sets: R (Regular) and T (Transparent) , i.e., $S = R \cup T$ and $R \cap T = \varnothing$;

- s_0 is the initial state;

- $\rightarrow \subseteq S \times S$ represents the transitions between states;

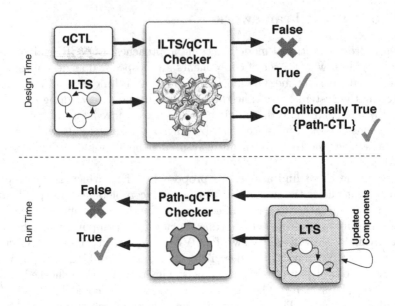

Fig. 2. The LOVER Framework

- $L : R \to \wp(A)$ is the labeling function that associates a subset of atomic propositions to each regular state.

The transparent states represent unknown components that, once specified, can be modeled using a special kind of LTS, namely LTS with single final state, i.e., a tuple $\langle S, s_0, s_F, \to, L \rangle$, where $s_F \in S$ is the final state. The initial state and the final state represent the unique entering and exiting points in and from the component, respectively. ILTS can be used to model dynamic systems in which some components are unspecified at design time or may change at run time. In other words, there is a big part of system specification that is known at design time, but there are some components that may be left undefined or may be dynamically replaced with other components. Figure 3 shows the ILTS of the motivating example, which is driven from the activity flow, presented in Section 2. Transparent state 5 represents the unavailable specification of Encryptor. The other states are labeled regarding the three message attributes: encrypted, failed, and sent.

3.2   Qualitative CTL and Path-Qualitative CTL

Qualitative CTL (qCTL) is a proper subset of CTL that excludes metrics by neglecting the operators EX and AX. Hence, the syntax of the language becomes:

$$\phi \to \ \phi \wedge \phi \mid \neg \phi \mid E \, \phi \, U \, \phi \mid E \, G \, \phi \mid p$$

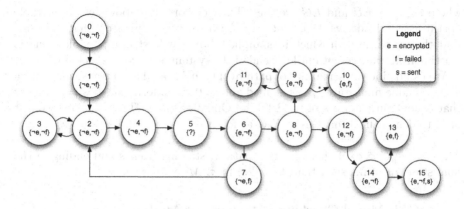

Fig. 3. The ILTS of the Secure Information Retrieval system

where $p \in AP$, EU and EG are the CTL operators whose semantics is briefly recalled below.

CTL is classically defined on a state of LTS $M = \langle S, s_0, L \rangle$ (M, $s \models \varphi$ means that φ holds in a state s of the LTS M) as follows:

- $M, s \models p \Leftrightarrow p \in L(s)$;
- $M, s \models \neg\varphi \Leftrightarrow M, s \not\models \varphi$
- $M, s \models \varphi_1 \wedge \varphi_2 \Leftrightarrow M, s \models \varphi_1$ and $M, s \models \varphi_2$;
- $M, s \models E\varphi_1 \cup \varphi_2 \Leftrightarrow$ if there exists a path π starting from s such that $\exists s_k \in \pi \mid M, s_k \models \varphi_2$ and $\forall s_i \in \pi$ with $i < k$, $M, s_i \models \varphi_1$;
- $M, s \models EG\ \varphi \Leftrightarrow$ if there exists an infinite path π starting from s such that $\forall s_i \in \pi$, $M, s_i \models \varphi$.

Notice that the classical boolean connectives ($\vee$, $\Rightarrow$ and $\Leftrightarrow$) and the temporal operators AU, AG, EF, and AF can be derived from the above sets of operators. As an example, let us consider the security and reliability properties presented in Section 2, using the set of atomic propositions $AP = \{s, e, f\}$, the meaning of which was explained above. The property "All messages are encrypted before being sent out over the network" can be expressed as $A(\neg sUe)$, meaning that there is no sending until the encryption is performed. The reliability property ("The system eventually recovers from any failure") can be instead expressed as $\neg EFEGf$, meaning that there does not exist a path in which eventually there will be a path in which there is a failure forever.

We formally define path-qCTL by adding a temporal operator to qCTL that allows the designer to predicate also on finite sequences of events. Path-qCTL will be used to describe the constraints that has to be guaranteed by the transparent components to assure the requirements validity. The syntax of the language is formally defined as follows:

$$\phi \rightarrow \phi \wedge \phi \mid \neg\phi \mid E\ \phi\ U\ \phi \mid E\ G\ \phi \mid E_p\ G\ \phi \mid p$$

where $p \in AP$, EU and EG are the CTL operators (the above set of derivable operators is still derivable)), E_PG is a fresh temporal operator, that indicates that the arguments, on which it is applied, holds at least in a possible scenario starting from the present until the end of the system behavior, i.e, the final state.

We can define the semantics of path-qCTL on M, a labelled transition system with a unique final state s_F, as defined above. If φ is a formula M, $s \models \phi$ means that ϕ holds in a state s of the LTS M. Omitting the qCTL operators, we just need to define the semantics of E_pG as follows

M, $s \models E_pG \phi \Leftrightarrow$ if there exists a path π, starting from s and ending in the final state s_F of M, such that, for all s_i in π, M, $s_i \models \phi$.

3.3   qCTL Model Checking of Incomplete Models

The core of LOVER is the qCTL model checking algorithm for incomplete models, described as ILTS. The basic idea is to modify the traditional explicit CTL model checking [3] in order to deal with transparent states. The algorithm takes as inputs a qCTL property and an ILTS. If the ILTS is a regular LTS, it behaves as the traditional approach on regular LTS, while if the ILTS contains transparent states, it computes the set of path-qCTL formulae that shall be guaranteed by the components modeled as transparent states.

More precisely, the algorithm works as follows. First, the qCTL formula is parsed and its parsing tree is derived. As usual, the leaves of the tree are propositions and the inner nodes are boolean and temporal operators. Similarly to CTL model checking, a bottom-up approach is applied to the tree to calculate the satisfactory states for each sub-formula, starting from the leaves of the tree. For each node of the tree, the set of the states in which the sub-formula holds is calculated by applying Algorithm 1.

Algorithm 1 is invoked for every subtree of the parsing tree, starting from the leaves. The algorithm takes as inputs a subtree T of the parsing tree (possibly the parsing tree itself), the formula φ, and the ILTS M on which the original formula is evaluated. The tree T is a binary tree, where a node representing a unary operator has a single son, while a node representing a binary operator has two sons. We use $T.S$ to refer to the set of states in M that satisfy the formula represented by the current subtree, $T.left$ and $T.right$ to refer to the left and the right subtrees of the current tree (when the root is a binary operator), and $T.son$ to refer to the subtree of the current tree (when the root is a unary operator). The elements of the ILTS M are referred as $M.S$ (states), $M.R$ (regular states), $M.T$ (transparent states), $M.Transitions$ (transition relation), and $M.L$ (labeling function).

The algorithm uses the set X (initialized in line 2) as a local set to store the elements that satisfy φ. Moreover, the set of constraints that are needed to satisfy the formula φ in a transparent state s are saved in a matrix $constr$. Each element $constr(\varphi, s)$ is a set of constraints in the form $[(\psi_1, state_1), \ldots, (\psi_n, state_n)]$, meaning that the formula φ holds in s if the path-qCTL formula ψ_1 holds in $state_1$, ..., and the path-qCTL formula ψ_n holds in $state_n$. For example, $constr(EGa, s) = \{[(EGa, s)], [(E_pGa, s), (EGa, s')]\}$ means that the formula

Algorithm 1. Node evaluation

```
1: evaluate(φ, T, M){
2:   X = ∅
3:   switch (φ){
4:     case φ ∈ AP :
5:       for all s ∈ M.S { constr(φ, s) = ∅; }
6:       for all s ∈ M.S {
7:         if (s ∈ M.R && p ∈ L(s)) {
8:           X = X ∪ {s};
9:         }elseif(s ∈ M.T){
10:          X = X ∪ {s};
11:          constr(φ, s) = constr(φ, s) ∪ {(Θp, s)}; }}
12:    case φ = ¬φ₁ :
13:      for all s ∈ M.R − T.son.R{
14:        X = X ∪ {s}; }
15:      for all s ∈ (T.son.S ∩ M.T) ∨ (s ∈ T.son.R ∧ constr(φ₁, s) ≠ ∅){
16:        X = X ∪ {s};
17:        constr(φ, s) = buildNeg(constr(φ₁, s)); }
18:    case φ = φ₁ ∧ φ₂ :
19:      for all s₁ ∈ T.left.S{
20:        for all s₂ ∈ T.right.S{
21:          if (s₁ = s₂){
22:            X = X ∪ {s₁};
23:            if(constr(φ₁, s₁) ≠ ∅ ∨ constr(φ₂, s₁) ≠ ∅){
24:              constr(φ, s) = ANDCombine(constr(φ₁, s₁), constr(φ₂, s₁)); }}}}
25:    case φ = Eφ₁Uφ₂ :
26:      for all s₂ ∈ T.right.S{
27:        X = X ∪ s₂
28:        if(s₂ ∈ T.right.S){constr(φ, s₂) = resolveRightUntil(φ₂, s₂)}
29:      X' = ∅;
30:      while(X'! = X){
31:        X' = X;
32:        for all s₁ ∈ T.left.S{
33:          if(∃s' ∈ X|(s₁, s') ∈ M.Transitions)
34:            X = X ∪ {s₁}
35:            π = buildPath(s₁, T.right.S)
36:            {constr(φ, s₁) = resolveLeftIUntil(constr(φ₁, s₁), π); }}}}
37:    case φ = EGφ₁ :
38:      S' = ∅;
39:      for all s ∈ M.T{
40:        S' = S' ∪ {{s}}; X = X ∪ {s};
41:        constr(φ, s) = resolveOutSCC(constr(φ₁, s); }
42:      for all sub_S ∈ ℘(T.son.S){
43:        if(sub_S is a scc){
44:          S' = S' ∪ {sub_S}; X = X ∪ sub_S;
45:          for all s ∈ sub_S{
46:            constr(φ, s) = resolveInSCC(constr(φ₁, s), subS); }}}
47:      for all sub ∈ S' ∪ M.T{
48:        X' = sub
49:        X'' = ∅;
50:        while(X''! = X'){
51:          X'' = X';
52:          for all s₁ ∈ T.son.S{
53:            if(∃s' ∈ X'|(s₁, s') ∈ M.Transitions)
54:              X' = X' ∪ {s₁}
55:              π = buildPath(s₁, T.right.S)
56:              constr(φ, s₁) = resolvePathGlobally(constr(φ₁, s₁), π); }}
57:        X = X ∪ X'; }
58:    }
59:  T.S = X;
60: }
```

EGa holds in the transparent state s either if the formula itself holds in the correspondent component or if the formula E_pGa holds in the correspondent component and EGa holds in the component represented by the transparent state s'. Roughly speaking, the elements of the set are conjunctions and the set is seen as a disjunction of such conjunctions. The evaluation algorithm is based on a switch on the value of the most external operator in φ (line 3). Considering the grammar of qCTL, there are five different cases: atomic proposition (lines 4–11), negated formulae (lines 12–17), conjunctions (lines18–24), EU formulae (lines 25–36), and EG formulae (lines 37–58).

If φ is an atomic proposition and T is a leaf, the value of $constr(\varphi, s)$ is initialized for all s. Note that this is the only case in which $constr(\varphi, s)$ is based on the value of the sub-formulae. Then, all the regular states labeled with φ are added to the set of states X in which the formula holds (lines 7-8). Moreover all the transparent states are added to X (line 10), together with an update of the correspondent $constr$ slot. In particular, for each transparent state s, the constraint Θp is added to $constr(\varphi, s)$(line 11). The symbol Θ represents a still non-identified path-qCTL operator, of which the kind will be resolved in the rest of the algorithm. The operator Θ indicates that a propositional formula, that is apparently evaluated on a state, will be evaluated on a component. If the propositional formula is inside a temporal formula, Θ will be resolved by the semantics of the outer operators.

If T is a subtree of which the root is a $\neg$ operator, i.e., φ is a formula of the form $\neg\varphi_1$, all the regular states that are not in the set of states in which φ_1 holds are added to the set X of states in which φ holds (line 13-14). The transparent states are always added to the set of states in which a formula holds together with a set of constraints (that however could also be unsatisfiable). Thus, every transparent state s is added to X. Moreover, the regular states in which the formula φ_1 conditionally holds are added to X. For both these kinds of states, the correspondent slot $constr(\varphi, s)$ is updated through the function $buildNeg(constr(\varphi_1, s))$ (lines 15-17). This function basically considers the "negation" of the set of constraints for φ_1 in s. At this stage, $\neg\Theta p$ is changed to $\Theta\neg p$, since the constraint comes from an untimed sub-formula. Note that the set represents a disjunction of constraints, while each element in square bracket represents a conjunction of constraints and this has to be considered in negating the set. For example the negation of $constr(EGa, s)$ considered above is $\{[(\neg EGa, s), (\neg E_pGa, s)], [(\neg EGa, s), (\neg EGa, s')]\}$.

When φ is a formula of the form $\varphi_1 \wedge \varphi_2$ and T is a subtree of which the root is a $\wedge$ operator, all the states that are both in the set of states in which φ_1 and φ_2 hold are added to the set X of states in which φ holds (line 19-23). If the added state contains a constraint w.r.t. the considered sub-formula, the correspondent constraint is built using the function $ANDCombine\ (constr(\varphi_1, s_1), constr(\varphi_2, s_1))$ (lines 23-24). This function basically considers the "conjunction" of the two sets, by simplifying the elements on the same state in the same constraint. At this stage, the conjunction of the elements Θp and $\Theta p'$ is considered as $\Theta(p \wedge p')$, because both the constraints come from an untimed formula. For example, if $\varphi =$

$EGa \wedge EaUb$, $constr(EGa, s)$ is defined as shown above and $constr(EaUb, s) = \{[(EaUb, s)], [(E_pGa, s), (EaUb, s')]\}$, then $constr(EGa \wedge EaUb, s)$ becomes $\{[(EaUb, s), (EGa, s)], [(E_pGa, s), (EGa, s), (EaUb, s')], [(EaUb, s), (E_pGa, s), (EGa, s')], [(E_pGa, s), (EaUb, s'), (EGa, s')]\}$.

If T is a subtree of which the root is an EU operator and φ is a formula of the form $E\varphi_1U\varphi_2$, the procedure is in two steps. First, all the states that are in the set of states in which φ_2 holds (T.right.S) are added to the set X of states in which φ holds. (line 26-27). If the added state s is transparent, the constraint of s for φ is updated using the function $resolveRightUntil(\varphi_2, s)$. This function transforms the elements of the form (x, s) that appears in $constr(\varphi_2, s)$ into $(E\varphi_1Ux, s)$. Note that the algorithm only changes the constraints connected to the current states and not the others on adjacent states of a constrained sequence. At this stage, if x has the form Θp or contains a Θ, the operator Θ is deleted. Second, X is updated by using φ_1 (lines 29-36). More precisely, we update X by adding in it the states, in which φ_1 holds (condition in line 32) and from which it is possible to reach a state in X (condition in line 33). The idea is that φ_1 holds in such states (these states can be either regular or transparent) and from them it is possible to reach directly the states in X, i.e., the states in which φ holds. For each added state, the path π that connects it to a state in the set in which φ_2 holds is computed (line 35). The path π is used to enrich the set of constraints that make φ hold in it. For this purpose, the algorithm uses the function $resolveLeftIUntil(constr(\varphi_1, s), \pi)$. This function adds to $constr(\varphi, s)$ a constraint composed by the conjunction of all the constraints x that makes φ_1 true in the transparent states of π (except the last one), after updating them in E_pGx. Again, if the original constraints contain Θ, the operator Θ is deleted.

Finally, if T is a subtree of which the root is an EG operator, i.e., φ is a formula of the form $EG\varphi_1$, all the transparent states are added to the set X of the states in which φ holds. Moreover, these states are added as singleton to the set S' that contains all the sets that represent strongly connected components, in which φ_1 always holds. Since, the added states are transparent, the correspondent set of constraints is updated using the function $resolveOutSCC(constr(\varphi_1, s))$ (lines 39-41). This function adds the constraint $EG\varphi_1$ to each of these states. Then as in the classical explicit model checking algorithm, for all the non-elementary possible subset in which φ_1 holds, if the subset is a strongly connected component, the set of the subset is added to S' and the states to X. If there exist transparent states in the added subset, their constraints are updated with the function $resolveInSCC(constr(\varphi_1, s), subS)$ (lines42-46). This function, for all the states in the subsets, adds a conjunction that includes for each state the constraint E_pGx, where x is the constraint that makes φ_1 hold in that state. Obviously, if the components only contain regular states, this constraint is empty. As the last step, analogously to what is done for operator EU, X is updated by using φ_1 and S' (lines 47-57). More precisely, starting from each strongly connected components in S', the set of the states in which φ_1 (condition in line 53) holds and from which it is possible to reach a state in which φ holds (condition in line 54) is added to X. Once a transparent node is added, the path

π that connects it to the strongly connected component in which φ_1 holds is computed (line 56), and using π (that contains also the considered strongly connected component), the set of constraints that makes φ hold in it, is updated using $resolvePathGlobally(constr(\varphi_1, s_1), \pi)$. This function works analogously to function $resolveLeftIUntil(constr(\varphi_1, s), \pi)$. In all the functions considered for this case, the operator Θp is automatically deleted.

After the evaluation algorithm is performed on the whole parsing tree from the leaves to the root, if the set of the states, that satisfy the root, contains the initial state of M, then the property φ holds constrained to $const(\varphi, s_0)$. If there is still an unresolved Θ in this set of constraints, it means that the initial state is a transparent state and that the property φ is untimed. In this case the untimed property that follows Θ has to hold in the initial state of the component representing the transparent state.

Sketching the Correctness of qCTL Algorithm for Incomplete Models
Here we informally describe the correctness of our algorithm by showing the equivalence between the classical checking of qCTL and the two-stage checking performed by LOVER. Our "proof" technique is based on the semantics of qCTL and path-qCTL. Basically, we show that checking a qCTL property φ on an ILTS with Algorithm 1 and imposing the obtained path-qCTL formulae to the components that are bound to the transparent states in the ILTS is equivalent to check the same property φ with the traditional qCTL algorithm on an *LTS*, obtained by substituting the transparent states in the original ILTS with the components bound to them.

Consider an LTS M and an ILTS M', obtained by removing k independent LTSs M_i^T (with $1 \leq i \leq k$) - starting from s_0^i with final state s_F^i - from M and replacing each of them with a transparent state s_i^T. An example, with $k = 2$, is shown in Figure 4, where the LTS M_1^T and M_2^T in M are abstracted through s_1^T and s_2^T in M'. A path π of M is called *compatible* with a path π' of M' if and only if π contains exactly the same (and in the same order) regular states of π' and, instead of the transparent states of π', it contains one of the possible paths that cross the graph obtained by substituting the transparent states with the actual components.

We want to show that proving a qCTL formula φ on M is equivalent to proving φ on M' using the LOVER approach.

Let us start by considering formulae of the form $E\varphi_1 U\varphi_2$. Checking the validity of this formula corresponds to check if $M, s_0 \models E\varphi_1 U\varphi_2$ holds, i.e., if there exists a path π starting from the initial state s_0 such that $\exists s_k \in \pi \mid M, s_k \models \varphi_2$ and $\forall s_i \in \pi$ with $i < k$, $M, s_j \models \varphi_1$. To show the correctness of Algorithm 1 is enough to show that, given a generic path π' in M', it satisfies $E\varphi_1 U\varphi_2$ and the components corresponding to the transparent states in M' satisfy the constraints obtained by LOVER if and only if there exists a path π of M, compatible with π', that satisfies $E\varphi_1 U\varphi_2$.

A generic path π' in M' can be as follows:

1. π' does not contain any transparent state s_i^T;

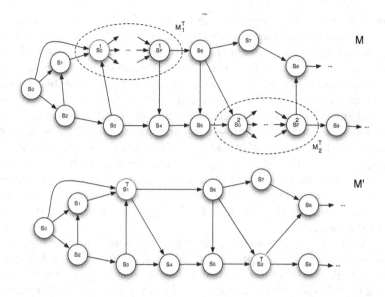

Fig. 4. An example of LTL and its corresponding ILT

2. the last state of π' is a transparent state;
3. π' contains transparent states, but the last state is not transparent;
4. π' contains transparent states, including the last position.

Obviously, case (4) is a generalization of cases (2) and (3), but since they are more intuitive, we will treat them separately (even if the proof for these cases are included in the proof for case (4)).

The first case is naive. Since there is no transparent state, Algorithm 1 behaves exactly as the classical model checking. The second case corresponds to π' containing only a transparent state at the end. Our algorithm will produce "yes" only if for all s_x in π' (excluded the last $s_{|\pi'|}$) $M', s_x \models \varphi_1$, exactly as required by the classical model checking algorithm. Moreover our algorithm will impose that $E\varphi_1 U\varphi_2$ holds in the component corresponding to $s_{|\pi'|}$ and this will happen only if exists a path π in M compatible with π' that satisfies $E\varphi_1 \cup \varphi_2$. The third case considers a path π' that contains a number of transparent states, but not at the end. Our algorithm will produce "yes" only if for all non-transient state s_x in π' (excluded the last $s_{|\pi'|}$) $M', s_x \models \varphi_1$, and $M', s_{|\pi'|} \models \varphi_2$. Moreover our algorithm will impose that $E_p G\varphi_1$ holds in the component corresponding to the transparent state of π'. All these requirements are satisfied if there exists a path π in M compatible with π' that satisfies $E\varphi_1 U\varphi_2$.

The last case is the most general case and corresponds to π' containing a number of transparent states, including the end. Our algorithm on such a path would first label the state with φ, using only φ_2. Among all the possible constraints that the labeling imposes, for the proof, we are only interested to the sets that include all the states through the end of π'^2. So, if $\pi' = s_0, s_1, ..., s_n$ and the sequence of transparent states in it is $[s_1', ..., s_m']$, for all $0 \leq i \leq n-1$, the set $constr(\varphi_2, s_i)$ can contain the constraint $[(sub_{\varphi_2}, s_j'), (sub_{\varphi_2}, s_{j+1}'), ..., (sub_{\varphi_2}, s_{m-1}'), (\varphi_2, s_m')]$, where s_j' is the first transparent state after s_i in π' and sub_{φ_2} is a subcondition needed to make φ_2 true in the current state. Moreover in s_n, $constr(\varphi_2, s_n)$ contains the constraint $[(\varphi_2, s_n)]$, where s_n is exactly the last transparent state s_m'. When our algorithm starts the labeling using also φ_1, each of the above constraints can be used to compute $constr(E\varphi_1 U\varphi_2, s_0)$, adding constraints of the form $[(E_p G\varphi_1, s_1'), ..., (E_p G\varphi_1, s_{j-1}'), (E(\varphi_1 U sub_{\varphi_2}), s_j'), (sub_{\varphi_2}, s_{j+1}'), ..., (sub_{\varphi_2}, s_{m-1}'), (\varphi_2, s_m')]$. Moreover, if such a constraint exists, the algorithm checks that all the regular states before the j-th transparent state satisfy φ_1 and all the regular states after the j-th transparent state satisfy sub_{φ_2}. A compatible path π satisfies $E\varphi_1 \cup \varphi_2$ if and only if it satisfies one of the previous constraints.

An analogous reasoning can be applied to $EG \varphi$, while the atomic proposition case and the boolean connectors need to be treated differently. When $\varphi \in AP$, φ holds in M if s_0 is labeled with φ. If s_0 is a regular state, then our algorithm will check exactly the same. If instead s_0 is included in an LTS substituted with a transparent state, the algorithm will come up with the constraint that in this component, that is exactly the same condition checked by the classical algorithm. Moreover, our algorithm deals with the boolean connectors as the classical one, only modifying the previously obtained constraints according to the connector semantics.

Notice that this is not a formal proof, but is an informal reasoning to show the equivalence of the two approaches.

3.4 Path-CTL Model Checking

To verify a path-qCTL property on an ILTS with unique final state, we need to observe that ILTS with a unique final state is a particular case of LTS and that the final state does not influence the verification of classical qCTL properties. Hence, since path-qCTL is qCTL with the extra temporal operator $E_p G$, we can readapt the classical CTL algorithm to deal with this new operator. Algorithm 2 shows a fragment of an evaluation function to deal with formulae φ of the form $E_p G\varphi_1$. The fragment uses the same notation and structure of Algorithm 1. The idea is that, starting from an LTS with final state M, the algorithm builds M' by delating the states where φ_1 does not hold and the transitions as a consequence (line 3). Then, a state s of M' is added to the set of states in which φ holds (line 7) if the final state s_F belongs to M' (line 4) and there exists at least a path from s to s_F in M' (line 6). This check can be done easily with a breadth-first search in $O(|M'.S|)$, making the overall evaluation $O(|M'.S|^2)$.

---

[2] We are looking at the satisfiability using the whole path; all the subpaths are considered separately as one of the possible four mentioned scenarios.

Algorithm 2. Checking formulae of the form $E_pG\varphi$

```
1: case($\varphi = E_pG\varphi_1$) :
2:   $S' = \{s \in M.S | s \in T.son.S\}$;
3:   $M' = M|_{S \leftarrow S'}$;
4:   if $s_F \in S'\{$
5:     for all $s \in S'\{$
6:       if $SearchPaths(s, s_F, M')\{$
7:         $X = X \cup \{s\}; \}\}\}$
```

4   Experimental Results

In this section, we present the applicability and scalability of the proposed approach in practice.

4.1   Tool Support and Applicability

We have developed a prototype tool to verify ILTSs against properties expressed in qCTL according to the algorithm presented in Section 3. The inputs of the tool are two files, which contain the ILTS and the qCTL property. The tool is capable to verify the property and report the output as a set of solutions[3]. Solutions are path-CTL properties that constrain the transparent states. The tool is also able to verify LTSs against properties expressed in path-CTL.

To demonstrate the applicability of our approach, we used the tool to verify the ILTS of the running example against the properties (presented in Section 2). Regarding the global security property $A(\neg s \cup e)$, the model checker returns two solutions that constrain a possible specification of the transparent state (state 5). The first solution is $\{S_5 \models A(\neg s \cup e)\}$, which means that the global property shall hold also in the specification. The second solution is $\{S_5 \models A_pG\neg s\}$. This property enforces the paths between the start and the end states of the specification to be labeled with $\neg s$.

Applying the verification algorithm to the second property returns only one solution: $\{S_5 \models \neg EFEGf\}$. Therefore, any component that is bound at run time to play the role of Encryptor shall satisfy this path-qCTL property.

4.2   Scalability

To see how our approach scales up with respect to the number of regular and transparent states, we performed a scalability experiment. To do so, we generated different models by concatenating the running example. Concatenation here means to produce a new ILTS by simply connecting the last state (state 15) of the ILTS to the first state of another copy of the ILTS. For example, the

---

[3] The tool is available online:
   https://sites.google.com/site/amirsharifloo/tool-lover

first concatenation results in an ILTS with 30 states in which two states are transparent. This way we generated larger models and applied the tool to verify the properties.

Figure 5 illustrates the result, which is obtained by running the experiment 100 times and computing the average. The result shows that the verification time of both properties exponentially grow. However, the verification time of the nested property grows faster as the number of states increases. The machine we used for the experiments had the following characteristics: OS = Mac, CPU=2.4 GHz Core 2 Duo, and RAM=4 GB.

Although in general the verification cost of the algorithm exponentially grows with respect to the number of transparent states, the specification topology is a key parameter that can significantly affect the total amount of the computation. Note that this is the verification time required at design-time. Obviously, it is more than a simple verification performed by an LTS model checker, since the algorithm calculates constraints, considering the combinations. Moreover, our tool is a prototype and the result can be improved by applying further optimizations. Despite such overhead at design-time, the verification cost of verifying unspecified components at run time is always less than the model-checking of the whole specification, and that is the main advantage of applying LOVER in practice. This is due to the fact that the verification at run-time phase is performed on the specifications of the components, which are much smaller than the entire one. Moreover, the constraints can be checked in parallel in order to speed up the verification.

Transparent	State	$A(\neg s \cup e)$	$\neg E \Diamond E \Box f$
1	15	0.105637	0.079811
4	60	0.76972	0.702177
7	105	3.156306	5.841801
10	150	8.659444	24.611509
13	195	19.197839	70.304578
16	240	36.051059	161.264
19	285	59.829017	326.778

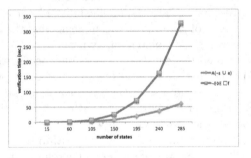

Fig. 5. The verification time for the properties (The table provides the precise values shown in the diagram.)

5   Related Work

There have been a set of approaches to formally specify adaptive systems and apply model checking techniques to verify their properties at design time [16]. To formally specify adaptive behaviors, Zhang et al. [19,20] introduce A-LTL (an extension of LTL). A-LTL adds an operator Adapt-operator which eases describing the properties that hold in the initial program and the adapted program. They also present a modular verification algorithm to verify an adaptive system against the formulae expressed in A-LTL [21]. The system is represented as a state machine in which the states present the system configurations and transitions are adaptation actions.

Adler et al. [2] propose an approach to modularly design and model adaptive embedded systems such that the system specification is suitable for verification analysis. The approach distinguishes between the part of the system that supports the functionality and the part that manages the adaptation, and focuses on specifying the adaptation behavior in order to verify the stability property of the adaptation process. Theorem proving techniques e.g. Isabelle/HOL are employed to verify the properties. The approach is extended in [15] to verify system properties with respect to environment constraints. To this end, the interaction among the system and the environment is modeled and is verified that the system properties are guaranteed assuming a maximal environment. This approach assumes that all the environmental behaviors can be predetermined in advanced so the verification of the properties are performed at design time. Although applying modular techniques reduces the verification costs, the approach assumes that the whole knowledge on the specification and the adaptations is available at design time.

Păsăreanu et al. [6,9] propose an approach to automatically generating assumptions for the environments of a component, and apply the technique for compositional verification. The output of the approach describes the environments in which a component will satisfy the expected properties. Our approach is different in the point that there exists a couple of unspecified components that make the specification incomplete and the verification unfeasible. What we do is to enforce those components with some constraints such that the global properties hold.

To verify the properties of dynamic component-based systems, there has been a trend of research based on black-box testing and monitoring at run time [18,17,7]. Xie and Zhe [18,17] propose a test-based approach for the verification of component-based systems, in which the behavior of some components is not specified. The system consists of a host system and a collection of unspecified components, which are represented as finite transition systems that synchronously communicate via a set of input/output symbols. An algorithm is used to derive a set of strings that unspecified components are supposed to generate through black-box testing. Although testing approaches do not lead to state explosion, applying them at run time is still challenging.

Run-time verification [11,14] an interesting area that addresses a problem similar to what we deal with in this paper. Runtime verification approaches assume that the implementation may be different from the specification, or the environment may change in such a way that the expected system properties violate. The aim of run-time verification is to ensure that the traces generated by the system satisfy the properties. To this end, the key idea is to generate specific elements, called *monitor*, to check the compliance at run time. Differently from model checking, run-time verification does not lead to state exploration, but it does not guarantee that the properties certainly hold.

6   Conclusion and Future Work

This paper presents a two-phase framework to efficiently verify adaptive systems, in which some components may dynamically change at run time. To support the framework, we developed formalisms, verification algorithms, and a prototype tool. We applied our approach to a running example, and evaluated the scalability by larger models.

This paper states the initial steps that we have taken to address the runtime model checking of dynamic systems. There are many directions to extend this work. At the moment, we are working to optimize the implementation and to explore a new symbolic approach. In the current paper, we have focused on qualitative CTL, but the future work is to support the full CTL by adding Next operator. Further steps are applying the approach to other case studies in different areas and extending the framework to support other temporal logics such as LTL.

Acknowledgments. We would like to thank Carlo Ghezzi for the fruitful discussions on this work. This research has been partially funded by the European Commission, Programme IDEAS-ERC, Project 227977-SMScom.

References

1. Smart Grids European Technology Platform, http://www.smartgrids.eu/
2. Adler, R., Schaefer, I., Schuele, T., Vecchié, E.: From Model-Based Design to Formal Verification of Adaptive Embedded Systems. In: Butler, M., Hinchey, M.G., Larrondo-Petrie, M.M. (eds.) ICFEM 2007. LNCS, vol. 4789, pp. 76–95. Springer, Heidelberg (2007)
3. Baier, C., Katoen, J.-P.: Principles of Model Checking (Representation and Mind Series). The MIT Press (2008)
4. Cheng, B.H.C., de Lemos, R., Giese, H., Inverardi, P., Magee, J. (eds.): Software Engineering for Self-Adaptive Systems. LNCS, vol. 5525. Springer, Heidelberg (2009)
5. Cimatti, A., Clarke, E., Giunchiglia, E., Giunchiglia, F., Pistore, M., Roveri, M., Sebastiani, R., Tacchella, A.: NuSMV 2: An OpenSource Tool for Symbolic Model Checking. In: Brinksma, E., Larsen, K.G. (eds.) CAV 2002. LNCS, vol. 2404, pp. 359–364. Springer, Heidelberg (2002)
6. Cobleigh, J.M., Giannakopoulou, D., Păsăreanu, C.S.: Learning Assumptions for Compositional Verification. In: Garavel, H., Hatcliff, J. (eds.) TACAS 2003. LNCS, vol. 2619, pp. 331–346. Springer, Heidelberg (2003)
7. Falcone, Y., Jaber, M., Nguyen, T.-H., Bozga, M., Bensalem, S.: Runtime Verification of Component-Based Systems. In: Barthe, G., Pardo, A., Schneider, G. (eds.) SEFM 2011. LNCS, vol. 7041, pp. 204–220. Springer, Heidelberg (2011)
8. Ghezzi, C.: Engineering evolving and self-adaptive systems: An overview. In: Software and Systems Safety - Specification and Verification, pp. 88–102 (2011)
9. Giannakopoulou, D., Păsăreanu, C.S., Barringer, H.: Assumption generation for software component verification. In: Proceedings of the 17th IEEE International Conference on Automated Software Engineering, ASE 2002 (2002)

10. Gold, N., Mohan, A., Knight, C., Munro, M.: Understanding service-oriented software. IEEE Software 21(2), 71–77 (2004)
11. Leucker, M., Schallhart, C.: A brief account of runtime verification. Journal of Logic and Algebraic Programming 78(5), 293–303 (2009)
12. Levis, P., Gay, D., Culler, D.: Active Sensor Networks. In: Proc. of the 2nd Symposium on Networked Systems Design & Implementation, vol. 2, pp. 343–356. USENIX Association (2005)
13. Pasareanu, C.S., Dwyer, M.B., Huth, M.: Assume-guarantee model checking of software: A comparative case study. In: Proceedings of the 5th and 6th International SPIN Workshops on Theoretical and Practical Aspects of SPIN Model Checking, pp. 168–183 (1999)
14. Roşu, G., Havelund, K.: Rewriting-based techniques for runtime verification. Automated Software Engg. 12(2), 151–197 (2005)
15. Schaefer, I., Poetzsch-Heffter, A.: Model-based verification of adaptive embedded systems under environment constraints. SIGBED 6(3), 9:1–9:4 (2009)
16. Schneider, K., Schuele, T., Trapp, M.: Verifying the adaptation behavior of embedded systems. In: SEAMS 2006, pp. 16–22 (2006)
17. Xie, G., Dang, Z.: Ctl model-checking for systems with unspecified finite state components. In: SAVCBS (2004)
18. Xie, G., Dang, Z.: An Automata-Theoretic Approach for Model-Checking Systems with Unspecified Components. In: Grabowski, J., Nielsen, B. (eds.) FATES 2004. LNCS, vol. 3395, pp. 155–169. Springer, Heidelberg (2005)
19. Zhang, J., Cheng, B.H.C.: Model-based development of dynamically adaptive software. In: ICSE 2006, pp. 371–380. ACM, New York (2006)
20. Zhang, J., Cheng, B.H.C.: Using temporal logic to specify adaptive program semantics. Journal of Systems and Software 79(10), 1361–1369 (2006)
21. Zhang, J., Goldsby, H.J., Cheng, B.H.C.: Modular verification of dynamically adaptive systems. In: AOSD 2009, pp. 161–172. ACM, New York (2009)

A Calculus for Quality

Hanne Riis Nielson, Flemming Nielson, and Roberto Vigo

DTU Informatics, Technical University of Denmark, Denmark
{riis,nielson,rvig}@imm.dtu.dk

Abstract. A main challenge of programming component-based software is to ensure that the components continue to behave in a reasonable manner even when communication becomes unreliable. We propose a process calculus, the Quality Calculus, for programming software components where it becomes natural to plan for default behaviour in case the ideal behaviour fails due to unreliable communication and thereby to increase the quality of service offered by the systems. The development is facilitated by a SAT-based robustness analysis to determine whether or not the code is vulnerable to unreliable communication. This is illustrated on the design of a fragment of a wireless sensor network.

Keywords: Distributed systems, availability of data, robustness, SAT-solving.

1 Introduction

One of the main challenges of component-based software development is to ensure that the distributed components continue to behave in a reasonable manner even when communication becomes unreliable. This is especially important for safety-critical software components in embedded systems and control software components that control part of our physical environment. With the advent of cyber-physical systems, in which software components are distributed throughout a physical system, the challenges will continue to grow in importance.

Considerable focus has been placed on how to ensure the integrity, confidentiality and authenticity of data communicated between components. In embedded systems this is easiest when communication takes place over cables shielded from other applications and used only for this purpose. However, increasingly cables are shared between many applications, including for example the infotainment system on cars, and often wireless communication needs to be employed as well, as when the control system needs to communicate with the pressure meter installed in the tyres. In health care applications there also is a trend to use wireless communication for interconnecting measuring apparatus with patient monitoring systems and with systems that dispense oxygen, saline or morphine. Solutions generally include the proper use of cryptographic communication protocols that can be proved secure using state-of-the-art analysis tools.

Less focus has been placed on how to ensure that the expected communication actually takes place. This is hardly surprising given the much more challenging

C.S. Păsăreanu and G. Salaün (Eds.): FACS 2012, LNCS 7684, pp. 188–204, 2013.
© Springer-Verlag Berlin Heidelberg 2013

nature of this problem. One dimension of the problem is to ensure that other control components continue to operate and for this it often suffices to use model checking techniques for proving the absence of deadlock and livelock in software components. Another dimension is to ensure that messages sent are in fact received and this is much harder. Over the internet the possibility of denial of service attacks is well-known — simply flooding the internet with messages beyond the capacity of the recipient thereby masking the proper messages. Wireless communication is open to the same attacks as well as interference with the frequency band and physically shielding the antennas of sender and receiver as they are distributed throughout a cyber-physical system. Indeed, it might seem that this problem cannot be solved by merely using computer science techniques.

What is feasible using computer science techniques is to ensure that software systems are hardened against the unreliability of communication. This calls for programming software components of distributed systems in such a way that one has programmed a default behaviour to be enacted when the ideal behaviour is denied due to the absence of expected communication. To this end we propose

- a process calculus, the Quality Calculus, for programming software components and their interaction, and
- a SAT-based analysis to determine the vulnerability of the processes against unreliable communication.

The Quality Calculus is developed in Section 2 and clearly inherits from calculi such as CCS [9] and the π-calculus [10]. Its main novelty is a binder specifying the inputs to be performed before continuing. In the simplest case it is an input guard $t?x$ describing that some value should be received over the channel t and should be bound to the variable x. Increasing in complexity we may have binders of the form $\&_q(t_1?x_1, \cdots, t_n?x_n)$ indicating that several inputs are simultaneously active and a quality predicate q that determines when sufficient inputs have been received to continue. As a consequence, when continuing with the process after the binder some variables might not have obtained proper values as the corresponding inputs have not been performed. To model this we distinguish between data and optional data, much like the use of option data types in programming languages like Standard ML. The construct case e of some(y) : P_1 else P_2 will evaluate the expression e; if it evaluates to some(c) we will execute P_1 with y bound to c; if it evaluates to none we will execute P_2. The expressiveness of the Quality Calculus is considered in Section 3 and an example in the context of a wireless sensor network is presented in Section 4.

The SAT-based [8] robustness analysis is developed in Section 5. It is based on the view that processes must be coded in such a way that error configurations are not reached due to unreliable communication; rather, default data should be substituted for expected data in order to provide meaningful behaviour in all circumstances. Of course, this is not a panacea — default data is not as useful as the correct data, but often better quality of service may be obtained when basing decisions on default or old data, rather than simply stopping in an error state. As an example, if a braking system does not get information about the spinning of the wheels from the ABS system, it should not simply stop

Table 1. The syntax of the Quality Calculus

$$P ::= (\nu c)\, P \mid P_1 \mid P_2 \mid 0 \mid b.P \mid t_1!t_2.P \mid A(e)$$
$$\mid \; \mathsf{case}\; e\; \mathsf{of}\; \mathsf{some}(y) : P_1 \; \mathsf{else}\; P_2$$

$$b ::= t?x \mid \&_q(b_1, \cdots, b_n)$$

$$t ::= y \mid c \mid g(t_1, \cdots, t_n)$$

$$e ::= x \mid \mathsf{some}(t) \mid \mathsf{none} \mid f(e_1, \cdots, e_n)$$
$$\mid \; \mathsf{case}\; e\; \mathsf{of}\; \mathsf{some}(y) : e_1 \; \mathsf{else}\; e_2$$

---

braking, rather it should continue to brake — perhaps at reduced effect to avoid blocking the wheels. The analysis attaches propositional formulae to all points of interest in the processes; they characterise the combinations of optional data that could be missing. This is useful for showing that certain error configurations cannot be reached; indeed, if the propositional formula is unsatisfiable then the corresponding program point cannot be reached. The availability of extremely efficient SAT-solvers makes this a very precise analysis method with excellent scalability.

We conclude and present our outlook on future work in Section 6.

2   Syntax and Semantics

Process calculi are useful for delineating a programming abstraction that focuses on specific challenges in the development of distributed systems. Calculi such as CCS [9] and the π-calculus [10] have provided profound insights into the nature of concurrent computation.

There are a least two approaches to the use of process calculi. One focuses on the universality of calculi such as the π-calculus and would explain the computational paradigms of interest by their encoding into the π-calculus (which is known to be Turing complete). The other focuses on explaining the computational paradigms of interest as primitives in a suitable process calculus in order to avoid modelling artifacts, analysis artifacts, or other intricacies due to the encoding. The latter approach has lead to recent calculi such as COWS [7], SOCK [6], SCC [2] and CaSPiS [3] for understanding service-oriented computation and have suggested several novel paradigms for how to deal with services and the increasingly important notion of quality of service. We follow the latter approach in developing a process calculus, the Quality Calculus, that enforces robustness considerations on software systems that execute in an open environment that does not always live up to expectations — possibly because anticipated communications do not take place (due to faults or denial of service attacks).

Syntax. A *system* consists of a number of process definitions and a main process:

$$\text{define } A_1(x_1) \triangleq P_1$$

$$\vdots$$

$$A_n(x_n) \triangleq P_n$$

$$\text{in} \quad P_*$$

Here A_i is the name of a process, x_i is its formal parameter, P_i is its body and P_* is the main process. The syntax of processes is given in Table 1. A *process* can have the form $(\nu c)\, P$ introducing a new constant c and its scope P, it can be a parallel composition $P_1 \mid P_2$ of two processes P_1 and P_2 and it can be an empty process denoted 0. An input process is written $b.P$ where b is a binder specifying the inputs to be performed before continuing with P. An output process has the form $t_1!t_2.P$ specifying that the value t_2 should be communicated over the channel t_1. A process can also be a call $A(e)$ to one of the defined processes with e being the actual parameter. Finally, a process can be a case construct whose explanation we defer to later. We shall feel free to dispense with trailing occurrences of the process 0.

The main novelty of the calculus is the *binder* b specifying the inputs to be performed before continuing. In the simplest case it is an input guard $t?x$ describing that some value should be received over the channel t and it will be bound to the variable x. Increasing in complexity we may have binders of the form $\&_q(t_1?x_1, \cdots, t_n?x_n)$ indicating that n inputs are simultaneously active and a *quality predicate* q determines when sufficient inputs have been received to continue. As an example, q can be $\exists$ meaning that one input is required, or it can be $\forall$ meaning that all inputs are required; these and other examples are summarised in Table 4. Even more complex cases arise when binders are nested, as in $\&_\forall(t_0?x_0, \&_\exists(t_1?x_1, t_2?x_2))$ that describes that input must be received over t_0 as well as one of t_1 or t_2. If we assume that our quality predicates can express all combinations of arguments then nested binders can always be unnested without changing the overall semantics; as an example $\&_\forall(t_0?x_0, \&_\exists(t_1?x_1, t_2?x_2))$ has the same effect as $\&_q(t_0?x_0, t_1?x_1, t_2?x_2)$ if $q(r_0, r_1, r_2)$ amounts to $r_0 \wedge (r_1 \vee r_2)$.

As a consequence, when continuing with the process P in $b.P$ some variables might not have obtained proper values as the corresponding inputs have not been performed. To model this we distinguish between *data* and *optional data*, much like the use of option data types in programming languages like Standard ML. In the syntax we use terms t to denote data and expressions e to denote optional data; in particular, the expression some(t) signals the presence of some data t and none the absence of data. Returning to the processes, the construct case e of some(y) : P_1 else P_2 will test whether e evaluates to some data and if so, bind it to y and continue with P_1 and otherwise continue with P_2.

Clearly more elaborate choices of syntax for expressions and terms are possible including the possibility of distinguishing between them using type systems. However, for simplicity we have opted for two syntactic categories and therefore we also distinguish between functions g returning data values and functions f

Table 2. The structural congruence of the Quality Calculus

$P \equiv P$	$P_1 \equiv P_2 \Rightarrow P_2 \equiv P_1$	$P_1 \equiv P_2 \wedge P_2 \equiv P_3 \Rightarrow P_1 \equiv P_3$
$P \mid 0 \equiv P$	$P_1 \mid P_2 \equiv P_2 \mid P_1$	$P_1 \mid (P_2 \mid P_3) \equiv (P_1 \mid P_2) \mid P_3$
$(\nu c)\, P \equiv P$ if $c \notin \mathsf{fc}(P)$	$(\nu c_1)\,(\nu c_2)\, P \equiv (\nu c_2)\,(\nu c_1)\, P$	$(\nu c)\,(P_1 \mid P_2) \equiv ((\nu c)\, P_1) \mid P_2$ if $c \notin \mathsf{fc}(P_2)$
$A(e) \equiv P[e/x]$ if $A(x) \triangleq P$	$P_1 \equiv P_2 \Rightarrow C[P_1] \equiv C[P_2]$	

returning optional data values. For expressions we additionally support a case construct much as for processes.

We need to impose a few well-formedness constraints on systems. For this we write $\mathsf{fc}(P)$ to denote the set of free constants in P, $\mathsf{fx}(P)$ to denote the set of free variables ranging over expressions, and $\mathsf{fy}(P)$ to denote the set of free variables ranging over terms. For a system of the form displayed above we require that $\mathsf{fx}(P_i) \subseteq \{x_i\}$, $\mathsf{fy}(P_i) = \emptyset$, $\mathsf{fx}(P_*) = \emptyset$, $\mathsf{fy}(P_*) = \emptyset$, and put no restrictions on $\mathsf{fc}(P_i)$ and $\mathsf{fc}(P_*)$.

Semantics. The semantics consists of a structural congruence and a transition relation [10]. The *structural congruence* $P_1 \equiv P_2$ is defined in Table 2 and expresses when two processes, P_1 and P_2, are congruent to each other. It enforces that processes constitute a monoid with respect to parallel composition and the empty process and it takes care of the unfolding of calls of named processes and scopes for constants. Finally, it allows replacement in contexts C given by:

$$C ::= [\,] \mid (\nu c)\, C \mid C \mid P \mid P \mid C$$

As usual, we apply α-conversion whenever needed in order to avoid accidental capture of names during substitution. The *transition relation*

$$P \longrightarrow P'$$

describes when a process P evaluates into another process P'. It is parameterised on a relation $t \rhd c$ describing when a term t evaluates to a constant c and a similar relation describing when an expression e evaluates to a constant that either has the form $\mathsf{some}(c)$ or is none; the definitions of these relations are straightforward and hence omitted. Furthermore, we make use of two auxiliary relations

$$c_1!c_2 \vdash b \to b'$$

for specifying the effect on the binder b of matching the output $c_1!c_2$, and

$$b ::_v \theta$$

Table 3. The transition rules of the Quality Calculus

$$\frac{t_1 \rhd c_1 \quad t_2 \rhd c_2 \quad c_1!c_2 \vdash b \to b' \quad b' ::_{\mathrm{ff}} \theta}{t_1!t_2.P_1 \mid b.P_2 \longrightarrow P_1 \mid b'.P_2}$$

$$\frac{t_1 \rhd c_1 \quad t_2 \rhd c_2 \quad c_1!c_2 \vdash b \to b' \quad b' ::_{\mathrm{tt}} \theta}{t_1!t_2.P_1 \mid b.P_2 \longrightarrow P_1 \mid P_2\theta}$$

$$\frac{e \rhd \mathsf{some}(c)}{\mathsf{case}\ e\ \mathsf{of}\ \mathsf{some}(y):P_1\ \mathsf{else}\ P_2 \longrightarrow P_1[c/y]}$$

$$\frac{e \rhd \mathsf{none}}{\mathsf{case}\ e\ \mathsf{of}\ \mathsf{some}(y):P_1\ \mathsf{else}\ P_2 \longrightarrow P_2}$$

$$\frac{P_1 \equiv P_2 \quad P_2 \longrightarrow P_3 \quad P_3 \equiv P_4}{P_1 \longrightarrow P_4} \qquad \frac{P_1 \longrightarrow P_2}{C[P_1] \longrightarrow C[P_2]}$$

$$\frac{t_1 \rhd c_1}{c_1!c_2 \vdash t_1?x_2 \to [\mathsf{some}(c_2)/x_2]}$$

$$\frac{c_1!c_2 \vdash b_i \to b_i'}{c_1!c_2 \vdash \&_q(b_1,\cdots,b_i,\cdots,b_n) \to \&_q(b_1,\cdots,b_i',\cdots,b_n)}$$

$$t?x ::_{\mathrm{ff}} [\mathsf{none}/x] \qquad [\mathsf{some}(c)/x] ::_{\mathrm{tt}} [\mathsf{some}(c)/x]$$

$$\frac{b_1 ::_{v_1} \theta_1 \quad \cdots \quad b_n ::_{v_n} \theta_n}{\&_q(b_1,\cdots,b_n) ::_v \theta_n \cdots \theta_1} \ \text{where } v = \llbracket q \rrbracket(v_1,\cdots,v_n)$$

for recording (in $v \in \{\mathsf{tt},\mathsf{ff}\}$) whether or not all required inputs of b have been performed as well as information about the substitution (θ) that has been constructed. To formalise this we extend the syntax of binders to include substitutions

$$b ::= \cdots \mid [\mathsf{some}(c)/x]$$

where $[\mathsf{some}(c)/x]$ is the substitution that maps x to $\mathsf{some}(c)$ and leaves all other variables unchanged. We write id for the identity substitution and $\theta_2\theta_1$ for the composition of two substitutions, so $(\theta_2\theta_1)(x) = \theta_2(\theta_1(x))$ for all x.

The first part of Table 3 defines the transition relation $P \longrightarrow P'$. The first clause expresses that the original binder is replaced by a new binder recording the output just performed; this transition is only possible when $b ::_{\mathrm{ff}} \theta$ holds, meaning that more inputs are required before proceeding with the continuation P_2. The second clause considers the case where no further inputs are required; this is expressed by the premise $b ::_{\mathrm{tt}} \theta$. In this case the binding is performed by applying the substitution θ to the continuation process. The next clauses are straightforward; they define the semantics of the case construct, how the structural congruence is embedded in the transition relation and how transitions take place in contexts.

The next group of clauses in Table 3 defines the auxiliary relation $c_1!c_2 \vdash b \to b'$. We have one clause for each of the two syntactic forms of b and the idea is simply to record the binding of the value received in the appropriate position.

Table 4. Quality predicates and their semantics

$$\begin{aligned}
[\![\forall]\!](r_1,\cdots,r_n) &= (|\{i \mid r_i = \mathsf{tt}\}| = n) &= r_1 \wedge \cdots \wedge r_n \\
[\![\exists]\!](r_1,\cdots,r_n) &= (|\{i \mid r_i = \mathsf{tt}\}| \geq 1) &= r_1 \vee \cdots \vee r_n \\
[\![\exists!]\!](r_1,\cdots,r_n) &= (|\{i \mid r_i = \mathsf{tt}\}| = 1) \\
[\![m/n]\!](r_1,\cdots,r_n) &= (|\{i \mid r_i = \mathsf{tt}\}| \geq m)
\end{aligned}$$

The auxiliary relation $b ::_v \theta$ is defined in the final group of clauses in Table 3. Here we perform a pass over the syntax of (the extended syntax of) the binder b evaluating whether or not a sufficient number of inputs has been performed (recorded in v) and computing the associated substitution θ. Table 4 gives examples of quality predicates to be used in the sequel together with their semantics; here we write $|X|$ for the cardinality of the set X.

Discussion. The semantics of Table 3 is a *rigid* semantics: The first time the top-level quality predicate holds the remaining inputs are no longer of interest and the computation can proceed. An alternative would be to use a *flexible* semantics and replace the two topmost rules of Table 3 with

$$\frac{t_1 \triangleright c_1 \quad t_2 \triangleright c_2 \quad c_1!c_2 \vdash b \to b'}{t_1!t_2.P_1 \mid b.P_2 \longrightarrow P_1 \mid b'.P_2} \qquad \frac{b ::_{\mathsf{tt}} \theta}{b.P \longrightarrow P\theta}$$

The first clause expresses that we may continue accepting inputs even when $b ::_{\mathsf{tt}} \theta$ holds, that is, after the top-level quality condition is met the first time. The second clause ensures that at any point where the quality condition is met we can decide to proceed with the continuation process. Thus there is a non-deterministic choice as to how many inputs are accepted beyond the minimum number. This becomes a bit tricky when using quality predicates that do not satisfy a monotonicity requirement, meaning that the quality condition may go from true to false once more inputs have been accepted; this is for example the case for $\exists!$ in Table 4. On top of this important difference between the rigid and the flexible semantics, they also differ in their "speed"; as an example, in the rigid semantics a single step is needed to perform the binding of a single input whereas two steps are needed in the flexible semantics. Clearly the *flexible* semantics admits all the behaviours of the *rigid* semantics as well as sometimes additional ones.

3   Expressiveness of Binders

The binding operator $\&_q(b_1,\cdots,b_n)$ is surprisingly powerful and in this section we show how the primitives of the Quality Calculus can be used to define a number of other constructs known from process calculi. In the other direction the Quality Calculus can be encoded into the π-calculus but it would seem that some binding operators would require an exponential expansion; as an example, $\&_{n/2n}(b_1,\cdots,b_{2n})$ indicating that half of the $2n$ arguments are needed would seem to require that the π-calculus encoding would need to enumerate subsets of $\{1,\cdots,2n\}$ with at most n elements.

Guarded sum. Let us consider the guarded sum $\Sigma_{i=1}^{n} t_i?x_i.P_i$ of processes that each wants to perform an input before proceeding with their continuation. It can easily be encoded in our calculus using the binding construct:

$$\Sigma_{i=1}^{n} t_i?x_i.P_i \triangleq \&_\exists(t_1?x_1,\cdots,t_n?x_n).$$
$$(\text{case } x_1 \text{ of some}(y_1)\colon P_1 \text{ else } 0 \mid$$
$$\vdots$$
$$\mid \text{case } x_n \text{ of some}(y_n)\colon P_n \text{ else } 0)$$

Here the quality predicate $\exists$ expresses that only 1 of the n inputs is required and we assume that no x_i occurs free in P_j when $i \neq j$.

To illustrate this in more detail let us consider the binary case $c_1?x_1.P_1 + c_2?x_2.P_2$ where the encoding amounts to:

$$c_1?x_1.P_1 + c_2?x_2.P_2 \triangleq \&_\exists(c_1?x_1, c_2?x_2).$$
$$(\text{case } x_1 \text{ of some}(y_1)\colon P_1 \text{ else } 0$$
$$\mid \text{case } x_2 \text{ of some}(y_2)\colon P_2 \text{ else } 0)$$

Let us assume that this process is in parallel with the process $c_1!c.Q$. Using Table 3 we have

$$c_1!c \vdash \&_\exists(c_1?x_1, c_2?x_2) \to \&_\exists([\text{some}(c)/x_1], c_2?x_2)$$

and

$$\&_\exists([\text{some}(c)/x_1], c_2?x_2) ::_{tt} [\text{some}(c)/x_1][\text{none}/x_2]$$

so we get

$$c_1!c.Q \mid (c_1?x_1.P_1 + c_2?x_2.P_2) \longrightarrow Q \mid P_1[\text{some}(c)/x_1][\text{none}/x_2]$$

We have assumed that x_2 does not occur free in P_1 and hence we have the result we would expect.

Generalised input binder. We now introduce a version of the binding operator that even though it does not need all inputs in order to proceed still will honour them – and thereby ensure that other processes will not become stuck for that reason. The new binding operator is written $\&_q^?(t_1?x_1,\cdots,t_n?x_n)$ and is defined by

$$\&_q^?(t_1?x_1,\cdots,t_n?x_n).P \triangleq \&_q(t_1?x_1,\cdots,t_n?x_n).$$
$$(P \mid \text{case } x_1 \text{ of some}(y_1)\colon 0 \text{ else } t_1?x_1$$
$$\vdots$$
$$\mid \text{case } x_n \text{ of some}(y_n)\colon 0 \text{ else } t_n?x_n)$$

Thus the idea is to spawn processes in parallel to the continuation P taking care of the inputs that were not necessary according to the quality predicate.

To illustrate this let us consider the binary case $\&_\exists^?(c_1?x_1, c_2?x_2)$ where the encoding amounts to:

$$\&_\exists^?(c_1?x_1, c_2?x_2).P \triangleq \&_\exists(c_1?x_1, c_2?x_2).$$
$$(P \mid \text{case } x_1 \text{ of some}(y_1)\colon 0 \text{ else } c_1?x_1$$
$$\mid \text{case } x_2 \text{ of some}(y_2)\colon 0 \text{ else } c_2?x_2)$$

Assume that this process is in parallel with the process $c_1!c.Q_1$. Then we get

$$c_1!c.Q_1 \mid \&_\exists^?(c_1?x_1, c_2?x_2).P$$
$$\longrightarrow^* Q_1 \mid P[\mathsf{some}(c)/x_1][\mathsf{none}/x_2] \mid c_2?x_2$$

Thus the process $c_2?x_2$ is ready to take care of a late arrival of the input; so we will for example have

$$c_2!c'.Q_2 \mid Q_1 \mid P[\mathsf{some}(c)/x_1][\mathsf{none}/x_2] \mid c_2?x_2$$
$$\longrightarrow Q_2 \mid Q_1 \mid P[\mathsf{some}(c)/x_1][\mathsf{none}/x_2]$$

showing that the unsuccessful process $c_2!c'.Q_2$ will not be stuck even though its output is neglected.

Internal nondeterministic choice. We now show how to encode a version of the general sum $\bigoplus_{i=1}^n P_i$ of processes modelling *internal nondeterministic choice* between the alternatives. The idea is to introduce n fresh channels d_i over which a fresh constant d is communicated and bound to fresh variables x_i and y_i and then to select one of the summands:

$$\bigoplus_{i=1}^n P_i \triangleq (\nu d_1) \cdots (\nu d_n) (\nu d)$$
$$(d_1!d \mid \cdots \mid d_n!d$$
$$\mid \&_\exists(d_1?x_1, \cdots, d_n?x_n).$$
$$(\mathsf{case}\ x_1\ \mathsf{of}\ \mathsf{some}(y_1)\colon P_1\ \mathsf{else}\ d_1?x_1 \mid$$
$$\vdots$$
$$\mid \mathsf{case}\ x_n\ \mathsf{of}\ \mathsf{some}(y_n)\colon P_n\ \mathsf{else}\ d_n?x_n))$$

The difference from the ordinary CCS sum is that the choices are not made according to the availability of inputs but rather an internal nondeterministic choice is performed as in CSP.

Again let us consider the binary case where the encoding amounts to:

$$P_1 \oplus P_2 \triangleq (\nu d_1) (\nu d_2) (\nu d)$$
$$(d_1!d \mid d_2!d$$
$$\mid \&_\exists(d_1?x_1, d_2?x_2).$$
$$(\mathsf{case}\ x_1\ \mathsf{of}\ \mathsf{some}(y_1)\colon P_1\ \mathsf{else}\ d_1?x_1$$
$$\mid \mathsf{case}\ x_2\ \mathsf{of}\ \mathsf{some}(y_2)\colon P_2\ \mathsf{else}\ d_2?x_2))$$

Let us assume that it is $d_1!d$ that is successful and as above we get

$$d_1!d \vdash \&_\exists(d_1?x_1, d_2?x_2) \to \&_\exists([\mathsf{some}(d)/x_1], d_2?x_2)$$

and

$$\&_\exists([\mathsf{some}(d)/x_1], d_2?x_2) ::_{\mathsf{tt}} [\mathsf{some}(d)/x_1][\mathsf{none}/x_2]$$

and therefore we get

$$P_1 \oplus P_2 \longrightarrow^* (\nu d_2) (\nu d) (d_2!d \mid P_1[\mathsf{some}(d)/x_1][\mathsf{none}/x_2] \mid d_2?x_2)$$
$$\longrightarrow P_1$$

Here we have used that neither x_1, x_2, y_1 nor y_2 occur free in P_1 and that $d_2!d \mid d_2?x_2 \longrightarrow 0$.

Generalised output prefix. Finally we introduce an operator that allows a process to learn which outputs have been delivered and then use a quality predicate to determine when to proceed. The idea is to introduce new channels that can be used for internal communication when the outputs have been accepted. The new operator is denoted $\&_q^!(t_1!t_1', \cdots, t_n!t_n')$ and it is defined using the $\&_q^?(\cdots)$ binding operator introduced above:

$$\&_q^!(t_1!t_1', \cdots, t_n!t_n').P \triangleq (\nu d_1) \cdots (\nu d_n) (\nu d)$$
$$(t_1!t_1'.d_1!d \mid \cdots \mid t_n!t_n'.d_n!d$$
$$\mid \&_q^?(d_1?x_1, \cdots, d_n?x_n).P)$$

Here we assume that the new constants and variables do not occur in the terms t_i and t_i' nor in the process P. This operator will ensure that the continuation process P can start when some of the outputs have taken place (as determined by the quality predicate q) and it will also ensure that remaining outputs are still ready to be performed so that other processes do not get stuck because of missing communication possibilities.

To illustrate this let us consider the binary case $\&_\exists^!(c_1!c_1', c_2!c_2')$ where the encoding amounts to:

$$\&_\exists^!(c_1!c_1', c_2!c_2').P \triangleq (\nu d_1) (\nu d_2) (\nu d)$$
$$(c_1!c_1'.d_1!d \mid c_2!c_2'.d_2!d$$
$$\mid \&_\exists(d_1?x_1, d_2?x_2).$$
$$(P \mid \textsf{case } x_1 \textsf{ of some}(y_1) \colon 0 \textsf{ else } d_1?x_1$$
$$\mid \textsf{case } x_2 \textsf{ of some}(y_2) \colon 0 \textsf{ else } d_2?x_2))$$

Assuming that this process is in parallel with the process $c_1?z_1.Q_1$ we get

$$c_1?z_1.Q_1 \mid \&_\exists^!(c_1!c_1', c_2!c_2').P$$
$$\longrightarrow Q_1[c_1'/z_1] \mid (\nu d_1) (\nu d_2) (\nu d)$$
$$(d_1!d \mid c_2!c_2'.d_2!d$$
$$\mid \&_\exists(d_1?x_1, d_2?x_2).$$
$$(P \mid \textsf{case } x_1 \textsf{ of some}(y_1) \colon 0 \textsf{ else } d_1?x_1$$
$$\mid \textsf{case } x_2 \textsf{ of some}(y_2) \colon 0 \textsf{ else } d_2?x_2))$$
$$\longrightarrow^* Q_1[c_1'/z_1] \mid P \mid (\nu d_2) (\nu d) (c_2!c_2'.d_2!d \mid d_2?x_2)$$

where we have used that neither x_1 nor x_2 occurs free in P. The resulting process is thus ready to handle the late communication over c_2; indeed we have

$$c_2?z_2.Q_2 \mid Q_1[c_1'/z_1] \mid P \mid (\nu d_2) (\nu d) (c_2!c_2'.d_2!d \mid d_2?x_2)$$
$$\longrightarrow^* Q_2[c_2'/z_2] \mid Q_1[c_1'/z_1] \mid P$$

showing that the additional machinery introduced ensures that all three processes can continue.

4   Motivating Example

We now consider a scenario inspired by [1] where a base station BS will communicate with a sensor node SN to obtain the value of a physical parameter, which has to be communicated to a central aggregating unit. In order to ease the presentation, we will take the liberty to use a polyadic version of the calculus.

The sensor node SN is defined by

$$\mathsf{SN} \triangleq 0 \oplus (\mathsf{sn}?(x_i, x_p).$$
$$\text{case } x_i \text{ of } \mathsf{some}(y_i)\colon$$
$$\text{case } x_p \text{ of } \mathsf{some}(y_p)\colon y_i!\mathsf{value}(y_p).\mathsf{SN} \text{ else } 0$$
$$\text{else } 0)$$

A basic node is equipped with a sensor able to measure one or more physical parameters (e.g. temperature, radioactivity) and a transceiver. As a node is typically powered by batteries, at some point in time it will die: this behaviour is captured by the possibility to non-deterministically evolve to 0 in the first line. While the node is alive, it waits for a request from the base station on channel sn, expecting the identity x_i of the sender and the name x_p of the parameter to be measured. The subsequent case constructs are used to extract the actual data, and then the measure is taken and communicated to the base station; the two else branches are in fact not reachable. The function value (which takes data as input and returns data) produces the result of measuring the intended parameter.

The base station will ask the sensor node to measure a physical parameter, and in the interest of its robustness we extend it with a process representing a local computer, able to estimate such a value. The local estimate will be communicated to the central unit and used whenever the sensor node does not respond. The local computer is defined by

$$\mathsf{LC} \triangleq \mathsf{lc}?x_e.\text{case } x_e \text{ of } \mathsf{some}(y_e)\colon \mathsf{lc}!\mathsf{guess}(y_e).\mathsf{LC} \text{ else } 0$$

and it uses the function guess (taking data and returning data) to estimate the value of the intended parameter; again, the case construct is used to extract the actual request and the else branch is not reachable.

The base station will put a limit on how long it will wait for a measure. In order to model this behaviour we make use of a time counter defined by

$$\mathsf{Clock} \triangleq \mathsf{set}?x_t.\mathsf{tick}!\checkmark.\mathsf{Clock}$$

where channel set is used to set a time-out, and the output of the constant $\checkmark$ signals that the prescribed amount of time has passed.

Finally, the base station is defined by the process

$$\mathsf{BS} \triangleq (\nu id)\,(\nu p)\,(\nu t)\, \&^!_{\exists}(\mathsf{lc}!p, \mathsf{sn}!(id, p)).\mathsf{set}!t$$
$$\&_\forall(\mathsf{tick}?x_t, \&^?_{\exists}(\mathsf{lc}?x_l, id?x_r))$$
$$\text{case } x_r \text{ of } \mathsf{some}(y_r)\colon {}^1\mathsf{cu}!y_r.\mathsf{BS} \text{ else}$$
$$\text{case } x_l \text{ of } \mathsf{some}(y_l)\colon {}^2\mathsf{cu}!y_l.\mathsf{BS} \text{ else } {}^3 0$$

where we have added some labels for later reference. In the first line the base station issues a request for a parameter p to the local computer and to the sensor node, identifying itself as id. The timer is set to the constant t as soon as one of the recipients has received the request. The second line waits for the deadline and for at least one value among the local estimate and the real measure. This behaviour is determined by the top-most quality predicate $\forall$, which requires that both inputs are successful, and by the inner quality predicate $\exists$, which insists that at least one of its two inputs is successful. As we are using the binding operator $\&_\exists^?(\ldots)$ the other input will be handled when (and if) it arrives. It is important to note that it is also possible that both values arrive before the time has passed. The third line tests whether or not the sensor node responded; if this is the case the value is communicated to the central unit, otherwise the local estimate is sent. Observe that in this formalisation the final else branch (labelled 3) is not reachable, as the requests built by the base station correctly match the inputs of SN and LC, and the latter always responds.

Discussion. Let us conclude by discussing two alternative choices for the binding construct in the second line of BS. One possibility is to use the binder

$$\&_{2/3}(\mathsf{tick}?x_t, \mathsf{lc}?x_l, id?x_r)$$

and this would require that at least one entity among the sensor network and the local computer has communicated a value before proceeding. Another possibility is to use

$$\&_\exists(\mathtt{tick}?x_t, \&_\exists^?(\mathtt{lc}?x_l, id?x_r))$$

and in this case we might end up having no value at all.

5   Robustness Analysis

The Quality Calculus provides the means for expressing dure care in always having default data availble in case the real data cannot be obtained — but it does not enforce it.

Our enforcement mechanism will be a SAT-based [8] robustness analysis for characterising whether or not variables over optional data do indeed contain data. The analysis attaches propositional formulae to all points of interest in the processes; the formulae characterise the combinations of optional data that could be missing. At key places one would like to demand that such formulae would always require default data to be available; this translates into demanding that certain logical formulae are unsatisfiable as determined by a SAT-solver.

The formulae encode optional data as booleans as follows. A value of the form some$(\cdot)$ is coded as tt and a value of the form none is coded as ff. We find it helpful to let $\overline{v}$ denote the boolean encoding of the value v, i.e. $\overline{\mathsf{some}(\cdot)} = \mathsf{tt}$ and $\overline{\mathsf{none}} = \mathsf{ff}$. As an example, the formula $x_1 \lor (x_2 \land x_3)$ indicates that either x_1 is available or both of x_2 and x_3 are available, the variables ranging over booleans.

The judgements. The main judgement of our analysis takes the form

$$\vdash \varphi @ P$$

Table 5. Robustness Analysis of the Quality Calculus

$$\vdash \mathsf{tt} @ P_* \qquad \vdash \mathsf{tt} @ P_1 \qquad \cdots \qquad \vdash \mathsf{tt} @ P_n$$

$$\frac{\vdash \varphi @ (\nu c)\, P}{\vdash \varphi @ P} \qquad \frac{\vdash \varphi @ (P_1 \mid P_2)}{\vdash \varphi @ P_1} \qquad \frac{\vdash \varphi @ (P_1 \mid P_2)}{\vdash \varphi @ P_2}$$

$$\frac{\vdash \varphi @ (b.P) \quad \vdash b \blacktriangleright \varphi_b}{\vdash (\exists \mathsf{bv}(b).\varphi) \wedge \varphi_b @ P} \qquad \frac{\vdash \varphi @ (t_1!t_2.P)}{\vdash \varphi @ P}$$

$$\frac{\vdash \varphi @ (\mathsf{case}\ e\ \mathsf{of}\ \mathsf{some}(y): P_1\ \mathsf{else}\ P_2) \quad \vdash e \triangleright \varphi_e}{\vdash \varphi \wedge \varphi_e @ P_1}$$

$$\frac{\vdash \varphi @ (\mathsf{case}\ e\ \mathsf{of}\ \mathsf{some}(y): P_1\ \mathsf{else}\ P_2) \quad \vdash e \triangleright \varphi_e}{\vdash \varphi \wedge \neg\varphi_e @ P_2}$$

$$\frac{\vdash \varphi @ P}{\vdash (\exists x.\varphi) @ P}\ \text{if}\ x \in \mathsf{fv}(\varphi) \setminus \mathsf{fv}(P) \qquad \frac{\vdash \varphi @ P}{\vdash \varphi' @ P}\ \text{if}\ \varphi \Leftrightarrow \varphi'$$

$$\vdash t?x \blacktriangleright x \qquad \frac{\vdash b_1 \blacktriangleright \varphi_1 \quad \cdots \quad \vdash b_n \blacktriangleright \varphi_n}{\vdash \&_q(b_1, \cdots, b_n) \blacktriangleright [\![q]\!](\varphi_1, \cdots, \varphi_n)}$$

$$\vdash x \triangleright x \qquad \vdash \mathsf{some}(t) \triangleright \mathsf{tt} \qquad \vdash \mathsf{none} \triangleright \mathsf{ff}$$

$$\frac{\vdash e_1 \triangleright \varphi_1 \quad \cdots \quad \vdash e_n \triangleright \varphi_n}{\vdash f(e_1, \cdots, e_n) \triangleright [\![f]\!](\varphi_1, \cdots, \varphi_n)}$$

$$\frac{\vdash e_0 \triangleright \varphi_0 \quad \vdash e_1 \triangleright \varphi_1 \quad \vdash e_2 \triangleright \varphi_2}{\vdash \mathsf{case}\ e_0\ \mathsf{of}\ \mathsf{some}(y): e_1\ \mathsf{else}\ e_2 \triangleright (\varphi_1 \wedge \varphi_0) \vee (\varphi_2 \wedge \neg\varphi_0)}$$

and the idea is that the formula φ describes the program point immediately before P. This is ambiguous in case there are multiple occurrences of the same subprocess in the system and the traditional solution is to add labels to disambiguate such occurrences but we dispense with this in order not to complicate the notation. The intended semantic interpretation of this judgement is that

$$\text{if} \vdash \varphi @ P \text{ and } P_* \rightarrow^* C[P\theta] \text{ then } \overline{\theta} \models \varphi$$

where $\overline{\theta}$ is the mapping obtained by pointwise application of the encoding $\overline{\cdot}$, and $\overline{\theta} \models \varphi$ denotes the truth of φ under the interpretation $\overline{\theta}$.

We will make use of two auxiliary judgements. One is for bindings

$$\vdash b \blacktriangleright \varphi$$

and the idea is that the formula φ describes the bindings of the variables that correspond to successful passing the binder b. The intended semantic interpretation of this judgement is that

$$\text{if} \vdash b \blacktriangleright \varphi \text{ and } b::_{\mathsf{tt}} \theta \text{ then } \overline{\theta} \models \varphi$$

The other auxiliary judgement is for expressions; it takes the form

$$\vdash e \triangleright \varphi$$

and the idea is that the formula φ describes the result of evaluating the expression e. The intended semantic interpretation of this judgement is that

$$\text{if } \vdash e \triangleright \varphi \text{ and } e \triangleright v \text{ then } \models (\varphi = \overline{v})$$

As usual, we write $\varphi_1 = \varphi_2$ as a shorthand for $(\varphi_1 \wedge \varphi_2) \vee (\neg\varphi_1 \wedge \neg\varphi_2)$.

The detailed definition. The formal definition of $\vdash \varphi @ P$ is given by the inference system in the topmost part of Table 5. It operates in a top-down manner (as opposed to a more conventional bottom-up manner) and gets started by an axiom $\vdash \mathsf{tt} @ P_*$ for the main process saying that it is reachable. Also we have an axiom for each of the defined processes; they have the form $\vdash \mathsf{tt} @ P_i$ thereby ensuring that the process definitions are analysed in all contexts.

The first inference rule expresses that if φ describes the program point just before a process of the form $(\nu c) P$ then it also describes the program point just before P. Then we have two rules for parallel composition: if φ describes the program point before $P_1 \mid P_2$ then it also describes the program point just before each of the two processes. The rule for bindings in more interesting; here we make use of the auxiliary analysis judgement $\vdash b \blacktriangleright \varphi_b$ explained below for analysing the binding b. The information φ describing the program point before $b.P$ is transformed into $(\exists \mathsf{bv}(b).\varphi) \wedge \varphi_b$ in order to describe the program point before P; the existential quantification captures that potential free occurrences of the bound variables of b in φ are no longer in scope. The rule for output should now be straightforward. The two rules for the case construct make use of the auxiliary analysis judgement $\vdash e \triangleright \varphi_e$ explained below for analysing the expression; this gives rise to a formula describing the outcome of the test being performed and this information is added to describe the program point just before the selected branch.

Finally, we have two inference rules for manipulating the formulae describing the program points. The first one allows us to existentially quantify over variables not occurring free in the process being described. The second allows us to replace a formula with a logically equivalent one.

In the case of binders the formula φ produced by the judgement $\vdash b \blacktriangleright \varphi$ denotes that succesful passing of the binder gives rise to the formula φ for characterising the availability of data as provided by the binder. In the detailed definition of $\vdash b \blacktriangleright \varphi$ presented in the second part of Table 5 we rely on the formula schemes $[\![q]\!](r_1, \cdots, r_n)$ of Table 4 for encoding the effect of quality predicates q.

The last part of Table 5 defines the judgement $\vdash e \triangleright \varphi$ for expressions and as already mentioned the idea is that the formula φ characterises the availability of data used in e. Also here we rely on formula schemes of the form $[\![f]\!](r_1, \cdots, r_n)$ for encoding the effect of functions f and we assume that they satisfy the following soundness and completeness property:

$$[\![f]\!](\overline{v_1}, \cdots, \overline{v_n}) = \overline{v} \quad \text{whenever} \quad f(v_1, \cdots, v_n) \triangleright v$$

Implementation. We have implemented this analysis by writing a program in Standard ML for computing the formulae at the program points of interest and next use the SAT [8] and SMT [5] solver Z3 [4] to determine whether or not the formulae are satisfiable. For the examples we have studied the answer is obtained in less than a second on an ordinary laptop computer.

The motivating example. Let us return to the base station BS of Section 4 where we now want to compute the analysis results for the program points identified by the three labels. Starting with $\vdash$ tt @ BS we obtain the following formulae at the labels:

$$1 : (x_1 \vee x_2) \wedge x_t \wedge (x_l \vee x_r) \wedge x_r$$
$$2 : (x_1 \vee x_2) \wedge x_t \wedge (x_l \vee x_r) \wedge (\neg x_r) \wedge x_l$$
$$3 : (x_1 \vee x_2) \wedge x_t \wedge (x_l \vee x_r) \wedge (\neg x_r) \wedge (\neg x_l)$$

where we used the same variable names used in the process in order to stress the relationship between the formulae produced by the analysis and the program points they describe, even if here the variables range over the boolean encoding of optional data. Observe that $(x_1 \vee x_2)$ refer to the generalised output prefix $\&_\exists^!(\mathsf{lc}!p, \mathsf{sn}!(id, p))$ encoded as shown in Section 3, $(x_t \wedge (x_l \vee x_r))$ is the condition for passing the quality binder in the second line, and the remainder identifies the condition for reaching the given label. We can then ask whether or not the process points decorated with labels are reachable, that is, whether or not the related formulae are satisfiable. Using Z3 we obtain the following satisfying substitutions:

$$1 : [x_2 \mapsto \mathsf{ff}; x_1 \mapsto \mathsf{tt}; x_l \mapsto \mathsf{tt}; x_r \mapsto \mathsf{tt}; x_t \mapsto \mathsf{tt}]$$
$$2 : [x_2 \mapsto \mathsf{ff}; x_1 \mapsto \mathsf{tt}; x_l \mapsto \mathsf{tt}; x_r \mapsto \mathsf{ff}; x_t \mapsto \mathsf{tt}]$$
$$3 : \text{not satisfiable}$$

This shows that the 0 process of BS will never be executed.

Let us conclude by considering the variants of the base station discussed at the end of Section 4. Using the binder $\&_{2/3}^?(\mathsf{tick}?x_t, \mathsf{lc}?x_l, id?x_r)$ we get slightly different formulae but the satisfiability results are the same as above: the formula for the process labelled 3 is unsatisfiable whereas the others have satisfying assignments.

Using the binder $\&_\exists(\mathsf{tick}?x_t, \&_\exists^?(\mathsf{lc}?x_l, id?x_r))$ we get the following formula for the process labelled 3:

$$3 : (x_1 \vee x_2) \wedge (x_t \vee x_l \vee x_r) \wedge (\neg x_r) \wedge (\neg x_l)$$

which is satisfiable using the substitution:

$$3 : [x_2 \mapsto \mathsf{ff}; x_1 \mapsto \mathsf{tt}; x_l \mapsto \mathsf{ff}; x_r \mapsto \mathsf{ff}; x_t \mapsto \mathsf{tt}]$$

The 0 process labelled 3 might thus be reachable. The above substitution gives us an indication of when this can happen: the binder $\&_\exists(\mathsf{tick}?x_t, \&_\exists^?(\mathsf{lc}?x_l, id?x_r))$ will be successful when $x_t = \mathsf{tt}$ meaning that the time has passed but it does not need to be the case that any of the schedules are available as reflected by $x_l = \mathsf{ff}$ and $x_g = \mathsf{ff}$. In this case the 0 process will in fact be reached and the BS process will terminate.

Formal correctness. We have argued informally that the analysis is correct with respect to the semantics and this is in line with how static analyses of programming languages are often presented. The main obstacle in giving a formal proof of correctness is that the semantics applies substitutions directly whereas the correctness statements talk about explicit substitutions. This is a well-known obstacle and at least two solutions are possible. One is to keep the semantics and correctness statements and to emulate the technically complex approach of [11]. Another is to modify the semantics to use explicit substitutions and perform a more direct proof of correctness leaving the technical complexities to proving the equivalence of the original semantics to the modified semantics. However, this technically complex development would provide little additional insight onto our approach.

6   Conclusion

Many of the errors in current software are due to an overly optimistic programming style. Programmers tend to think of benign application environments and hence focus on getting the software to perform as many functions as possible. To a much lesser extent they consider malign application environments and the need to focus on avoiding errors that can be provoked by outside attackers.

This is confounded by the fact that key software components are often developed in one context and then ported to another. The Simple Mail Transfer Protocol (SMTP) is a case in point. Originally developed in benign research or development environments, where few would be motivated to misuse the protocol and could easily be reprimanded if doing so, it has become a key constituent of the malign environment provided by the global internet where many users find an interest in misusing the protocol, and where it is extremely difficult to even identify offenders.

Future programming languages and programming environments need to support a more robust (pessimistic) programming style: What conceivably might go wrong probably will go wrong. A major cause of disruption is due to the communication between distributed sofware components. There is an abundant literature on methods and techniques for how to prevent attackers from learning secrets (confidentiality) or from telling lies (integrity, authenticity). Hence our focus considers how to mitigate the consequences of attackers, nature or misfortune preventing expected communication from taking place. This calls for a very robust way of programming systems where there always are default data available for allowing the system to continue its operation as best as it can (rather than simply terminate with an error or get stuck in an input operation).

We believe that the Quality Calculus presents the core ingredients of a process calculus supporting such defensive (robust) programming. To assist in analysing the extent to which robustness has been achieved we have developed a SAT-based robustness analysis, that indicates the places where errors can still arise in spite of robust programming, and where additional hardening of the code may be called for.

Acknowledgement. The research has been supported by MT-LAB, a VKR Centre of Excellence for the Modelling of Information Technology, and by IDEA4CPS, supported by the Danish Foundation for Basic Research.

References

1. Anand, M., Ives, Z., Lee, I.: Quantifying eavesdropping vulnerability in sensor networks. In: Proceedings of the 2nd International Workshop on Data Management for Sensor Networks, DMSN 2005, pp. 3–9. ACM (2005)
2. Boreale, M., Bruni, R., Caires, L., De Nicola, R., Lanese, I., Loreti, M., Martins, F., Montanari, U., Ravara, A., Sangiorgi, D., Vasconcelos, V., Zavattaro, G.: SCC: A Service Centered Calculus. In: Bravetti, M., Núñez, M., Zavattaro, G. (eds.) WS-FM 2006. LNCS, vol. 4184, pp. 38–57. Springer, Heidelberg (2006)
3. Bruni, R.: Calculi for Service-Oriented Computing. In: Bernardo, M., Padovani, L., Zavattaro, G. (eds.) SFM 2009. LNCS, vol. 5569, pp. 1–41. Springer, Heidelberg (2009)
4. de Moura, L., Bjørner, N.: Z3: An Efficient SMT Solver. In: Ramakrishnan, C.R., Rehof, J. (eds.) TACAS 2008. LNCS, vol. 4963, pp. 337–340. Springer, Heidelberg (2008)
5. de Moura, L., Bjørner, N.: Satisfiability modulo theories: introduction and applications. Commun. ACM 54(9), 69–77 (2011)
6. Guidi, C., Lucchi, R., Gorrieri, R., Busi, N., Zavattaro, G.: SOCK: A Calculus for Service Oriented Computing. In: Dan, A., Lamersdorf, W. (eds.) ICSOC 2006. LNCS, vol. 4294, pp. 327–338. Springer, Heidelberg (2006)
7. Lapadula, A., Pugliese, R., Tiezzi, F.: A Calculus for Orchestration of Web Services. In: De Nicola, R. (ed.) ESOP 2007. LNCS, vol. 4421, pp. 33–47. Springer, Heidelberg (2007)
8. Malik, S., Zhang, L.: Boolean satisfiability from theoretical hardness to practical success. Commun. ACM 52(8), 76–82 (2009)
9. Milner, R.: A Calculus of Communication Systems. LNCS, vol. 92. Springer, Heidelberg (1980)
10. Milner, R.: Communicating and Mobile Systems: the Pi-Calculus. Cambridge University Press (1999)
11. Nielson, F., Nielson, H.R., Bauer, J., Nielsen, C.R., Pilegaard, H.: Relational Analysis for Delivery of Services. In: Barthe, G., Fournet, C. (eds.) TGC 2007. LNCS, vol. 4912, pp. 73–89. Springer, Heidelberg (2008)

Model Checking of Qualitative Sensitivity Preferences to Minimize Credential Disclosure*

Zachary J. Oster, Ganesh Ram Santhanam, Samik Basu, and Vasant Honavar

Department of Computer Science, Iowa State University, Ames, Iowa 50011, USA
{zjoster,gsanthan,sbasu,honavar}@iastate.edu

Abstract. In most client-server interactions over the Web, the server requires the client to disclose certain credentials before providing the client with the requested service (server policy). The client, on the other hand, wants to minimize the sensitivity of the set of credentials disclosed (client preference). We present a qualitative preference formalism based on conditional importance networks (CI-nets) for representing and reasoning with client preferences over the relative sensitivity of sets of credentials. The semantics of CI-net preferences is described using a preference graph over the set of credentials for which the preferences are expressed. We develop a model checking-based approach for analyzing the preference graph, efficiently verifying whether one set of credentials is more sensitive than another (dominance testing). Further, we identify the least (minimum) sensitive set of information that may be disclosed by the client to get access to the desired service. We present a technique based on iterative verification and refinement of the preference graph for computing a sequence of credential sets, ensuring that a credential set with higher sensitivity is never returned before one with lower sensitivity. We present a prototype implementation and preliminary simulation results.

1 Introduction

In online transactions, a client often must choose from multiple servers that provide some desired service. Typically, each server expects to verify a set of the client's credentials (as specified by the server's access control policy) before allowing access to the requested service. As the servers may hold different access control policies, they may demand different sets of credentials from the client; some sets of credentials may be more *sensitive* to the client than others, in the sense that they compromise the client's privacy to a greater degree.

This induces a preference on the sets of credentials that the client can disclose. Given a set of servers providing the same service, the client will prefer a server requiring the disclosure of a less sensitive set of credentials over a server requiring the disclosure of a more sensitive credential set.

For all except the smallest sets of possible credentials, it is impractical for the client to explicitly specify preferences over all possible combinations of credentials. Even if the client has only four credentials, he or she would need to

---

* This work is supported in part by U.S. National Science Foundation grants CCF0702758 and CCF1143734.

C.S. Păsăreanu and G. Salaün (Eds.): FACS 2012, LNCS 7684, pp. 205–223, 2013.
© Springer-Verlag Berlin Heidelberg 2013

assert preferences over $2^4 = 16$ combinations of credentials. A more practical approach would be to specify preferences over individual credentials, which can then be used to reason about preferences over sets of credentials. This reduces the decision-making burden on the client while still allowing him or her to access a desired service from the server that requires the least sensitive set of credentials.

Existing approaches to this problem, including [4,7,14], assume that the client has a priori knowledge of the access control policy of the server. However, in practice some servers may restrict the disclosure of their access control policies [1], especially when the client may be able to infer sensitive information by looking at the server's policy. For example, a server storing medical records may wish to release the records of a patient A suffering from a certain disease only to specialist doctors who are qualified to treat the illness. The server may thus require clients (in this case doctors) requesting access to patient A to present credentials certifying that they are licensed doctors who are qualified to treat A's disease. However, disclosing this requirement may allow any client to infer that A is suffering from that ailment, violating privacy laws. In such settings, the server has to protect its policy from being fully or partially disclosed to its clients.

Given the privacy preferences of a client that is totally or partially ignorant of the server's requirements, the client can access the service while minimizing disclosure of the client's credentials by providing increasingly sensitive credential disclosure sets (beginning from the least sensitive set) until the client finds one that is accepted by the server. Thus there is a need for algorithms and formal methods that compute a sequence of successively next-best (more sensitive) credential disclosure sets based on the sensitivity preferences of the client.

Driving Problem. In this paper, we address two important problems in the context of these scenarios. First, we use an intuitive formalism for representing and reasoning with the client's sensitivity preferences over the credentials. We claim that it is natural for clients to specify their preferences over credentials using an expressive preference language, namely *conditional importance networks (CI-nets)* [2]. CI-nets can represent

- *Monotonicity Preference*: disclosing less information is preferred to disclosing more information
- *Set-Based Relative Importance Preference*: disclosing one set of credentials is always preferred to disclosing another set of credentials
- *Conditional Relative Importance Preference*: given the presence or absence of certain credentials in the disclosure set, including one set of credentials in the disclosure set is preferred to including another set of credentials

Second, we introduce a model checking-based technique for finding a sequence of successively next-most-preferred (more sensitive) credential disclosure sets with respect to the CI-net preferences specified by the client. This new technique is built upon our previous work on dominance testing via model checking for CP-nets [11], which are related to but less expressive than CI-nets.

Contributions. The contributions of our work are summarized as follows:

1. We employ a formal preference language and semantics based on CI-nets to represent the client's preferences over the sensitivity of the credentials.
2. We show how model checking techniques for preferential dominance testing (finding whether one set of credentials is preferred over another) can be used to find the least sensitive (most preferred) set of credentials that the client would like to disclose and that the server will accept. This is done by repeatedly finding the next-best (next-least-sensitive) set of credentials and seeing whether the server will accept this credential set.
3. We present an implementation and preliminary experiments to show the practical feasibility of our approach.

Organization. The rest of the paper is organized as follows. Section 2 motivates the addressed problems and the proposed solution using a simple example. Section 3 describes the syntax and semantics of CI-nets. Section 4 presents our approach to finding the most preferred sets of credentials according to the sensitivity preferences of the client, as well as a model checking-based technique for ordering the sets of credentials based on their relative sensitivities. Section 5 describes our implementation and summarizes the results of our initial experiments. Section 6 discusses related techniques from the existing literature. Section 7 summarizes the paper and presents some directions for future work.

2   Illustrative Example

Consider a client who is interested in obtaining some financial quote (e.g., auto and/or home insurance, mortgage, etc.) using an online service. Suppose that there are multiple servers that provide the required service, and each server's access control policy requires a combination of several credentials from the client before granting access to the service. We consider four such credentials: the client's name, residential address, bank account number, and bank routing number.

The client has some qualitative preferences over the relative importance of his credentials based on their sensitivity. The rationale behind these preferences is that the client would like to make it impossible (or at least difficult) for a third party to perform any financial transaction maliciously posing as the client. Therefore, from the client's perspective, the objective is to choose the server that provides the desired financial service by requiring the least sensitive set of client credentials. Consider the following qualitative preferences specified by the client:

P1. If my bank account number is disclosed to the server, I would rather give my address than my bank's routing number to the server. This is because my bank account number along with the bank routing number identifies my bank account precisely, and hence it is highly sensitive information compared to my bank account number and address.

P2. If I have to disclose my address without having to disclose my name, then I would prefer giving my bank's routing number over my bank account number. However, this preference does not hold when I have to disclose my name along with my address, because the combination of my name, address, and bank routing number is not any less sensitive than my name, address, and bank account number. In both cases, a malicious party needs to guess one of the credentials – bank account number or bank routing number – to gain access to important financial information.

P3. Because I would like to protect as many details as possible regarding my bank account, when I don't have to disclose my bank account number I would provide my name and address rather than my bank's routing number.

Based on these preferences, the client can identify successively more sensitive sets of credentials (starting from the empty set) and verify whether a set of credentials is sufficient to satisfy the access control policy of any server providing the desired service. Any server that accepts this least sensitive acceptable set of credentials may be selected to provide the service to the client.

3   Background: CI-Nets

We use *conditional importance networks* (CI-nets) [2] to capture and reason with the client's preferences over the set of credentials in terms of their sensitivity. CI-nets allow a client to clearly and precisely specify sensitivity among credentials.

3.1   Syntax

Let V denote the set of credentials over which the client expresses his/her preferences. A CI-net C is a collection of conditional importance statements of the form $S^+, S^- : S_1 \succ S_2$, where S^+, S^-, S_1, and S_2 are pairwise disjoint subsets of V and where $S_2 \neq \emptyset$. Informally, given two sets of credentials which both include the set S^+ and exclude S^-, the set that contains all of the credentials in S_1 is preferred (relatively less sensitive) to the set that contains all of the credentials in S_2.

Recall the preference P1 described in Section 2 that *"if my bank account number is disclosed to the server, I would rather give my address than my bank's routing number to the server"*. It is expressed as the following CI-net statement:

$$\{Bank\ Account\ Number\}, \{\} : \{Address\} \succ \{Bank\ Routing\ Number\} \quad (1)$$

Similarly, the preference P2 that *"if I have to disclose my address without having to disclose my name, then I would prefer giving my bank's routing number over my bank account number"* is expressed in the language of CI-nets as:

$$\{Address\}, \{Name\} : \{Bank\ Routing\ Number\} \succ \{Bank\ Account\ Number\} \quad (2)$$

3.2   Semantics

The ceteris paribus ("all else being equal") semantics [2] provides a way to use the statements in a CI-net to reason about preferences over various sets of credentials. The semantics of preferences described using a CI-net C over a set of credentials V is given in terms of a strict partial order (irreflexive and transitive) relation $\succ$ over the powerset of V such that:

1. $\succ$ is monotonic, i.e., $\gamma \subset \gamma' \Rightarrow \gamma \succ \gamma'$
2. For each CI-net statement $S^+, S^- : S_1 \succ S_2$,
   $\gamma \subseteq [V \setminus (S^+ \cup S^- \cup S_1 \cup S_2)] \Rightarrow \gamma \cup S^+ \cup S_1 \succ \gamma \cup S^+ \cup S_2$

In the original CI-net formalism [2], a set is preferred to its subset, i.e., it is always preferred to have more elements in a set. We reverse the direction of monotonicity (see item 1 above) in the semantics because in our context it is always better to disclose fewer credentials. Further, note that allowing $S_2 = \emptyset$ combined with monotonicity could permit preferences where a set is preferred to itself. In order to ensure the strict partial ordering of preferences, we do not allow $S_2 = \emptyset$ in the syntax (see Section 3.1).

Going back to the CI-net preference statement P1 in our example, by the rule in item 1 above, the set of credentials {*Name, Address, Bank Account Number*} is preferred to the set {*Name, Bank Account Number, Bank Routing Number*} according to ceteris paribus semantics. Similarly, a ceteris paribus interpretation of the preference statement P2 in our example CI-net can be used to reason that the set of credentials {*Address, Bank Routing Number*} is less sensitive than (therefore more preferred to) the set {*Address, Bank Account Number*}.

CI-Nets for Preferences over Credential Disclosure Sets. CI-nets are a natural choice for modeling client preferences over sets of credentials for the following reasons:

1. Preferences in CI-nets are monotonic. According to the semantics of CI-nets, a set of credentials is preferred to all of its proper supersets. The client would typically like to protect as many credentials as possible (ideally all) from being disclosed.
2. The CI-net semantics induces a strict partial order among the subsets of credentials with respect to the CI-net preference statements of the client. Thus, it is possible to order the subsets of credentials in a way that is consistent with the semantics of a CI-net. Such an ordering can be used to search for less sensitive sets of credentials that fulfill the server's requirement ahead of the ones that are more sensitive.

4   Finding the Most Preferred Set of Credentials

We present a method for automatically identifying a most preferred set γ of credentials that the client has to disclose in order to satisfy the server's requirement, such that there exists no other credential set γ' that (a) is preferred to (less sensitive than) γ and (b) fulfills the server's requirement. Our method consists of the following two processes:

1. *Decide:* Automatically decide the preference of a set of credentials over another, where preferences are specified using CI-nets (Section 4.1).
2. *Order:* Use the above decision process to automatically identify the preference ordering of sets of credentials, starting from the most preferred sets and ending in the least preferred ones (Section 4.4).

210   Z.J. Oster et al.

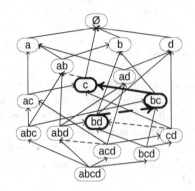

a = Name
b = Address
c = Bank Routing Number
d = Bank Account Number

P1. $\{d\}, \{\}$: $\{b\} \succ \{c\}$
P2. $\{b\}, \{a\}$: $\{c\} \succ \{d\}$
P3. $\{\}, \{d\}$: $\{a, b\} \succ \{c\}$

Fig. 1. Induced preference graph and CI-net preference statements for the preferences given in Section 2, with the improving flipping sequence from {*Address, Bank Account Number*} to {*Bank Routing Number*} shown in bold.

4.1 Dominance Testing

Given two choices (of sets of credentials), deciding the preference of one choice over the other is referred to as *dominance testing*. Dominance testing is known to be PSPACE-complete [2,6]. Recently, in [11], we have demonstrated an effective model checking [5] based approach to dominance testing for certain families of preferences, such as TCP-nets [3]. In this paper, we follow a similar approach for dominance testing between choices (of sets of credentials) where preferences are represented using CI-nets. This approach relies on alternate semantics of CI-nets given in terms of an *improving flipping sequence*, analogous to the worsening flipping sequence defined in [2].

Definition 1 (Improving Flipping Sequence [2]). *A sequence of credential sets* $\gamma_1, \gamma_2, \cdots \gamma_{n-1}, \gamma_n$ *is an* improving flipping sequence *with respect to a set of CI-net statements if and only if, for* $1 \leq i < n$, *either*

1. *(Monotonicity Flip)* $\gamma_{i+1} \subset \gamma_i$; *or*
2. *(Importance Flip) there exists a conditional importance statement* S^+, S^- : $S_1 \succ S_2$ *in the CI-net for which all of the following hold:*
   (a) $\gamma_{i+1} \supseteq S^+$, $\gamma_i \supseteq S^+$, $\gamma_{i+1} \cap S^- = \gamma_i \cap S^- = \emptyset$;
   (b) $\gamma_{i+1} \supseteq S_1$, $\gamma_i \supseteq S_2$, $\gamma_{i+1} \cap S_2 = \gamma_i \cap S_1 = \emptyset$;
   (c) $\gamma = V \setminus (S^+ \cup S^- \cup S_1 \cup S_2) \Rightarrow \gamma \cap \gamma_{i+1} = \gamma \cap \gamma_i$.

In the above definition, condition (1) states that disclosing a set of credentials is always preferred to disclosing its superset. (2) states that if the set S^+ of credentials are disclosed and the set S^- of credentials are not disclosed, then disclosing the set S_1 of credentials is preferred to disclosing the set S_2 of credentials, all other disclosures being identical (which is ensured by condition (2c)). Given a CI-net C and two sets γ and γ' of credentials, we say that γ is preferred to γ', denoted by $C \models \gamma \succ \gamma'$, if and only if there is an improving flipping sequence with respect to C from γ' to γ (Proposition 1, [2]).

In our example CI-net (right side of Figure 1), we can thus say that the set *{Bank Routing Number}* is preferred to the set *{Address, Bank Account Number}*. This is because the set *{Address, Bank Account Number}* has an improving (importance) flip to the set *{Address, Bank Routing Number}* (see preference P2 in Section 2 and its CI-net representation, Equation 2 in Section 3), which in turn has an improving (monotonicity) flip to *{Bank Routing Number}*.

From the above definition, one can construct a graph where each node corresponds to a set of credentials and each directed edge from one node to another denotes an "improving flip", capturing the fact that the set of credentials at the destination node is preferred to the set of credentials at the source node. This graph is referred to as the *induced preference graph* [2].

Definition 2 (Induced Preference Graph). *Given a CI-net C over a set of credentials V, the* induced preference graph $\delta(C) = (N, E)$ *is constructed as follows. The nodes N correspond to the powerset of V, and for a pair $\gamma, \gamma' \in N$, the directed edge $(\gamma, \gamma') \in E$ indicates an improving (monotonicity or importance) flip from γ to γ' as per the CI-net semantics (Definition 1) such that $\gamma' \succ \gamma$.*

Figure 1 presents the CI-net statements representing the preferences over credentials specified in Section 2, along with the corresponding induced preference graph. The solid edges between sets of credentials in this graph correspond to monotonicity flips and the dotted edges correspond to importance flips. Each path in the graph corresponds to an improving flipping sequence.

A set γ' of credentials *dominates* (i.e., is preferred to) another set γ with respect to CI-net C if and only if the node corresponding to γ' in $\delta(C)$ is reachable from γ. For example, the set *{Bank Routing Number}* is preferred to the set *{Address, Bank Account Number}* due to the existence of the path $bd \to bc \to c$, which is highlighted in Figure 1. The induced preference graph of a CI-net is *consistent* if and only if it is cycle-free.

4.2 Kripke Structure Modeling of CI-Net Semantics

We use the Cadence SMV symbolic model checker [8] to verify reachability (and therefore dominance) from one node to another in the induced preference graph. There are three primary advantages in using Cadence SMV for testing dominance. First, Cadence SMV is equipped with (symbolic or BDD-based) algorithms that allow for efficient state-space exploration of large graphs. Second, Cadence SMV can verify properties (beyond simple reachability) in expressive temporal logic (e.g., CTL and LTL), a capability that we will use in Section 4.4 to obtain a preference ordering over sets of credentials. Finally, the SMV input language allows us to directly encode the CI-net preference statements. The induced preference graph is then automatically constructed by the model checker to answer dominance (verification) queries. The model checker takes as input a Kripke structure $\langle S, S_0, T, L \rangle$, where S is the set of states, $S_0 \subseteq S$ is the set of start states, $T \subseteq S \times S$ is the set of transition relations, and L is a labeling function mapping each state in S to a set of propositions that hold at that state.

In our encoding, we represent each credential (say, x_i) as a proposition, where the value of the proposition is true when the credential is disclosed and false when the credential is not disclosed. The propositions are uninitialized, which allow the model checker to consider all possible valuations of propositions as initial states of the Kripke structure. Given a set of CI-net statements C, the Kripke structure K_C representing the induced preference graph $\delta(C)$ contains states that are labeled with the truth values of the set of credential propositions x_i and two types of helper Boolean variables: a set of Boolean variables h_i and a Boolean variable g.

SMV Input Language: Role of Helper Variables. In SMV, a Kripke structure is encoded using a set of variables, their possible initial valuations, and a set of transition relations. Each transition relation describes the valuation of the variable based on certain conditions on the current state variable-valuations. For instance, consider a Kripke structure with two Boolean variables a and b.

```
                          next(a) := case
                                     a = b :  !a;
init(a) := 0;                        1     : a;
                          esac;
```

This SMV specification states that the initial valuation of a is 0, while the initial valuation of b can be either 0 or 1 since it is not explicitly given. The corresponding Kripke structure has two different start states: one where a and b are equal to 0 and another where a is equal to 0 and b is equal to 1. Furthermore, the transition relation (described by the **next** operation) states that the value of a is toggled only when the valuations of a and b are equal in the current state. The absence of **next** definitions for b indicates that the valuation of b can change non-deterministically whenever a change in state occurs in the Kripke structure.

In the encoding of $\delta(C)$ as a Kripke structure K_C, attributes over which the CI-net statements are specified are encoded as Boolean variables in K_C. Each state in K_C corresponds to a node in $\delta(C)$: if $x_3 \wedge x_4$ holds (evaluates to true) in a state in K_C, that state corresponds to the node annotated with x_3 and x_4 in $\delta(C)$. Next, note that the existence of a given edge in $\delta(C)$ depends on the contents of the source and destination nodes (improving flip, see Definition 1). Direct encoding of such edges in SMV requires encoding of transitions in K_C where the **next** operation on each variable (describing the enabling condition of the transitions) includes conditions that depend on the variables' values in the next states. Encoding such conditions in SMV may lead to circular dependencies between **next** operations for two or more variables. For instance,

```
next(a) :=  case                next(b) :=  case
            next(b) : !a;                   next(a) : !b;
            1       : a;                     1       : b;
            esac;                           esac;
```

From the above encoding, it is not clear what valuation a and b should have in the next state when the current state valuations of the variables are equal to 1.

Role of h_i. In order to correctly encode the edges of $\delta(C)$ as transitions in K_C, we have used one auxiliary variable h_i for each proposition x_i. Each h_i is encoded such that if h_i is 0 (false) in the current state, then in the next state the valuation of x_i cannot change; otherwise, the valuation of x_i may change in the next state if a condition corresponding to a CI-net preference statement is satisfied. The h_i variables are all initialized to 0 and the model checker performs updates to the h_is non-deterministically. For instance, the semantics of the CI-net statement $\{d\}, \{\} : \{b\} \succ \{c\}$ (preference P1 from Section 2, resulting in edges $cd \to bd$ and $acd \to abd$ in $\delta(C)$) can be encoded in the SMV language as

```
next(b) := case
                h_a = 0            -- a does not change in next state
         &  b = 0 & h_b = 1   -- b can change in the next state
         &  c = 1 & h_c = 1   -- c can change in the next state
         &  d = 1 & h_d = 0   -- d does not change in next state
                : 1
            ...
         esac;
next(c) := case
                h_a = 0            -- a does not change in next state
         &  b = 0 & h_b = 1   -- b can change in the next state
         &  c = 1 & h_c = 1   -- c can change in the next state
         &  d = 1 & h_d = 0   -- d does not change in next state
                : 0
            ...
         esac;
```

The enabling conditions are identical in both cases to ensure that the valuations of b and c are updated under identical conditions as specified by the CI-net, i.e., when $d = 1$ in the current and next states (ensured by $h_d = 0$ in the current state) and when the valuation of a is unaltered in the current and next states (ensured by $h_a = 0$ in the current state). Further, $c = 1$ and $h_c = 1$ in the current state, which allows the value of c to change in the next state; similarly, $b = 0$ and $h_b = 1$ in the current state, which allows for the toggling of b in the next state.

In this way, the semantics of CI-nets as given in Definition 1 is directly encoded as SMV specifications. This encoding eliminates the need to manually construct the induced preference graph $\delta(C)$; instead, the model checker automatically constructs and explores the Kripke model representing $\delta(C)$.

Role of g. Within the above encoding, the different valuations of each h_i for the same valuation of each x_i correspond to states in K_C that allow different ways in which the valuation of that x_i can be changed. Consequently, K_C contains multiple states where an identical set of x_i's hold true; all of these states correspond to one node in $\delta(C)$. Transitions between these states do not change the valuation of any x_i and, therefore, do not correspond to any edge in $\delta(C)$.

The variable g is set to 1 (true) whenever a transition traversed in K_C results in a change in the valuation of at least one of the x_i's (i.e., when a transition in K_C corresponds to an edge in $\delta(C)$). Conversely, if a transition in K_C does not indicate a change in any of the x_i variables, the variable g is set to 0 (false). Consider the following SMV code, which updates g based on the CI-net statements that encode the preferences expressed in Section 2:

```
next(g) := case
        -- Guards corresponding to P1, where g will be set to 1 :
                    h_a = 0 -- a does not change in next state
          & b = 0 & h_b = 1 -- b can change in the next state
          & c = 1 & h_c = 1 -- c can change in the next state
          & d = 1 & h_d = 0 -- d does not change in next state
              : 1 -- g is set to 1 indicating that this transition
                  -- corresponds to a change in "b" or "c"
        ...

        -- Guards corresponding to P2, where g will be set to 1 :
        ...
        -- Guards corresponding to P3, where g will be set to 1 :
        ...

        1: 0 -- default case : if no variables change, then g is 0
    esac;
```

Note that these are precisely the same conditions under which b changes to 1 (true) and c changes to 0 (false), as defined in the previous SMV code excerpt. The code in this excerpt sets g to 1 whenever the conditions for changing the value of b and c are satisfied. The full next(g) block contains conditions for setting g to 1 when any monotonicity or importance flip causes one or more variables to change; we have omitted the remaining conditions to save space. The 1 condition at the end of the block sets g to 0 if no other condition is met, i.e., if no variables change during the specified transition. In Section 4.4, we show how the variable g can be used directly to compute the ordering of preferred solutions.

Figure 2 shows how the data variables x_i, the helper variables h_i, and the change variable g interact within the Kripke structure K_C for a node in the induced preference graph $\delta(C)$ containing variables a and b. The most preferred node in $\delta(C)$ is the empty set, while the least preferred node is the set of all elements; nodes containing a and b are intermediate nodes. Each node in $\delta(C)$ is modeled by a set of interconnected states in K_C. In Figure 2, we have expanded and shown the set of states in K_C that corresponds to one node (where $a = 1$ and $b = 0$) in $\delta(C)$. The expanded node is divided into two subsets of states: the left subset a_g represents the set of states where $g = 1$, while the right subset $a_{\neg g}$ represents the set of states where $g = 0$. There are four states in both subsets, one for each possible valuation of the two Boolean variables h_a and h_b. Any state in a_g can be reached from some state in K_C that represents the node where $a = 1$ and $b = 1$ in $\delta(C)$. States where $h_a = 1$ and $h_b = 0$ move to states in K_C where $a = 0$ and $b = 0$, regardless of g's value. All other states in a_g can move to some state in $a_{\neg g}$ by a transition in K_C; however, since $g = 0$ in all states in $a_{\neg g}$, any transition to or between the states in $a_{\neg g}$ does not correspond to any edge in $\delta(C)$. Note that, as in a_g, the state

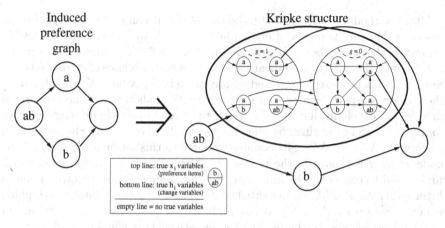

Fig. 2. Diagram of a Kripke-structure encoding of part of an induced preference graph

in $a_{\neg g}$ where $h_a = 1$ and $h_b = 0$ has transitions to states where $a = 0$ and $b = 0$. The rest of the Kripke structure K_C is constructed similarly: each node in $\delta(C)$ corresponds to a set of states in K_C, where the number of states in the set is exponential in the number of variables (credentials) in $\delta(C)$. Further details of the SMV encoding process may be found on this paper's website at http://fmg.cs.iastate.edu/project-pages/credentials.html.

Theorem 1. *Given a CI-net C, a Kripke structure K_C constructed as described in this subsection preserves the semantics of the induced preference graph $\delta(C)$ of the CI-net.*

Proof. Consider the induced preference graph $\delta(C)$ for CI-net C as defined in Definition 2. Each state in K_C maps onto exactly one node in $\delta(C)$. Furthermore, given two nodes $\gamma, \gamma' \in \delta(C)$ and two states $s, s' \in K_C$ where s maps to γ and s' maps to γ', there exists a directed edge $(\gamma, \gamma') \in \delta(C)$ if and only if both (1) there exists a transition $s \to s' \in K_C$ and (2) $g = 1$ in state s'. This transition $s \to s'$ models the improving flip (γ, γ') in the induced preference graph. □

4.3   Model Checking for Verifying Consistency and Dominance

Given a CI-net C, we use the method in Section 4.2 to specify the corresponding Kripke model K_C for input to the Cadence SMV model checker. We begin by verifying that the induced preference graph $\delta(C)$ modeled by K_C is consistent (i.e., cycle-free). This is done by checking K_C against the LTL formula F G($g = 0$), which is satisfied if and only if every path from the initial state in K_C eventually reaches a point where no x_i variable ever changes (i.e., g is always 0) in any future state.[1] If a cycle exists in the induced preference graph, then every state in the cycle always has at least one outgoing transition from that state where $g = 1$, indicating that a variable is changing; this violates the consistency property.

---

[1] Details of LTL syntax and semantics can be obtained in [10].

After the model K_C is verified to be consistent, it can be used for preference reasoning. For any two sets of credentials γ and γ', we use the following CTL formula to check whether γ' is preferred to γ: $X \Rightarrow \text{EF}(X')$, where X (resp. X') is the propositional formula indicating the presence or absence of credentials in γ (resp. γ'). This property is satisfied by any state in K_C where X holds true and where there is a path leading to a state where X' holds true.[2] If the property is satisfied, we conclude that γ' is preferred to γ. An improving flipping sequence from γ to γ' can be obtained by querying the model checker with the negation of the formula $X \Rightarrow \text{EF}(X')$. The counter-example to this formula returned by the model checker is a path in the Kripke structure that proves dominance, which can be used to construct the improving flipping sequence. On the other hand, if the property $X \Rightarrow \text{EF}(X')$ is not satisfied, then there exists no improving flipping sequence from γ to γ', i.e., γ' is *not* preferred to γ. In the CI-net used in our example (see Section 2), the model checker returns true when queried with the formula $(acd \Rightarrow \text{EF}(bd))$, which verifies that bd is preferred to or dominates acd. When we query the model checker with the CTL formula $\neg(acd \Rightarrow \text{EF}(bd))$, it yields a counter-example corresponding to either the path $acd \rightarrow cd \rightarrow bd$ or the path $acd \rightarrow abd \rightarrow bd$. Either path gives a proof of the dominance of bd over acd.

We find the most preferred set of credentials by verifying the CTL property $\text{EF}(g = 1)$ for all states in K_C. This property is satisfied at a state s in K_C if and only if s can reach any state (including itself) where g evaluates to 1 (true). The property is not satisfied at states in K_C that correspond to the *top-most node* (containing the most preferred set of credentials) of the induced preference graph (see, for instance, Figure 1). This is because the top-most node in $\delta(C)$ does not contain any outgoing edges. Any one of the states in K_C that corresponds to the top-most node in $\delta(C)$ is identified by Cadence SMV as a counterexample, proving the unsatisfiability of the property $\text{EF}(g = 1)$. In our running example, this query returns the state where variables a, b, c, and d are false, which corresponds to the empty set of credentials. This reflects the fact that not disclosing any credentials at all is the most preferred option.

4.4   Preference Ordering over Credential-Sets

Once the induced preference graph $\delta(C)$ is modeled as a Kripke structure K_C, our next objective is to order the sets of credentials from most to least preferred. Note that $\delta(C)$ specifies a strict partial order between sets of credentials. The ordering we obtain is a total order consistent with this strict partial order. We achieve this by performing model checking on the model K_C and its modifications against CTL properties. The steps in our approach are as follows.

1. We verify all states in K_C against the CTL property $\text{EF}(g = 1)$, which returns the most preferred set of credentials (say γ_i) from the top of $\delta(C)$. Since $\delta(C)$ is a strict partial order, it may have multiple elements at the top.

---

[2] Details of CTL syntax and semantics can be obtained in [5].

Any state that corresponds to any one of the top elements will be returned as a counterexample (proving the unsatisfiability of the CTL property).

2. Let $\gamma_1, \gamma_2, \ldots, \gamma_n$ be the sequence of sets of credentials that has been obtained so far (as the total order consistent with the partial order presented in $\delta(C)$). We define the following formula

$$I = \bigvee_{i=1}^{n} \bigwedge_j (x_{ij}) \tag{3}$$

where x_{ij} is the proposition representing the presence or absence of the jth credential in the set γ_i. We then query the model checker to verify whether the modified CTL property $\text{EF}(g = 1) \vee I$ holds true in all states of K_C. The property is satisfied by a state s in K_C if and only if (a) s can reach some state (including itself) where $g = 1$ or (b) s corresponds to nodes $\gamma_1, \gamma_2, \ldots, \gamma_n$ in $\delta(C)$. If the property is not satisfied by s, then s cannot reach a state where g is set to true and s does not correspond to nodes $\gamma_1, \gamma_2, \ldots, \gamma_n$.

3. If the model checker returns false, then it identifies (as a counterexample) a state corresponding to a set of credentials γ_{n+1}, which is at least as preferred as one of the previously identified sets of credentials $\gamma_1, \gamma_2, \ldots, \gamma_n$. In this case, we iterate Step 2 using the new sequence $\gamma_1, \gamma_2, \ldots, \gamma_{n+1}$. Otherwise, the property is satisfied by all states in K_C, meaning there exists no set of credentials that is at least as preferred as one of the elements in $\gamma_1, \gamma_2, \ldots, \gamma_n$. If this occurs, we remove from the Kripke structure K_C all states corresponding to the credential sets $\gamma_1, \gamma_2, \ldots, \gamma_n$ (obtained by iterating Step 2 so far) by adding $\neg I$ (see Equation 3) to the Kripke structure as an invariant (the model checker only considers the states where the invariant holds). Thus, the reduced model corresponds to the induced preference graph where the nodes corresponding to $\gamma_1, \gamma_2, \ldots, \gamma_n$ are not considered. We then iterate starting from Step 1 until the invariant results in a model where no states are considered by the model checker.

Note that in Step 2, the states in the model corresponding to $\gamma_1 \ldots \gamma_n$ are *not considered* as counterexamples by the model checker, as I is added as a disjunction to the property $\text{EF}(g = 1)$. This enables us to obtain the top-most nodes one by one in sequence without altering the model. However, when all the top-most nodes are obtained, we *remove* the states corresponding to $\gamma_1 \ldots \gamma_n$ from the model in Step 3 (by adding the $\neg I$ as an invariant to the current model). This modification of the model makes it possible for us to obtain the next set of top-most nodes in the subsequent iteration. We explain the above steps using the example $\delta(C)$ presented in Figure 1.

Iteration 1: The Kripke structure K_C encoding of $\delta(C)$ is first model-checked with the property $\text{EF}(g = 1)$ following Step 1 above. The result (counterexample) obtained is the top-most element $\gamma_{11} = \emptyset$. In Step 2, model checking is performed again with the property $\text{EF}(g = 1) \vee I$, where $I = (\neg a \wedge \neg b \wedge \neg c \wedge \neg d)$ corresponds to the absence of any credentials ($\gamma_{11} = \emptyset$). The property is satisfied because all states except the one corresponding to $\gamma_{11} = \emptyset$ can reach a state where $g = 1$ (true). As per Step 3, we remove from K_C the states corresponding to the node $\gamma_{11} = \emptyset$ by adding $\neg I = (a \vee b \vee c \vee d)$ as an invariant to K_C. As a result, we have forced the model checker to consider only the states where the invariant holds (the invariant does not hold at states corresponding to γ_{11}). This can be viewed as an updated K_C, which encodes a $\delta(C)$ where the nodes $((a), (b), (d))$ are at the top (as Figure 1, but with the $\emptyset$ node and its incoming edges removed).

Iteration 2: Step 1 is performed again with the updated model, and the model checker returns as a counterexample one of the states that corresponds to either (a), (b), or (d). Note that such a state is identified non-deterministically by the model checking algorithm. Suppose that the state corresponding to (a) is obtained as a counterexample. So far, we have $\gamma_{11} = \emptyset$ (from the previous iteration) followed by $\gamma_{21} = (a)$ in our total ordering of sets of credentials. Proceeding to Step 2, we have a new $I = (a \wedge \neg b \wedge \neg c \wedge \neg d)$. When model checking is performed again, one of the states corresponding to either (b) or (d) is obtained as a counterexample. Suppose that a state corresponding to $\gamma_{22} = (b)$ is returned.

We proceed to perform Step 2 again with $I = (a \wedge \neg b \wedge \neg c \wedge \neg d) \vee (\neg a \wedge b \wedge \neg c \wedge \neg d)$. The model checker returns a counterexample state corresponding to the node $\gamma_{23} = (d)$. Proceeding further, Step 2 is again performed using $I = (a \wedge \neg b \wedge \neg c \wedge \neg d) \vee (\neg a \wedge b \wedge \neg c \wedge \neg d) \vee (\neg a \wedge \neg b \wedge \neg c \wedge d)$. At this point, the model checker fails to find any counterexamples for the property $\mathtt{EF}(g = 1) \vee I$. In Step 3, we remove all the states corresponding to the nodes (a), (b), and (d) by adding to K_C the invariant $\neg I = (\neg a \vee b \vee c \vee d) \wedge (a \vee \neg b \vee c \vee d) \wedge (a \vee b \vee c \vee \neg d)$ to the model (in conjunction with the invariant $(a \vee b \vee c \vee d)$ used to remove the node $\emptyset$ in iteration 1), and we start a new iteration from Step 1. So far, we have obtained an ordering of sets of credentials $\gamma_{11} = \emptyset, \gamma_{21} = (a), \gamma_{22} = (b), \gamma_{23} = (d)$.

The iterative process (starting from Step 1) is illustrated in Table 1. The iteration is continued until including an invariant in K_C results in an empty model (i.e., a model with no states). The number of such iterations is equal to the height of the partial order in $\delta(C)$. In the example (Figure 1), it is equal to 9. Each such iteration obtains a sequence of sets of credentials that are equally preferred (or indistinguishable as per the given preferences). For instance, in iteration 3, we obtain the equally preferred sets (ab) and (ad). Such elements are obtained by iterating Step 2 multiple times. The maximum number of iterations starting at Step 2 is equal to the width of the partial order in $\delta(C)$. In the example (Figure 1), it is equal to 3.

The main advantage of using this method is that a total ordering of sets of credentials is obtained without performing all possible pairwise comparisons. Instead, systematic updates to the model corresponding to the induced preference graph and repeated model checking using a CTL property are used to automatically and effectively find the total order over the sets of credentials.

Finding Preferred Sets of Credentials with Sensitivity Thresholds. We have presented a technique for using sensitivity preferences to generate a sequence or ordering of sets of credentials such that less (or equally) sensitive sets of credentials are obtained prior to more sensitive sets of credentials based on

Table 1. Steps in finding the ordering of sets of credentials for example in Section 2

#	Iteration	Query	Result	Action
1.	Iteration 1	$\mathbf{EF}(g = 1)$	[ ]	$I = (\bar{a}\bar{b}\bar{c}\bar{d})$
2.		$\mathbf{EF}(g = 1) \vee I$	−	Revise model by adding $\neg I$ as invariant
3.	Iteration 2	$\mathbf{EF}(g = 1)$	[a]	$I = (a\bar{b}\bar{c}\bar{d})$
4.		$\mathbf{EF}(g = 1) \vee I$	[b]	$I = (a\bar{b}\bar{c}\bar{d}) \vee (\bar{a}b\bar{c}\bar{d})$
5.		$\mathbf{EF}(g = 1) \vee I$	[d]	$I = (a\bar{b}\bar{c}\bar{d}) \vee (\bar{a}b\bar{c}\bar{d}) \vee (\bar{a}\bar{b}\bar{c}d)$
6.		$\mathbf{EF}(g = 1) \vee I$	−	Revise model by adding $\neg I$ as invariant
7.	Iteration 3	$\mathbf{EF}(g = 1)$	[ab]	$I = (ab\bar{c}\bar{d})$
8.		$\mathbf{EF}(g = 1) \vee I$	[ad]	$I = (ab\bar{c}\bar{d}) \vee (a\bar{b}\bar{c}d)$
9.		$\mathbf{EF}(g = 1) \vee I$	−	Revise model by adding $\neg I$ as invariant
10.	Iteration 4	$\mathbf{EF}(g = 1)$	[c]	$I = (\bar{a}\bar{b}c\bar{d})$
11.		$\mathbf{EF}(g = 1) \vee I$	−	Revise model by adding $\neg I$ as invariant
12.	Iteration 5	$\mathbf{EF}(g = 1)$	[ac]	$I = (a\bar{b}c\bar{d})$
13.		$\mathbf{EF}(g = 1) \vee I$	[bc]	$I = (a\bar{b}c\bar{d}) \vee (\bar{a}bc\bar{d})$
14.		$\mathbf{EF}(g = 1) \vee I$	−	Revise model by adding $\neg I$ as invariant
15.	Iteration 6	$\mathbf{EF}(g = 1)$	[abc]	$I = (abc\bar{d})$
16.		$\mathbf{EF}(g = 1) \vee I$	[bd]	$I = (abc\bar{d}) \vee (\bar{a}b\bar{c}d)$
17.		$\mathbf{EF}(g = 1) \vee I$	−	Revise model by adding $\neg I$ as invariant
18.	Iteration 7	$\mathbf{EF}(g = 1)$	[abd]	$I = (ab\bar{c}d)$
19.		$\mathbf{EF}(g = 1) \vee I$	[cd]	$I = (ab\bar{c}d) \vee (\bar{a}\bar{b}cd)$
20.		$\mathbf{EF}(g = 1) \vee I$	−	Revise model by adding $\neg I$ as invariant
21.	Iteration 8	$\mathbf{EF}(g = 1)$	[acd]	$I = (a\bar{b}cd)$
22.		$\mathbf{EF}(g = 1) \vee I$	[bcd]	$I = (a\bar{b}cd) \vee (\bar{a}bcd)$
23.		$\mathbf{EF}(g = 1) \vee I$	−	Revise model by adding $\neg I$ as invariant
24.	Iteration 9	$\mathbf{EF}(g = 1)$	[abcd]	$I = (abcd)$
25.		$\mathbf{EF}(g = 1) \vee I$	−	Revise model by adding $\neg I$ as invariant
26.		$\mathbf{EF}(g = 1)$	−	No more states to explore. Terminate.

the preferences of the client. As we have shown, such an ordering can be used to select a server from many that provide similar services. However, this ordering by itself does not allow clients to prevent highly sensitive sets of credentials from being disclosed. In many settings, clients may want to add additional constraints to prevent such unacceptable disclosures. One way to express these constraints is to specify, in addition to the preferences, one or more "threshold" sets of credentials which indicate the *maximum* sensitivity of information that the client would like to disclose. In other words, the client will consider disclosing sets of credentials in order of their sensitivity, as long as they are not more sensitive than the threshold(s). Our model-based technique can seamlessly incorporate such thresholds by extending the property to $\mathbf{EF}(g = true) \vee \mathbf{EX}\ \mathbf{EF}(\bigvee_i t_i)$, where t_is denote the credential sets describing the thresholds.

5   Implementation and Experiments

5.1   Overview of Framework

We have implemented our approach to finding the most preferred set of credentials with respect to the client's sensitivity preferences in a Java-based framework. Our framework consists of two primary modules:

1. A *pre-processor* module that uses two sub-modules to produce input to the model checker, namely:
   (a) *Parser:* Reads CI-net statements specified in a text input file.
   (b) *Translator:* Automatically translates CI-net statements to generate the SMV input model.
2. A *reasoning driver* module that coordinates preference reasoning. Its two sub-modules invoke the Cadence SMV model checker [8] to do different tasks:
   (a) *Consistency Checker:* Checks the consistency of CI-nets, returning true if and only if the CI-net is consistent.
   (b) *Rank Order Generator:* Takes the model generated by the pre-processor, generates appropriate temporal properties, and invokes the Cadence SMV model checker [8]. After the first run of the model checker, it reads the output of the model checker, appropriately updates the property or refines the model (by including invariants), and repeatedly invokes the model checker until all ordered results are obtained.

5.2   Experimental Setup

For our experiments, we generated random CI-nets with between 5 and 20 variables (denoting the disclosure of credentials) and either 5 or 10 CI-net statements. We tested the consistency of each sample CI-net generated according to these combinations of variables and statements; consistency is necessary to ensure that the induced preference graph does not contain any loops. We collected 20 consistent samples for each combination of variables and statements being considered, then applied the algorithm described in Section 4 to find the top 25 (next-)most preferred sets of credentials for each randomly generated sample. Our experiments were performed and results were recorded on a Dell Latitude E5420 with an Intel Core i5-2410M 2.30 GHz dual-core CPU and 4 GB of RAM, running a 64-bit Windows 7 operating system.

To examine the practical feasibility of our approach, we collected time and memory usage data from the Cadence SMV model checker for each sample tested in the experiment. We observed that consistency checking was much more resource-intensive than identifying next-most-preferred credential sets, especially with 16 or more variables; however, with 15 or fewer variables, consistency checking generally used less than one second and 7 MB of memory (for 5 statements) or a few seconds and 15 MB of memory (for 10 statements). To identify each next-most-preferred set of credentials given up to 18 variables and 5 statements (or up to 16 variables and 10 statements), the model checker generally used less than 300 ms of time and less than 7 MB of memory; however, resource usage can increase significantly once these bounds are passed. The amounts of resources required to identify the next-most-preferred set in each case remain relatively stable regardless of whether the overall most-preferred credential set or the 25th-most-preferred set is being obtained. These results show that our approach is feasible for use in practical applications.

Data from our experiments and a prototype version of our tool are available at http://fmg.cs.iastate.edu/project-pages/credentials.html.

6 Related Work

In the past, cost-based approaches [4] for minimizing credential disclosure have been proposed. These approaches assign higher cost to more sensitive credentials of the client; the objective is to minimize the cost associated with disclosing a set of credentials while satisfying the server's requirements. Similarly, the point-based approach in [14] assigns points to each credential based on the trustworthiness of the client, and the client values its credentials with a private score. The approaches in [4] and [14] use quantitative valuations to model preferences; in our view, qualitative valuations are better for representing the naturally qualitative preferences in this setting. Kärger et al. developed an expressive logic-based preference formalism [7] for specifying qualitative privacy preferences over the user's credentials, which can be used to minimize the sensitivity of the disclosed credentials. In contrast to all of these approaches, which require the client to have a priori knowledge of the server's access control policy, our method is able to minimize disclosure of the client's credentials even when all or part of the access control policy is unavailable to the client.

A similar problem arises in online trust negotiation [12,13,15], where a client iteratively negotiates with a server in order to determine the least sensitive set of credentials that is acceptable to the server. Our approach can be applied within such automatic trust negotiation frameworks, even when negotiating with servers that have partially or fully protected access control policies.

Our earlier work in [11] introduced a new technique for using model checking to compute dominance between two outcomes when preferences are expressed in CP-nets. This paper builds on the ideas in [11] to solve two different problems using model checking: in addition to computing dominance when preferences are expressed in CI-nets, we also compute the sequence of next-most-preferred outcomes. Our work in [9] addresses a related problem in the domain of goal-oriented requirements engineering, while this paper focuses on the details of the modeling strategy and the method of computing next-most-preferred sets in order to minimize the sensitivity of credentials disclosed by a client to the server.

7 Summary and Discussion

In this paper, we introduced a new approach based on the CI-net [2] formalism for representing and reasoning with a client's sensitivity preferences over credentials. We have developed a model checking-based technique for finding a sequence of successively next-preferred (more sensitive) credential disclosure sets with respect to CI-net preferences specified by the client. Our approach involves encoding the semantics of a CI-net as a model in the input language of the Cadence SMV model checker, then querying the model checker with temporal logic formulas to check the consistency of the CI-net preferences and to obtain the top-k ranked sets of credentials such that less sensitive credentials are returned before more sensitive ones. We have presented an implementation and performed experiments that show the practical feasibility of our approach for computing consistency and finding the top 25 sets of credentials when given CI-nets of varying sizes.

Our approach can be used in client-server negotiation settings such as choosing the most preferred server to provide a service (such that least-sensitive credentials are disclosed), as well as in online trust negotiation where clients incrementally disclose sensitive credentials while negotiating with servers that have partially or fully protected access control policies. We are now seeking "real-world" industrial applications where we can compare the performance of our approach against existing solutions to these problems. Our future plans also involve developing techniques that take into account server preferences for obtaining some client credentials over others along with the client's sensitivity preferences.

References

1. Ardagna, C.A., De Capitani di Vimercati, S., Foresti, S., Neven, G., Paraboschi, S., Preiss, F.-S., Samarati, P., Verdicchio, M.: Fine-Grained Disclosure of Access Policies. In: Soriano, M., Qing, S., López, J. (eds.) ICICS 2010. LNCS, vol. 6476, pp. 16–30. Springer, Heidelberg (2010)
2. Bouveret, S., Endriss, U., Lang, J.: Conditional importance networks: A graphical language for representing ordinal, monotonic preferences over sets of goods. In: Boutilier, C. (ed.) IJCAI, pp. 67–72 (2009)
3. Brafman, R.I., Domshlak, C., Shimony, S.E.: On graphical modeling of preference and importance. J. Artif. Intell. Res. (JAIR) 25, 389–424 (2006)
4. Chen, W., Clarke, L., Kurose, J., Towsley, D.: Optimizing cost-sensitive trust-negotiation protocols. In: INFOCOM, pp. 1431–1442 (2005)
5. Clarke, E., Grumberg, O., Peled, D.: Model Checking. MIT Press (January 2000)
6. Goldsmith, J., Lang, J., Truszczynski, M., Wilson, N.: The computational complexity of dominance and consistency in CP-nets. JAIR 33, 403–432 (2008)
7. Kärger, P., Olmedilla, D., Balke, W.-T.: Exploiting Preferences for Minimal Credential Disclosure in Policy-Driven Trust Negotiations. In: Jonker, W., Petković, M. (eds.) SDM 2008. LNCS, vol. 5159, pp. 99–118. Springer, Heidelberg (2008)
8. McMillan, K.L.: Cadence SMV (software). Release 10-11-02p1 (2002), http://www.kenmcmil.com/smv.html
9. Oster, Z.J., Santhanam, G.R., Basu, S.: Automating analysis of qualitative preferences in goal-oriented requirements engineering. In: Alexander, P., Pasareanu, C.S., Hosking, J.G. (eds.) ASE, pp. 448–451. IEEE (2011)
10. Pnueli, A.: The temporal logic of programs. In: FOCS, pp. 46–57. IEEE Computer Society (1977)

11. Santhanam, G.R., Basu, S., Honavar, V.: Dominance testing via model checking. In: AAAI, pp. 357–362. AAAI Press (2010)
12. Winsborough, W., Seamons, K., Jones, V.: Automated trust negotiation. In: Proceedings DARPA Information Survivability Conference and Exposition, DISCEX 2000, vol. 1, pp. 88–102. IEEE (2000)
13. Winsborough, W.H., Li, N.: Safety in automated trust negotiation. In: IEEE Symposium on Security and Privacy, pp. 147–160. IEEE Computer Society (2004)
14. Yao, D., Frikken, K.B., Atallah, M.J., Tamassia, R.: Private information: To reveal or not to reveal. ACM Trans. Inf. Syst. Secur. 12, 6:1–6:27 (2008)
15. Yu, T., Winslett, M., Seamons, K.E.: Interoperable strategies in automated trust negotiation. In: Reiter, M.K., Samarati, P. (eds.) ACM Conference on Computer and Communications Security, pp. 146–155. ACM (2001)

IBOS: A Correct-By-Construction Modular Browser*

Ralf Sasse[1], Samuel T. King[2], José Meseguer[2], and Shuo Tang[2]

[1] Institute of Information Security, ETH Zurich, Switzerland
ralf.sasse@inf.ethz.ch
[2] University of Illinois at Urbana-Champaign, USA
{kingst,meseguer,stang6}@illinois.edu

Abstract. Current web browsers are complex, have enormous trusted computing bases, and provide attackers with easy access to computer systems. This makes web browser security a difficult issue that increases in importance as more and more applications move to the web. Our approach for this challenge is to design and build a correct-by-construction web browser, called IBOS, that consists of multiple concurrent components, with a small required trusted computing base. We give a formal specification of the design of this secure-by-construction web browser in rewriting logic. We use formal verification of that specification to prove the desired security properties of the IBOS design, including the address bar correctness and the same-origin policy.

Keywords: Browser security, same-origin policy, rewriting logic.

1 Introduction

The modern web browser has become a popular target for attackers of computer systems [20,11,13,12,16] – two key factors contribute to this trend. First, browsers are complex software artifacts that are riddled with security vulnerabilities. For example, Internet Explorer, Chrome, Safari, Opera, and Firefox had over 500 new security vulnerabilities combined in 2010 [16]. Second, browsers are the primary way users access the wide array of current web-based applications. Web-based applications are collections of web pages that people use in concert to carry out common computing tasks. As users continue to use browsers for more fundamental computing needs, the browser itself contains more valuable data, such as banking credentials, login information, and credit card numbers, presenting an enticing target for attackers of computer systems.

Current research efforts into more secure web browsers help to deal with the complexity of browsers themselves by decomposing them into smaller components. The OP web browser [7], Gazelle [19], Chrome [2], and ChromeOS [6] propose new browser architectures for separating the functionality of the browser

---

* This work was done while the first author was at the University of Illinois.

C.S. Păsăreanu and G. Salaün (Eds.): FACS 2012, LNCS 7684, pp. 224–241, 2013.
© Springer-Verlag Berlin Heidelberg 2013

from security mechanisms and policies. This privilege separated architecture enables a small program, called a *browser kernel*, to enforce browser security policies without relying on the correct operation of the millions of lines of code used to implement the browser. In addition to these alternative browser architectures, the IBOS system [17] extends these modularity principles to the operating system to remove almost all traditional operating system (OS) components and services from the browser's trusted computing base (TCB).

In this work we first present the design of IBOS, which is highly modular, with the browser kernel being separated from all other processes. Our presentation includes a discussion of the browser's security goals, in particular the ability to enforce security policies, like the same-origin policy (SOP), and a trusted user interface, to prevent address bar manipulation. The browser is also resilient against having some of its components subverted, due to its modular structure and central trust in the kernel only.

We give a formal specification of IBOS in rewriting logic [10], showing its modular structure and its communication paths. The formal specification is executable in the Maude tool [5], which is a high-performance implementation of rewriting logic. The IBOS security properties mentioned above are then model checked in Maude for suitable bounds. Furthermore, we prove that the bounded model-checking results thus obtained do actually extend to the unbounded case, i.e., the full operation of the browser. In this way we prove that the browser design implements SOP correctly and that its address bar cannot be spoofed, i.e., it will always show the URL for the content on screen. Our analysis did find an easy to correct bug related to how the display memory is handled, which makes browser tabs inoperable, as their content does not update anymore.

Organization. The rest of this paper is organized as follows. Section 2 will show some preliminaries on rewriting logic and the Maude tool. In Section 3 we explain the IBOS system including its design and security properties. Section 4 presents a high-level picture of the formal specification of IBOS. In Section 5 we show the formal verification of the security goals of IBOS. Finally, in Section 6 we discuss related work and present some conclusions.

2   Preliminaries

In this paper, we follow the classical notation and terminology from [18] for term rewriting, and from [10] for rewriting logic. Rewriting logic specifications are rewrite theories, $\mathcal{R} = (\Sigma, E \cup Ax, R)$, with $(\Sigma, E \cup Ax)$ an equational theory. Σ is the set of typed function symbols, sorts, and subsorts, while the equations E together with the axioms Ax specify the set of *states* of $\mathcal{R}$ as an algebraic data type. This equational theory represents the deterministic part of the system, while the rules R represent the concurrent aspects and work on top of that data type. The rewrite theory $\mathcal{R}$ provides both a *mathematical model* and an *executable semantics* by term rewriting.

The *Maude* tool [5] is a high-performance implementation of rewriting logic. It allows equational specification in *functional modules*, corresponding to equational theories $(\Sigma, E \cup Ax)$, and full rewrite theories $\mathcal{R} = (\Sigma, E \cup Ax, R)$ can be specified as *system modules*. In functional modules other modules can be included, sorts and subsorts can be declared and operator symbols can be defined, possibly with equational attributes (called axioms) like associativity, commutativity and/or identity. Sorts, subsorts, conditional equations and memberships define the computations that are possible. Reasonable executability requirements are needed to make a module *admissible* (see [5, Sections 4.6 and 6.3]), including termination (modulo axioms), ground confluence and sort-decreasingness. Then, Maude can execute the module by equational simplification modulo the axioms, where the equations in E are used as rules from left to right and Maude's built-in matching modulo the axioms Ax leads for each term t to its canonical form with a least sort. For functional modules this yields the algebra of canonical forms $Can_{\Sigma/E \cup Ax}$ which is isomorphic to the initial algebra semantics given by $T_{\Sigma/E \cup Ax}$ (see [5, Sections 4.6-4.8]). Equational simplification modulo axioms is executed by the `reduce` command in Maude. Maude also has built-in support for the modeling of objects, in the `CONFIGURATION` module, which we use here.

In order to be admissible, a system module has to, in addition to its equational component being admissible, satisfy the ground coherence requirement of its rules R with respect to equations in E and also needs to ensure that all variables in rules can be instantiated by (incremental) matching. Such a module can be executed in Maude by rewriting with the rules and oriented equations modulo axioms Ax. This yields an initial reachability model $\mathcal{T}_R$ whose states are elements of $Can_{\Sigma/E \cup Ax}$ and whose transitions are rewrites. Rewrites in a system module are performed in Maude by the `rewrite` command, which is position fair and rule fair. Breadth-first search is also available using the `search` command. A linear temporal logic (LTL) model checker is built-in for verification of safety and liveness properties.

3 Illinois Browser Operating System

We present the formal verification of the design and implementation of an experimental operating system called the Illinois Browser Operating System (IBOS) [17]. IBOS is an operating system and a browser co-designed to drastically reduce the trusted computing base (TCB) for a web browser and to simplify the browsing system. We first give a brief introduction about the background of the state-of-the-art of web browser security, then describe the architecture and design principles of IBOS to show why its component-based design is suitable for formal verification, and finally explain its key security properties related to the browser components that we are going to verify.

3.1 Web Browser Security Background

The web is now the dominant platform for delivering interactive application to hundreds of millions of users. Web browsers have become the *de facto* operating system for hosting these web-based applications (web apps). On the one hand, the current web introduces a rich set of features enabling a variety of web apps, such as banking, shopping, social networking, etc. On the other hand, these features inevitably increase the complexity of web apps and browsers. Due to the complexity and outdated design of traditional browsers, attackers are able to carry out web-based attacks against web apps, browsers, and operating systems.

As explained in the introduction, the use of a browser kernel is highly advised. But, even when retrofitting a small such kernel to a browser, it still has to rely on the underlying operating system. In contrast, IBOS takes the modular design one step further to extend the principle to the operating system itself, introducing a small browser and operating system kernel that is the sole TCB of the whole system. The TCB makes it feasible to formally verify some of the key properties of web browsers, such as the same-origin policy.

The primary security policy that all modern browsers implement is the same-origin policy (SOP). The same-origin policy acts as a non-interference policy to ensure that web apps from different origins are isolated from each other. An origin is often defined as the <protocol, domain, port> tuple of the URL of a web app. Under the same-origin policy, a malicious web app from `attacker.com` should not be able to alter content and access sensitive information from `bank.com`. Unfortunately, due to their design, Chrome, Internet Explorer, Safari, and Firefox have to enforce the policy by using a number of checkers spread around the whole code base that consists of millions lines of code. Evidence shows that all of them have had trouble implementing the policy correctly [4].

3.2   IBOS Architecture

IBOS proposes a highly modularized architecture of operating system and web browser by embracing principles from microkernel design. By exposing browser abstractions at the operating system kernel level, IBOS is able to remove all traditional OS and browser components and services from the TCB of the systems.

Figure 1 shows the architecture of IBOS. The IBOS architecture uses a thin kernel for managing hardware and facilitating message passing between processes. The system includes all traditional OS and browser components such as device drivers (e.g., networking interface card (NIC) driver), browser engines used for rendering web apps, and storage subsystem for storing cookies.

Some of the key goals of IBOS are the following, see [17] for all the goals and more detail:

– Security decisions happen at the lowest possible level: small TCB.
– Enough browser states and events exposed, so as to allow for security policy checking; this makes IBOS flexible to allow new browser security policies.

A key property of the IBOS browser is that *all communication*, i.e., all messages sent or received, *get transmitted through the* IBOS *kernel*. This is because the message passing is implemented as system calls, which of course go the the microkernel operating system, which is tightly integrated with the IBOS kernel. The components of the IBOS architecture which we want to highlight are the following three:

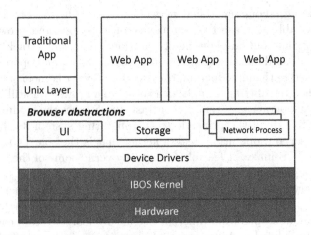

Fig. 1. IBOS Architecture

- **The IBOS Kernel.** The IBOS kernel builds upon the L4Ka microkernel and is the central component of the IBOS web browser. It takes care of traditional OS tasks, e.g., process creation and application memory management. Message passing is based on the L4Ka::Pistachio message passing implementation, forcing all messages through the kernel, and specifically allows the checking of the security policies. Some of these policies are shown in Section 3.3
- **Network Process.** The network process is responsible for HTTP requests. It transforms HTTP data into a TCP stream and in turn into a series of Ethernet frames which are passed to the NIC driver.
- **Web Apps.** A new web app is created for each individual page visit of the user; specifically, whenever a link is clicked or a new URL is entered into the address bar. A web app sends out the HTTP request to the network process, parses HTML and runs JavaScript and renders web content to a tab. Each web app is labeled with the origin of the HTTP request used at creation.

3.3 Security Goals

The modularized design and the small size of the TCB of IBOS enable the use of formal methods to verify the design's correctness. IBOS' use of small, simple, and exposed APIs allows us to model the system and reason about it. Using formal methods, we are able to check if the IBOS design preserves its security goals during an attack.

In IBOS, the goal is to minimize the TCB for web browsers and to simplify browser-based systems. To quantitatively evaluate its effort, the authors count the LOC in the IBOS TCB to be approximately 42K lines of code, which includes both the L4Ka kernel and integrated browser kernel. While the L4Ka kernel itself should also be formally verified to provide the security guarantee, we argue that it is a replaceable part in the TCB and there is already a verified kernel (seL4 [9]) in the L4 family that exposes a similar API that IBOS can use. As a result, in this paper we focus on proving the security properties based on the browser kernel design and implementation, and assume correct microkernel behavior.

Overall, we are going to verify the *same-origin policy* design in IBOS by verifying that the following invariants are upheld:

1. The kernel must route network requests from web page instances to the proper network process.
2. The kernel must route Ethernet frames from the network interface card (NIC) to the proper network process.
3. Ethernet frames from network processes to the NIC must have an IP address and TCP port that matches the origin of the network process.
4. HTTP data from network processes to web page instances must be from acceptable origins.
5. Network processes for different web page instances must remain isolated.
6. Isolation of the browser chrome (UI elements) and web page content displays.
7. Only the current tab can access the screen, mouse, and keyboard.
8. All components can only perform their designated functions.
9. The URL of the current tab is displayed to the user.

The same-origin policy is given by properties (1)–(7). Property (8) is another good property for IBOS, while property (9) aids in verifying property (7). Another important IBOS property we will verify is *address bar correctness*, that is, the address displayed in the address bar is always correct and cannot be spoofed.

3.4   Comparing the IBOS Approach to Commercial Browsers

IBOS enforces strong security guarantees by implementing a small kernel and exposing browser-related abstractions at the kernel level. By doing so, IBOS is able to ensure all critical browser-related messages pass through the kernel, which enforces security policies. Although commercial browsers, such as Chrome and ChromeOS [6], also use a browser kernel to validate messages, this browser kernel still runs on commodity operating systems and can only be as secure as the underlying OS and system services. In contrast, IBOS has only a small kernel in its trusted computing base, which is what makes our modeling and verification effort feasible.

For performance, one concern is that the exclusive use of message passing in IBOS would cause a slowdown compared to traditional commercial browsers, such as Internet Explorer and Firefox. However, the authors show that the page loading speed of an unoptimized IBOS prototype is roughly equivalent to Chrome and Firefox for 6 popular web sites. Moreover, Chrome also uses message passing for most of the communication between its components, showing that using message passing in a browser implementation can be practical.

Although browser-based operating systems do limit the apps one can run on their system, we anticipate a system like IBOS being used in the same way users use ChromeOS where all user interface components are implemented using a browser.

4   Formal Specification of IBOS

Maude specifications were used systematically in the design of IBOS before its code was developed. Furthermore, we developed a more detailed formal specification of IBOS by doing a detailed study of the IBOS C++ source code to reflect all important details. This detailed specification was then subjected to thorough review by a joint team of modelers and developers to ensure that it faithfully reflected the implementation, and, in one case, to detect an implementation flaw. In this way, the formal specification has been further refined during this phase. Thus, we made sure that the original design intentions, the source code, and the formal specification matched correctly.

For the full formal model with detailed explanations see the PhD thesis [15]. In this section we point out key properties and give a general flavor of the model. At the top level, our state space is made up of objects with an object identifier, a type, and a set of attributes. Each network process, web app, and the kernel is modeled as a single object. Each of these components runs in parallel and is independent, except for communication. We show the form of the distributed state of the model in Figure 2. In that figure all objects outside the kernel are shown as rectangles. Note that pipes are a special kind of object that connects the objects at its left and right end. Other than that, arrows show connectivity. The ellipses inside the kernel contain relevant pieces of the kernel, that are not objects themselves, i.e., they are not independent components. There will of course be multiple instances of objects for most classes, except for the NIC, display and web app manager.

Let us start by looking at the kernel in more detail, particularly at the message passing mechanism. First, we present more information on the messages. All messages are passed as system calls of the underlying micro kernel operating system, where the browser-specific part of the message is encapsulated in the system call. The message part specific to the browser has the following format, which we call the payload of the encapsulating system call:

```
op payload : Oid Oid MsgType String  -> Payload [ctor] .
```

The arguments of payload are the sender (as Oid), the receiver (as Oid), the message type (as MsgType), and an argument commonly containing the URL that is requested or sent (as String). We have simplified a little here and left out some extra arguments that are in the model, but which are not relevant for the present purposes. The sort Oid is that of object or process identifiers. Each web app, network process, etc., has a unique Oid. Note that the correct sender Oid is enforced by the kernel, as it knows which process sent the system call encapsulating this payload.

The actual message is then built using the payload and system call type:

```
op msg : SyscallType Payload -> Message [ctor] .
op OPOS-SYSCALL-FD-SEND-MESSAGE : -> SyscallType .
```

where OPOS-SYSCALL-FD-SEND-MESSAGE is the most commonly used type of system call for sending browser messages.

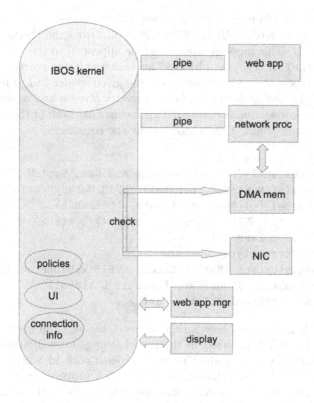

Fig. 2. IBOS Model State

To model the fact that the kernel knows which process actually sent a message (as a system call) and to make sure that in the model no two processes can send messages directly to each other, but are forced to send messages via the kernel, the model defines one pipe object per process (using the same Oid as the associated process), which contains two one-way pipes, going to the kernel from the process and going to the process from the kernel:

```
op pipe : -> Cid [ctor] .

op fromKernel : MessageList -> Attribute [ctor] .
op toKernel : MessageList -> Attribute [ctor] .
```

Let us show an example pipe object for the process with 1050 as Oid with two buffers which currently holds no message (mt) going either way:

```
< 1050 : pipe | fromKernel(mt), toKernel(mt) >
```

Suppose this process wants to send, for example, the message:

```
msg(OPOS-SYSCALL-FD-SEND-MESSAGE, payload(1050, 256,
    MSG-FETCH-URL, l(http,dom("test"),port(81))))
```

This message comes from web app 1050 and goes to network process 256, sending the message to fetch a URL (MSG-FETCH-URL) from the (fictional) domain http://test:81. This message would then be appended to the list of messages held in toKernel in the pipe object. The kernel enforces correct sender Oid based on the pipe's id by simply changing the given sender Oid, if necessary.

As part of the policy checking when a network process and a web app communicate, their connection is checked. This means that both of them need to be linked to the same origin. This is modeled by the equation:

```
eq < kernel-id : kernel |
    handledCurrently(checkConnection(Num:Nat, Num':Nat, M)) ,
    weblabels(pi(Num':Nat, L:Label), WPIS:WebappProcInfoSet) ,
    networklabels(pi(Num:Nat, L:Label, L':Label),
                  NPIS:NetworkProcInfoSet) , Att >
 =  < kernel-id : kernel |
    handledCurrently(M) ,
    weblabels(pi(Num':Nat, L:Label), WPIS:WebappProcInfoSet) ,
    networklabels(pi(Num:Nat, L:Label, L':Label),
    NPIS:NetworkProcInfoSet) , Att > .
```

The property being checked here is that the receiving web app with id Num':Nat is associated to a URL L:Label in the kernel storage for web app connections weblabels, and that the sending network process with id Num:Nat is associated with the same URL L:Label in the network process connection storage networklabels. Then the message is simply being passed on, by dropping the checkConnection wrapper around the message M. The kernel is only handling one thing at a time, which is stored in handledCurrently. Once the current instruction has been dealt with, any of the currently incoming messages can become the next message to be executed. This is modeled by the rule:

```
rl [kernelReceivesOPMessage] :
   < kernel-id : kernel |
       handledCurrently(mt) , msgPolicy(MP), Att >
   < ID : pipe | toKernel(msg(ST:SyscallType,
       payload(N, N', M:MsgType, S:String)), ML) , Att2 >
=> < kernel-id : kernel |
     handledCurrently(policyAllows(msg(ST:SyscallType,
         payload(ID, N', M:MsgType, S:String)), MP)) ,
     msgPolicy(MP), Att >
  < ID : pipe | toKernel(ML) , Att2 > .
```

Note that the kernel does not take the message to be dealt with directly, but wraps the actual message inside the policyAllows operator, together with the set of message policies MP as an extra argument, which is an attribute of the kernel wrapped in msgPolicy. Also, in the message the sender id N, which was given by the sender, is forcibly changed to the actual sender id ID, which is the process id of the pipe (and thus the associated process).

For the network process we are using (as does IBOS) the process ids 256 through 1023. The attributes of a network process are:

```
op returnTo : ProcId -> Attribute [ctor] .
op in : LabelList -> Attribute [ctor] .
op out : LabelList -> Attribute [ctor] .
```

The returnTo attribute stores the process id of the web app that this network process will return data to, while the attributes in and out hold the lists of labels (representing URLs) that the network process will ask data from and has received data from already. We simplify here by using a URL to represent its data, instead of using its actual HTML code.

For web apps we are using the process ids 1024 through 1055 with attributes:

```
op rendered : Label -> Attribute [ctor] .
op URL : Label -> Attribute [ctor] .
op loading : Nat -> Attribute [ctor] .
```

The label inside rendered is the URL for which the web app has put the data on the screen, provided it is the active web app. The label inside URL is the location where this web app wants to load data from. loading is just a binary flag indicating whether the web app has already sent a request to load data. Initially, the rendered field for a new web app will be empty, and loading is 0, meaning that it has not yet started to load. The following equation sends the message to start loading:

```
eq < N : proc | rendered(L) , URL(L') , loading(0) , Att >
   < N : pipe | toKernel(ML) , Att2 >
 = < N : proc | rendered(L) , URL(L') , loading(1) , Att >
   < N : pipe | toKernel(ML, msg(OPOS-SYSCALL-FD-SEND-MESSAGE,
        payload(N, network-id, MSG-FETCH-URL, L'))) , Att2 > .
```

The message is sent to fetch the data from URL L' and the loading attribute changes to 1. On return of the requested data, rendered will change to L'.

The hardware pieces of Figure 1, video card, NIC, etc., are not modeled in any detail. Only the NIC is modeled, and it receives target URLs from the memory set aside for this purpose through the kernel, and then, after a potential delay, returns the representation of the resulting data.

This model uncovered an issue with the display memory, which turned out to be a bug. It was found in the model and could then be fixed in both model and implementation. The issue was that when switching web apps, the newly active web app would sometimes not get access to the actual display memory, which would then simply stay blank. The model let us figure out how and why this happened. This is not a security concern, but actually a usability issue, as the tab in question becomes useless, but cannot be abused for malicious purposes.

5   Formal Verification of IBOS Security

The verification of IBOS design security is based on the formal model explained in the prior section. We simply assume that the underlying microkernel operating

234 R. Sasse et al.

system performs its functions correctly. Of course, in order to not have to rely on this we could instead use seL4 [9], which has been verified.

An important property for a web browser is the trustworthiness of user interface elements. This is crucial to counter spoofing attacks. Particularly, the address bar needs to be trustworthy, so that the user always knows which site is currently being visited. It is truly important to know whether the currently visited site is really his/her banking web site, where entering credentials is fine, or if it is instead a phishing web site, where if the user enters his/her account information monetary loss is imminent. We all know that it is possible, even simple, for malicious attackers to create phishing web sites that are indistinguishable on the surface from the real web sites. A careful user should be able to trust the address bar, to prevent such phishing from succeeding. Also see [3,15] about the address bar spoofing possibilities we found in an analysis of Internet Explorer.

Similarly important is the correct implementation of security policies in the browser. The same-origin policy, presented in Section 3.3, is one such policy that assures the user that his private information, say from a banking web site, will not be leaked to another web site, with possibly malicious intentions.

As IBOS has been designed with security in mind, our goal in this section is not just to find possible flaws that could be abused by attackers. Our goal actually is to be able to prove that no such address bar spoofing attacks are possible, as well as to verify the correct implementation of SOP. First, let us show the operator which drives the search, simulating user input, `inspect-space`:

```
op inspect-space :  -> Configuration .
eq inspect-space = < testMsg : testMsg | cmd( inspect ) > .
```

where `testMsg` is a wrapping process, which allows this to be put at the top level of our multi-set of processes, and `cmd` is a wrapper allowing this to follow the usual way of storing information in process attributes. The key here is the `inspect` command. We will call the rules for `inspect` the *trigger rules*, and write them as R_T. All other rules belong to the *internal rules* of the model, written as R_I. We are working modulo the equations E. So we are actually rewriting with $\to_{R_{(I \cup T)/E}}$, which can be split into $\to_{R_{I/E}}$ and $\to_{R_{T/E}}$. We will use the shorthands $\to_I$ and $\to_{I/E}$ (resp. $\to_T$ and $\to_{T/E}$) to represent $\to_{R_{I/E}}$ (resp. $\to_{R_{T/E}}$).

```
op inspect : -> Cmd .
op inspect : Nat -> Cmd .
rl inspect => inspect(3) .
rl inspect(0) => mtCmdList .
rl inspect(s(N:Nat)) => new-url , inspect(N:Nat) .
rl inspect(s(N:Nat)) => switch-tab , inspect(N:Nat) .
```

This shows that `inspect` is unrolled step by step. The number 3 can of course be changed, but that number is picked in particular so that two web apps can be created and the tab can then be switched as well. At each step either a `switch-tab` or `new-url` will be generated. This simulates user input. As `inspect` is defined by rules, the `search` command will create all possible combinations.

We omit how `new-url` gets assigned a new URL and how `switch-tab` picks any of the web apps to be the new active web app.

Internal Normalization Between Trigger Rules. We observe that there is no interference between internal rules I and trigger rules T, i.e., we can re-order them in any way we please. In particular, we like to normalize with the internal rules after each execution of a trigger rule. That means, for execution using both internal rules and trigger rules, $\rightarrow^*_{(T \cup I)}$, we will rearrange that to $\rightarrow_T \rightarrow^!_I$ $\ldots \rightarrow_T \rightarrow^!_I \ldots \rightarrow_T \rightarrow^*_I$, where $\rightarrow^!_T$ denotes a terminating subsequence. The last set of internal rules does not have to be carried all the way to normalization, to take into account the fact that the combination of trigger and internal rules might not normalize either. Let us state this formally as a lemma, noting that by $\rightarrow^i_{T/E}$ we mean the i-th use of a rule from T/E:

Lemma 1. *Given terms s_1 and s_2, for any chain of rewrites of the form $s_1 \rightarrow^*_{(T \cup I)/E} s_2$, with n uses of trigger rule, we can rearrange that sequence, using the same rewrites, to $s_1 \rightarrow^1_{T/E} \rightarrow^!_{I/E} \cdots \rightarrow^i_{T/E} \rightarrow^!_{I/E} \cdots \rightarrow^n_{T/E} \rightarrow^*_{I/E} s_2$.*

This lemma is based on the minimal overlap of the trigger rules in T and the internal rules in I. In particular, no trigger rule step is ever influenced by any internal rule step, that is, trigger rule steps can either be taken, or not taken, independently of anything happening with the internal rules. Conversely, a trigger rule step may enable additional internal rule steps to be taken, but does not disable internal rule steps that have been available already. The entire proof for this is included in [15]. We can now consider the effect of each trigger rule on the state by itself. We let the model do all internal computations until finished before using another trigger rule step.

5.1   Address Bar Correctness Verification

Address bar correctness in the model means that the content of the displayed page is always from the address which is displayed in the address bar. In our model, the kernel keeps track of the address bar by means of the data stored in the `displayedTopBar`. The source of the content being displayed is stored in the display process abstraction, which has the `displayedContent` field to store the information. The content of both these fields needs to be the same at all times. Only when there currently is no content in one of the two field, which is modeled by the `about-blank` URL, the other one can have any value.

To motivate the property of address bar correctness, note that the address bar, and the content as stored in the display process, are both stateless objects. They have no memory, but only know what is stored in them right now.

Both the address bar and the display content are only changed due to the current web app interacting with the kernel when created or when the tab is switched to it. To create a mis-match between the two, two different URLs are all that is needed, which can be provided by just two web apps. This allows us to make the reduction that only the last two web apps that are on the screen need to be taken into account. The rest of the browser model state and the length of the run of the browser model is irrelevant and thus can be abstracted away.

Assume we needed to consider a third web app, then that would only be the case if that web app made a change to either of the two objects in question; but then one of the other two does not make a change (or does a duplicate one), so then that other web app becomes irrelevant and we are back to the case of two web apps. If there was a way for more than two web apps to create such a mis-match, then the deciding last step (we would stop at such a mis-matching point) must be either a new web app being added or the tab being switched. But then, that whole trace of actions and number of web apps can be simplified to just the state before that last action, with only the old active web app and the new active web app taken into account to create the exact same mis-match. Now we can focus on the interaction of only two web apps, which requires search up to depth three, due to the need of also allowing a tab switch.

We now present our theorem for the address bar correctness.

Theorem 1. *The property of address bar correctness holds for any rewrite sequence, using any number of trigger rule steps.*

For the detailed proof, see [15]. We will show that bounded model checking analysis of all sequences with at most 3 trigger rules finds no possible violation. So, the address bar is correct for all sequences with at most 3 trigger rules. A reduction from longer sequences to sequences of at most length 3 then proves the theorem. This means that the correctness extends to sequences with *any* number of trigger rules being used. Let us start with that lemma, which is proved by a detailed case analysis using Lemma 1, see [15].

Lemma 2 (Reduction). *Any sequence of trigger rule steps that leads to a violation of the address bar correctness and uses 4 or more trigger rule steps can be reduced by a step. This yields that all possible trigger rule sequences leading to a violation must be of length 3 or less.*

Now that we have the reduction to 3 trigger rule steps, we can use bounded model-checking to analyze this finite state space. We start the model-checking search for potential attacks, in the form of a mismatch of these two fields, from an initialized kernel, together with the driver `inspect-space`. We are looking for any configuration in which there is a mismatch between the value of `displayedTopBar` and `displayedContent`. If no solution to this search is found, then there is no attack for this bounded case.

```
search init-simp-kernel
inspect-space =>* X:Configuration
  < kernel-id : kernel | Att:AttributeSet ,
          displayedTopBar(URL:Label) >
  < display-id : proc |
    displayedContent(URL':Label), Att2:AttributeSet >
such that URL:Label =/= URL':Label
      and  URL:Label =/= about-blank
      and  URL':Label =/= about-blank .
```

Indeed, when we run this search command we find no solutions as result:
No solution.
states: 247743 rewrites: 3663864 in 247886ms cpu
(248055ms real) (14780 rewrites/second)

Together with the reduction lemma, Lemma 2, this completes the proof.

Bounded model-checking is indeed required here, as the active web app can change the content on screen after the address bar has been set. Of course, that web app is associated to the URL in the address bar in the kernel, so the kernel will not allow the web app to access any other origins and thus the address bar correctness will hold.

5.2   Same-Origin Policy Verification

After the proof of the address bar correctness we now prove that IBOS implements the same-origin policy correctly, that is, that it satisfies properties (1)–(7) in Section 3.3. We will now look more closely at those security requirements which result in the browser implementing SOP.

To analyze the SOP property of our browser, we use the model of the internal logic of the browser we have introduced; it includes the policies being enforced by the kernel. We already noted that all messages go through the kernel and thus are subject to being checked with respect to the policies. We then also have to create canonical messages that different components can try to send to each other. That is, we need a small set of messages that is *generic*, so that the instances of these generic messages can cover all messages. Then the analysis can in fact verify that none of those messages can reach disallowed destinations. We again use a reduction to a limited number of required trigger steps and then use model checking to show the property for this smaller state space.

See Section 3.3 for the whole list of SOP properties. Let us consider the first property of SOP in more detail:

- (1) *The kernel must route network requests from web page instances to the proper network process.*

Let us first motivate at a high level why this should be true before we state the lemma and show the model-checking analysis afterwards. Simply said, each web page instance and each network process have an associated URL which identify them to the kernel, in addition to their actual process id. This URL is the URL they are allowed to communicate with. Now, whenever a web page instance tries to communicate with a network process, the kernel checks the process id and associated URL for both. For this purpose, the kernel stores a mapping of process id to URLs. If no appropriate network process exists, a new one will be created by the kernel. In practice, the kernel (and its modeling) enforces that only matching processes communicate. For checking property (1) we look at each message that is received by any network process and compare the URLs of sender and receiver using the kernel's mapping. Note that sender and receiver names cannot be forged as these are their process ids and enforced by the kernel based on the underlying guarantees of the operating system.

Indeed, the execution for property (1) does not make use of a history of what happened before, but only of the current assignment of each process to URL. We can abstract away from a long sequence of network requests to simply one single network request. As the state is generic and the correctness of the property only depends on one network request, if we can show the absence of errors for this one network request, we know that any arbitrary number of them still will not exhibit any errors. Otherwise, we could take just that network request which triggers the error and use it to get the error by itself, contradicting the fact that we show that no single message creates an error.

Checking property (1) then boils down to checking executions (up to some depth of input), from canonical starting points, to see whether there is a mismatch between URLs in the resulting configuration for any message. If there is no mis-match for all starting points, then all communications have been legal and property (1) is actually proved. We can limit the depth of execution, i.e., the number of messages being considered, and still be complete. Each message is generic and representative of a set of messages. The reason we can limit the depth is that if the property would turn out to be possibly violated at an arbitrary number of messages, then that final message triggering the failure will only have one source process and one destination process. That violation can then be boiled down to the triggering network request, and the setup for those involved two processes, which would be a total depth of three actions.

Now we can state the theorem for SOP, whose detailed proof is given in [15]:

Theorem 2. *The Same-Origin Policy holds for any rewrite sequence, using any number of trigger rule steps.*

The proof of this theorem consists of the proofs for all of the SOP properties (1)–(7). To illustrate this we give the lemma for property (1).

Lemma 3. *The property (1) holds for any rewrite sequence, using any number of trigger rule steps.*

The proof we give is based on the number of trigger rule steps needed to find a violation. We have used bounded model-checking to show there is no violation up to the bound. Assume there is a violation, then we pick one of the sequences that lead to such a violation with the smallest number of trigger rule steps. That number must be bigger than the bound. We then analyze that sequence and we find at least one step that is not needed. By that we mean that after removing this one trigger rule step the same violation is still reached, but now the sequence is one trigger rule step shorter. This contradicts that we pick the sequence with the smallest number of trigger rule steps and thus there is no violation for any number of trigger rule steps. We can state this as a reduction lemma again:

Lemma 4 (Reduction). *Any sequence of trigger rule steps that leads to a violation of property (1) and uses 4 or more trigger rule steps can be reduced by a step. Thus, all possible trigger rule sequences leading to a violation of property (1) must be of length 3 or less.*

The proof in [15, Chapter 4] explains this reduction by which we extend the bounded model-checking proof for sequences with at most three triggers to sequences with *any* number of triggers in detail.

The following search returns no solution, meaning that no illegal (according to SOP) communication happened.

```
search init-simp-kernel inspect-space =>*
X:Configuration < N:Nat : pipe | toKernel(ML:MessageList) ,
    fromKernel(msg(OPOS-SYSCALL-FD-SEND-MESSAGE,
        payload(Num:Nat, N:Nat, MSG-FETCH-URL, L1:Label)),
        ML':MessageList) , Att:AttributeSet >
< kernel-id : kernel | Att2:AttributeSet ,
    weblabels(pi(Num:Nat,L1':Label), WAPIS:WebappProcInfoSet) ,
    networklabels(pi(N:Nat, L2':Label, L2:Label),
                    NPIS:NetworkProcInfoSet) ,
    displayedTopBar(URL:Label) >
such that  L1:Label =/= L2:Label or L1':Label =/= L2':Label .
```

As the above bounded model-checking did not return any violations, no illegal messages were passed. All network requests indeed end up going to the proper network processes. This bounded model-checking analysis proves the base cases of up to 3 trigger steps, while together with the reduction lemma, Lemma 4, this yields the proof for all possible sequences.

The model contains about 20 rules and 60 equations and the bounded model-checking takes between 10 and 20 minutes to check each property.

For all of the remaining properties (2)–(9) we give similar proofs in [15]. We omit their statement and explanation due to space reasons in this paper. Altogether, this shows that the SOP is correctly implemented for the IBOS formal specification, and thus for the IBOS design.

6   Related Work and Conclusions

Let us consider some previous work formally verifying the design or implementation of operating system kernel and browsers. In seL4 [9], the authors use a self-developed framework to verify the correctness of a L4 type microkernel, which provides the foundation of further proof of systems built on top it, such as our work in this paper. Heiser *et al.* discuss some possibilities in system security once one has a truly trustworthy kernel [8]. One of those possibilities is providing even stronger security guarantees for a web browser, like we do in this paper. On the browser side, the designers of the OP browser [7] use formal methods to verify some security properties of their design, in particular, they are concerned with whether or not the security indicators behave as expected. Formal methods have also been used to check properties of the status bar and address bar in Internet Explorer [3]. Akhawe *et al.* also propose an abstract formal model of web security and use it to analyze the security of several web apps [1]. However, even though those approaches improve the security of the corresponding systems, these systems still rely on a large TCB that could not be verified.

In our work we were able to obtain an executable specification of the IBOS design thanks to the substantially smaller TCB of the web browser. This was key to prove security properties of the IBOS design.

In this paper we present a correct-by-construction browser with analysis of its correctness at the design level. For this, we show how useful a formal specification of such a modular piece of software is. It allowed us to first find bugs, to fix them, and then to prove correctness of the address bar and the same-origin policy.

There are a few follow up projects that would be useful as future work. First, now that a design that has been analyzed in detail exists, it would be highly desirable to analyze the implementation using (semi-)automatic source code verification tools such as matching logic [14]. Another way of further increasing the confidence in IBOS would be to actually use the proven secure microkernel seL4 or to develop a new proof of security for IBOS' underlying microkernel. In the other direction, it would also be interesting to consider generating source code from the model directly, i.e., code synthesis.

Acknowledgments. This research was partially supported by NSF Grant CCF 09-05584 and AFOSR Grant FA8750-11-2-0084 as well as by grant N0014-09-1-0743 from the Office of Naval Research, AFOSR MURI grant FA9550-09-01-0539, NSF grant CNS 0831212, and by Intel through the ISTC for Secure Computing.

References

1. Akhawe, D., Barth, A., Lam, P.E., Mitchell, J., Song, D.: Towards a formal foundation of web security. In: Proceedings of the 2010, 23rd IEEE Computer Security Foundations Symposium, CSF 2010, pp. 290–304. IEEE Computer Society, Washington, DC (2010)
2. Barth, A., Jackson, C., Reis, C., The Google Chrome Team: The security architecture of the chromium browser (2008), http://crypto.stanford.edu/websec/chromium/chromium-security-architecture.pdf
3. Chen, S., Meseguer, J., Sasse, R., Wang, H.J., Wang, Y.-M.: A systematic approach to uncover security flaws in GUI logic. In: IEEE Symposium on Security and Privacy, pp. 71–85. IEEE Computer Society (2007)
4. Chen, S., Ross, D., Wang, Y.-M.: An analysis of browser domain-isolation bugs and a light-weight transparent defense mechanism. In: Ning, P., di Vimercati, S.D.C., Syverson, P.F. (eds.) ACM Conference on Computer and Communications Security, pp. 2–11. ACM (2007)
5. Clavel, M., Durán, F., Eker, S., Lincoln, P., Martí-Oliet, N., Meseguer, J., Talcott, C.: All About Maude - A High-Performance Logical Framework. LNCS, vol. 4350. Springer, Heidelberg (2007)
6. Google Inc. Chromium OS (2010), http://www.chromium.org/chromium-os
7. Grier, C., Tang, S., King, S.T.: Secure web browsing with the OP web browser. In: Proceedings of the 2008 IEEE Symposium on Security and Privacy, pp. 402–416 (May 2008)
8. Heiser, G., Ryzhyk, L., Von Tessin, M., Budzynowski, A.: What if you could actually trust your kernel? In: Proceedings of the 13th USENIX Conference on Hot Topics in Operating Systems, HotOS 2013, pp. 27–27. USENIX Association, Berkeley (2011)

9. Klein, G., Andronick, J., Elphinstone, K., Heiser, G., Cock, D., Derrin, P., Elka-duwe, D., Engelhardt, K., Kolanski, R., Norrish, M., Sewell, T., Tuch, H., Win-wood, S.: seL4: Formal verification of an operating-system kernel. Commun. ACM 53(6), 107–115 (2010)
10. Meseguer, J.: Conditional rewriting logic as a unified model of concurrency. Theoretical Computer Science 96(1), 73–155 (1992)
11. Moshchuk, A., Bragin, T., Gribble, S.D., Levy, H.M.: A crawler-based study of spyware on the web. In: Proceedings of the 2006 Network and Distributed System Security Symposium (NDSS) (February 2006)
12. Provos, N., Mavrommatis, P., Rajab, M.A., Monrose, F.: All your iFRAMEs point to us. In: Proceedings of the 17th Usenix Security Symposium, pp. 1–15 (July 2008)
13. Provos, N., McNamee, D., Mavrommatis, P., Wang, K., Modadugu, N.: The ghost in the browser: Analysis of Web-based malware. In: Proceedings of the 2007 Workshop on Hot Topics in Understanding Botnets (HotBots) (April 2007)
14. Rosu, G., Stefanescu, A.: Matching logic: a new program verification approach. In: Taylor, R.N., Gall, H., Medvidovic, N. (eds.) ICSE, pp. 868–871. ACM (2011)
15. Sasse, R.: Security Models in Rewriting Logic for Cryptographic Protocols and Browsers. PhD thesis, University of Illinois at Urbana-Champaign (July 2012), http://hdl.handle.net/2142/34373
16. Symantec. Symantec internet security threat report (2011), http://www.symantec.com/business/threatreport
17. Tang, S., Mai, H., King, S.T.: Trust and protection in the illinois browser operating system. In: Arpaci-Dusseau, R.H., Chen, B. (eds.) OSDI, pp. 17–32. USENIX Association (2010)
18. TeReSe (ed.): Term Rewriting Systems. Cambridge University Press (2003)
19. Wang, H.J., Grier, C., Moshchuk, A., King, S.T., Choudhury, P., Venter, H.: The multi-principal OS construction of the Gazelle web browser. In: Proceedings of the 2009 USENIX Security Symposium (August 2009)
20. Wang, Y.-M., Beck, D., Jiang, X., Roussev, R., Verbowski, C., Chen, S., King, S.: Automated Web Patrol with Strider HoneyMonkeys: Finding Web sites that exploit browser vulnerabilities. In: Proceedings of the 2006 Network and Distributed System Security Symposium (NDSS) (February 2006)

Guided Search for Deadlocks
in Actor-Based Models

Steinar Hugi Sigurdarson, Marjan Sirjani,
Yngvi Björnsson, and Arni Hermann Reynisson

School of Computer Science, Reykjavik University

Abstract. Model checking is used to uncover errors by searching the state space of a model. Informed search algorithms use heuristic strategies with problem-specific knowledge to find solutions efficiently. Generally, such heuristics estimate the distance from a given state to a goal state. In this paper, we present seven heuristics for guiding search algorithms through the state-space of actor-based models to a deadlock. In many cases, our methods can find a deadlock more efficiently than uninformed searches. The A* search algorithm guarantees an optimal solution and returns the shortest counter-example when used with an admissible heuristic. These methods are supported by a tool that performs directed search for the deadlock property. The objective is to detect errors that might not be found by simulation or by conventional model checkers before reaching an upper bound or state-space explosion.

1 Introduction

Building reliable software systems is a complicated and important challenge of modern engineering. Software systems nowadays are mostly reactive, concurrent, and distributed. Even small such systems can exhibit complex behavior where standard testing techniques often fall short of finding potential problems. Model checking, through a systematic verification of the entire state-space, may help to discover hard to find flaws in such systems. However, model checking comes with its own set of problems. Even relatively simple reactive systems may have huge state-spaces, many orders of magnitude larger than the memory of conventional computers can store. Such state-space explosion can be somewhat alleviated with techniques such as symmetry and partial order reduction [4], but the exponential growth still remains.

Directed model checking is one of the key techniques developed to address the state-space explosion problem [7,12,18,9]. Heuristics are used to expand the state-space in a selective fashion, where states more likely to violate a required property are expanded early. Although this does not save time to verify the entire system, it may find bugs earlier. In practice, such use of model checking is just as useful as proving a property [32].

The actor model is among the pioneering ones to address concurrent and distributed applications [13], and is getting more and more popular in practice

C.S. Păsăreanu and G. Salaün (Eds.): FACS 2012, LNCS 7684, pp. 242–259, 2013.
© Springer-Verlag Berlin Heidelberg 2013

[20,15,16]; for example, Erlang [10] and Scala [28] are two widely used programming languages that have applied the actor model of concurrency. The pure asynchronous actors can be used as encapsulated components for modeling event-driven systems and service-oriented software. Actors send messages (events) to each other which are put in the message buffers of the receiver actor. Each actor takes a message (event) from the buffer and executes the corresponding method or service. Although we can see the increasing use of actors in applications ranging from networks to multi-core programming, little has been done on analyzing actor- based models [29,27]. Because of the asynchronous nature of communication in actor models and the message queues, the state space explosion is more likely to happen rapidly, making directed model checking a good candidate for finding flaws in such systems.

In this paper we present a directed model-checking approach for actor-based models. We use the actor-based language Rebeca [30] and extend Modere [19], the model checking tool of Rebeca, to use directed model checking. The resulting model checker, Guided-Modere, provides a flexible framework with interchangeable search algorithms and heuristics. We experiment with two commonly used informed search algorithms, A* and pure heuristic search, and introduce several heuristics for guiding them. The objective is to find a possible deadlock state, before exhausting the computer's memory. Moreover, we aim to find the shortest, or a relatively short, counter-example reproducing the error found.

In a closed actor model (where there is no input to the system and the environment is modeled as an actor), a deadlock happens only when the message queues of all actors are empty, i.e., there is no event left to handle. This feature of actors is the basis of our proposed heuristics for guiding the search: to look for a state where the message queues are empty. The ideas behind our proposed heuristics are based on getting closer to such state: we look for a state where there are less messages in the queues of all the actors, or a state with more actors with empty queues, or a state which is in a path that shows a trend of decreasing messages, or a state where the last executed actor has a smaller queue. Our experiments show that Guided-Modere on average outperforms its unmodified counter part.

Contribution. To summarize our contribution, in this work we

- proposed seven heuristics suitable for a guided search to find possible deadlocks in an actor-based model,
- implemented different search strategies and the heuristics in Guided-Modere, as an extension of the Rebeca model checking tool,
- performed experiments over a set of case studies to show the effectiveness of the heuristics and some of their combinations under various conditions.

Structure of the Paper. In Section 2 we give an overview of the relevant background, including model checking, state space reduction techniques, the actor model, and heuristic search algorithms. In Section 3 we introduce the proposed heuristics, and the experimental results are introduced in Section 4. Section 5 covers related work. We give a summary of the work and our general results in the discussion and conclusion section, Section 6. Future work is presented in Section 7.

2   Background

When you run a model checker on a model to check a specific property, the result may be that the property is valid, the property is invalid together with a counter-example, or the model checker may exhaust available computing resources (memory or time). If the property is validated it means that the model checker has been able to explore the entire state-space and has concluded that the model satisfies the given property. On the other hand, if the outcome was invalid, the model checker has reached a state in which the provided property is violated. Ideally, the model checker will return some form of a counter-example showing a set of reproducible actions which will result in the violation of the property. In the case when execution is terminated prematurely because of the memory or allotted time being exhausted, no information about the validity of the model can be derived.

2.1   Model Checking and State-Space Explosion

Traditional model checking tools exhaustively search the state space using either depth first (DFS) or breadth first (BFS) algorithms. Modere, a model checking tool for Rebeca [19], can exhaustively check for deadlocks and LTL properties against Rebeca models. It is implemented with a variation of DFS called Nested DFS and fitted with optimizations such as partial order reduction, to counter against state explosion.

The state-space for a model can grow exponentially. A major disadvantage of model checking is how poorly it scales. Symbolic model checking [2], partial order reduction and symmetry [25], and model abstraction [3] are among techniques that have been used to tackle state space explosion. Also, directed model checking is a bug-hunting technique where selection from the enumerated successor states is prioritized in order to find short counter examples quickly. Model checking algorithms exploit the specification of properties to lead the search towards their falsification. This approach is driven by the success of directed state space exploration in the field of artificial intelligence and is among the key technologies to overcome the state- space explosion problem in model checking [9].

Here, we focus on directed search for the deadlock property in actor-based models.

2.2   Actor Model

In the actor model *actors* are treated as the universal primitives of concurrency. Instead of threads, the actor model uses objects as units of distribution and concurrency which provides a simple and natural concurrency model. Actors are self-contained and communicate through fair asynchronous message passing. Actors can be created dynamically and the topology of the system changes dynamically [14,1,30].

In a response to a message an actor can send a finite number of messages to actors it knows, create a finite number of new actors and designate the behavior for the next message it will process. More importantly, all of the actors in the system can perform these actions concurrently and no assumptions are made regarding the order in which they occur.

Rebeca [30,29] is an actor-based language and is designed for the verification of distributed concurrent systems. A Rebeca model consists of a finite number of rebecs (actors) which communicate via asynchronous message passing. Reactive systems are typically not expected to halt, hence the terminal states represent a design error and are not desired. Actor systems continue their execution as long as there are messages to handle. If we have a closed actor model, with no input from outside, a deadlock happens when all the message queues are empty.

2.3   Search Algorithms and Heuristics

In practice, finding a bug with a model checker can be more useful than proving a property [32]. Informed search algorithms use heuristic strategies with problem-specific knowledge to find solutions more efficiently than uninformed algorithms. Generally, such heuristics estimate the distance from a given state to a goal state.

We consider two of the most commonly used informed search algorithms, pure heuristic search and A* search, which belong to a family of *best- first search* algorithms. They use an *evaluation function*, denoted by $f(n)$ where n is a node in the search tree, to prioritize the fringe, i.e. to decide which node to expand next.

This evaluation function considers the estimated cost to reach a goal state from the current state, denoted as $h(n)$, and the cost to reach the current state from the initial state, denoted as $g(n)$. The function $h(n)$ is refered to as the heuristic function and $g(n)$ as the path cost function. For a goal state, $h(n) = 0$ and $g(n)$ is the length from the initial state the the goal state.

For pure heuristic search only the heuristic function is used to decide which action to choose, thus $f(n) = h(n)$. The A* algorithm uses the path-cost function $g(n)$ as well, thus $f(n) = g(n) + h(n)$ [24]. A* search is optimal for admissible heuristics, described below, and is guaranteed to return a shortest counter example if a goal state exists and is found before reaching state-explosion.

Experience has shown that for some problems A* search spends a great amount of time exploring paths with insignificant difference in cost. The requirement of optimality causes the algorithm to spend time choosing between candidates with roughly the same cost. We may wish to relax the requirement of optimality in exchange for a quicker solution. We do that by using a weighted variant of the A* algorithm, Weighted-A* search [24]. It adds weight factor w to the evaluation function, $f(n) = (1 - w)\, g(n) + w\, h(n)$. By varying w the desired mixture between relying on the heuristic and finding the shortest counter-example can be achieved. Higher value of w will put more responsibility on the heuristic and reduce the chance of an optimal solution and vice versa. The factors 0, $\frac{1}{2}$ and 1 would correspond to uniform cost, A* search and pure heuristic search, respectively. In this study, Weighted-A* search is used to relax the requirement of optimality. Thus, our experiments will use $w \in [\frac{1}{2}, 1]$.

The efficiency of informed search is largely based on the quality of the heuristic function used. A heuristic strategy is *admissible* (or *optimistic*) if it never overestimates the distance from a given state to the nearest goal state. This is important if we want to guarantee that the first solution found is optimal, i.e. that no shorter solution exists. Model checkers using DFS search tend to return longer paths which makes it more difficult for the user to identify the error. In practice, a relatively short path will usually suffice. However, non-admissible heuristics can be useful and are widely used [6]. *Consistent*, or *monotone*, heuristics are monotonically non-decreasing along the shortest path to a goal state. The estimated distance from a state n to a goal state will never exceed the estimated distance of its successor state q to the goal state and the cost of traversing between n and q. Formally, heuristic function $h(n)$ is consistent if and only if for every node n and every successor q of n,

$$h(n) \leq c(n, q) + h(q),$$

where $c(n, q)$ is the cost of traversing from n to q. A consistent heuristic function is always admissible, but an admissible strategy can be inconsistent [24].

When searching with inconsistent but admissible heuristics we must be careful when discarding previously expanded states if we wish to guarantee optimality. A node on the closed list (the list of already expanded states), may have a greater estimated total distance to a goal state than a new state, in which case we must re-open it. In theory, exponential increase in the number of expanded nodes may occur, however, in practice it rarely happens [9].

3   Deadlock Detection Heuristics for Actor Models

A Rebeca model is expressed semantically as a labeled transition system $\mathcal{M} = \langle S, A, T, s_0 \rangle$ where S is the set of global states, A is the set of actions, T is the set of transitions and s_0 is the set of initial states. A state in Rebeca is defined as the combination of the local states of all rebecs in the system, $s = \Pi_{j \in I} r_j$, where I is the set of rebecs. The local state of a rebec r_j is identified by the values assigned to its state variables, v_j, and the contents of its message queue, m_j, including information about the sender, destination message server and parameters. We say that rebec r_j is enabled when the number of messages in its queue, $|m_j|$, is greater than zero.

In general, a deadlock is a situation where two or more actions are waiting for each other to finish. The actor model is event-driven and Rebeca only allows asynchronous message passing. Thus, the system cannot deadlock as long as there are events driving it. A rebec will never wait for a process to finish, access to a shared resource, or a reply from another rebec. The system will run into a deadlock state if and only if there are no enabled rebecs, that is, $\sum_{j \in I} |m_j| = 0$, assuming the model has no terminal states. All of our heuristics exploit this fact and share the intention of driving the search towards states which are more likely to result in a deadlock. In the tool-supported subset of Rebeca dynamic creation and deletion of rebecs are not allowed.

We define and implement seven heuristics, presented in the following sections. All of the heuristics are admissible. In the literature, admissible heuristics are often assumed consistent, implying that consistency is desirable. Only two of the heuristics are consistent: Queue Size and Empty Queue. Although generally considered worse for A* search, recent studies have shown that inconsistency can be beneficial. Inconsistent heuristics are able to escape regions of poor heuristic values before incurring significant cost [33]. However, due to reopening of states and the relatively low heuristic values returned by our inconsistent heuristics they are not expected to perform well with A* search and are intended for pure heuristic search only.

The state of the system at node n is referred to as n_{state} and the single parent state of n as n_{parent}. We refer to the number of rebecs in n_{state} as $|n_{state}|$. The cost of an action is fixed to 1.

3.1 Queue Size (QS)

Expand the state where the sum of the number of messages in the message queues of all rebecs is the smallest. The number of messages on queue in a state is the lower bound for number of actions required to reach a deadlock state. That is, if no new messages will be sent, the number of actions required to drive a system to a deadlock state from a given state s is equal to the number of unprocessed messages in s. The *Queue Size* heuristic uses the total number of unprocessed messages in the system as the estimated distance to a goal state, preferring states with few messages to states with many. The Queue Size heuristic is formally defined in Equation 1.

$$h(n) = \sum_{j \in n_{state}} |m_j|. \tag{1}$$

Between every node n and its successor node q exactly one message has been removed from the message queue of an enabled rebec (in n), and zero or more messages have been sent (added to rebecs in q). The cost of an action is $c(n,q) = 1$, and therefore $h(n) \leq c(n,q) + h(q)$ holds for every n in the search tree. A goal state n will have no messages, $h(n) = 0$. Given the above we know that $h(n)$ is *consistent* and, therefore, also *admissible* and will return an optimal solution when used with A* search.

3.2 Empty Queue (EQ)

Expand the state which has the most disabled rebecs. The *Empty Queue* heuristic assigns better heuristic values to states based on the number of disabled rebecs, where a state with all rebecs disabled will receive the best heuristic value and a state with no disabled rebecs will receive the worst value. This drives the search towards paths closer to a deadlock state and possibly with smaller branching factors, depending on the number of non-deterministic choices made by the enabled rebecs. The idea of this heuristic is similar to the deadlock heuristic of

PROVAT[22] and H_{ap} in HSF- SPIN[7]. This strategy is formally defined in Equation 2.

$$h(n) = |n_{state}| - \sum_{j \in n_{state}} \begin{cases} 0 & if \ |m_j| > 0, \\ 1 & otherwise. \end{cases} \tag{2}$$

Initial states will receive heuristic values equal to the number of rebecs in the system, since all of them are enabled. For every node n and every successor q of n, we know n can have at most one more enabled rebec than q. That is, at most one more rebec has become disabled. Thus, this heuristic is consistent and will not require reopening of states when guiding an A* search.

3.3 Current Queue (CQ)

Expand the state where the current rebec has the smallest message queue. We refer to the last executed rebec as the *current* rebec of a state. The *Current Queue* heuristic aims to "drain" rebecs by favoring nodes whose current rebec has the smallest message queue. The intention is to make the execution less fair, focusing on rebecs becoming disabled and thus potentially reduce the branching factor along the path. The *branching factor* of a node n is affected by the number of enabled rebecs and number of non-deterministic choices made in n_{state}. The heuristic is defined in Equation 3.

$$h(n) = \sum_{j \in n_{state}} \begin{cases} |m_j| & if \ j = current, \\ 0 & otherwise. \end{cases} \tag{3}$$

In Equation 3, *current* is the message queue of the most recently executed rebec in state n_{state}. A search path using this heuristic function should empty out rebecs with the smallest queues before proceeding to those with more messages which might reactivate the rebec again. Once a rebec has become disabled the node will receive a heuristic value equal to the second smallest queue at best. Between such nodes the condition for consistent heuristics is broken. It never overestimates the distance to the nearest goal and is therefore admissible.

3.4 Reductive Queue (RQ)

Expand the state where the number of messages is decreasing or not increasing. Essentially, message servers that do not send any messages can cause deadlocks in Rebeca models. The *Reductive Queue* heuristic utilizes this fact by comparing the total number of messages of a state and its parent. States are categorized as follows: 1. Number of messages has been reduced. 2. Number of messages has not changed. 3. Number of messages has increased.

States in each category receive the best, neutral and worst heuristic value, respectively. The initial states do not have a valid parent and are all assigned a value equal to the number of rebecs in the system.

$$p = \sum_{k \in n_{parent}} |m_k|$$

$$q = \sum_{j \in n_{state}} |m_j|$$

$$h(n) = \begin{cases} best & if \ q < p \\ neutral & if \ q = p \\ worst & otherwise \end{cases} \tag{4}$$

We choose the values for *best*, *neutral* and *worst* in Equation 4 as 0, $\lfloor \frac{1}{2} \sum |m_j| \rfloor$ and $\sum |m_j|$, respectively. The heuristic is not consistent as the difference between resulting heuristic values of two consecutive states can be greater than the added cost (which is 1) if the two states have different heuristic values. Since the size of the message queue is the upper limit it will never return a value greater than the path cost to the nearest goal. Therefore, we know that the Reductive Queue heuristic is admissible.

3.5 Reductive Queue with Memory (RM)

Expand the state where the number of messages is decreasing or not increasing. Use the history of rebecs to break ties. The *Reductive Queue* heuristic strategy will only identify and favor a state immediately after performing reducing number of messages. This variant of the heuristic keeps track of how often a rebec has decreased or increased number of messages in the past. When no decrease or increase has taken place, the state will receive the *neutral* heuristic value, as before, but with a discount based on how likely executions of this rebec are to reduce number of messages. This requires only two additional integers for each rebec in the system and has insignificant impact on memory usage and execution time.

A state receiving maximum discount would get the heuristic value $\frac{1}{2}neutral$ which, in this case, is equal to *best*. However, that can only happen if a state has a reduced number of messages on every execution and the discount would not apply. Should a rebec have a reduced number of messages on every other execution, the value of a non-decreasing state would be $\frac{3}{4}neutral$. To maintain admissibility no penalty is given to rebecs which are likely to have increased size of the message queue. This heuristic is defined formally in Equation 5. Again we choose the values for *best*, *neutral* and *worst* as 0, $\lfloor \frac{1}{2} \sum |m_j| \rfloor$ and $\sum |m_j|$, respectively.

$$p = \sum_{k \in n_{parent}} |m_k|,$$

$$q = \sum_{j \in n_{state}} |m_j|,$$

$$h(n) = \begin{cases} best & if \ q < p, \\ \frac{1}{2}neutral + \frac{1}{2}(1 - \frac{reductions_r}{executions_r})neutral & if \ q = p, \\ worst & otherwise. \end{cases} \tag{5}$$

The discount is meant to serve as a tie-breaker between two non-reducing and non-increasing states. For the same reason as *Reductive Queue*, this heuristic is not consistent.

3.6 Queue Difference (QD)

Expand the state where the fewest messages were sent. This heuristic strategy is identical to the *Reductive Queue* strategy except for the returned values. Instead of returning *best*, *neutral* and *worst* it relies on the number of messages created by the last action. This strategy will assign worse values for each additional message that is sent while the Reductive Queue heuristic assigns the same value to all states sending more than 1 message. The heuristic is defined formally in Equation 6.

$$h(n) = 1 + \sum_{j \in n_{states}} |m_j| - \sum_{k \in n_{parent}} |m_k|. \tag{6}$$

This strategy will violate the requirement for consistency when $\sum_{j \in n_{state}} |m_j| > 1 + \sum_{k \in n_{parent}} |m_k|$. This will happen every time a message server sends more than one message. Thus, this heuristic is not consistent. As the path cost from a state to a goal state will never be less than the number of messages created the strategy is admissible. The number of messages sent is usually far smaller than the total number of messages left to be processed. Because of how small the heuristic values are, compared to the path cost, A* search behaves similar to breadth-first search with this heuristic and will expand more nodes than better informed search algorithms. This behavior could be overcome by upscaling, but doing so would sacrifice the admissibility. Thus, the heuristic strategy is not expected to return satisfying results with A* search but has good potentials with pure heuristic search and, perhaps, weighted A* search with a sufficiently small weight factor.

Initial states receive a value of 1, as if no difference took place. Should we count each initialization as a sent message, returning a heuristic value equal to the number of rebecs, chances are that only one rebec would ever be expanded at level 1 since the successor states would almost certainly have lower values.

3.7 Queue Difference with Memory (QM)

Expand the state where the fewest messages were sent. Use the history of rebecs to break ties. The *Queue Difference* strategy suffers from the same problem as *Reductive Queue* when it comes to states which have not affected the total number of messages. We define a heuristic which is similar to *Reductive Queue with Memory* except that it keeps track of the difference in the number of messages instead of only incrementation and reduction. A rebec sending as many messages as it consumes will have a memory value of 0 while a rebec only consuming messages but sending none would have a memory value of 1. The heuristic is defined formally in Equation 7.

$$p = \sum_{k \in n_{parent}} |m_k|$$

$$q = \sum_{j \in n_{state}} |m_j|$$

$$h(n) = \begin{cases} 1 + q - p - (1 - \frac{reductions_r}{executions_r}) & if \ q = p \\ 1 + q - p & otherwise \end{cases} \tag{7}$$

When the difference in messages is 0, a state will receive a discount based on the the history of the rebec, called memory value. The maximum discount has the same effect on the heuristic value as half a message. However, that can only happen when a rebec has a negative difference, i.e. -1, on every execution and, therefore, the discount would not apply. Thus, the discount range is equal to 0 to 0.5 messages.

As before, the discount is only used as a tie-breaker for equal states. The aim is to favor rebecs which have a history of decreasing the total number of messages when the model checker has two or more otherwise equally-valued states. To maintain admissibility, no penalty is given to rebecs having, on average a positive difference, and, of course, no discount either. For the same reasons as the Queue Difference heuristic, this one is not consistent.

As with the non-memory version, due to the extreme underestimating of the heuristic, it is not expected to perform well with A* search but has good potential with pure heuristic search.

4   Guided-Modere and Experimental Results

Guided-Modere is an extension of Modere, the standard model checker for Rebeca, and was developed over the course of this research. The goal was to create a flexible framework to study the efficiency of heuristic search for Rebeca models with respect to execution time, length of counter-examples, and number of expanded nodes which affect both memory usage and execution time.

The implementation includes several variations of our heuristics, pure heuristic search algorithm, two A* search algorithms and three blind search algorithms.

4.1   Test Models

We ran our experiments on various problems and protocols from the literature. Each of them was modeled in Rebeca and verified for deadlock freedom before adding errors occurring at different places in the state-spaces. Many commonly experienced modeling errors will be discovered at certain depth in the search tree, no matter which path in the search tree is chosen. For such errors DFS is always equally good and faster than guided search. More interesting in the context of this study are errors which occur only in rare situations, preferably in models with a relatively large state-space. These errors might be missed by simulation or conventional model checkers before reaching an upper bound or state-space explosion. The test models presented have a reasonably large state-spaces with deadlock errors occurring at different depths in their search tree, depending on the path chosen.

Self-Stabilizing Token Ring. We experimented with two different variations of a Dijkstra's self-stabilizing token ring [5]. Such a ring has a unique predefined leader. By defining two distinct nodes as leaders, we have introduced a deadlock error. Eventually the leaders will have distinct values and the nodes between them share the value with the leader that is its closest ancestor. Both leaders will wait (forever) for receiving a value equal to their own before increasing the value and passing on the token. The second variation is a token ring with an incorrectly configured node which breaks the ring. Within a finite number of steps the model is guaranteed to deadlock. The two token rings have 6 and 5 nodes, respectively.

Dining Philosophers. The Dining Philosophers is another problem, originally presented by Dijkstra as five computers competing for access to five shared drives, but presented as five philosophers by Hoare in [17]. We experimented with the problem both without taking any measure to prevent deadlocks and by allowing the philosophers to forget the dinner. If all philosophers forget the dinner, the system is in a deadlock state.

Needham-Schroeder Public-Key Protocol. The Needham-Schroeder Public-Key Protocol is a well-known communication protocol providing mutual authentication of two clients communicating over an insecure network using a trusted server for key exchange [23]. Clients generate nonces, single-use keys to prevent replay attacks, on two separate occasions. First, when a client initiates communication and second when a client responds to a communication initiated by another client. By using the same memory slot to store the nonce, regardless of which case it was created in, an error is introduced that may occur when both clients initiate communication at the same time and the messages are processed in a specific order. In these cases, both clients have an incorrect nonce for each other the system will deadlock.

4.2   Results

Table 1 shows the result for different heuristics and algorithms. For each search the number of expanded nodes, length of the counter-example found and average execution time is shown. The experiments were executed on Dual Core Intel(R) Xeon(TM) CPU 3.20GHz processors and 2GB RAM computers. Execution time results are averaged over 20 executions. Modere's default bound for maximum depth is 10,000; Guided-Modere has no such limit.

We first contrast the performance of the different heuristics. For the pure-heuristic search algorithm all heuristics return for the most part relatively short counter examples, often optimal or close to optimal. Of those the Queue Size (QS) and Empty Queue (EQ) heuristics find the counter-examples on average the fastest. These two heuristics also performed the best for the A*-based algorithms, where QS is on average slightly better for both A* and Weighted A* ($w = 0.8$).

Table 1. Results for pure heuristic, A*, Weighted-A*, breadth-first, and Modere's Nested Depth-First search, with and without partial order reduction (PO). For each row bold numbers mark the best result.

	Pure Heuristic							A*		WA*		BFS	Modere	
	QS	EQ	CQ	RQ	RM	QD	QM	QS	EQ	QS	EQ	BFS	M_{PO}	M
Token ring w/two leaders (TR2L)														
Nodes	29	31	5882	31	29	131	131	262,355	834,609	86	1588	4,147,805	26,205	244,673
Length	17	18	23	15	17	17	17	13	13	17	20	13	13	13
Time (ms)	30	29	1062	28	32	55	56	58,043	164,134	41	254	359,106	795	19,215
Token ring w/broken relation (TRBR)														
Nodes	31	14	315	191	31	54	54	15,595	113,340	63	372	236,769	35	35
Length	14	11	14	18	14	11	11	11	11	14	11	11	15	15
Time (ms)	25	21	57	34	26	29	29	2263	9191	28	45	12,906	26	26
Dining Philosophers (DP)														
Nodes	230	863	1205	213	609	748	540	198,596	232,372	1724	5156	388,234	31	31
Length	31	76	31	31	76	31	31	31	31	31	31	31	31	31
Time (ms)	25	21	147	64	120	127	110	25,522	29,622	224	545	38,091	49	49
Forgetful Philosophers (FP)														
Nodes	16	16	2119	86	30	873	1777	94,074	105,076	2305	6436	911,149	3,057,183	-
Length	16	16	16	16	16	16	16	16	16	17	16	16	21	-
Time (ms)	36	36	302	60	44	211	379	26,973	30,446	362	890	169,271	338,532	-
Needham-Schroeder (NS)														
Nodes	973	108	238	974	973	335	120	788	784	830	850	1203	1576	1691
Length	18	18	18	18	18	18	18	18	18	18	18	18	450	450
Time (ms)	81	35	40	87	94	51	38	74	74	76	76	82	269	278

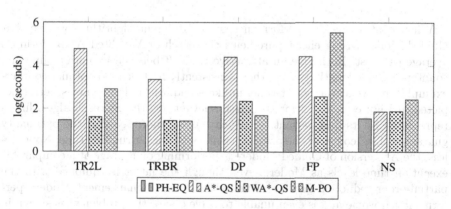

Fig. 1. Average execution times for pure heuristic search with empty queue heuristic (PH-EQ), A* with queue size heuristic (A*-QS), Weighted-A* with queue size heuristic (WA*-QS) and Modere with partial-order reduction (M-PO), for the five case studies shown in Table 1

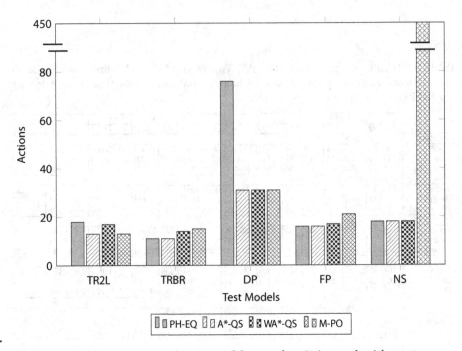

Fig. 2. Length of counter examples returned for pure heuristic search with empty queue heuristic (PH-EQ), A* with queue size heuristic (A*-QS), Weighted-A* with queue size heuristic (WA*-QS) and Modere with partial-order reduction (M-PO), for the five case studies shown in Table 1

When contrasting the performance of the different algorithms we see that Guided Modere using either pure-heuristic search or Weighted A* perform on average the best. Both give an attractive tradeoff between execution time and counter-example length, that is, they consistently find close to optimal counter-examples in a relatively short time, unlike standard Modere. This is better depicted in Figures 1 and 2 for the most relevant algorithms (each algorithm is represented by its best variant [1]). We can furthermore see that the optimality guarantee of A* comes at the price of a somewhat longer running time. Nonetheless, the A* version of Guided Modere is performing on average at a comparable execution time levels as Modere, even though the latter is equipped with the partial-order reduction improvement (without that enhancement Modere performs much worse and is even unable to solve one of the problems, as shown in the last column of Table 1).

In terms of node expansions per second there is a significant difference between models and search algorithms due the to different overhead in maintaining the

---

[1] The breadth-first search algorithm, included in the table for a base-line comparison, is omitted from the figures, but it requires up to an order of magnitude longer to find optimal paths than its A*-based counterparts.

priority lists used by the guided searches and the cost of evaluating the heuristics. Overall, standard Modere performs similarly or better than Guided-Modere for satisfied, deadlock-free, models.

5   Related Work

Some form of directed model checking has been presented from the beginning of model checking. *Approver*, first implemented in 1977, is assumed to be the first automated verification tool for communication protocols and used directed search for verification of safety properties [9]. In addition to classical communication protocols it was also capable of verifying other concurrency systems such as mutual exclusion algorithms. It used techniques dedicated to bug-finding instead of traditional depth-first or breadth-first search.

The PROVAT strategy presented in [22] has several heuristics, all of which depend only on the send and receive operations. They cover the selection of states from the open list, selecting between actions available from a specific state and deciding whether to discard particular states. The heuristic proposed for finding deadlocks is similar to our Empty Queue heuristic. When selecting a transition the deadlock heuristic always selects a transition performing a receive operation, choosing the one with the fewest messages. This corresponds to the behavior of our Current Queue heuristic, but in a different context.

In 1998, Yang and Dill published a paper on validation with guided search. They presented a strategy called Target Enlargement which was very effective for some models [32]. The idea was to make the target states bigger by computing their pre-image, the states that in one cycle can reach an error state, until the computer's memory limitation was reached. If the heuristics found problems, they usually did so in fewer states than breadth-first and depth-first search. They also show that their approach is more likely to find an error before state-space explosion occurs. In addition to Target Enlargement, they propose a heuristic using hamming distance as search metric. Their third technique, called Tracks, is similar to Target Enlargement except it uses approximate pre-images of error states based on subsets of the state variables, focusing on the main state variables which control the behavior of the system. The fourth technique, Guideposts, relies on hints provided by the designer. The number of guideposts a path passes through is used as guidance for the search.

Edelkamp, Leue, and Lluch-Lafuente coined the term *directed model checking* in their paper on HSF-SPIN [7]. Based on SPIN and its Promela modeling language, HSF-SPIN used A*, best-first search (referred to as pure heuristic search in this paper) and an improved NFDS algorithm to verify safety and a large class of LTL-specified liveness properties. They present a formula-based heuristics for different classes of properties. One of them, called H_{ap}, is used for finding deadlocks and is virtually identical to our Empty Queue heuristic. Other heuristics aim at violation of liveness and safety properties, and allow designer-devised heuristics where the protocol designer can alter the definition of heuristics and explicitly define which states are dangerous. Without designer intervention, all reads, sends and conditions are considered dangerous. The paper includes test results for variety of protocols.

Groce and Visser presented heuristic-guided model checking of Java programs in [12] using Java PathFinder. They presented seven different heuristics, in short, based on the number of executions of branches and byte-code instructions, branch coverage, number of blocked threads, amount of interleaving, thread preference and non-determinism avoidance (choose-free). Additionally, they allow developers to define their own heuristic functions or declare certain states "boring" or "interesting" by adding statements to the model in question.

In [18] predicate abstraction is used to generate heuristics for the verification of networks of extended timed automata in Uppaal. They built the entire abstract state-space before starting the search. During the search, states are mapped to their counterpart in the abstracted state-space and the error distance of the counterpart used as a heuristic estimate.

Our research was limited to A* and pure heuristic search, but other informed search algorithms have been applied to model checking as well. IDA* search (Iterative-Deepening A*) [21] has been successfully used in model checking [8] and has been demonstrated to perform well in general with inconsistent heuristics [33]. K-beam search and the non-pruning alternative k-best search [11] have been successfully applied to model checkers [12,31]. MA* (Memory-bounded A*) and SMA* (Simplified-MA*) are designed to overcome the impractical memory requirements of A*. Simply put, once the search runs out of memory it expands the best node on the open list and prunes off the worst node [26]. All of these algorithms would be worthwhile experimenting with in Guided-Modere as a future work. The Weighted A* search could potentially be improved by dynamic weighting. Rather than keeping the weight constant throughout the search the heuristics could have the most weight initially, reducing it as the search gets deeper into the search tree [24]. This approach provides an upper bound for the length of solution with respect to the optimal solution. Thus, the requirement for optimality could be relaxed up to a specific point, with regard to an optimal solution. In other words, the number of actions in the counter-example returned would never be more than, for example, twice that of an optimal solution.

6   Discussion and Conclusion

The methods presented in this paper provide the ability to guarantee shortest counter-examples for deadlocks more efficiently than the conventional breadth-first search. Without the requirement of optimality and by exploring the state-space more efficiently, these methods may find deadlock errors in models, where standard depth-first search would suffer state-space explosion.

We have presented seven heuristics which guide actor-based models towards deadlock states. Our experimental results indicate that in many cases they can significantly reduce the number of node expansions required before finding an error state. We have shown their ability to produce shorter counter-examples than the conventional depth-first search and in fewer node expansions than the optimal breadth-first search. For models with large state-spaces, blind searches could exhaust the computer's memory before reaching a goal, failing to find a deadlock error if one exists. The proposed guided searches presented might reach that deadlock state before the state-space explosion occurs. Of the heuristics the Queue Size one showed the best overall performance regarding both node expansion and execution time.

The requirement of optimality causes considerable overhead, and by removing that by using pure heuristic search only a fraction of the states A* search explored were expanded, while still returning close to optimal counter examples. Weighted A* with $w = 0.8$ was a good balance between the two objectives, returning near-optimal counter-examples with fewer expansions than traditional A* search.

7   Future Work

Further experiments can be done with Guided-Modere using the implemented heuristics. One possibility is to use one or more heuristics in combination to get potentially even more informed search guidance. One could even create combinations targeting specific deadlock scenarios.

Heuristics based on information provided by the designer have been implemented in [12] and [7], for example. Such a heuristic could be implemented for Guided-Modere. The model designer could tag message servers as either interesting or boring. Then the heuristic would guide the search such that states processing interesting messages are chosen over those processing a boring one. This strategy could be implemented by enabling either flags or annotations in the Rebeca code or by the identification of specific message servers at run-time.

Modere implements partial-order reduction. Such a reduction would benefit the informed search algorithms and further reduce node expansions.

The study focuses only on the message queue and its relation to the deadlock property. The next big step would be developing property-based heuristics and performing heuristic search for violations of safety properties for actor-based models. Furthermore, applying the hybrid A*+Improved-Nested-DFS search algorithm presented in [8] would enable the verification of liveness properties as well. The Target Enlargement technique proposed in [32] or predicate abstraction such as proposed in [18] could result in reduced exploration. Both these approaches could also benefit the search for violations of the deadlock property.

Acknowledgement. The work on this paper has been partially supported by the projects "Timed Asynchronous Reactive Objects in Distributed Systems: TARO" (nr. 110020021) and "General Problem Solving Agents" (nr. 100039022) of the Icelandic Research Fund.

References

1. Agha, G.A., Mason, I.A., Smith, S.F., Talcott, C.L.: A foundation for actor computation. Journal of Functional Programming 7(1), 1–72 (1997)
2. Burch, J., Clarke, E., McMillan, K., Dill, D., Hwang, L.: Symbolic model checking: 10^20 states and beyond. In: [1990] Proceedings. Fifth Annual IEEE Symposium on Logic in Computer Science, vol. (4976), pp. 428–439 (1986)
3. Clarke, E.M., Grumberg, O., Long, D.E.: Model checking and abstraction. ACM Transactions on Programming Languages and Systems 16(5), 1512–1542 (1994)
4. Clarke, E.M., Grumberg, O., Peled, D.A.: Model Checking. The MIT Press, Cambridge (1999)
5. Dijkstra, E.: Self-stabilizing systems in spite of distributed control. Communications of the ACM 17(11), 643–644 (1974)
6. Dräger, K., Finkbeiner, B., Podelski, A.: Directed model checking with distance-preserving abstractions. International Journal on Software Tools for Technology Transfer 11(1), 27–37 (2009)
7. Edelkamp, S., Lafuente, A., Leue, S.: Directed explicit model checking with HSF-SPIN. In: Proceedings of the 8th International SPIN Workshop on Model Checking of Software, pp. 57–79. Springer-Verlag New York, Inc. (2001)
8. Edelkamp, S., Leue, S., Lluch-Lafuente, A.: Directed explicit-state model checking in the validation of communication protocols. International Journal on Software Tools for Technology Transfer (STTT) 5(2), 247–267 (2004)
9. Edelkamp, S., Schuppan, V., Bošnački, D., Wijs, A., Fehnker, A., Aljazzar, H.: Survey on Directed Model Checking. In: Peled, D.A., Wooldridge, M.J. (eds.) MoChArt 2008. LNCS, vol. 5348, pp. 65–89. Springer, Heidelberg (2009)
10. Erlang. Erlang Programming Language Homepage, http://www.erlang.org
11. Felner, A.: Improving search techniques and using them on different environments. Science (February 2001)
12. Groce, A., Visser, W.: Heuristics for model checking Java programs. International Journal on Software Tools for Technology Transfer 6(4), 260–276 (2004)
13. Hewitt, C.: Description and theoretical analysis (using schemata) of PLANNER: A language for proving theorems and manipulating models in a robot. MIT Artificial Intelligence Technical Report 258, Department of Computer Science. MIT (April 1972)
14. Hewitt, C.: Viewing control structures as patterns of passing messages. Artificial Intelligence 8(3), 323–364 (1977)
15. Hewitt, C.: Orgs for scalable, robust, privacy-friendly client cloud computing. IEEE Internet Computing 12(5), 96–99 (2008)
16. Hewitt, C.: Actorscript(tm): Industrial strength integration of local and nonlocal concurrency for client-cloud computing. CoRR, abs/0907.3330 (2009)
17. Hoare, C.A.R.: Communicating sequential processes. Communications of the ACM 21(8), 666–677 (1978)
18. Hoffmann, J., Smaus, J.-G., Rybalchenko, A., Kupferschmid, S., Podelski, A.: Using Predicate Abstraction to Generate Heuristic Functions in UPPAAL. In: Edelkamp, S., Lomuscio, A. (eds.) MoChArt IV. LNCS (LNAI), vol. 4428, pp. 51–66. Springer, Heidelberg (2007)
19. Jaghoori, M.M., Movaghar, A., Sirjani, M.: Modere: The model-checking engine of Rebeca. In: Proceedings of the 21st Annual ACM Symposium on Applied Computing (SAC 2006), Software Verificatin Track, pp. 1810–1815 (April 2006)

20. Karmani, R.K., Shali, A., Agha, G.: Actor frameworks for the jvm platform: a comparative analysis. In: PPPJ 2009: Proceedings of the 7th International Conference on Principles and Practice of Programming in Java, pp. 11–20. ACM, New York (2009)
21. Korf, R.: Depth-first iterative-deepening: An optimal admissible tree search. Artificial Intelligence 27(1), 97–109 (1985)
22. Lin, F.J., Chu, P.M., Liu, M.T.: Protocol verification using reachability analysis: the state space explosion problem and relief strategies. In: Proceedings of the ACM Workshop on Frontiers in Computer Communications Technology - SIGCOMM 1987, pp. 126–135 (1988)
23. Needham, R.M., Schroeder, M.D.: Using encryption for authentication in large networks of computers. Communications of the ACM 21(12), 993–999 (1978)
24. Pearl, J.: Heuristics: intelligent search strategies for computer problem solving. Addison-Wesley (1984)
25. Peled, D.: Combining Partial Order Reductions with On-the-fly Model-checking. In: Dill, D.L. (ed.) CAV 1994. LNCS, vol. 818, pp. 377–390. Springer, Heidelberg (1994)
26. Russell, S.: Efficient memory-bounded search methods. In: Proceedings of the 10th European Conference on Artificial Intelligence (1992)
27. Sabouri, H., Sirjani, M.: Slicing-based reductions for Rebeca. In: Proceedings of FACS 2008. Electr. Notes Theor. Comput. Sci., vol. 260, pp. 209–224 (2010)
28. Scala. Scala Programming Language Homepage, http://www.scala-lang.org
29. Sirjani, M., Jaghoori, M.M.: Ten Years of Analyzing Actors: Rebeca Experience. In: Agha, G., Danvy, O., Meseguer, J. (eds.) Formal Modeling: Actors, Open Systems, Biological Systems. LNCS, vol. 7000, pp. 20–56. Springer, Heidelberg (2011)
30. Sirjani, M., Movaghar, A., Shali, A., de Boer, F.: Modeling and verification of reactive systems using Rebeca. Fundamenta Informatica 63(4), 385–410 (2004)
31. Wijs, A.J., Lisser, B.: Distributed Extended Beam Search for Quantitative Model Checking. In: Edelkamp, S., Lomuscio, A. (eds.) MoChArt IV. LNCS (LNAI), vol. 4428, pp. 166–184. Springer, Heidelberg (2007)
32. Yang, C.H., Dill, D.L.: Validation with guided search of the state space. In: Proceedings of the 35th Annual Conference on Design Automation Conference - DAC 1998, pp. 599–604 (1998)
33. Zahavi, U., Felner, A., Schaeffer, J., Sturtevant, N.: Inconsistent heuristics. In: Proceedings of the National Conference on Artificial Intelligence, vol. 22, p. 1211. AAAI Press, MIT Press, Menlo Park, Cambridge (1999, 2007)

Assumption Generation for Asynchronous Systems by Abstraction Refinement

Qiusong Yang[1], Edmund M. Clarke[3], Anvesh Komuravelli[3], and Mingshu Li[1,2]

[1] National Engineering Research Center of Fundamental Software
[2] State Key Laboratory of Computer Science
Institute of Software, Chinese Academy of Sciences
Beijing 100190, China
[3] Computer Science Department, Carnegie Mellon University
Pittsburgh, PA 15213, USA
{qiusong,mingshu}@nfs.iscas.ac.cn, {emc,anvesh}@cs.cmu.edu

Abstract. Compositional verification provides a way for deducing properties of a complete program from properties of its constituents. In particular, the assume-guarantee style of reasoning splits a specification into assumptions and guarantees according to a given inference rule and the generation of assumptions through machine learning makes the automatic reasoning possible. However, existing works are purely focused on the synchronous parallel composition of Labeled Transition Systems (LTSs) or Kripke Structures, while it is more natural to model real software programs in the asynchronous framework. In this paper, shared variable structures are used as system models and asynchronous parallel composition of shared variable structures is defined. Based on a new simulation relation introduced in this paper, we prove that an inference rule, which has been widely used in the literature, holds for asynchronous systems as long as the components' alphabets satisfy certain conditions. Then, an automating assumption generation approach is proposed based on counterexample-guided abstraction refinement, rather than using learning algorithms. Experimental results are provided to demonstrate the effectiveness of the proposed approach.

1 Introduction

Compositional verification provides a way for deducing properties of a complete program from properties of its constituents and it is a promising technique to address the state explosion problem. In particular, the assume-guarantee reasoning splits a specification into assumptions and guarantees [1]. A typical rule for assume-guarantee reasoning has the form of $\langle\varphi\rangle P\langle\phi\rangle$, where the *assumption* φ constrains the behavior of the environment and the *guarantee* ϕ specifies the behavior of the component P when φ is ensured. The rule means that in any execution where the environment behaves according to φ, it is guaranteed that P

C.S. Păsăreanu and G. Salaün (Eds.): FACS 2012, LNCS 7684, pp. 260–276, 2013.
© Springer-Verlag Berlin Heidelberg 2013

behaves according to ϕ. For example, the following inference rule was proved in [2] for *synchronous* composition of Kripke Structures against properties ACTL*.

$$\frac{M_1 \parallel A \models G \ (\langle A \rangle M_1 \langle G \rangle)}{M_1 \parallel M_2 \models G \ (\langle \rangle M_1 \parallel M_2 \langle G \rangle)} \qquad (1)$$

To prove that $M_1 \parallel M_2 \models G$, where $\parallel$ denotes the synchronous parallel composition operator, it is first to show that G is satisfied in $M_1 \parallel A$, assuming that its environment satisfies the assumption A. Then, the assumption A will be discharged on the other component M_2 by checking if $M_2 \preceq A$, where $\preceq$ is a strong simulation relation between two components. If the assumption is much smaller than M_2, checking $M_1 \parallel A \models G$ and $M_2 \preceq A$ might be more efficient than directly checking $M_1 \parallel M_2 \models G$.

However, in earlier works, human intervention was required to get an assumption satisfying an assume-guarantee rule. As it requires the interaction with an expert user, devising a proper assumption is not easy, even if not impossible, to accomplish for nontrivial verification problems. The pioneering work [3] presented an automatic assume-guarantee reasoning framework, in which the weakest assumption [4], represented as a finite-state automaton, is automatically learned using the L^* algorithm [5]. Since then, the problem of generating assumptions automatically has been extensively studied.

Prior work can be categorized according to the following three dimensions: system model, compositional pattern and learning algorithm used.

- System Model. Most of existing works [3,6,7,8,9,10] use *Labeled Transition Systems (LTSs)* as system models. In [11], *Kripke Structures* are used instead.
- Compositional Pattern. Existing works are focused purely, as least as we know, on the *synchronous* composition of LTSs or Kripke Structures. For LTSs, synchronous composition[1] usually allows the non-common actions between parallel components to be interleaved, while the executions of common actions must be synchronized [3,6,7,8,9,10]. Similarly, all components are forced to make transitions simultaneously in the synchronous composition of Kripke Structures [11].
- Learning Algorithm. As only safety properties are considered in most of existing works, the assumptions can be modeled as finite state automata and the L^* algorithm and its variants are used for learning a regular set through membership and equivalence queries [3,6,7,8,9,10]. As a Kripke Structure is normally defined through its initial and transition predicates, the CDNF algorithm [12] is employed to learn Boolean functions in [11]. The CDNF algorithm can exactly learn a Boolean function by continuously asking membership and equivalence queries to a teacher, who can precisely answer every query.

---

[1] It should be noted that some authors called it as *asynchronous composition* of LTSs. In this paper, we only think a definition allowing interleaving on *common* actions as an asynchronous composition.

In this paper, for *asynchronous* systems, we propose an *alternative* approach for the automatic assumption generation based on predicate abstraction and interpolation, *instead of* using learning algorithms. That we are focused on asynchronous systems here is because real software programs are more naturally modeled as asynchronous systems, while synchronous models are more amenable to hardware systems. A concise example will be provided in the next section to demonstrate the differences between synchronous and asynchronous compositions. On the other side, the reason we propose an alternative to traditional learning-based approaches is that learning algorithms normally have a very high computational complexity. The running time of L* is bounded by a polynomial of n and m [5], where n denotes the number of states of the target automaton and m denotes the length of the longest counterexample, and CDNF bounded by a polynomial of the minimal CNF and DNF size of the target formula. However, in the assume-guarantee reasoning of asynchronous systems, the parameter n and the minimal CNF or DNF size are exponential in the number of global and local variables in the worst case.

The contribution of our paper is the following. First, we prove that the inference rule (1) holds for asynchronous systems with a redefined simulation relation between two components. The standard simulation relation in assume-guarantee reasoning, such as [9,10], is defined as the inclusion of trace languages, implying that, if $M_1 \preceq M_2$, the projection of every behavior of M_1 on the alphabet of M_2 is also a behavior of M_2. Under the asynchronous circumstances, the trace language inclusion induced simulation relation will be not monotonic with respect to the parallel composition operator, i.e. $M_1 \preceq M_2 \not\Rightarrow M_1 \parallel M_3 \preceq M_2 \parallel M_3$, which is essential for proving the inference rule (1), as a component can transit to an arbitrary state because of *jumps* in which shared variables are modified by other components while local variables are left untouched. The simulation relation introduced in Section 3 requires that the simulation relation is maintained between two components even if they make jumps, rather than real transitions.

Second, a method automating the assumption generation is proposed. The assumption A starts with the coarsest predicate abstraction, which is defined over a set of predicates over variables of M_2, such that $M_2 \preceq A$. Then, the assumption A will be refined in a series of iterations. In each iteration, $M_1 \parallel A \models G$ will be checked first. If it holds, we will have $M_1 \parallel M_2 \models G$. Otherwise, a finite counterexample will be returned as a result of $M_1 \parallel A \not\models G$. Then, we will check if the counterexample's projection on A is also feasible in M_2. If so, the algorithm can terminate as a real counterexample is found. Otherwise, a refined assumption, denoted as A', will be generated based on a new predicate obtained through counterexample analysis, using interpolation techniques. At the same time, the refinement ensures that: 1) $M_2 \preceq A'$. 2) A' contains strictly less behaviors than A in the sense that the counterexample will be not feasible in $M_1 \parallel A'$. When the algorithm terminates, an assumption satisfying the two premises of rule (1) is obtained, implying the property holds, or a real counterexample is found.

Finally, experimental results are provided to demonstrate that the proposed approach outperforms typical learning approaches based on CDNF.

Related Work. Since the first approach for automatic assume-guarantee reasoning based on automata learning was proposed [3], there have been extensive studies on the automatic assumption generation for compositional verification. These include devising new inference rules [6], extensions and optimizations of the L* algorithm [13,14], automatic refinement of the assumption's alphabet [15], symbolic methods for assume-guarantee reasoning [16,17], implicit learning based on CDNF [11] and minimal separating automata-based reasoning [18,19]. However, as discussed before, all these works are focused only on the synchronous parallel composition of LTSs or Kripke Structures, while it is more natural to model real software programs in the asynchronous framework. The rules that have been used for synchronous systems might not hold when asynchronous composition is considered. The reasoning framework must also be changed accordingly.

Our assumption generation method given in Section 4 is essentially based on the CEGAR(CounterExample Guided Abstraction Refinement) [20]. In [21], the authors also present a CEGAR-based method for assume-grantee reasoning, instead of using learning algorithms. Similarly, a CEGAR-based method for the assume-guarantee reasoning of probabilistic systems is given in [22]. However, those works are also focused on the synchronous parallel composition of LTSs.

2   Preliminary Definitions

In this section, preliminary definitions and notations used in the rest of the paper are given. LTSs are not selected as system models because it is more natural to model an asynchronous system with *shared variable structures*.

Shared Variable Structures. An SVS $M = (\eta, \zeta(\eta), \tau(\eta, \eta'))$, simplified as (η, ζ, τ), consists of the following components:

- $\eta = \{u_1, \cdots, u_m\}$: A finite set of Boolean variables, containing data and control variables. The set of *states* of M are the valuations over η, denoted as 2^η. For a state $s \in 2^\eta$, we use the notation $s_{|\eta_1}$, with $\eta_1 \subseteq \eta$, to denote the projection of s on η_1. For a set $S \subseteq 2^\eta$, then $S_{|\eta_1} = \{s_{|\eta_1} | s \in S\}$.
- $\zeta(\eta)$: The *initial predicate* characterizing the initial states. All valuations over η such that the initial predicate evaluates to true are the initial state of M.
- $\tau(\eta, \eta')$: The *transition predicate* relating the values η of state $s \in 2^\eta$ to the values η' in a successor state $s' \in 2^\eta$. There is a transition from s to s', denoted as $s \to s'$, if and only if $\tau(s, s')$ evaluates to true.

Parallel Composition. We also need to decide how to combine those processes into a concurrent system. Let $M_1 = (\eta_1, \zeta_1, \tau_1)$ and $M_2 = (\eta_2, \zeta_2, \tau_2)$ be two SVSs. The *asynchronous* and *synchronous* parallel compositions of M_1 and M_2 are denoted as $M = M_1 \|_a M_2$ and $M = M_1 \|_s M_2$, respectively. They agree on the definitions of η and ζ as follows:

- $\eta = \eta_1 \cup \eta_2$. The variables of the combined system are union of those of the components. The set of states of M is $2^{\eta_1 \cup \eta_2}$. It should be noted that we use

$s \in 2^{\eta_1 \cup \eta_2}$ to represent a state of M instead of (s_1, s_2), with $s_1 \in 2^{\eta_1}$ and $s_2 \in 2^{\eta_2}$, as (s_1, s_2) is a state of M only if they agree on the shared variables in $\eta_1 \cap \eta_2$.

- $\zeta = \zeta_1 \wedge \zeta_2$. For a state s of M, it is the initial state of M if and only if $s_{1_{\eta_1}}$ and $s_{1_{\eta_2}}$ are the initial states of M_1 and M_2, respectively. That is, $\zeta_1(s_{1_{\zeta_1}}) = true$ and $\zeta_2(s_{1_{\zeta_2}}) = true$.

As for the transition predicate τ, it is respectively defined as follows:

- In **asynchronous** composition, $\tau = \tau_1 \vee \tau_2$. For states s and s' of $M_1 \parallel_a M_2$, $s \to s'$ if and only if $\tau_1(s_{1_{\eta_1}}, s'_{1_{\eta_1}})$ or $\tau_2(s_{1_{\eta_2}}, s'_{1_{\eta_2}})$. During the transition, exactly one component, either M_1 or M_2, will make a move. If only $\tau_1(s_{1_{\eta_1}}, s'_{1_{\eta_1}})$ $(\tau_2(s_{1_{\eta_2}}, s'_{1_{\eta_2}}))$ evaluates to true, we say that $s \to s'$ is resulted from a transition of M_1 (M_2). If both $\tau_1(s_{1_{\eta_1}}, t_{1_{\eta_1}})$ and $\tau_2(s_{1_{\eta_2}}, t_{1_{\eta_2}})$ evaluates to true, then M_1 or M_2 will be non-deterministically selected to make a move.
- In **synchronous** composition, $\tau = \tau_1 \wedge \tau_2$. For states s and s' of $M_1 \parallel_s M_2$, $s \to s'$ if and only if $\tau_1(s_{1_{\eta_1}}, s'_{1_{\eta_1}})$ and $\tau_2(s_{1_{\eta_2}}, s'_{1_{\eta_2}})$. The components M_1 and M_2 will make a move simultaneously .

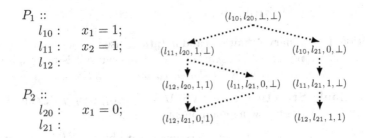

$P_1 ::$
    $l_{10} :$ $x_1 = 1;$
    $l_{11} :$ $x_2 = 1;$
    $l_{12} :$

$P_2 ::$
    $l_{20} :$ $x_1 = 0;$
    $l_{21} :$

Fig. 1. Process P_1 and P_2 **Fig. 2.** Composition of M_1 and M_2

With the short program provided in Fig. 1, we give a sense of SVSs and demonstrate the difference between synchronous and asynchronous compositions. The Boolean variable x_1 is shared between the two processes P_1 and P_2. P_1 has also a local Boolean variable, named x_2. We can construct two SVSs $M_1 = (\eta_1, \zeta_1, \tau_1)$ and $M_2 = (\eta_2, \zeta_2, \tau_2)$ to receptively represent P_1 and P_2 as follows:

- $\eta_1 = \{x_1, x_2, pc_{11}, pc_{12}\}$ and $\eta_2 = \{x_1, pc_2\}$, where pc_{11}, pc_{12} and pc_2 are variables introduced to encode the program counters of P_1 and P_2. The term $!pc_{11} \wedge !pc_{12}$ corresponds to l_{10}, $pc_{11} \wedge !pc_{12}$ to l_{11}, $!pc_{11} \wedge pc_{12}$ to l_{12}, $!pc_2$ to l_{20}, and pc_2 to l_{21}.
- $\zeta_1 = !pc_{11} \wedge !pc_{12}$ and $\zeta_2 = !pc_2$, The valuation 00 of pc_{12} and pc_{11} corresponds to l_{10}, 01 to l_{11}, and so on.
- $\tau_1 = ((!pc_{11} \wedge !pc_{12} \wedge pc'_{11} \wedge !pc'_{12} \wedge x'_1 \wedge x'_2 = x_2) \vee (pc_{11} \wedge !pc_{12} \wedge !pc'_{11} \wedge pc'_{12} \wedge x'_2 \wedge x'_1 = x_1))$ and $\tau_2 = (!pc_2 \wedge pc'_2 \wedge !x'_1)$.

Let $\perp$ denote an arbitrary value of 1 or 0. The only path of M_1 can be represented as $(l_{10}, \perp, \perp) \rightarrow (l_{11}, 1, \perp) \rightarrow (l_{12}, 1, 1)$, where the first element of each state records the value of PC_1 and the other two elements record the values of x_1 and x_2. M_2's only path is $(l_{20}, \perp) \rightarrow (l_{21}, 0)$. The parallel composition of M_1 and M_2 is given in Fig. 2, in which a dotted edge represents a transition that could only occur in the asynchronous composition. However, the synchronous composition does not have any transitions because there is no state in $M_1 \parallel_s M_2$ such that x_1 evaluates to true *and* false at the same time.

Interpolant. Let (C_1, C_2) be a pair of sets of clauses, where a *clause* is a disjunction of literals and a *literal* is either a Boolean variable or its negation. If C_1 and C_2 are inconsistent, meaning that the conjunction of C_1 and C_2 is unsatisfiable. An interpolant for an inconsistent pair (C_1, C_2) is a formula $\mathcal{I}$ with the following properties:

- $C_1 \Rightarrow \mathcal{I}$.
- $\mathcal{I} \wedge C_2$ is unsatisfiable.
- $\mathcal{I}$ is defined over the common variables of C_1 and C_2.

In practice, an interpolant can be generated from a proof by resolution that C_1 and C_2 are inconsistent. Several SMT solvers, such as MathSAT [23] and iZ3 [24], have included supports for interpolant generation. The generation procedure is actually very simple and can be finished in linear time [25].

3   Compositional Verification of Asynchronous Systems

Let $M_1 = (\eta_1, \zeta_1, \tau_1)$ and $M_2 = (\eta_2, \zeta_2, \tau_2)$ be shared variable structures with $\eta_2 \subseteq \eta_1$ [2]. We define a *simulation relation* $(\preceq)$ between two shared variable structures, using which we show that the inference rule (1) is sound and complete. One fundamental requirement of this is that the simulation relation should be compositional, i.e. whenever $M_1 \preceq M_2$, we have that $M_3 \parallel M_1 \preceq M_3 \parallel M_2$ for any other shared variable structure M_3 (maybe under some suitable extra assumptions). For simplicity, we will use $\parallel$ to denote $\parallel_a$ from here on.

Let $H \subseteq 2^{\eta_1} \times 2^{\eta_2}$. First, we consider *strong simulation*[3] [26], which is widely used in compositional reasoning, and show that it is not compositional for *asynchronous* systems.

Definition 1 (Strong Simulation [26]). *H is a strong simulation w.r.t a set of observable variables $\eta_o \subseteq \eta_2$ iff for $s \in 2^{\eta_1}, t \in 2^{\eta_2}$, $H(s, t)$ implies*

- *$s_{|\eta_o} = t_{|\eta_o}$, and*
- *for every $s' \in 2^{\eta_1}$ with $\tau_1(s, s')$, there exists a $t' \in 2^{\eta_2}$ such that $\tau_2(t, t')$ and $H(s', t')$.*

---

[2] This assumption comes naturally from the target application of assume-guarantee reasoning.

[3] A less restricted version of it appears in [11]; we will comment on it later in the section.

$M_1 \preceq_{\eta_o} M_2$ iff there is a strong simulation H such that for every $s_1^0 \in 2^{\eta_1}$ with $\zeta_1(s_1^0)$, there exists $s_2^0 \in 2^{\eta_2}$ with $\zeta_2(s_2^0)$ and $H(s_1^0, s_2^0)$.

In other words, every transition in M_1 is *simulated* by some transition of M_2. If this is everything, compositionality may not hold of asynchronous systems because a transition in $M_3 \parallel M_1$ resulting from a transition in M_3 can change the values of some variables common between M_1 and M_3[4].

To see this, let us consider a simple example. Let $\eta_1 = \eta_2 = \eta_o = \{x_1, x_2\}$. Let $\zeta_1 = \zeta_2 = (!x_1 \wedge !x_2)$. Also, let

$$\tau_1 = (!(!x_1 \wedge x_2) \wedge (!x_1' \wedge !x_2'))$$
$$\vee ((!x_1 \wedge x_2) \wedge (x_1' \wedge x_2')),$$
$$\tau_2 = (!x_1' \wedge !x_2').$$

It is easy to see that $M_1 \preceq_{\eta_o} M_2$ with $H = \{(\langle 0,0 \rangle, \langle 0,0 \rangle)\}$ as the strong simulation. Now, let $M_3 = (\eta_3, \zeta_3, \tau_3)$ with $\eta_3 = \{x_2\}$, $\zeta_3(0)$ and $\tau_3 = x_2'$.

Consider $M_3 \parallel M_1$ and the initial state $\langle 0,0 \rangle$. If M_3 takes a step, $M_3 \parallel M_1$ goes from $\langle 0,0 \rangle$ to $\langle 0,1 \rangle$. This step can also be taken in $M_3 \parallel M_2$. Now, let M_1 take a step and from τ_1 defined above, $M_3 \parallel M_1$ moves to $\langle 1,1 \rangle$. But the only transitions from $\langle 0,1 \rangle$ in $M_3 \parallel M_2$ are to either $\langle 0,0 \rangle$ (if M_2 takes a step) or $\langle 0,1 \rangle$ (if M_3 takes a step), neither of which is compatible with $\langle 1,1 \rangle$.

To fix this problem, we add a condition to the definition of simulation relation resulting in the following.

Definition 2 (Strong Jump Simulation). *H is a strong jump simulation w.r.t. a set of observable variables $\eta_o \subseteq \eta_2$ iff for $s \in 2^{\eta_1}, t \in 2^{\eta_2}$, $H(s,t)$ implies*

- *$s_{|\eta_o} = t_{|\eta_o}$, we also say that s and t are compatible on η_o, and*
- *for every $s' \in 2^{\eta_1}$ with $\tau_1(s,s')$, there exists a state $t' \in 2^{\eta_2}$ such that $\tau_2(t,t')$ and $H(s',t')$, and*
- *for every $s' \in 2^{\eta_1}$ such that $s' \restriction_{\eta_1 \backslash \eta_o} = s \restriction_{\eta_1 \backslash \eta_o}$, there exists a state $t' \in 2^{\eta_2}$ such that $t' \restriction_{\eta_2 \backslash \eta_o} = t \restriction_{\eta_2 \backslash \eta_o}$ and $H(s',t')$.*

$M_1 \preceq_{\eta_o}^{\mathcal{J}} M_2$ iff there is a strong jump simulation H such that for every $s_1^0 \in 2^{\eta_1}$ with $\zeta_1(s_1^0)$, there exists $s_2^0 \in 2^{\eta_2}$ with $\zeta_2(s_2^0)$ and $H(s_1^0, s_2^0)$.

When the context is clear, $\preceq_{\eta_o}^{\mathcal{J}}$ will be written as $\preceq^{\mathcal{J}}$. Thus, in addition to being a strong simulation, a strong jump simulation needs M_2 to simulate any *jump* in M_1 which keeps the values of the variables in $\eta_1 \backslash \eta_o$, where $\backslash$ denotes the set minus operator, intact while changing the remaining variables arbitrarily. Such a jump effectively models any asynchronous transition in a system which M_1 is part of.

Now, it is not hard to see that in the example considered above, $M_1 \not\preceq M_2$. This is because a jump in M_1 from $\langle 0,0 \rangle$ to $\langle 0,1 \rangle$ can not be simulated by a similar jump in M_2 as the only transition from $\langle 0,1 \rangle$ in M_2 is back to $\langle 0,0 \rangle$.

---

[4] This is not possible in *synchronous composition* [11], because such a transition would be synchronized in both M_3 and M_1.

In fact, $\preceq^{\mathcal{J}}$ is compositional as we show below. The left part of Fig. 3 shows the relation between η_1, η_2 and η_3, in general. We observe that when $M_3 \parallel M_1$ takes a step, the variables in the region marked $\stackrel{?}{=} \emptyset$ can be changed for which there may not be a corresponding step in $M_3 \parallel M_2$ to a compatible state. For this reason, this region is assumed to be empty, leading to the assumption $\eta_1 \cap \eta_3 \subseteq \eta_2$ (note that this also holds in the above example); see the right part of the figure. As we will see soon, this is not an unreasonable assumption.

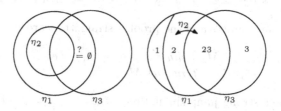

Fig. 3. Inclusion Relationships between Sets

Lemma 1. *If $M_1 \preceq^{\mathcal{J}}_{\eta_{23}} M_2$ and $\eta_1 \cap \eta_3 \subseteq \eta_2$, where $\eta_{23} = \eta_2 \cap \eta_3$, then $M_3 \parallel M_1 \preceq^{\mathcal{J}}_{\eta_3} M_3 \parallel M_2$.*

Proof. The assumption $\eta_1 \cap \eta_3 \subseteq \eta_2$ divides the space of the state variables into the four disjoint regions shown in Fig. 3 and given a state, we identify the corresponding components of the state by using the notation in the figure for subscripts. For example, the components for a state s in $M_3 \parallel M_1$ are identified as s_1, s_2, s_{23} and s_3.

Let H_{12} be a strong jump simulation between M_1 and M_2 satisfying the condition for the initial states. We show that $H = \{(s,t) | s \in 2^{\eta_1 \cup \eta_3}, t \in 2^{\eta_2 \cup \eta_3}, H_{12}(s_{23} \cdot s_2 \cdot s_1, t_{23} \cdot t_2), s_3 = t_3\}$ witnesses $M_3 \parallel M_1 \preceq^{\mathcal{J}}_{\eta_{23}} M_3 \parallel M_2$, where $\cdot$ denotes that concatenation of two state vectors. Let $H(s,t)$. We need to first show the three conditions of Definition 2 for H to be a strong jump simulation. Note that the target simulation relation is respect to η_3. So, any jump in $M_3 \parallel M_1$ or in M_1 needs to only keep the variables in $\eta_1 \setminus \eta_3$ intact.

By the assumption on H, $s_3 = t_3$ and $H_{12}(s_{23} \cdot s_2 \cdot s_1, t_{23} \cdot t_2)$. As H_{12} only has compatible pairs, the latter implies that $s_{23} = t_{23}$. Together, $s_{1_{\eta_3}} = t_{1_{\eta_3}}$.

Let $s \to s'$ be a transition in $M_3 \parallel M_1$. This can be due to a step in M_1 or in M_3.

In the first case, we have that $s_{23} \cdot s_2 \cdot s_1 \to s'_{23} \cdot s'_2 \cdot s'_1$ in M_1. As $H_{12}(s_{23} \cdot s_2 \cdot s_1, t_{23} \cdot t_2)$, there is a transition $t_{23} \cdot t_2 \to t'_{23} \cdot t'_2$ in M_2 with $H_{12}(s'_{23} \cdot s'_2 \cdot s'_1, t'_{23} \cdot t'_2)$. This transition in M_2 also means the transition $t \to t_3 \cdot t'_{23} \cdot t'_2 = t'$ exists in $M_3 \parallel M_2$. As $s_3 = t_3$, clearly $H(s', t')$.

In the second case, where the step is in M_3, we have that $s_3 \cdot s_{23} \to s'_3 \cdot s'_{23}$ in M_3. As $s_3 = t_3$ and $s_{23} = t_{23}$ from above, $t_3 \cdot t_{23} \cdot t_2 \to s'_3 \cdot s'_{23} \cdot t_2 = t'$ in $M_3 \parallel M_2$. Now, $s_{23} \cdot s_2 \cdot s_1 \to s'_{23} \cdot s_2 \cdot s_1$ is a jump. As $H_{12}(s_{23} \cdot s_2 \cdot s_1, t_{23} \cdot t_2)$, there exists a state $t'_{23} \cdot t_2$ of M_2 such that $H_{12}(s'_{23} \cdot s_2 \cdot s_1, t'_{23} \cdot t_2)$. Similarly, it also implies that $t'_{23} = s'_{23}$. As $s'_3 = s'_3$, clearly $H(s', t')$.

Finally, if there is a jump $s_3 \cdot s_{23} \cdot s_2 \cdot s_1 \to s_3' \cdot s_{23}' \cdot s_2 \cdot s_1$ in $M_3 \parallel M_1$. It is the same to the second case given above.

The condition on the initial states can easily be checked.   □

Finally, we show that the inference rule (1) is sound and complete for shared variable structures. In order to do so, we show that $\preceq^{\mathcal{J}}$ is reflexive and that it preserves LTL properties.

Lemma 2. $\preceq^{\mathcal{J}}$ is reflexive, i.e. $M \preceq^{\mathcal{J}} M$ for any shared variable structure M.

Proof. We only have jumps and the proof is straightforward.   □

Lemma 3. Let $M_1 \preceq_{\eta_o}^{\mathcal{J}} M_2$ (with $\eta_o \subseteq \eta_2 \subseteq \eta_1$). Let f be an LTL formula defined over η_o. Then, $M_2 \models f$ implies $M_1 \models f$.

Proof. Let H be a strong jump simulation witnessing $M_1 \preceq_{\eta_o}^{\mathcal{J}} M_2$. As H is also a strong simulation and, for $H(s,t)$, an atomic proposition of f is labeled in s if and only if it is labeled in t, preservation follows [27].   □

Theorem 1 (Compositional Verification). Let G be an LTL formula defined over η_G. Let $\eta_I = (\eta_1 \cap \eta_2)$. If $\eta_G \subseteq \eta_1 \cup \eta_I$ and $\eta_I \subseteq \eta_A \subseteq \eta_2$, then the inference rule

$$\frac{M_1 \parallel A \models G \qquad M_2 \preceq_{\eta_I}^{\mathcal{J}} A}{M_1 \parallel M_2 \models G} \tag{2}$$

is sound and complete.

Proof. *Soundness.* Assume $M_1 \parallel A \models G$ and $M_2 \preceq_{\eta_I}^{\mathcal{J}} A$. Lemma 1 gives us $M_1 \parallel M_2 \preceq_{\eta_1}^{\mathcal{J}} M_1 \parallel A$. From the former and $\eta_G \subseteq \eta_1 \cup \eta_I$, Lemma 3 gives us $M_1 \parallel M_2 \models G$.

Completeness. Assume $M_1 \parallel M_2 \models G$. Let $A = M_2$. From Lemma 2, $M_2 \preceq_{\eta_I}^{\mathcal{J}} M_2$. The other premise is what we just assumed.   □

Note that the assumptions on the variables in the above theorem are quite reasonable and $\eta_1 \cap \eta_2 \subseteq \eta_A$ means that η_A should include all the common variables of M_1 and M_2 which is what is expected of an assumption.

4   Automatic Assumption Generation

Let $M_1 = (\eta_1, \zeta_1, \tau_1)$, $M_2 = (\eta_2, \zeta_2, \tau_2)$, $A = (\eta_A, \zeta_2, \tau_2)$ and G be an LTL formula defined over the alphabet η_G. Let $\eta_I = \eta_1 \cap \eta_2$ and $\eta_G \subseteq \eta_1 \cup \eta_I$. They will be fixed in the rest of this section. Although the rule (2) holds for all LTL formulae, we will only consider G as safety properties from here on to ensure that a finite counterexample is returned when $M_1 \parallel A \models G$ does not hold. As discussed later, the work presented is this paper can be easily extended to liveness properties.

The basic idea of our algorithm is the following. The assumption A starts with the coarsest over-approximation. Then, the assumption A will be refined in a series of iterations. In every iteration, $M_1 \parallel A \models G$ will be model checked first. If it holds, we will have $M_1 \parallel M_2 \models G$, as A is an over-approximation of M_2, and the algorithm terminates. Otherwise, a finite counterexample will be returned as a result of $M_1 \parallel A \not\models G$. Then, we will check if the counterexample's projection on A is also feasible in M_2. If so, the algorithm can terminate as a real counterexample is found. Otherwise, a refined version of A, denoted as $A' = (\eta'_A, \zeta'_A, \tau'_A)$, will be generated based on counterexample analysis. At the same time, the refinement has the following two properties: 1) $M_2 \preceq A'$, i.e. the updated assumption is still an over-approximation of M_2. 2) A' contains strictly less behaviors than A in the sense that the counterexample will be not feasible in $M_1 \parallel A'$. Then, the algorithm enters into the next iteration. The termination of the algorithm is guaranteed by the completeness of the inference rule (2).

Alphabet Selection. In those works on assume-guarantee reasoning of synchronous compositions with systems being modeled as LTSs, the alphabet η_A of the assumption can be a strict subset of η_2 and contains only those common variables between M_1 and M_2 and those variable necessary to prove the property, i.e. $\eta_A = (\eta_G \cup \eta_1) \cap \eta_2$. Even a smaller alphabet is used in [28] with the help of alphabet refinement techniques. However, when $M_1 \parallel A \models G$ does not hold and the assumption is refined based on the returned counterexample, the counterexample analysis in an asynchronous environment, in which systems are modeled as SVSs, requires that $\eta_A = \eta_2$. The rational behind the alphabet selection is the following.

Assume that $\eta_A \subset \eta_2$, i.e η_A is a strict subset of η_2. When a counterexample to $M_1 \parallel A \models G$ is returned, the assumption must be refined to make the counterexample infeasible in $M_1 \parallel A'$. In any way, some transition, assuming that $s \to s'$, that is enabled in A will be disabled in the refined assumption A'. The problem is that for every transition $t \cdot s \to t' \cdot s'$ of M_2, where $t, t' \in 2^{\eta_2 \setminus \eta_A}$, no transitions in A' are available to simulate it. In the case of LTSs, it is different because, if a transition labelled with an action is removed from A, another transition with the same label might still exist. For the same reason, the assumption generation approach given in [11], which uses the CDNF algorithm to learn an assumption represented as SVS, also assumes that $\eta_A = \eta_2$.

Predicate Abstraction. If $\eta_A = \eta_2$, the assumption A satisfying the premise $M_2 \preceq^{\mathcal{J}} A$ will be not "smaller" than M_2. To solve the problem, we use predicate abstraction to compress the states of the assumption. Let $\mathcal{AP}$ be a set of predicates over $\bar{\eta}_2 = \eta_2 \setminus \eta_I$ (recall that $\eta_I = \eta_1 \cap \eta_2$). Those variables in η_I are not included because they are used for interacting with the component M_1. The equivalence relation induced from $\mathcal{AP}$ over the set $2^{\bar{\eta}_2}$ is denoted as $\equiv_{\mathcal{AP}}$.

Given a set of predicates $\mathcal{AP}$ over $\bar{\eta}_2$, an existential abstraction of M_2, denoted as $M_2^{\mathcal{AP}} = (\eta_I \cup \bar{\eta}_2, \varsigma_{\mathcal{P}}, \tau_{\mathcal{P}})$, is defined as the following:

- For $s_1 \in 2^{\bar{\eta}_2}$ and $s_2 \in 2^{\eta_I}$, $\varsigma_{\mathcal{P}}(s_1 \cdot s_2)$, if there exists a state $t_1 \cdot s_2$ of M_2, where $t_1 \in 2^{\bar{\eta}_2}$, such that $t_1 \in [s_1]_{\equiv_{\mathcal{AP}}}$ and $\zeta_2(t_1 \cdot s_2)$.

– For $s_1, s_1' \in 2^{\bar{\eta}_2}$ and $s_2, s_2' \in 2^{\eta_I}$, $\tau_{\mathcal{P}}(s_1 \cdot s_2, s_1' \cdot s_2')$ if there exist $t_1, t_1' \in 2^{\bar{\eta}_2}$ such that $\tau_2(t_1 \cdot s_2, t_1' \cdot s_2')$, $t_1 \in [s_1]_{\equiv_{\mathcal{AP}}}$, and $t_2 \in [s_1']_{\equiv_{\mathcal{AP}}}$.

where $[s]_{\equiv_{\mathcal{AP}}}$ denotes an equivalence class of $\equiv_{\mathcal{AP}}$. By introducing predicate abstraction, we can reduce the size of M_2 from $2^{|\eta_2|}$ to $2^{|\mathcal{AP}|+|\eta_I|}$, where $|S|$ denotes the size of a set S. Normally, the size of η_I is small for a well designed system.

Lemma 4. *For a set of predicates $\mathcal{AP}$ over $\bar{\eta}_2$ and the induced existential abstraction $M_2^{\mathcal{AP}}$ of M_2 from it, $M_2 \preceq_{\eta_I}^{\mathcal{J}} M_2^{\mathcal{AP}}$.*

Proof. Let $H = \{(s,t) | s \in 2^{\eta_2}, t \in 2^{\bar{\eta}_2}, s_{\eta_I} = t_{\eta_I}, s_{1\bar{\eta}_2} \in [t_{1\bar{\eta}_2}]_{\equiv_{\mathcal{AP}}} \}$.

Assumption Initialization. The set $\mathcal{AP}$ will be *initialized to the empty set*. The abstraction of M_2 induced from the empty set will be used as our coarsest over-approximation.

Assumption Refinement. Let $p = v_0, v_1, \cdots, v_k$ be a path of $M_1 \parallel M_2$, where v_i is a valuation over $\eta_1 \cup \eta_2$. Some transitions are executed as a result of the executions of M_1, while others as a result of M_2. The projection of p on M_1 (M_2) is obtained by removing details about those transitions and states not related to any transitions of M_1 (M_2) and projecting those remained states onto η_1 (η_2). It should be noted that a projection is not necessarily a path of a component. For example, $p' = \langle 0,0 \rangle \xrightarrow{P_1} \langle 1,0 \rangle \xrightarrow{P_2} \langle 0,0 \rangle \xrightarrow{P_1} \langle 0,1 \rangle$ is a path of the program given in Fig. 1, where the labels on transitions indicate the SVS, P_1 or P_2, to be executed. The projection of p' on P_1 is $p'' = \langle 0,0 \rangle \xrightarrow{P_1} \langle 1,0 \rangle \rightsquigarrow \langle 0,0 \rangle \xrightarrow{P_1} \langle 0,1 \rangle$, where $\rightsquigarrow$ denotes a *jump*. In the jump, the shared variable x_1 is changed by P_2 while the local variable x_2 is left untouched. It is easy to see the jump is not feasible in M_1.

Definition 3 (η-$\mathcal{J}$-Path). *A projection including transitions and jumps, in which the variables contained in η are left untouched, is called an η-$\mathcal{J}$-path.*

If $M_1 \parallel A \models G$ does not hold, a counterexample will be returned by a model checker. Let $ce = v_0, v_1, \cdots, v_k$ be the counterexample's projection on A. As we use the equivalence classes of $\equiv_{\mathcal{AP}}$ to represent the set of states of $2^{\bar{\eta}_2}$, rather than enumerating them explicitly, every state of ce belongs to $2^{\mathcal{AP} \cup \bar{\eta}_2}$. From previous discussions, we know that ce is an η_{J_1}-$\mathcal{J}$-path, where $\eta_{J_1} = \eta_A \setminus \eta_1$. Then, we will have to decide if ce feasible in M_2 by checking if there exists a η_{J_2}-$\mathcal{J}$-path $p = s_0, s_1, \cdots, s_k$ in M_2, where $\eta_{J_2} = \eta_2 \setminus \eta_1$, such that:

– $\zeta_2(s_0)$, $[s_{0_{1\bar{\eta}_2}}]_{\equiv_{\mathcal{AP}}} = v_{0_{1\mathcal{AP}}}$, and $s_{0_{1\eta_I}} = v_{0_{1\eta_I}}$.
– If $v_i \rightarrow v_{i+1}$ is a *transition* or an η_{J_1}-jump of ce, then $[s_{i_{1\bar{\eta}_2}}]_{\equiv_{\mathcal{AP}}} = v_{i_{1\mathcal{AP}}}$, $s_{i_{1\eta_I}} = v_{i_{1\eta_I}}$, $[s_{i+1_{1\bar{\eta}_2}}]_{\equiv_{\mathcal{AP}}} = v_{i+1_{1\mathcal{AP}}}$, $s_{i+1_{1\eta_I}} = v_{i+1_{1\eta_I}}$, and $\tau_2(s_i, s_{i+1})$ if $v_i \rightarrow v_{i+1}$ is a real transition.

If such an η_{J_2}-$\mathcal{J}$-path is found, the counterexample to $M_1 \parallel A \models G$ is guaranteed to be feasible in $M_1 \parallel M_2$, as $\eta_1 \cap \eta_2 \subseteq \eta_A$ ensures that all common variables

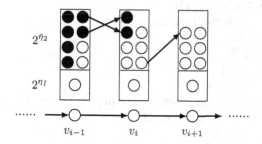

Fig. 4. Counterexample Analysis

between M_1 and M_2 are included in η_A. Thus, $M_1 \parallel M_2 \not\models G$ and the algorithm will terminate. Otherwise, the assumption A has to be refined to exclude the counterexample.

In reverse to the existential abstraction given before, a concretization function γ will be defined as the following:

$$\gamma(v) = \{s \cdot t | s \in 2^{\bar{\eta}_2}, t \in 2^{\eta_I}, [s]_{\equiv_{\mathcal{AP}}} = v_{1_{\mathcal{AP}}}, \text{ and } t = v_{1_{\eta_I}}\} \tag{3}$$

In Fig. 4, the path ce is shown at the bottom, while the set of concrete states $\gamma(v_i)$ corresponding to every state v_i is shown above. All concrete states have the same values over η_I, but different over $\bar{\eta}_2$. Let $R_0 = \{s | s \in 2^{\bar{\eta}_2}, s \in \gamma(v_0), \text{ and } \zeta_2(s)\}$. Thus, R_0 denotes the set concrete states corresponding to the initial abstract state. Then, R_i for $i \geq 1$ is recursively defined as follows:

- if $v_{i-1} \to v_i$ is a transition of ce, then $R_i = \{s | s \in 2^{\bar{\eta}_2}, s \in \gamma(v_i), \exists t \in R_{i-1} : \tau_2(t, s)\}$.
- if $v_{i-1} \to v_i$ is a jump of ce, then $R_i = \{s | s \in 2^{\bar{\eta}_2}, s \in \gamma(v_i), \exists t \in R_{i-1} : s_{1_{\bar{\eta}_2}} = t_{1_{\bar{\eta}_2}}\}$.

Every set R_i actually defines those concrete states that can be reachable along the counterexample. If the counterexample ce is not feasible in M_2, there's no corresponding transition in M_2 for some *transition* $v_i \to v_{i+1}$ of ce. Then, we will have:

$$R_i \cap (\tau_2^{-1}(\gamma(v_{i+1})) \cap \gamma(v_i)) = \emptyset \tag{4}$$

where τ_2^{-1} denotes the pre-image calculation. As shown in Fig. 4, there is at least one sate $s \in \gamma(v_{i+1})$ which is reachable from some states of $\gamma(v_i)$. However, none of those states of $\gamma(v_i)$ are included in R_i.

Because two states respectively from R_i and $\tau_2^{-1}(\gamma(v_{i+1})) \cap \gamma(v_i)$ agree on their projections on η_I, the equation (4) implies that the intersection between $R_{i_{1_{\bar{\eta}_2}}}$ and $(\tau_2^{-1}(\gamma(v_{i+1})) \cap \gamma(v_i))_{1_{\bar{\eta}_2}}$ is also empty. As we can symbolically compute the two sets, let f_1 and f_2 be the Boolean formulae representing R_i and $\tau_2^{-1}(\gamma(v_{i+1})) \cap \gamma(v_i)$, respectively. Let $\mathcal{F}_1 = \exists \eta_I : f_1$ and $\mathcal{F}_2 = \exists \eta_I : f_2$. We know that $\mathcal{F}_1 \wedge \mathcal{F}_2$ is unsatisfiable. Then, let $\mathcal{I}$ be the interpolant of $(\mathcal{F}_1, \mathcal{F}_2)$, which is defined over $\bar{\eta}_2$. We will add the interpolant I into $\mathcal{AP}$ as a new predicate and refine the assumption according to the augmented $\mathcal{AP}$.

Algorithm AAG(M_1, M_2, G)
Let $\mathcal{AP} = \emptyset$ be a set of predicates over $\bar{\eta}_2$.
while *TRUE* **do**
    Let $A = M_2^{\mathcal{AP}}$.
    Check if $M_1 \parallel A \models G$.
    if $M_1 \parallel A \not\models G$ **do**
        Let ce be the counterexample's projection on A
        Check if ce is feasible in M_2.
        if ce is feasible **do**
            $M_1 \parallel M_2 \not\models G$ and terminate.
        else
            Calculate interpolant based on formula (4).
            Add the interpolant to $\mathcal{AP}$.
    else
        $M_1 \parallel M_2 \models G$ and terminate.

Fig. 5. Interpolant-based Compositional Model Checking

Lemma 5. *The counterexample ce will be not feasible in the new assumption.*

The whole algorithm, named AAG (asynchronous assume-guarantee), is presented in Fig. 5. For the algorithm, we have the following theorem:

Theorem 2. *The algorithm will terminate. When the algorithm terminates, if $M_1 \parallel M_2 \not\models G$, a real counterexample will be returned and, otherwise, an assumption A such that $M_2 \preceq^{\mathcal{J}} A$ and $M_1 \parallel A \models G$ will be found.*

Proof. Termination. If a real counterexample or an assumption such that $M_2 \preceq^{\mathcal{J}} A$ and $M_1 \parallel A \models G$ is found, the algorithm will terminate. Otherwise, the assumption A converges to M_2 in at most $|\bar{\eta}_2|$ iterations and the algorithm terminates.

When the algorithm terminates, $M_1 \parallel M_2 \not\models G$ if a real counterexample is returned. Otherwise, an assumption satisfying the two premises of rule (2) will be reached. The correctness of $M_1 \parallel M_2 \models G$ is guaranteed by theorem 1.   □

5   Experimental Results

Our algorithm AAG, presented in Fig. 5, has been implemented in the C language. We use NuSMV [29] to check the premise $M_1 \parallel A \models G$ and MathSAT [23] to, given two inconsistent clauses, calculate an interpolant which will be added to the set of existing predicates. To make a comparison with learning-based algorithms, we also adapted the CDNF-based approach proposed in [11] to learn the Boolean initial and transition predicates of an assumption. The work is selected to be compared with because it also uses shared variable structures, rather than LTSs, as system models although it is purely focused on synchronous

Table 1. Experimental Results

Problems	Truth	CDNF					AAG			
		MQs	EQs	ζ_A	τ_A	Time(s)	ARs	ζ_A	τ_A	Time(s)
Inverter-1-2	T	221	45	2	9	0.49	1	2	9	0.03
Inverter-2-2	F	99	20	2	9	0.18	1	1	7	0.02
Inverter-3-2	T	211	45	2	9	0.53	1	2	9	0.04
Inverter-4-2	F	99	20	2	9	0.22	1	1	7	0.01
Inverter-1-4	T	1393	184	4	15	7.13	4	5	17	0.10
Inverter-2-4	F	749	98	2	7	2.19	1	1	9	0.03
Exclusive-3-1	T	348	53	4	11	0.17	1	2	7	0.15
Exclusive-2-2	T	5263	396	4	13	10.67	5	6	17	0.2
Exclusive-3-3	T	×	×	×	×	×	8	8	22	0.66

parallel compositions. The authors also showed that their approach outperforms interpolation-based monolithic model checking [30].

The examples we consider are systems consisting of multiple threads, i.e. $M = M_1 \parallel M_2 \parallel \cdots \parallel M_n$ for some finite n. We arbitrarily divide such a system into two sub-systems, say by composing the first i threads $(M_1 \parallel \cdots \parallel M_i)$ and composing the rest of the threads $(M_{i+1} \parallel \cdots \parallel M_n)$ for some $1 \leq i \leq n$. These two composed models serve as M_1 and M_2 of the inference rule (2). Several auxiliary variables are introduced in M_2 to ensure that the executions are fair in the sense that every enabled thread of $M_{i+1} \parallel \cdots \parallel M_n$ will be executed infinitely often. We use the notation XXXX-a-b to denote the above described partition of a verification problem, where XXXX is the name of the problem, a and b denote the number of threads in M_1 and M_2, respectively. The experimental systems used here are the asynchronous version of a *ring* of inverters and the semaphore-based exclusive access, which are distributed with NuSMV. The property verified for the first example states that any inverter will infinitely often output data and receive data for its neighbors, while the property for the second one states that no two processes are in the critical section at the same time.

The experimental results are summarized in Table 1. The CDNF algorithm needs to ask membership queries (MQs) to a teacher on whether the initial predicate or transition predicate evaluates to true for a given valuation to Boolean variables. By asking an equivalence query (EQ), the learning algorithm can get an affirmative answer, i.e. the submitted conjecture is an assumption satisfying the premises of the inference rule, or a counterexample. In our AAG algorithm, only abstraction refinements (ARs) are necessary. The size of generated assumptions are measured in the number of Boolean variables of ζ_A and τ_A, denoted as $|\zeta_A|$ and $|\tau_A|$, respectively. The execution time is measured in seconds. The columns labelled with crosses indicate that the CDNF-based algorithm does not terminate in 30 minutes. The experiments were run on a Macbook Pro laptop with a 2.2 GHz Intel Core i7 CPU and 4GB of memory running Mac OS X.

The experiment results confirm the results presented in [10], showing that a learning algorithm takes normally 90 percent of the time. The learning algorithms

CDNF asks a huge amount of queries to learn a formula. Normally, answering a membership query needs to solve a SAT problem or do a simulation check, while equivalence queries are more specific to the application domain and tend to be even more expensive. On the contrary, the AAG algorithm just "mechanically" calculates an abstraction and then checks if the second premise of the inference rule is satisfied. As discussed above, it is required that $\eta_A = \eta_2$ in the CDNF-based assume-guarantee learning. It is possible to obtain an assumption smaller than M_2 only when the verified property does not hold. As our algorithm introduces an abstraction over not shared variables of M_2, the generated assumption can be smaller than M_2 even if a property holds, as shown in some cases. It's also possible that the generated assumption is greater than M_2 when some *redundant predicates* are produced. A predicate is redundant if it is implied by the conjunction of some predicates that are produced later. In general, our approach outperforms the CDNF-based assume-guarantee reasoning.

6   Conclusion

As a promising technique to tackle the state explosion problem, compositional verification of concurrent systems based on assume-guarantee reasoning has been studied extensively. Inference rules play a key role in assume-guarantee reasoning as they tell how to verify a system by checking its constituents. However, the most widely used inference rule used in the literature has only been proved for synchronous systems. Based on a new simulation relation introduced in this paper, we prove that the rule holds for asynchronous systems as long as the alphabets of the components satisfy certain constraints. Then, an automating assumption generation approach is proposed based on counterexample-guided abstraction refinement, rather than using learning algorithms. Our approach is compared with the CDNF-based assume-guarantee reasoning algorithm.

Although only safety properties are considered in Section 4, the inference rule (2) allows liveness properties. The techniques given in [20] for identifying spurious loop counterexamples can be used for refining abstractions when liveness properties are taken into account. In addition, some lazy or approximate abstraction strategies might replace the exact existential abstraction used in our current implementation, which is normally very expensive.

Acknowledgements. The work was partially supported by the National Natural Science Foundation of China under grant Nos. 60903051, 61003028 and the Knowledge Innovation Program of the Chinese Academy of Sciences under grant No. ISCAS2009-DR09.

The first author's academic visit to the Computer Science Department of Carnegie Mellon University is supported by the Foundation for Selected Young Scientists Studying Abroad, Chinese Academy of Sciences. Thanks are also due to the Carnegie Mellon University for providing the infrastructure during the first author's visit.

References

1. Pnueli, A.: In transition from global to modular temporal reasoning about programs. In: Apt, K.R. (ed.) Logics and Models of Concurrent Systems, pp. 123–144. Springer-Verlag New York, Inc., New York (1985)
2. Grumberg, O., Long, D.E.: Model checking and modular verification. ACM Trans. Program. Lang. Syst. 16, 843–871 (1994)
3. Cobleigh, J.M., Giannakopoulou, D., Păsăreanu, C.S.: Learning Assumptions for Compositional Verification. In: Garavel, H., Hatcliff, J. (eds.) TACAS 2003. LNCS, vol. 2619, pp. 331–346. Springer, Heidelberg (2003)
4. Giannakopoulou, D., Păsăreanu, C.S., Barringer, H.: Assumption generation for software component verification. In: Proceedings of the 17th IEEE International Conference on Automated Software Engineering, ASE 2002, p. 3. IEEE Computer Society, Washington, DC (2002)
5. Angluin, D.: Learning regular sets from queries and counterexamples. Inf. Comput. 75(2), 87–106 (1987)
6. Barringer, H., Giannakopoulou, D.: Proof rules for automated compositional verification through learning. In: Proc. SAVCBS Workshop, pp. 14–21 (2003)
7. Giannakopoulou, D., Păsăreanu, C.S., Barringer, H.: Assumption generation for software component verification. In: Proceedings of the 17th IEEE International Conference on Automated Software Engineering, ASE 2002, pp. 3–12. IEEE Computer Society, Washington, DC (2002)
8. Bobaru, M.G., Păsăreanu, C.S., Giannakopoulou, D.: Automated assume-guarantee reasoning by abstraction refinement. In: [31], pp. 135–148
9. Păsăreanu, C.S., Giannakopoulou, D., Bobaru, M.G., Cobleigh, J.M., Barringer, H.: Learning to divide and conquer: applying the L* algorithm to automate assume-guarantee reasoning. Form. Methods Syst. Des. 32, 175–205 (2008)
10. Cobleigh, J.M., Avrunin, G.S., Clarke, L.A.: Breaking up is hard to do: An evaluation of automated assume-guarantee reasoning. ACM Trans. Softw. Eng. Methodol. 17(2), 7:1–7:52 (2008)
11. Chen, Y.F., Clarke, E.M., Farzan, A., Tsai, M.H., Tsay, Y.K., Wang, B.Y.: Automated Assume-Guarantee Reasoning through Implicit Learning. In: Touili, T., Cook, B., Jackson, P. (eds.) CAV 2010. LNCS, vol. 6174, pp. 511–526. Springer, Heidelberg (2010)
12. Bshouty, N.H.: Exact learning boolean functions via the monotone theory. Inf. Comput. 123, 146–153 (1995)
13. Chaki, S., Gurfinkel, A.: Automated assume-guarantee reasoning for omega-regular systems and specifications. Innov. Syst. Softw. Eng. 7, 131–139 (2011)
14. Chaki, S., Strichman, O.: Optimized L*-Based Assume-Guarantee Reasoning. In: Grumberg, O., Huth, M. (eds.) TACAS 2007. LNCS, vol. 4424, pp. 276–291. Springer, Heidelberg (2007)
15. Gheorghiu Bobaru, M., Păsăreanu, C.S., Giannakopoulou, D.: Automated Assume-Guarantee Reasoning by Abstraction Refinement. In: Gupta, A., Malik, S. (eds.) CAV 2008. LNCS, vol. 5123, pp. 135–148. Springer, Heidelberg (2008)
16. Alur, R., Madhusudan, P., Nam, W.: Symbolic Compositional Verification by Learning Assumptions. In: Etessami, K., Rajamani, S.K. (eds.) CAV 2005. LNCS, vol. 3576, pp. 548–562. Springer, Heidelberg (2005)
17. Sinha, N., Clarke, E.: SAT-based compositional verification using lazy learning. In: Damm, W., Hermanns, H. (eds.) CAV 2007. LNCS, vol. 4590, pp. 39–54. Springer, Heidelberg (2007)

18. Gupta, A., Mcmillan, K.L., Fu, Z.: Automated assumption generation for compositional verification. Form. Methods Syst. Des. 32(3), 285–301 (2008)

19. Chen, Y.-F., Farzan, A., Clarke, E.M., Tsay, Y.-K., Wang, B.-Y.: Learning Minimal Separating DFA's for Compositional Verification. In: Kowalewski, S., Philippou, A. (eds.) TACAS 2009. LNCS, vol. 5505, pp. 31–45. Springer, Heidelberg (2009)

20. Clarke, E.M., Grumberg, O., Jha, S., Lu, Y., Veith, H.: Counterexample-guided abstraction refinement for symbolic model checking. J. ACM 50(5), 752–794 (2003)

21. Bobaru, M.G., Pasareanu, C.S., Giannakopoulou, D.: Automated assume-guarantee reasoning by abstraction refinement. In: [31], pp. 135–148

22. Komuravelli, A., Păsăreanu, C.S., Clarke, E.M.: Assume-Guarantee Abstraction Refinement for Probabilistic Systems. In: Madhusudan, P., Seshia, S.A. (eds.) CAV 2012. LNCS, vol. 7358, pp. 310–326. Springer, Heidelberg (2012)

23. MathSAT, http://mathsat.fbk.eu/

24. iZ3, http://research.microsoft.com/en-us/um/redmond/projects/z3/iz3.html

25. Bonet, M.L., Pitassi, T., Raz, R.: Lower bounds for cutting planes proofs with small coefficients. J. Symb. Log. 62(3), 708–728 (1997)

26. Milner, R.: An algebraic definition of simulation between programs. Technical report, Stanford, CA, USA (1971)

27. Clarke Jr., E.M., Grumberg, O., Peled, D.A.: Model checking. MIT Press, Cambridge (1999)

28. Gheorghiu, M., Giannakopoulou, D., Păsăreanu, C.S.: Refining Interface Alphabets for Compositional Verification. In: Grumberg, O., Huth, M. (eds.) TACAS 2007. LNCS, vol. 4424, pp. 292–307. Springer, Heidelberg (2007)

29. NuSMV, http://nusmv.fbk.eu/

30. McMillan, K.L.: Interpolation and SAT-Based Model Checking. In: Hunt Jr., W.A., Somenzi, F. (eds.) CAV 2003. LNCS, vol. 2725, pp. 1–13. Springer, Heidelberg (2003)

31. Gupta, A., Malik, S. (eds.): CAV 2008. LNCS, vol. 5123. Springer, Heidelberg (2008)

Author Index